# Hail Columbia!

# Hail Columbia!

## *American Music and Politics in the Early Nation*

LAURA LOHMAN

OXFORD
UNIVERSITY PRESS

Oxford University Press is a department of the University of Oxford. It furthers the University's objective of excellence in research, scholarship, and education by publishing worldwide. Oxford is a registered trade mark of Oxford University Press in the UK and certain other countries.

Published in the United States of America by Oxford University Press
198 Madison Avenue, New York, NY 10016, United States of America.

© Oxford University Press 2020

All rights reserved. No part of this publication may be reproduced, stored in a retrieval system, or transmitted, in any form or by any means, without the prior permission in writing of Oxford University Press, or as expressly permitted by law, by license, or under terms agreed with the appropriate reproduction rights organization. Inquiries concerning reproduction outside the scope of the above should be sent to the Rights Department, Oxford University Press, at the address above.

You must not circulate this work in any other form
and you must impose this same condition on any acquirer.

CIP data is on file at the Library of Congress
ISBN 978-0-19-093061-5

1 3 5 7 9 8 6 4 2

Printed by Sheridan Books, Inc., United States of America

*To my parents*

# Contents

# List of Illustrations

# Acknowledgments

This book could not have been completed without support and assistance from many sources. The research and writing were made possible by a sabbatical leave and an unpaid leave from California State University, Fullerton. Generous funding through the New England Regional Fellowship Consortium enabled me to conduct archival research at several institutions, including the Maine Historical Society, the Rhode Island Historical Society, Mystic Seaport, and the Connecticut Historical Society. While my initial research interest in music commemorating the Tripolitan War and Algerian Captivity subsequently expanded into a larger study of political expression through music in the early nation, this book would not have been written without the support of the New England Regional Fellowship Consortium. Additionally, its publication has been supported by the Claire and Barry Brook Endowment of the American Musicological Society, funded in part by the National Endowment for the Humanities and the Andrew W. Mellon Foundation.

Essential to the research was assistance from the staffs of several libraries and historical societies. These include the University of Virginia Albert and Shirley Small Special Collections Library, the American Antiquarian Society, the Maine Historical Society, the Rhode Island Historical Society, the Connecticut Historical Society, Mystic Seaport, and the University of Pennsylvania Library at the Kislak Center for Special Collections, Rare Books and Manuscripts.

At Oxford, I am particularly indebted to Suzanne Ryan and Victoria Kouznetsov who shepherded the manuscript through the review process and provided substantive feedback on my work at a critical early stage. This book has also been shaped by the generosity of individual scholars who championed the study of early American music, offered helpful guidance toward secondary literature, and provided constructive feedback on earlier drafts. In particular, I thank David Hildebrand, Mark Evan Bonds, and Wayne Shirley, as well as the anonymous readers whose insightful and generous feedback has significantly shaped the final product.

# About the Companion Website

www.oup.com/us/hailcolumbia

Oxford has created a website to accompany *Hail Columbia! American Music and Politics in the Early Nation*. As you read, please use this website to access audio recordings, additional images, and additional lyrics of the music discussed in the book. In the text, Oxford's symbol ▶ indicates that such materials have been made available online.

# Introduction

Personal attacks. Vulgar language. Inventive narratives. Exaggerated claims. Public protests. Language to embarrass, demean, bully, and weaken political opponents. Accusations made in the lowest of tones, and circulated through the most rapid of media.

This description of the contemporary American political scene and its daily discourse aptly captures that of the nation's first decades. And music was one of its essential forms of expression. From Thomas Jefferson and Abigail Adams to a New York cabinet maker and the son of a radical itinerant preacher, Americans created, consumed, critiqued, praised, performed, and preserved music that served all these political functions and more. Songwriters carried out political debates in verse, Americans shamed their compatriots with instrumental "rough music," and politically charged music brought men to blows. This music reached Americans through popular media of the day, including newspapers, broadsides, and street theater. The early American retweet was the reprinting of lyrics through networks of partisan newspaper editors and the sharing of newspapers in personal correspondence. The remix and sample of the day were songwriters' reworking and quoting of popular songs to make their political jabs.

George Washington, Abigail Adams, and Thomas Jefferson all noted music's political power—its ability to express emotional connections between the American people and their president, to unite Americans in times of political crisis, and to mark the triumphant ascendance of a once-despised opposition party. Recognizing this power, early Americans used music as a discursive tool during every major political development. As the young nation grew in population, territory, and commerce, its leaders faced domestic and international challenges ranging from the government's structure to impressment of seamen. These challenges, and causes for celebration, came amid the nearly constant threat of embroilment in European war and deep insecurity about a large republic's viability. Americans responded by using this music to protest, stifle protest, propagandize, and vie for political dominance. Through music, they persuaded, intimidated, lauded, legitimated,

*Hail Columbia*. Laura Lohman, Oxford University Press (2020). © Oxford University Press.
DOI: 10.1093/oso/9780190930615.001.0001

and demonized their fellow Americans based on their political beliefs and actions. Through music, they debated crucial questions about citizens' roles and rights, the government's structure, and the pursuit of peace and prosperity. While pursuing these political ends, they used music to construct powerful narratives about the nation's history, values, and institutions; to celebrate the accomplishments of country, community, and individual; and to reinforce a sense of identity in national and partisan terms.

Why did Americans turn to music for political expression? Music's value was encapsulated by diplomat, poet, and Connecticut Wit Joel Barlow, who estimated that "one good song is worth a dozen addresses or proclamations." A New Hampshire Republican declared that an electioneering song would "have more influence upon the minds of some, than whole volumes of rational arguments, couched in the most elegant language." Such assessments were fueled by mid-eighteenth-century conceptions of rhetoric that convinced John Adams and his contemporaries of the "primacy of sound over sense in the moving of passions." Songwriters and newspaper editors acknowledged that verse helped ideas stick in Americans' minds. Accordingly, newspaper editors sometimes placed songs prominently on the first page above the fold.[1] Music could address an "aggregate of patriotic spirit," the lack of which was a significant charge against the nation's character.[2] Affirming music's value, songwriters were rewarded with and sought political positions, reminding political leaders of their cultivation of public support through song.[3]

Music was also used for political purposes because it enabled communal performance. Marches coordinated street theater and processions. Song, unlike poetry, joined community voices in shared expression. Singing in meeting houses, taverns, homes, theaters, and streets synchronized Americans in shared action and expression of commitment to political principles.[4] While profit certainly motivated music's circulation in print and theater performance, and while songwriters shared their songs with presidents hoping for recognition or appointment, these motives do not negate music's significance in expressing and shaping Americans' ideas about the nation and their place in it as political actors. Music's importance in communally acknowledging and defining the nation is seen in songwriters' enjoining community members—through lyrics themselves—to hail, acclaim, or "sing the praises of" the nation, as foregrounded in this book's title.

Communal performance and music's potential to "harmonize" Americans were useful amid a pervasive discourse of discord.[5] A common command in songs was "unite!"—regardless of the songwriter's party or majority-minority position. Unity was called for and displayed through song during national crises and before elections, with the desired unity serving partisan ends. Partisanship was tied up with a particular envisioning of the nation and its values. So communal performance often entailed an expression of allegiance to a nation as understood through a partisan lens.

Music's ability to arouse feelings of allegiance in communal settings was noted by political leaders and partisan organizers. In 1803, Levi Lincoln stressed "feeling" when reporting to Thomas Jefferson on Massachusetts Republicans' anniversary celebrations of Jefferson's inauguration. When calling a "Patriotic Ode" by William C. White "one of the most animating and best composed songs" he had encountered on such an occasion, Lincoln stressed that his assessment drew on "feeling" rather than "judgment or taste." Lincoln's commentary reflected music's relevance for the sensibility that Knott has shown to be intimately connected with the Revolution and founders' efforts to shape the nation. White's direct, energetic lyrics and repetitious, rhythmic, reflexive commands to enliven the celebration illustrated music's ability to shape Americans' sentiments through perceptual sensibility, particularly in communal performance.[6]

Early Americans' characterization of such songs as "patriotic" and "national" should not obscure their political and partisan work. Through such adjectives, Americans commonly referenced feelings music was to arouse and equated a partisan community with a national one. Americans deemed partisan music "patriotic" and "national" when anticipating growing political power, responding to political marginalization, and desiring America to be perceived as independent of, and a peer or superior to, European powers. Written and performed before elections, in celebration of election victories, and on political anniversaries, "patriotic" and "national" songs were often integral to gaining and reinforcing the political power needed to realize the particular vision of the nation they described.

Music shaped Americans' visions of the nation through performance, imagination, and print. Through public festive culture and popular political culture, music helped form a "national identity and national consciousness."[7] Music was part of what Purcell called a "public culture, including memories of a shared past, [that] allowed people to create images of their 'communion' as they imagined their connections with one another to form national allegiances."[8] The imagined nation was tied up with its members' connections to it and music shaped both. Early Americans understood music's contributions to envisioning the nation, as seen in the Connecticut Wits' preface to a song in the mock epic *The Anarchiad*. These conservative Yale humorists argued that people's feelings and beliefs about the nation make the nation, and they stressed song's role in shaping those beliefs and feelings. The Wits singled out songs designed "to excite the feelings of patriotism" and noted that "this species of poetry, accompanied with music calculated for and understood by the multitude, may have as much influence on their manners, as the civil institutions of legislation." As an example, the Wits highlighted the British, who "seem to have sung themselves into a belief that their naval prowess is invincible. And this belief has contributed not a little to establish their empire on the main."[9] The Wits' argument highlights the discourse surrounding music and its ability to shape powerful concepts of nation and national potential. Part of this came through music's regular integration in the newspapers that many scholars have noted as contributing to an imagined community.[10] There was not one such community but many overlapping ones. These included local communities that aligned with and spanned partisan divisions, and national communities fostered by networks of newspapers, many partisan.

Along with envisioning the nation, music invited communal participation in articulating powerful political narratives about the nation. These narratives explained who was included in the nation, who had political legitimacy, how the nation originated, how it was developing, and where it fit in a larger global arena of revolution and competition for power. These musical narratives commonly relied on long-standing techniques of propaganda, including techniques honed in the Revolutionary era, such as gladwords and the reduction of complex issues to dualistic choices between good and evil. Songwriters of both parties constructed historical narratives invoking people, events, and music from the revolutionary past to justify contemporary political actions and shape Americans' political opinions, perceptions, and actions in their present. Inventive narratives were often spurred by crisis, such as foreign threat or an unprecedented change of national leadership.

Americans' use of music for political expression was rooted in long-established and transatlantic practices. A 1765 engraving attributed to Henry Dawkins highlights six such practices (see Figure I.1). First, a ubiquitous practice was singing new lyrics to well-known tunes. The new lyrics about a 1765 election in Pennsylvania were to be sung to the tune of the British song, "Of Good English Beer, Our Songs We'll Raise." Repurposing old melodies for new lyrics was a centuries-old practice brought from Britain to the

A New Song Suitable to the Season,
To The Tune of Good English Beer.

Of Good Honest Souls, our Songs lets Raise,
We've Right at our free Elections;
To Vote for all those that Most doth Please,
Nor Value New Ticket Objections.
Of those Honest Hearts loud Fame hath Spoke.
They'll neer be Enslaved By P— n Sir.
They'll secure all our Rights, by the L—d its no Joke,
In Council with Honest Old Ben Sir.

Chorus.
Then to them Crown our Bowls,
Our Plenteous Brown Bowls,
And toss them of Clever, to All true British Souls,
To all True Loyal Souls, and Old ticket, Old ticket for ever,
Huzza Old Ticket, Huzza Old Ticket,
Huzza Old Ticket, Old Ticket for Ever.

2
The Election's now Past We've Got the Day,
Hark, Hark, to the New Ticket cries Sir;
They're down in the Mouth they Soulk & Say,
"We've lost it by Telling of Lies Sir."
They're future Attempts We will Disdain,
We're fixt in Our Resolution;
Come let us Agree, and Our Agents maintain,
Then Safe is Our Constitution.

Chorus.
Then, to them Crown our Bowls,
Our Plenteous Brown Bowls;
And toss them of Clever, to all true British Souls,
to all true White Oak Souls & Old ticket, Old Ticket for ever
Huzza Old Ticket, Huzza Old Ticket,
Huzza Old Ticket, Old Ticket for Ever.

3
To them let us fill a Glass and Sing,
We Old Ticket Men are Hearty;
Four Hundred and more we've Bang'd them sore
So Care not a Figg for their Party.
Come now Drink about lets see it all Out,
With Hearts as light as a Feather;
And Chearfully Laugh, at the Author a Calf
Of the Bombastick Piece Bellweather.

Chorus.
Then to them Crown our Bowls,
Our Plenteous Brown Bowls
And toss them of Clever, to all true British Souls,
To all Heart of Oak Souls, th' Old ticket Old ticket for ever
Huzza Old Ticket, Huzza Old Ticket,
Huzza Old Ticket, Old Ticket for Ever.

FINIS.

**Figure I.1.** "A New Song Suitable to the Season, to the Tune of Good English Beer," 1765. The Library Company of Philadelphia.

colonies. If no tune was specified, it could often be inferred from a familiar textual refrain, such as "Derry down," or a familiar stanza structure. The fact that the consumer was expected to find a tune in such cases but occasionally struggled was exposed by one printer who indicated "Tune—Find one" and another who, exceptionally, suggested three different tunes when a reader was stumped.[11] Early Americans called new lyrics written to an existing melody a paraphrase or parody. The term "parody" was especially applied when the songwriter emulated earlier lyrics and adapted them to a new topic, often as satire. Modern music scholars call a new song written to an existing melody a contrafact or contrafactum.

Reuse of existing music was essential to political music's accessibility, for it enabled amateurs to create new music in rapid response to political developments. To capture this accessibility, creating a contrafact is described here as "reworking" an existing song. Americans reworked popular English, Irish, Scotch, and French songs, excerpts from George Frideric Handel's oratorios, religious music, and American songs from the colonial and Revolutionary eras. Repurposed melodies familiar to readers today include "God Save the King" (still used for "My Country 'Tis of Thee"), "Yankee Doodle," and "Anacreon in Heaven." With the American "Hail Columbia," these tunes recur through the chapters that follow. ▶ New lyrics to existing tunes could be sung with or without an added bass line, and with or without instrumental accompaniment.

Some tunes were reworked so often that we can trace a song's genealogy. Francis Scott Key's "The Star-Spangled Banner," written to fit the melody of the British drinking song "Anacreon in Heaven," invoked by association not only those British lyrics but also other American political lyrics written to the same melody and remaining in Americans' memories. New lyrics like Keys's can be traced back in time, considering how they related to and could be heard in dialogue with previous lyrics connected through a shared melody and available through memory, oral transmission, or written transmission. Conversely, a commonly used melody like "Anacreon in Heaven" can be traced forward in time, exploring how it gained new meanings by association with new lyrics. As Schrader noted when reviewing Revolutionary era songs, tunes acquired new layers of meaning "when combined with a text associated with emotional occasions"; Goodman specifically traced such accretion in treatments of "God Save the King."[12] Tracing such connections is not merely an intellectual exercise, as songwriters referred to pre-existing songs through poetic meter, stanza structure, and vocabulary to make their points. Invoking older songs by reference to a shared melody and textual features enhanced an argument and entertained an audience amid heated partisan debates.

Second, as Dawkins's engraving makes clear, music was used for political purposes from the colonial period. The engraving captures the use of song to celebrate an election victory in Philadelphia. In 1765, the Old Ticket, candidates put forward by Benjamin Franklin's Assembly Party or Quaker Party, defeated the New Ticket of the Proprietary Party. The election followed Franklin's efforts to replace the Penn brothers' proprietary government with a royal colonial government and was complicated by the Stamp Act. The song celebrates the "honest" Old Ticket's victory and implicitly challenges the falsehoods spread about Franklin's party through New Ticket propaganda. The song also includes a shout out to the White Oaks, rich merchants who funded the Old Ticket's campaign.

Before, during, and after the Revolutionary War, songwriters wrote election-related, narrative, and hortative songs. Through music, colonial and Revolutionary era Americans protested specific British legal measures. American songwriters took existing tunes laden with royal associations, like "God Save the King," and reworked them to call for the king's defeat, deliberately playing on emotional associations with the tune and the tune's ability to magnify powerful intertextual references. Other colonial era songwriting techniques sustained into the early national period included vernacular language, mythological and biblical references, satire, parody, hyperbole, stereotypes, exaggerated contrasts, and the hollow gladwords typical of propaganda.[13] Revolutionary era catchwords like "liberty," "freedom," and "independence" remained staples after the war's end, but they soon promoted the values and ideologies of emerging political parties.

Third, as the engraving shows, the tavern was a gathering site in which song, talk, drinking, smoking, and political activity coalesced. Treating voters to alcohol was a common practice for getting votes. After the Revolution, the tavern remained a site of political expression by hosting casual gatherings and celebratory dinners. The tavern often doubled as post office, particularly in rural areas, where it connected the post, stagecoach, and newspapers that were key attractions and carried songs across the states. While taverns were largely the purview of men, other venues, such as theaters, meeting houses, and outdoor community celebrations, drew women, and political music circulated in women's musical manuscripts and publications targeting women.[14]

Fourth, Dawkins's engraving captures how political music reached Americans through intersections of orality and literacy. Men in the tavern sing the recurring chorus together, with no need to attend to the broadside containing the lyrics and no need for music notation to sing the tune. Dawkins departed from his model, a London illustration circulated with "Old English Beer," by conveying which part of the song the Americans were singing and having them look directly at the reader, as if enjoining the reader to join the chorus.[15] While scholars of the early republic long focused on print culture, Looby noted "a distinct counterculture in the literature of the period that valorizes the grain of the voice in addition to, or instead of, the silence of print." Looby stressed the "saliency, in many of the texts of the period, of vocal utterance as a deeply politically invested phenomenon of the social world." As Smith and others have noted, and as Dawkins's engraving makes clear, print was not necessarily conceived as a silent medium. Texts for oral delivery were marked with careful attention to how they would be heard and speech was understood as having rhythm from the careful use of pause, segmentation, and cadence.[16] Song lyrics were circulated, explicitly at times, to be read, said, or sung. Consumed and heard multiple ways, therefore, they contributed to a rich early American soundscape in which life was shaped and meanings were expressed by varied sounds ranging from songs and bells to street noise and thunder.[17]

While political music was both sung and read, the absence of explicit musical indication does not necessarily mean that verses were not sung. Some verses circulated without explicit musical indication, but other sources confirm their musical performance.[18] Take the broadside *Ode for Election-Day, 1792* in the Evans Early American Imprint Collection. The broadside contains only poetry—no indication of a tune, a common refrain, or explicit direction that the words were to be sung. One might conclude that the ode was to be read aloud or recited were it not for locating the music in a unique manuscript music book containing a three-part setting composed by psalmodist Timothy Olmsted and preserved by the Connecticut Historical Society.

In addition to circulating through inexpensive broadsides, political music reached Americans of varied ranks through newspapers, songsters containing lyrics, more costly song collections with music notation, and sheet music. Americans were obsessed with newspapers for their political content, and those who could not afford a subscription borrowed or stole copies from neighbors; subscribed but left the bill unpaid; or frequented public spaces, such as taverns, marketplaces, and coffeehouses, where newspapers' contents were shared aloud.[19] Magazines, manuscripts, copybooks, and personal collections have also preserved this music.

Political music in the early nation sustained a fifth technique seen in the engraving—leveraging other voices to makes one's political argument. While emulating a London illustration attached to "Old English Beer," Dawkins added a devil, a dog, and an African American. The devil's voice reinforces the proclaimed honesty of Franklin's party. Pompey, an African American, comments on the fun in celebrating the victory over the largely Presbyterian Proprietary party. Distinguished in physical form, the devil speaks like the gentlemen; Pompey, dressed in alignment with the status of the men he serves, is distinguished through dialect. With the rise of the Jeffersonian party and Federalists receding to a regional presence in the early nineteenth century, representation of African American speech, music, and political practice resurfaced as techniques for making a political argument and engaging like-minded partisans. Such techniques reinforced the oral aspects of the music's circulation; rendition of dialect supported a performative recreation of sounds, speech, and song in alignment with the political argument made in print.

With Dawkins's engraving and later music incorporating African American characters, performances of race and power documented on slave ship decks and southern plantations extended into print and performance in spaces like taverns. Rather than insurrection as mounted by slaves through drumming, singing, and dancing at the Stono River in South Carolina in 1739, Dawkins's engraving depicts acquiescence. While the archive presents challenges, as Sesay has noted, in "recovering the thoughts and expressions of the enslaved," it also enables closer consideration of how African American voices were represented as enfranchised Americans and their supporters battled through political arguments.[20] Through song, African American voices were used to discredit political enemies in increasingly specific, elaborate, and varied ways.

Finally, Dawkins's engraving illustrates one of the greatest challenges in studying political music in the early nation: its anonymous and pseudonymous circulation. Both before and after the Revolution, much music appeared without mention of its creators. Leveraging information scattered in newspapers, letters, diaries, and manuscripts, this study provides attributions for songs that were previously discussed with no indication of who wrote them or with incorrect information, and it builds on these attributions to deepen interpretations of key songs.

Americans responsible for creating, circulating, interpreting, and performing political music in the early nation were often not professional musicians. Among them are many surprises. They include presidents and founders, a first lady, a future Supreme Court justice, lawyer-elites, African American activists, shopkeepers, printers, craftsmen, actresses, theater fans, and a weaver-turned-teacher and ornithologist. Professional musicians like Alexander Reinagle and Benjamin Carr were crucial to the performance, composition, and printing of much music. Yet one of the things that made music a powerful medium for shaping concepts of the nation and debating its principles was music's accessibility to those working in other professions.

Two recurring figures illustrate the range of Americans who engaged in making political music: Jonathan Mitchell Sewall and Susanna Haswell Rowson. For decades, Jonathan Mitchell Sewall (1748–1808) created songs for his Portsmouth, New Hampshire, community where his Gates Street home still stands. Sewall represents a common figure in early American political music—an educated gentleman, lawyer, and dedicated Federalist. He was a staple contributor to Portsmouth life, regularly writing verses for July 4 and other important community celebrations, typically from a strongly Federalist perspective. While Sewall's verse was later deemed uneven, his reputation in his lifetime stemmed from his writing's timeliness.[21] Along with Francis Hopkinson, Sewall was one of several writers of Revolutionary songs who continued to produce songs in the early national period. Best known today as a novelist, Susanna Rowson (1762–1824) wrote lyrics for several widely printed songs, including ones with political significance. Born in Portsmouth, England, Susanna Haswell crossed the Atlantic several times before returning to settle in the United States in 1793. In addition to acting, Susanna penned plays and wrote odes, epilogues, and songs, several of which were set to music and then published by George Willig. She collaborated with leading Philadelphia musicians such as Alexander Reinagle, and she could boast having Benjamin Franklin, Martha Washington, and Mathew Carey among the subscribers to her publications.[22]

As Sewall's and Rowson's cases make clear, a diverse group of Americans used music to shape ideas about the nation and its politics. These included men and women, native-born and immigrant, white and black. Rowson was unusual in attaching her name to her work, thereby helping to clarify the contributions of women, who more commonly wrote verse anonymously. Women may have also written and submitted verse under pseudonyms, including masculine pseudonyms, and for this reason pseudonymous works are discussed without assigning a gender to the writer. Harder to capture, based on extant sources, are detailed and specific accounts of how free blacks and slaves engaged with political music in the early nation. Slaves and free blacks in the North were often fiddlers, drummers, and French horn players who accompanied dancing and songs in taverns and street theater. Blacks were integral members of religious congregations in the North, where religious and political expression often intertwined. Free blacks enjoyed large public community events, such as the street theater of the heady days following the French Revolution, and they sat in the same areas as whites to enjoy Philadelphia theater performances. Furthermore, music was integral to the election of black governors in New England states and abolition celebrations.[23]

The rarity of detailed descriptions of musical performances from this period hinders interpretation of music's role in many such events. We know, for example, that the festivities surrounding the election of black governors included people playing fiddles, fifes, drums, banjos, and African instruments as well as singing and dancing, but more detailed accounts of the music performed and its impact appear elusive. Compounding this challenge is limited information about many individuals whose names were attached to music-making. A case in point is the Philadelphia songwriter Michael Fortune. Fortune has been variously described as an African American, a Catholic, and an immigrant arriving from northern Ireland around 1790. Fortune was a writer of Jeffersonian songs, songs for middling rank domestic entertainment, and lyrics sung in abolition celebrations organized by Philadelphia's African American activists. The writer's unclear identity hinders interpretation of his role, motives, and aspirations in engaging in such intriguingly varied musical production.

Despite a lack of detail in many cases, it is clear that Americans used several musical genres for political purposes in the early nation. These included ballads, songs, odes, Handelian excerpts, psalms, satires, marches, and battle sonatas. Narrative ballads were distinguished from sentimental, expressive, convivial, or descriptive songs. The designation "ode" was applied to both songs and multimovement vocal music in which tuneful "airs" and choruses alternated with "recitatives," verse sung to a melody that resembled speech in rhythm and intonation. Such multimovement works were intended to be sung either with instrumental accompaniment or a cappella.[24] Some American multimovement odes extended an English court tradition expressing loyalty to a reigning monarch. While the term "ode" also designated poetry to be read or recited, this account generally considers odes that were sung or intended to be sung. Musical satire was not necessarily intended to be sung but could be enjoyed by being read aloud or silently; its musical basis remained critical in conveying a writer's political point. Instrumental marches were used in public processions, greetings of political leaders, and convivial gatherings; often the exact marches performed were not specified in surviving accounts. Other instrumental music included battle sonatas for keyboard and "rough music," the centuries-old, transatlantic practice of performing instrumental music to shame those who violated community norms. The most common example was "The Rogue's March."

Through these varied genres and performance settings, this book addresses political uses of music in the early nation chronologically. As explored in the first two chapters, music was a tool of propaganda and protest. Chapter 1 considers how Americans used music to craft what Jones and Onuf have called the "central" and "founding myth of the American nation," the drafting and ratification of the Constitution.[25] Focusing on the period 1783–1792, the chapter examines how music was used as a tool of propaganda as debates over financial problems culminated in efforts to restructure the government through the Constitution. As advocates of a more powerful federal government repeatedly turned to musical propaganda, songwriters wrote music to contain popular protest, urge ratification, define the relationship between the people and the new federal government, and promote allegiance to the newly structured government during Washington's first term as president. Focusing on his second term, chapter 2 analyzes how Americans used music to express oppositional political values. Republicans challenged the Federalists' premise that people must defer to the wisdom of elite elected officials. Following the French Revolution, Americans voiced their political opposition in song through a cosmopolitan language of natural rights inspired by Thomas Paine. While Federalists perceived democracy as something to be curtailed, their emerging Republican opponents advocated broad public participation in politics and "universal principles" of liberty and equality. By performing, reworking, and printing music in a broader transatlantic context, Americans disseminated ideals of popular cosmopolitanism as a framework for domestic political opposition and resisted growing British influence. Federalists and Republican challengers used music to promote opposing visions of the American republic and political participation in it.

As seen in the middle two chapters, Americans leveraged music to circulate narratives of partisan dominance. Chapter 3 examines how Federalists used music to articulate a powerful narrative of legitimacy through relentless presentation of Federalist heroes and Republican villains during the intensely partisan atmosphere of John Adams's presidency. Songwriters expressed a surge of federalism, nationalism, and militarism in support of Federalist projects through both ephemeral songs and "patriotic" hits like "Hail Columbia." Despite Federalists' efforts to destroy domestic political "faction," Republicans refused to be silenced. They used many of the same symbols, strategies, and tunes to promote different causes and inspire oppositional political action through music. Sonically representing the Republican takeover of the administration with Jefferson's election, songwriters articulated a new narrative of Republican ascendance and political legitimacy. Counteracting years of Federalist assaults and their caricature of the "dangerous Democrat," Republicans foregrounded a new image of Jefferson, cast Federalists as evildoers, and stressed laudable Republican values. As explored in chapter 4, they creatively reworked songs symbolizing Federalist power and moving in transatlantic circulation, and they adapted rhetorical and narrative techniques from Federalist precedents. Marginalized Federalists contested this narrative with cutting satire, personal attacks, and a sectional counternarrative.

With music, Americans also addressed critical political questions about the nation's place in the world and articulated powerful narratives of national development. Although Federalists' national impact waned, partisanship and opposition resurged as Jefferson's and Madison's administrations struggled with severe trade restrictions during the Napoleonic wars. Focusing on the period 1806–1811, chapter 5 examines how Americans used music to address critical political questions in this time of naval depredations, failed diplomacy, and economic devastation: What should the makeup and purpose of the navy be? How should the nation form an alliance with a European power? Can the nation avoid embroilment in a major European war? Music provided an engaging medium not only to address these questions within the first party system but also to prioritize the nation's goals, including peace, prosperity, and isolationism. As seen in chapter 6, once the War of 1812 broke out, Americans obscured partisan and sectional divisions by circulating a large volume of selective accounts of the war that ignored reversals of Republican policy and highlighted the Republican administration's success in bringing peace with a navy of Federalist design. Understood in the context of the previous chapters, Key's "The Star-Spangled Banner" illustrates the sonic transcendence of ideological and partisan debate. The American nationalism that it came to symbolize developed not only in a transatlantic context but also alongside strong regional and other allegiances.[26] Following years of economic stress and partisan strife, Americans used music to portray the nation as self-sufficient, militarily competent, and united in feeling.

Whether offering political satire, cutting criticism, tribute to national heroes, or narratives of national growth, music was an essential part of early

American political culture. Americans used music to voice protest, propagandize, claim political legitimacy, and circulate powerful national myths. With music, Americans debated the nature of the republic, the structure of its government, the meaning of liberty, and the nation's relationship to European powers. Americans did so over three decades that witnessed the development of the first party system, the first peaceful transfer of power from one administration to another, and the replacement of a political system based on deference and apparent disinterestedness with one based on broader suffrage and electioneering. Americans' widespread and continuous use of music for these political ends attests to music's ability to engage listeners through both idealism and humor, to convey complex meanings through interrelated texts, and to gather Americans in communal political action and expression. *Hail Columbia!* reveals not only how Americans acclaimed and acknowledged the nation through music but also how they conceptualized the nation through music. While often perceived as ephemeral or aesthetically inferior, this music played a central role in shaping Americans' understandings of the nation.

## Notes

1. Arthur M. Schlesinger, "A Note on Songs as Patriot Propaganda 1765–1776," *William and Mary Quarterly* 11, no. 1 (January 1954): 79; Walpole *Political Observatory*, 22 August 1808; Jay Fliegelman, *Declaring Independence: Jefferson, Natural Language & the Culture of Performance* (Stanford, CA: Stanford University Press, 1993), 42–3; Frank Landon Humphreys, *Life and Times of David Humphreys*, vol. 1 (St. Clair Shores, MI: Scholarly Press, 1971), 397–8; Middletown *Middlesex Gazette*, 6 February 1790; Providence *Columbian Phenix*, 8 April 1809; Boston *New England Palladium*, 23 July 1802.
2. Clinton *Ohio Register*, 29 March 1814.
3. William Coleman, "'The Music of a Well Tun'd State': 'The Star Spangled Banner' and the Development of a Federalist Musical Tradition," *Journal of the Early Republic* 35, no. 4 (Winter 2015): 620; "To Thomas Jefferson from Joseph Croswell, February 1803," *Founders Online*, http://founders.archives.gov/documents/Jefferson/01-39-02-0511; "To Thomas Jefferson from Michael Fortune, 29 August 1825," *Founders Online*, http://founders.archives.gov/documents/Jefferson/98-01-02-5495; "To Thomas Jefferson from Michael Fortune, 8 October 1825," *Founders Online*, http://founders.archives.gov/documents/Jefferson/98-01-02-5580.
4. Hudson *Bee*, 11 June 1805; Boston *Repertory*, 2 September 1808; Newport *Rhode Island Republican*, 8 November 1809.
5. Kirsten E. Wood, "'Join with Heart and Soul and Voice': Music, Harmony, and Politics in the Early American Republic," *American Historical Review* 119

(October 2014): 1086–8, 1092; H[avilah] Farnsworth, *An Oration on Music* (Cooperstown: Elihu Phinney, 1795), 17–19.

6. Worcester *National Aegis*, 9 March 1803; "To Thomas Jefferson from Levi Lincoln, 15 March 1803," *Founders Online*, http://founders.archives.gov/documents/Jefferson/01-40-02-0052; Worcester *Massachusetts Spy*, 13 April 1803; Wood, "'Join with Heart," 1087–8, 1093–6, 1098, 1103, 1106–7, 1113; Sarah Knott, *Sensibility and the American Revolution* (Chapel Hill: University of North Carolina Press, 2012), 9–11.
7. Len Travers, *Celebrating the Fourth: Independence Day and the Rites of Nationalism in the Early Republic* (Amherst: University of Massachusetts Press, 1997); David Waldstreicher, *In the Midst of Perpetual Fetes: The Making of American Nationalism, 1776–1820* (Chapel Hill: University of North Carolina Press, 1997); Simon P. Newman, *Parades and the Politics of the Street: Festive Culture in the Early American Republic* (Philadelphia: University of Pennsylvania Press, 1997).
8. Sarah J. Purcell, *Sealed with Blood: War, Sacrifice, and Memory in Revolutionary America* (Philadelphia: University of Pennsylvania Press, 2002), 6.
9. Luther G. Riggs, ed., *The Anarchiad* (Gainesville, FL: Scholar's Facsimiles, 1967), 25.
10. Benedict Anderson, *Imagined Communities: Reflections on the Origins and Spread of Nationalism* (New York: Verso, 1991), 7–65; Jeffrey L. Pasley, *"The Tyranny of Printers": Newspaper Politics in the Early American Republic* (Charlottesville: University Press of Virginia, 2001), 12, 53; Jonathan Gross, ed., *Thomas Jefferson's Scrapbooks: Poems of Nation, Family, and Romantic Love* (Hanover, NH: Steerforth Books, 2006), 505; Seth Cotlar, *Tom Paine's America: The Rise and Fall of Transatlantic Radicalism in the Early Republic* (Charlottesville: University of Virginia Press, 2011), 13–14, 16–17, 23, 29–30.
11. Boston *Massachusetts Mercury*, 22 January 1793; Boston *Independent Chronicle*, 27 October 1808; Boston *Republican Gazetteer*, 9 October 1802.
12. Arthur F. Schrader, "Songs to Cultivate the Sensations of Freedom," in *Music in Colonial Massachusetts, 1630–1820: A Conference Held by the Colonial Society of Massachusetts*, 105–56 (Boston: The Society, distributed by the University Press of Virginia, 1980); Glenda Goodman, "Transatlantic Contrafacta, Musical Formats, and the Creation of Political Culture in Revolutionary America," *Journal of the Society for American Music* 11, no. 4 (November 2017): 392–419.
13. Robert James Branham, "'God Save the _____!' American National Songs and National Identities, 1760–1798," *Quarterly Journal of Speech* 85, no. 1 (February 1999): 27–8; Richard Crawford, *America's Music Life: A History* (New York: W. W. Norton, 2001), 67; Sylvia G. L. Dannett, *The Yankee Doodler* (South Brunswick, NJ: A. S. Barnes, 1973), 134–7; Frank Moore, *Songs and Ballads of the American Revolution*. 1855. Reprint (New York: Arno Press, 1969), 103–5, 109–11; Gillian B. Anderson, ed., *Freedom's Voice in Poetry and Song* (Wilmington, DE: Scholarly Resources, 1977), 614–17, 620–2.
14. Peter Thompson, *Rum Punch and Revolution: Taverngoing and Public Life in Eighteenth-Century Philadelphia* (Philadelphia: University of Pennsylvania Press, 1999), 97–8, 137, 141, 165; Alan Taylor, "'The Art of Hook & Snivey': Political Culture in Upstate New York during the 1790s," *Journal of American History* 79,

no. 4 (1993): 1388, 1392; Richard R. John and Thomas C. Leonard, "The Illusion of the Ordinary: John Lewis Krimmel's *Village Tavern* and the Democratization of Public Life in the Early Republic," *Pennsylvania History* 65, no. 1 (Winter 1998): 87–96; Albert Stoutamire, *Music of the Old South: Colony to Confederacy* (Rutherford, NJ: Fairleigh Dickinson University Press, 1972), 55, 261; Cotlar, *Tom Paine's America*, 53; Michael Merrill and Sean Wilentz, eds., *The Key of Liberty: The Life and Democratic Writings of William Manning, "A Laborer," 1747–1814* (Cambridge, MA: Harvard University Press, 1993), 54–5; New York *American Minerva*, 11 April 1794; Isaac Holmes, *An Account of the United States of America, Derived from Actual Observation during a Residence of Four Years in That Republic* (London: Caxton Press, 1823), 135–6; Polly Elvira Bouchell, *Music Book of Polly Elvira Bouchell*. 2 vols. Salem, North Carolina, 1811; *The New Ladies Memorandum-Book for the Year 1794* (London: James Evans, 1793).

15. *Calliope, or English Harmony*, vol. 2 (London: John Simpson, n.d.), 109.
16. Christopher Looby, *Voicing America: Language, Literary Form, and the Origins of the United States* (Chicago: University of Chicago Press, 1996), 3; Mark M. Smith, *Listening to Nineteenth-Century America* (Chapel Hill: University of North Carolina Press, 2001), 8; Fliegelman, *Declaring Independence*, 4–27.
17. Fredericktown *Republican Advocate*, 27 October 1808; Clark Hunter, ed., *The Life and Letters of Alexander Wilson* (Philadelphia: American Philosophical Society, 1983), 289; Richard Cullen Rath, *How Early America Sounded* (Ithaca, NY: Cornell University Press, 2003).
18. Boston *Columbian Centinel*, 17, 24 October 1792; *Boston Gazette*, 29 October 1792; *Ode for the 23rd of October, 1792* ([Boston]: n.p., 1792).
19. Charles G. Steffen, "Newspapers for Free: The Economies of Newspaper Circulation in the Early Republic," *Journal of the Early Republic* 23, no. 3 (Autumn 2003): 388–96; Marcus Daniel, *Scandal and Civility: Journalism and the Birth of American Democracy* (New York: Oxford University Press, 2009), 7, 14, 84; Cotlar, *Tom Paine's America*, 13–14, 29–30; Thomas C. Leonard, *News for All: America's Coming-of-Age with the Press* (New York: Oxford University Press, 1995), 3–32; Joanne B. Freeman, *Affairs of Honor: National Politics in the New Republic* (New Haven, CT: Yale University Press, 2001), 123–6; Alexander Wilson, *The Poems and Literary Prose of Alexander Wilson, the American Ornithologist*, vol. 1 (Paisley, Scotland: A. Gardner, 1876), 154; Pasley, *Tyranny of Printers*, 7–8.
20. Katrina Dyonne Thompson, *Ring Shout, Wheel About: The Racial Politics of Music and Dance in North American Slavery* (Urbana, IL: University of Chicago Press, 2014), 42–101; Chernoh M. Sesay Jr., "Mapping Intersectionality, Imagining Music, and Excavating America's African Archives," *Journal of the Early Republic* 38, no. 2 (Summer 2018): 329–31.
21. Charles Henry Bell, *The Bench and Bar of New Hampshire* (Boston: Houghton Mifflin, 1894), 630; Albert Stillman Batchellor, ed., *Early State Papers of New Hampshire*, vol. 22 (Concord: Ira C. Evans, 1893), 845–7; Concord *Courier of New Hampshire*, 16 January 1801.

22. Elias Nason, *A Memoir of Mrs. Susanna Rowson, with Elegant and Illustrative Extracts from Her Writings in Prose and Poetry* (Albany, NY: Joel Munsell, 1870), 33–4, 49, 72–3, 77, 89–90, 100–4, 114, 117–18, 123, 141.
23. Eileen Southern, *The Music of Black Americans: A History* (New York: W. W. Norton, 1997), 25–52; Jenna M. Gibbs, *Performing the Temple of Liberty: Slavery, Theater, and Popular Culture in London and Philadelphia, 1760–1850* (Baltimore: Johns Hopkins University Press, 2014), 39; Orville Platt, "Negro Governors," *New Haven Historical Society Quarterly* 6 (1900): 318–35; Newport *Guardian of Liberty*, 30 May 1801.
24. Daniel Mendoza de Arce, *Music in North America and the West Indies from the Discovery to 1850: A Historical Survey* (Lanham, MD: Scarecrow Press, 2006), 106.
25. Peter S. Onuf, *The Origins of the Federal Republic: Jurisdictional Controversies in the United States, 1775–1787* (Philadelphia: University of Pennsylvania Press, 1983), xiii; Robert F. Jones, "Economic Opportunism and the Constitution in New York State: The Example of William Duer," *New York History* 68, no. 4 (October 1987): 359.
26. Purcell, *Sealed with Blood*, 9; Cotlar, *Tom Paine's America*, 49–114.

# 1

# Musical Propaganda in the Era of the Constitution

After the Revolutionary War, American songwriters outlined the nation's future with ebullient optimism. Yet their optimistic portrayals obscured the country's many challenges, including an economic depression and European commercial restrictions. American wages dropped beginning in 1785 and did not recover significantly until 1791. The nation's bad trade balance, especially with Britain, contributed to a loss of specie and spurred heavy reliance on credit. These problems were compounded by land speculation and ultimately a bursting of the credit bubble. Despite this precarious financial situation, American songwriters envisioned a glorious future: they promised naval triumphs, even though the nation lacked a functioning navy, and they touted the nation's hard-won liberty, even though American sailors were enslaved when merchant vessels were seized by Algerian pirates.[1] Such idealistic portrayals could not alter the reality that ordinary citizens were struggling and the nation could not pay its debts.

State and national leaders prompted vigorous debate over the financial problems impacting individuals, states, and the central government. These debates culminated in efforts to restructure the government through the Constitution. Both proponents and critics of the Constitution valued the press, which, as Pasley explains, was understood to be "the most important means available of managing or manufacturing public opinion, the legitimating force behind the new governments." George Washington clearly understood the value of circulating propaganda in the press, for he stressed to his friend and advisor David Humphreys that "the recommendation of [the Constitution] by good pens should be *openly*, I mean, publickly afforded in the Gazettes."[2] Under pseudonyms like "Federalist" and "Centinel," leading thinkers developed arguments for and against ratification, and these were printed and reprinted in newspapers throughout the states.

Advocates of a more powerful federal government repeatedly turned to musical propaganda to make their case. They used music to craft what Jones

*Hail Columbia*. Laura Lohman, Oxford University Press (2020). © Oxford University Press.
DOI: 10.1093/oso/9780190930615.001.0001

and Onuf have called the "central" and "founding myth of the American nation" around the drafting and ratification of the Constitution.[3] With music, they delegitimated popular protest, portrayed the Constitution as the work of the people and essential to save the nation, and then prescribed the people's relationship to the restructured federal government as deference to elites consistent with an elitist, deferential republicanism. As ratification by nine states ensured that the Constitution would go into effect, songwriters proclaimed a "new era" and articulated the nation's first president as a focal point for cultivating popular allegiance to a far more powerful federal government, a government designed by elites and put into effect by circumventing one of the nation's founding documents.

Music supported this federalist project as both text and sound. An engaging tool for shaping opinion, new songs invited participation. Leveraging music's intertextual potential, songwriters enhanced their political argument by making connections to historical, functional, or topical musical precedent. Printers circulated propagandist lyrics to discredit protestors seen as endangering the early republic and federalists carefully deployed instrumental music and song in the American soundscape to promulgate order. When performed and heard, music showcased the sensibility that, as Knott has demonstrated, was fundamental to connecting American "selves and society in a harmonious whole." Communal singing aligned with physiological notions of sensibility, enacted order, and articulated a vision of the nation.[4] Not surprisingly, then, federalist songwriters enjoined their community members to hail, acclaim, and "sing the praises of" the nation, its principles, its leaders, and its newly conceived federal government.

## Containing Popular Protest

Efforts to restructure the federal government stemmed from the country's financial problems. The states needed to pay their share of Revolutionary War debts to Congress and other creditors. So states had raised taxes—and not with restraint, but to three to four times colonial-era levels. Some states facilitated citizens' payment of taxes by issuing paper money and offering debt relief. Other states moved in the opposite direction, hindering payment by insisting on collecting taxes in scarce gold and silver coin. Exacerbating the situation, once the credit bubble burst, local creditors hounded cash-strapped farmers and uncompensated veterans to pay their debts. When they could not pay, time-consuming and expensive court proceedings increased farm foreclosures and bankruptcies. Massachusetts forcefully pursued tax collection. Despite a Springfield newspaper's warning that the state government would have to choose between relaxing tax measures or precipitating a crisis, Governor James Bowdoin pursued the latter path and pushed the state legislature to collect taxes more forcefully. This push, enabled by the lack of well-organized party opposition, ultimately resulted in the most dramatic, extreme, and visible manifestation of problems simultaneously occurring in other states.[5]

While easterners celebrated their progress through events like the completion of the Charlestown Bridge, residents of western Massachusetts chafed under increasing pressures for tax and debt collection amid the shortage of hard currency. Citizens—including landowners, town leaders, and Revolutionary War officers—pursued the reform of oppressive state laws and consciously carried on the traditions of colonial regulators who had sought to check (or "regulate") elite and distant governments, prevent the confiscation of land, and restore communal order.[6] Spurred by a new state government and legislation that enriched the few to the detriment of many, Massachusetts regulators sought to change the state constitution and obtain a more responsive state government. From the summer of 1786, they protested at courts—the most visible symbol of state authority in western Massachusetts—to prompt the state legislature to consider reforms. The regulators' concerns encompassed the lack of hard currency, tax collection methods, unequal taxation, payment of debts, and measures that had enriched the wealthy, including the handling of government securities held in volume by elite speculators. About a quarter of the Massachusetts population participated in the regulation. Regulators responded to a state constitution that had created an aristocratic state government antithetical to the local governance favored in western Massachusetts. When the regulators' pursuit of state legal reform was answered by the rejection of their requests, raids by armed elites, organization of federal troops, and more suppressive legislation, the regulators sought to overthrow the unsympathetic and unresponsive state government. State troops organized at Governor Bowdoin's urging were funded—and, in some cases, led—by eastern elites—the very people to whom the regulators felt too much money and power had already shifted. Following a conflict with the regulators at the Springfield arsenal in late January 1787, these state troops, led by Benjamin Lincoln, marched at night through an early February blizzard to surprise and disperse the regulators at Petersham.[7]

In response to the regulators' actions—actions commonly known as Shays's Rebellion—songwriters created music to combat and contain this type of popular protest. Songwriters conveyed a vivid, threatening picture of the regulators. As part of a multifaceted approach to suppressing such protest—including military, legislative, and public relations strategies—songwriters produced music to prevent the regulators from being seen as positive role models and to justify the stringent military and legislative measures taken against them.

The songwriter "Bombardilla" demonized the regulators by reworking "I'm Old Mad Tom," a mad song circulated in the London song collection *The Lark* of 1740 and subsequent song collections.[8]▶ By selecting this tune, "Bombardilla" underscored the "leveling" agenda and lack of reason attributed to the regulators. "Bombardilla" specifically offered this reworking of "I'm Old Mad Tom" as a response to yeoman regulator Thomas Grover. Through prose commentaries portraying Grover as insane, vain, and cowardly, "Bombardilla" framed the new lyrics and turned the voice of the British "Old Mad Tom" into Thomas Grover. In reworking the song, "Bombardilla" had the crazy Grover and his colleagues overturning the state constitution, disregarding state laws, and intending to unseat judges at gunpoint to achieve their goals. "Bombardilla" portrayed the regulators' goal of moving the legislature as self-interested and illogical. The proposed move was intended to address prohibitive travel and lodging costs for western residents to engage with the state government and the challenges that western state legislators faced in supervising their private affairs from the coast. "Bombardilla" hyperbolized the danger of the regulators' actions in the penultimate verse, as "mad Tom" promised to rip the eastern hills "from the foundation . . . and hurl them on this nation" if his demands were not met. At a time when the republic's survival was seen to depend on the willingness of virtuous citizens to sacrifice their own interests for the community's good, the regulators—as portrayed in such propaganda—embodied the antithesis of republican ideals by engaging in self-interested, reckless action that jeopardized law, order, and safety.[9]

Such musical denunciations extended to Connecticut, New Hampshire, and New York, where protests had already occurred and could recur as the rebels dispersed from Petersham. In New Hampshire, small farmers and others hard-hit by the postwar depression could not access political positions and, like the Massachusetts regulators, they first used petitions and later physical and military confrontation to urge political leaders to address the debilitating economic conditions. In Exeter, townspeople who wanted legislative consideration of petitions for paper currency armed themselves and surrounded the legislature's meeting house; they ultimately clashed with local volunteers and militia called by John Sullivan, president of New Hampshire and chair of the state senate. The nearly forty insurgents captured by the militia were marched to the town jail to "The Rogue's March," a tune and drumbeat of British origin traditionally used to publicly shame and expel those committing significant violations in military and civilian life ⯈.[10] So great was song's power as propaganda that one poet penned a fictional singing competition to demonize the regulators as self-interested miscreants who flocked to plunder like crows to carrion. Another songwriter, whose work was first printed in Albany, just forty miles from a Massachusetts skirmish, touted the regulators' disregard for the law and state constitution. In reality, the regulators acted not with disregard for the Massachusetts constitution but from dissatisfaction with its elitism, evidenced by exclusionary property requirements for voting and holding office. Undermining the regulators' credibility, the songwriter portrayed their agenda as ridiculous and unrealistic goals based on a flawed understanding of the nation's domestic and international challenges. Foolishly, the songwriter explained, the regulators envisioned judges doing work for no pay, a miraculous defeat of the French in a subsequent war after failing to repay their loans, and a western Massachusetts town like Pelham or Glasgow becoming the state capital.[11]

Among the songs circulating across state lines was a Massachusetts song that mocked well-known regulators by name and misrepresented the regulators and their goals (see Figure 1.1). Although the named regulators included unpaid veterans (Daniel Shays and Luke Day), the songwriter portrayed the men as drunk, lazy riffraff and criminals who aspired to be political leaders and were intent on turning society upside down, dressing the governor in an apron and jerkin, and making the "ruffle-shirts" bow to the regulators. The songwriter falsely asserted that the regulators sought a leveling revolution to redistribute wealth and power (in fact, they simply sought to *stop* further enrichment of the wealthy at the expense of the average American). Outlining the consequences of the regulators' plans, the songwriter predicted violence, anarchy, and tyranny of the mob. The songwriter lent a sense of frenzy to their exploits by setting the lyrics to an energetic British hunting song in 6/8 time (a pace similar to "Little Miss Muffet"). The tune was named after a legendary British hunting horse, "Black Sloven." Printed in Britain in 1770, "Black Sloven"

# OETICKS.

A SONG—(Tune '*Black Sloven*,')
*Dedicated to the lovers of wit—the friends to mirth and good government.*

COME, come my bold boxers, 'tis liberty calls
Hark, hark, how ſhe luſtily bawls, and bawls!
It is high time if ever for mobbing 'twas time;
To mobing, ye chicks of dame Liberty run;
Scour up the old *whinyard*, and bruſh the old *gun*;
Freedom we'll chime,
While Tag, Rag, and Bobtail,
Lead up our decorum, Huzza!

Sure theſe are the plaguieſt of all plaguy times,
When *villains* muſt hang for their crimes, their crimes,
And debtors a gauntlope of bailiffs, muſt run;
When *rulers* will *govern*, and *we* muſt *obey*,
And *law* down our gullets is cramm'd every day--
Rap, Rap,—'tis a dun!
The ſheriff's behind him,
We'll gag him, and bind him, huzza!

When the *rum* is all out, and the *cyder* runs low,
And the taverns won't ſell for *ditto, ditto*,
And a man for his victuals muſt work like a dog;
*Paper-money*, and *cheating by law*, have both fled,
To Rhode-Iſland to hive in their Governor's head.
Come, come, tother *mug*!
Here a health to our *maſter*;
Talk leſs and drink faſter, huzza!

**Figure 1.1.** "Come, come my bold boxers." Northampton *Hampshire Chronicle*, 20 March 1787. Readex/NewsBank.

had been reworked in America on the Revolution's eve, performed by military musicians during war, and recorded in American musicians' tune books, including that of the young flute player John Quincy Adams ▶. This hunting song helped conjure the American songwriter's vision of a mob irrationally rushing to act and enhanced the regulators' intent to "ride o'er Lawyers and Judges." Filled with violent, realistic imagery and restricted to one- and two-syllable words, the new lyrics and tune captured a frenzied

Then haſte to our chiefs, ſuch as never were ſeen,
With hats and with *noddles*, ſo *green* ſo *green*,
There's the *Hind*† that's let looſe of true Naph-
tali breed,
There are *Shayſes* and *Dayſes*, and ſuch pretty
things,
And *Grovers* and *Wheelers*, and *Parſons* and Kings,
Yet diſmal to read!
Our poor brother *Shattuck*,
Was fell'd with a mattock, heigh ho!

We've *would-be* aſſembly-men, capt's and ſquires,
And the train that *Sir Richard* inſpires, inſpires,
With the ſpirit of *Ely*, our genius and guide.
No longer in priſon our gentlemen lurk;
Nor run from the Sheriff, nor live by hard work;
Gaily we'll ride,
O'er Lawyers and Judges,
And the Court drudges, Huzza!

Then Senates and Courts to our friend Beelzebub,
We'll drive with the muſquet, and club, and club,
And in *apron* and *jerkin* our Governor dreſs:
To ſet in the ſaddle we've men that know how,
And make all your *ruffle-ſhirts* foot it and bow;
The World ſhall confeſs
We've ſpirits in *hogſheads*,
And cunning in *fox-heads*, Huzza!

Thus no longer with *ſtocks*, and with *pillories* vex'd
Nor with work, jail, or ſheriff, perplex'd, per-
plex'd,
The mobmen ſhall rule, and the great men obey,
The world upon wheels ſhall be all ſet *agog*,
And blockheads and knaves, hail the reign of
(King *Log*.
Under his ſway,
Shall Tag, Rag, and Bobtail,
Lead up our decorum, Huzza.

**Figure 1.1.** Continued.

effort of uneducated, irreverent miscreants to turn society upside down. The horrifying portrayal of the frenetic lyrics was made all the more disturbing by a simultaneously circulated account of the regulators' engagement with Lincoln's army, an account that characterized the regulators as ill-suited for leadership and operating with a faulty notion of liberty based on lust rather than reason—an inversion that the songwriter emphasized in the song's opening two lines.[12]

In addition to demonizing the regulators, songwriters and printers trumpeted efforts to suppress them. An "Ode on the suppression of the REBELLION, raised against this Commonwealth" proudly announced that the Massachusetts turmoil had ended. Benjamin Russell, federalist editor of the *Massachusetts Centinel*, magnified the significance of state troops' dispersal of the regulators by circulating not just ordinary song lyrics but the lyrics of a seven-movement ode. In this case, "ode" signified a ceremonial musical genre long used in Britain to express loyalty to reigning monarchs and mark important events. The "Ode on the suppression of the REBELLION" included a series of recitatives and airs, a trio, and final chorus. It was actually a retooling of a British ode written by poet laureate Colley Cibber and set to music by the Master of the Royal Band Maurice Greene more than forty years earlier. In choosing this model, the anonymous Massachusetts propagandist who wrote the new lyrics not only selected a formal, courtly genre suitable for conveying grand praise but specifically evoked a parallel event from British history: the suppression of the Jacobite Rebellion of 1745 by King George II's son William. This suppression had prompted Cibber's original lyrics. Likely finding the lyrics in an older magazine, the American retooled them to proclaim the regulators' suppression, "'Tis done!" and lavish praise on Lincoln and the state's "Rulers," the most "belov'd," for their handling of the insurgency. Despite a lack of truly heroic military action to laud, the second air insisted, for political purposes, "'Tis he, 'tis he! the pride of fame,/Great LINCOLN all the shouts proclaim!/'Tis he, with *Rebel* laurels crown'd!/'Tis him the hills and vales resound!" The Massachusetts propagandist deemed the regulators' efforts "vain" attempts to subvert laws and stressed the "happiest peace" that would ensue as the "State again resumes her smile." Although the regulators acted in an established tradition of applying popular pressure on the government, as propagandists, the creators and circulators of lyrics like the ode insisted that such actions were anti-republican and not to be tolerated.[13]

## Reframing the Debate

The protests were not simply suppressed but were used to reframe debates over the federal government. While the regulators saw themselves as political actors capable of solving problems, propagandists of ratification cast the regulators as the problem. Propagandists made the regulators effective antiheroes to justify the restructuring of the federal government initially spurred by debates over the nation's financial problems. This recasting of the regulators provided a powerful backdrop for the drafting and ratification of the Constitution.

The efforts of Massachusetts regulators and their peers in other states coincided with leaders' interstate efforts to improve trade regulation, commercial laws, and other aspects of federal government.[14] The Annapolis convention, called in early 1786 and held in September, was intended to address trade regulation. Instead, it called for a second, more comprehensive interstate convention on reconstitution of the federal government in May 1787. That second convention, intended to revise the Articles of Confederation, instead generated a new document and avoided the difficult task of gaining approval of all state legislatures as required to amend the Articles of Confederation.[15] The new document, the Constitution, which outlined a more powerful national government and a less stringent approval procedure, was sent by the Confederation Congress to the states in late September 1787 for ratification by state conventions.

As political leaders corresponded between the two interstate conventions, they shared ideas for a federal government with greater authority to regulate the nation's financial matters—including taxes, currency, and the protection of creditors—and concern over the protestors' goals. The federalists, supporters of a more powerful federal government, viewed the state legislatures' measures very differently than did protestors. Ordinary Americans like the regulators were frustrated by tax legislation that transferred wealth from taxpayers and debtors to private creditors and elite government bondholders while hindering the agricultural work that they saw as necessary to improve the nation's economy. In contrast, federalist leaders—who saw the ability of individuals and the government to borrow as key to improving the economy and growing the nation into an industrial-commercial empire modeled after and capable of rivaling Britain—were dismayed by the federal government's inability to enforce taxation to pay the war debt. These federalists saw popular protest as worsening the situation by pressuring state legislatures to provide tax relief. Superintendent of Finance Robert Morris tried to establish federal powers of taxation in the early 1780s with the impost, an import duty to pay the principal and interest on the federal war debt, but the approval of all state legislatures, required to amend the

Articles of Confederation, was unachievable. Meanwhile, states had begun assuming federal debt, the reverse of efforts pursued by proponents of the industrial-commercial vision, and state legislatures faced continuing popular pressure to provide tax relief. The protest in Massachusetts set off alarms and was perceived and portrayed by federalists as an "excess of democracy" through which average people could unwisely influence the government and infringe on private liberty by damaging or confiscating property. In the *Connecticut Courant*, federalist Noah Webster declared, "I was once as strong a republican as any man in America. *Now* a republic is among the last kinds of governments I should choose. I should infinitely prefer a limited monarchy, for I would sooner be subject to the caprice of one man, than to the ignorance and passions of a multitude."[16] Federalists used the escalating conflict with the regulators as vivid justification for instituting a stronger national government with additional powers that they considered essential for national growth.

A leading example of such propaganda was *The Anarchiad*, a mock epic poem by the Connecticut Wits David Humphreys, Joel Barlow, John Trumbull, and Lemuel Hopkins. They issued *The Anarchiad* in installments from October 1786, when Shays's Rebellion was escalating and newspapers were circulating the Annapolis Convention's calls for meetings to revise the Articles of Confederation.[17] *The Anarchiad* pretended to be a recently discovered ancient poem in which a "prophetic bard" predicted the return of Chaos during the reader's time. From the first installment, the Wits invoked recent protests as justification for a more powerful federal government. Installments quickly expanded from the bard's visions of mobs overtaking Massachusetts to the destruction of the union and government. The Wits peppered the epic with attacks on populist measures and New Englanders who preferred maintaining less centralized powers and more democratic control.

After the fourth installment invoked the fundamental battle between good and evil—between the "guardian of the clime" Hesper and Anarch—the fifth installment called the people to help save the nation from Anarch's destructive forces. This installment was a song by David Humphreys titled "The Genius of America." Writing new words to the tune "The Watery God," or "Neptune's Resignation" (a British song about a naval battle of 1759), Humphreys hyperbolically juxtaposed the nation's remarkable progress in civilizing the land and its predicted reversion into Chaos. ▶ Where once "rove the naked tribes embrown'd,/Who feed on living gore" . . . "To midnight orgies, off'rings dire,/The human sacrifice in fire,/A heavenly light succeed[ed]/But lo! What horrors intervene." Humphreys implored the people to save the nation from the impending anarchy of rebellion, civil war, and populism, declaring "Ye FATHERS! Spread your fame afar!/'Tis yours to still the sounds of war,/And bid the slaughter cease;/The people hamlets wide extend,/The harvests spring, the spires ascend,/'Mid grateful songs of peace!" Humphreys's call to the people expanded on the first installment, in which the Wits had echoed Alexander Pope's mock epic *The Dunciad* to link the regulators' actions to efforts to reconstitute the federal government. Instead of the restoration of Chaos's "empire," following Pope, the Wits had their bard declare the restoration of Chaos's "constitution."[18] The Wits thus implied that if the people would not support their leaders and representatives in restructuring the federal government, the "anarchists" would do it for them, with dire, chaotic consequences.

As Humphreys's work demonstrates, music was a tool of propaganda used by the most well-connected political and military leaders. Humphreys was not a detached propagandist: he commanded the Connecticut militia that was readied, along with federal troops raised under the guise of an incipient war with Native Americans, to suppress the Massachusetts regulators, and he served in the Connecticut General Assembly. A confidant of George Washington since the Revolutionary War, Humphreys had spent several weeks with him at Mount Vernon preparing a biography and reflecting on the state of the nation. He also briefed Washington, the future president of the Constitutional Convention, on both *The Anarchiad* and regional protests. Well aware of how perceptions of recent protests could help shift more powers to the federal government, Humphreys, like other federalists, turned to music and verse as effective means of promoting his political views.[19]

## Promises and Fearmongering

The Wits issued *The Anarchiad* in installments until September 1787 as the federal convention was ending with a signed Constitution ready to be distributed for ratification by state convention. From early October, pro- and anti-ratification songs began appearing—as did pseudonymous essays of writers like "Federalist" and "Centinel." Advocates of ratification had the advantage in volume of material and tactics. This was especially clear in Pennsylvania, where federalists were so determined to control the discourse that they suppressed records of the debates in the state's ratification process.[20]

The few extant songs opposing ratification came from the presses of middling rank newspaper printers who stressed democracy, freedom of the press, and egalitarian ideals. These included Eleazer Oswald and Thomas Greenleaf, printers of the Philadelphia *Independent Gazetteer* and the *New York Journal*.[21] Opposition songs in their newspapers memorialized the efforts of antifederalists, who advocated less centralization of powers and more democratic control. Yet the songs' impact was limited, for rather than arguing against ratification or undermining the federalists, their writers lauded vandalism and efforts to stall ratification proceedings. One song touted the political battle waged on a sign outside a Philadelphia tavern. The attack came in April 1788 after six states had ratified the Constitution and a Rhode Island referendum rejected it. The "Federal Sign" showed the thirty-nine signing delegates to the "General Convention in all their different attitudes framing the proposed Constitution." Opponents of ratification attacked the sign with paint, the songwriter said, to make the honored signers look like criminals at the gallows. The sign was washed and repainted, but persisting in their opposition, townspeople tried to set it on fire and threatened to damage the tavern.[22]

Although many American leaders had reached agreement on the shape and significance of a stronger national government, advocates of ratification faced a challenge: they had to convince a population fearful of centralized government that additional centralization of powers was required. Like essayists, propagandists in verse urged ratification with bold promises, fearmongering, and misleading and false statements.[23] But they carefully selected older songs to rework to enhance their argument and rhetorical strategy. At times still invoking the regulators, songwriters used music to shape perceptions of efforts to reconstitute the national government and cultivate popular support for the Constitution.

From the beginning of the ratification process, songwriters stressed that the Constitution would help solve the nation's financial problems. The unnamed Boston writer of "The Grand Constitution: or, the Palladium of Columbia" offered a relentlessly optimistic portrayal of the "empire's" future gains under the Constitution (see Figure 1.2).[24] The songwriter portrayed the Constitution as the nation's escape and palladium, or safeguard, from all evils. The songwriter crafted new words to "Heart of Oak," a rousing British theatrical song written in 1759 by David Garrick and William Boyce. Garrick's lyrics honored a critical naval victory in Britain's Seven Years' War with France. Filled with "arrogance and jingoism" in Pencak's forthright assessment, "Heart of Oak" became an iconic British song by the century's

## CASTALIAN FOUNT.

THE

## GRAND CONSTITUTION:

Or, *The* PALLADIUM *of* COLUMBIA:

A NEW FEDERAL SONG.

Tune—" *Our Freedom we've won,*" &c.

FROM ſcenes of affliction—Columbia oppreſt—
Of credit expiring—and commerce diſtreſt,
Of nothing to do—and of nothing to pay—
From ſuch diſmal ſcenes let us haſten away.
*Our Freedom we've won, and the prize let's maintain*
*Our hearts are all right—*
*Unite, Boys, Unite,*
*And our* EMPIRE *in glory ſhall ever remain.*

The Muſes no longer the cypreſs ſhall wear—
For we turn our glad eyes to a proſpect more fair:
The ſoldier return'd to his ſmall cultur'd farm,
Enjoys the reward of his conquering arm.
" *Our Freedom we've won,*" &c.

Our trade and our commerce ſhall reach far and wide,
And riches and honour flow in with each tide,
*Kamſchatka* and *China* with wonder ſhall ſtare,
That the *Federal Stripes* ſhould wave gracefully there.
" *Our Freedom we've won,*" &c.

With gratitude let us acknowledge the worth,
Of what the CONVENTION has call'd into birth,
And the Continent wiſely confirm what is done
By FRANKLIN the ſage, and by brave WASHINGTON.
" *Our Freedom we've won,*" &c.

The wiſe CONSTITUTION let's truly revere,
It points out the courſe for our EMPIRE to ſteer,
For oceans of bliſs do they hoiſt the broad ſail,
And *peace* is the current, and *plenty* the gale.
" *Our Freedom we've won,*" &c.

With gratitude fill'd—let the great Commonweal
Paſs round the full glaſs to Republican zeal—
From ruin—their judgment and wiſdom well aim'd,
Our liberties, laws, and our credit reclaim'd.
" *Our Freedom we've won,*" &c.

Here Plenty and Order and Freedom ſhall dwell,
And your *Shayſes* and *Dayſes* won't dare to rebel—
Independence and culture ſhall graciouſly ſmile,
And the *Huſbandman* reap the full fruit of his toil.
" *Our Freedom we've won,*" &c.

That theſe are the bleſſings, Columbia knows—
The bleſſings the Fed'ral CONVENTION beſtows.
O! then let the People confirm what is done
By FRANKLIN the ſage, and by brave WASHINGTON.
*Our Freedom we've won, and the prize will maintain*
*By Jove we'll Unite,*
*Approve and Unite—*
*And huzza for* Convention *again and again.*

**Figure 1.2.** "The Grand Constitution: or, the Palladium of Columbia." Boston *Massachusetts Centinel*, 6 October 1787. Readex/NewsBank.

end.[25] The melody was popularized in America when John Dickinson used it for his 1768 "The Liberty Song," and it was commonly used for hortative texts to rouse fighting spirit during the Revolutionary era. ▶ Here the melody was used to rouse support for the Constitution. The Boston songwriter sustained the original naval topic and hyped the Constitution by likening it to a compass that would guide the nation through "oceans of bliss," promising "*peace* is the current, and *plenty* the gale." The reconstituted government would address expiring credit and distressed commerce and reclaim "liberties, laws, and our credit," promises appealing to mechanics, artisans, merchants, and shipbuilders. Targeting another key group, the songwriter promised that the veteran would enjoy "the reward of his conquering arm," implying that the Constitution would provide financial benefit for unpaid soldiers. Yet this rosy portrayal obscured the fact that some of the same individuals responsible for denying payment to ordinary soldiers—while better-off officers received huge payments in federal bonds—were also behind the writing and advocacy of the Constitution. Moreover, the songwriter's determined portrayal of the Constitution as *the* solution to the nation's ills obscured the fact that numerous solutions had been proffered, including monarchy, regional republics, and amendments to the Articles of Confederation.[26]

Federalist songwriters also argued, like the Connecticut Wits, that a more powerful federal government was needed to avoid the republic's destruction. As Maier has explained, proponents of this greater centralization of authority saw a "crippled national government; state authority trampled into the dust; a people incapable of self-government; a revolutionary cause on the brink of failure. . . . [T]he entire future of the United States was at stake." Promulgating this vision, federalists warned of mobs, state rivalries, and anarchy. Writing to fellow New Yorker Henry van Schaack, federalist Philip Schuyler maintained that without stronger central government, the republic would degenerate into "despotism, arbitrary monarchy, aristocracy, or what is still worse, an oligarchy." Arguing that the Constitution would prevent such dire consequences, the writer of "The Grand Constitution: or, the Palladium of Columbia" specifically related the Constitution to the bogeymen created from Shays's Rebellion, an event seen as so valuable to the ratification campaign that some federalists wished that it had lasted longer. Promising that a greater centralization of powers would protect the people and prevent "anarchy" (as in local pressure on state governments to change their policies on particular issues), the songwriter pledged, "Here Plenty and Order and Freedom shall dwell/And your *Shayses* and *Dayses* won't dare to rebel."

Even though events in Massachusetts were prompted by overly aggressive state debt-elimination efforts—not a lack of central authority—federalist propagandists used those events to cast the Constitution as necessary to create "order." Through such portrayals, the federalists not only rejected states' achievement of order through other means, such as debt relief and the issuing of paper currency, but also diverted attention from the Constitution's reduction of state powers.[27]

Proponents of ratification strengthened their argument by portraying the antifederalists as conspiring foes of order, stability, and freedom. Songwriters accused opponents of ratification of furthering a British-funded espionage effort to ruin the nation.[28] By conjuring such a dire set of coordinated threats, federalists could present the proposed restructuring of the government as a welcome preserver of the nation's hard-won freedoms. A songwriter reworking Thomas Paine's revolutionary-era "Liberty Tree" described a collection of internal and external threats to its "budding" and "blooming" branch. ▶ The federalist songwriter warned, "'Tis a tale most prophane,/How a wicked assemblage of powers—/Riot, Discord and Britain are uniting amain,/To cut down this garden of ours." Yet the nation would be freed from this conspiracy of popular insurgency, sectional and state jealousy, and British commercial restrictions, for "Our CONSTITUTION confirm—it firmly shall fix,/ Its idol—our LIBERTY TREE." Such representations of the Constitution as a means of preserving and nurturing liberty—which, for federalists, was defined in economic terms—diverted attention from a strong national government's potential to harm, reduce, or take away other freedoms, such as democracy and freedom of speech, press, and religion.[29] Moreover, by reworking and recontextualizing Revolutionary War songs, writers made failure to ratify the Constitution seem like failure to preserve the war's hard-won gains. Introducing one such song with the exhortation that "It is as essential that we now UNITE, to save our Country, as it once was to resort TO ARMS to defend it," a New York newspaper editor not only portrayed the Constitution as an extension of the war but also tapped into a concern, documented as early as 1783, that peace and the lack of external threat would likely weaken the bonds of union. Federalists made up for that lack through their rhetoric of crisis and conspiracy—threatening forces that they maintained could only be controlled through ratification. As Onuf has explained, the federalists' rhetoric "created a new reality by juxtaposing and synthesizing different and previously unconnected kinds of violence and disorder and by treating them all as symptoms of an unconstitutional problem."[30]

Casting opponents of ratification as conspirators intent on the young nation's ruin was just one federalist tactic. Proponents of ratification had already dealt a huge blow to their opponents by misleadingly dubbing them "antifederalists," a term that denied their support for the existing federal government and inaccurately cast them as obstructionists without any plans of their own. Federalist songwriters demonized the antifederalists as "imps of war" and "vile screaming owls of faction," delegitimizing opposition despite the long-standing place of "faction" and oppositional activity in American culture. While the New York assembly remained divided over ratification, local propagandists accused opponents of ratification of being willing to "undo" the nation for their own gain and being the source of all evil. Such federalist verses were intended not only to weaken the reputations and influence of antifederalists in the public's eye but also to intimidate them. In New York, as in other states, proponents of ratification benefited from newspaper editors' circulation of ample federalist material.[31]

Federalist propagandists targeted individuals who could oppose ratification in the states' conventions. In Connecticut, where newspaper editors circulated almost exclusively federalist material, proponents of ratification still aimed to end the political career and influence of their leading opponents, most notably General James Wadsworth. Wadsworth had been elected a delegate to the Confederation Congress and served as a member of Connecticut's Council, Speaker of the House, and comptroller, establishing himself as a significant figure in his state's political landscape. Wadsworth opposed federal taxation and a federal standing army, and he lauded Rhode Island, which was seen by federalists as the epitome of populist evils. He staunchly opposed the Constitution in the ratifying convention, where he represented the farmers of New Haven County. Already mocked by the Connecticut Wits as Anarch's lieutenant "Wronghead" in *The Anarchiad*, Wadsworth was further vilified in the anonymous song "A Parody on the Death of General Wolfe."▶ Writing a close parody of Thomas Paine's song on the death of the British General James Wolfe in 1759 during the French and Indian War, the unnamed federalist songwriter opened with a disgusting and chaotic scene in Anarch's retreat where Wronghead still wept for Daniel Shays more than a year after the regulators dispersed. In Paine's original, which Americans could recall, Britannia "mourned for her Wolfe," and "The walls of her cell she had sculptured around/With the feats of her favorite son;/And even the dust, as it lay on the ground,/Was engraved with the deeds he had done." In contrast, as Wadsworth deplored Shays's fate, "The walls of the hall were bespatter'd around,/With the juices of pursley [purslane] and peas,/And even the dust, as it lay on the ground,/Was imprinted with bed-bugs and fleas."[32] By using such vivid imagery, and by establishing such contrast with the heroic Wolfe, the federalist songwriter made clear that antifederalists like Wadsworth were no caretakers of the nation.

Other lyrics, while attacking leading antifederalists, emphasized how their supposed self-interest endangered states and the union. As George Washington explained to David Humphreys, opposition to ratification would be sizable "because the importance and sinister views of too many characters will be affected" by the restructured government. Following this line of thinking, another spin-off of *The Anarchiad* portrayed Wadsworth and New York antifederalist John Lamb as united in opposing the Constitution through a shared desire to preserve their personal power. The unnamed federalist songwriter contrived a genre within a genre to make this point—a newsboy's address in verse for the new year, which contained an oyster-catcher's song, in essence, a work song. The fictitious oyster-catcher's song recounted a dialogue between the two antifederalists who met under moonlight. The songwriter showed that self-interest endangered the union by enabling some states to take advantage of others. As the song foregrounded the willingness of Wadsworth and Lamb to work together—for example, in distributing other states' antifederalist propaganda in Connecticut—it made the Connecticut antifederalist Wadsworth look foolish for collaborating with the New York Collector of Customs Lamb, who obsessed over his state's potential loss of import duties under the Constitution, duties that were derived in part at New Jersey's and Connecticut's expense. Connecticut suffered through Lamb's self-interest, as he happily "let imperial [New] York still rule the sea,/And leave our posts to Clinton and to me." While Collector of Customs Lamb, antifederalist New York Governor George Clinton, and their state would still thrive from commerce and import duties, Wadsworth would let his own state eke out a meager existence from its poor soil as long as he could retain his personal power. Through the oyster-catcher's song, the federalist writer not only vilified Wadsworth, but also highlighted the foolishness of perpetuating a system of government that could allow states' interests to continue unabated.[33]

While today it may be difficult to imagine the Constitution as something that had to be fought for, it is important to place federalists' propaganda in perspective. Half the population opposed the Constitution, and while some states—particularly those at an economic disadvantage due, for example, to the import duties imposed by neighboring states—ratified it quickly and easily, in others ratification was hard-fought. In the latter states, crucial factors leading to ratification were propaganda and coverage in the press. Proponents of the Constitution dominated the states' ratification processes and surrounding discourse, including musical discourse. Intolerant of opposition, federalists controlled the information disseminated through notes of ratification proceedings, pulled subscriptions and advertisements in newspapers that printed oppositional material, and loaded newspapers with pro-Constitution writings, including songs. Federalists' songs contributed to an overblown sense of crisis that enabled ratification, including circumvention of the Articles of Confederation. Such songs were not merely humorous or malicious. They were engaging tools for justifying and enacting a significant restructuring of the government. Songwriters created these political musical statements through carefully crafted intertextual references and reworkings of relevant musical models accessible to Americans through oral and written transmission.[34]

## Celebrating Ratification

Federalists promptly celebrated states' ratification of the Constitution. Celebrations offered ritual closure of ratification debates and proclaimed federalist victory. Cultivating broader acceptance of the Constitution and the newly structured government was important not only because of ongoing antifederalist challenges but also because non-ratification by any state could result in a partial union, entailing new commercial rivalries.[35] As states ratified, songwriters and printers used celebratory music as interstate propaganda to pressure remaining states to ratify, usher in a post-debate period of allegiance to the newly structured government, and articulate a social hierarchy under the Constitution.

In one frequently reprinted song, "A Yankee" recounted Massachusetts's debates, ratification, and celebration as new propagandist lyrics to the tune of "Yankee Doodle" (see Figure 1.3).[36]▶ Following Pennsylvania's protracted ratification process, Massachusetts's ratification—despite the narrow margin—was cause for celebration. It also exemplified how federalists could succeed in other states, particularly those without anticipated financial benefits as an incentive to ratify. The "Yankee" promoted ratification and allegiance to the new government by calling for the opposition's silence and lauding Boston's approach to amendments. In Pennsylvania, discussion of

POETRY.

The Grand Federal Edifice.

Tune—*Yankee Doodle.*

THE 'Vention did in Boſton meet,
But ſtate-houſe could not hold 'em,
So then they went to Fed'ral-ſtreet,
And there the truth was told 'em—
*Yankee doodle, keep it up!*
*Yankee doodle, dandy,*
*Mind the muſic and the ſtep,*
*And with the girls be handy.*

They ev'ry morning went to prayer,
And then began diſputing,
Till oppoſition ſilenc'd were,
By arguments refuting.
*Yankee doodle, keep it up!* &c.

Then 'ſquire Hancock, like a man
Who dearly loves the nation,
By a concil'atry plan,
Prevented much vexation.
*Yankee doodle,* &c.

He made a *woundy* fed'ral ſpeech,
With ſenſe and elocution;
And then the 'Vention did beſeech
'T adopt the conſtitution.
*Yankee doodle,* &c.

The queſtion being outright put,
(Each voter independent)
The fed'raliſts agreed t'adopt,
And then propoſe amendment.
*Yankee doodle,* &c.

The other party ſeeing then
The people were againſt 'em,
Agreed like honeſt, faithful men,
To mix in peace amongſt 'em.
*Yankee doodle,* &c.

The Boſton folks are *deucid* lads,
And always full of notions;
The boys, the girls, their mams and dads,
Were fill'd with joy's commotions.
*Yankee doodle,* &c.

So ſtraight way they proceſſion made,
Lord! how *nation* fine, ſir!
For ev'ry man of ev'ry trade
Went with his tools——to dine, ſir.
*Yankee doodle,* &c.

JOHN FOSTER WILLIAMS in a ſhip,
Join'd in the ſocial band, ſir,
And made the laſſes dance and ſkip,
To ſee him ſail on land, ſir.
*Yankee doodle,* &c.

Oh then a *whapping* feaſt begun,
And and all hands went to eating;
They drank their toaſts, ſhook hands & ſung,
Huzza!! for 'Vention meeting.
*Yankee doodle,* &c.

Now politicians of all kinds,
Who are not yet decided,
May ſee how Yankees ſpeak their minds,
*And yet are not divided.*
*Yankee doodle,* &c.

Then from this ſample let 'em ceaſe
Inflammatory writing,
For FREEDOM, HAPPINESS and PEACE,
*Is better far than fighting.*
*Yankee doodle,* &c.

So here I end my fed'ral ſong,
Compos'd of thirteen verſes,
May agriculture flouriſh long,
And commerce fill our purſes!
*Yankee doodle, keep it up!*
*Yankee doodle, dandy,*
*Mind the muſic and the ſtep,*
*And with the girls be handy.*

**Figure 1.3.** "The Grand Federal Edifice." Charleston *City Gazette,* 1 April 1788. Readex/NewsBank.

amendments had slowed ratification; the "Yankee" highlighted by contrast the approach suggested by Governor Hancock: ratify now and agree to amend later. This approach, which Holton has called the federalists' "most effective tactic," simultaneously validated and contained interest in amendments while sustaining the expectation that antifederalists would silence themselves and let the ratification process continue unobstructed. Selecting "Yankee Doodle" gave the songwriter the perfect opportunity to write, with a nod to the tune's earlier lyrics and vocabulary, an extended, wide-eyed observational account of this approach to amendments and its effects. Through the song's thirteen-verse structure, a symbolic feature noted in the final verse, the "Yankee" presented a clear expectation that all thirteen states would ratify. Any state opposing or resisting ratification would break the union, the preservation of which was a major justification for ratification.[37] The "Yankee" articulated an expectation of, and a path toward, reunification at the state level by tracing Massachusetts's progression from debate, through ratification, and on to unifying celebration in which "ev'ry man of ev'ry trade went with his tool" to process and then "dine." Boston's celebration—which included an elaborate procession with floats and banners—played a crucial role in the narrative offered by the "Yankee": the celebration's joy, toasts, and songs fostered unity during a transition from a period of debate to one of allegiance to the newly reconstituted government.

Other celebratory musical propaganda came from prominent Philadelphian Francis Hopkinson. The son of a well-placed English resident of Philadelphia, Hopkinson (1737–91) was an early American gentleman with a talent for political propaganda and music. He graduated from what would become the University of Pennsylvania and entered the bar in 1761. Connections with Benjamin Franklin, Governor John Penn, the bishop of Worcester, and the British prime minister's wife gave Hopkinson lucrative positions, financial support, and an escape to England during violence over the Stamp Act. After returning in 1767 to Philadelphia, Hopkinson ran a dry-goods store and obtained a sinecure as a Delaware customs collector, a post that provided him income while he lived in New Jersey as a "country gentleman." Supporting the revolution, Hopkinson signed the Declaration of Independence and wrote political propaganda, deploying his talents for satire, parody, whimsy, wit, and music. He wrote "Battle of the Kegs," a song mocking the British for firing in panic at the patriots' floating mines in the Delaware River, mines that Hopkinson and his colleagues conceived to send down river to blow up British ships moored at Philadelphia. ▶ Hopkinson's lyrics were sung, likely to the tune of "Yankee Doodle" or "Maggy Lauder," by officers in the war. Hopkinson's famous song only hinted at his musical talents. He studied harpsichord and organ; organized and performed in concerts; compiled, composed, and adapted hymns and psalms; and wrote secular vocal music. The latter included songs dedicated to George Washington, odes, and a cantata on American independence. His musical manuscripts and library reflect a strong influence of eighteenth-century Italian music, prompting Richard Crawford to liken Hopkinson's taste to that of "a cultivated Englishman."[38]

Hopkinson wrote federalist propaganda in both prose and verse. He issued a prose allegory "The New Roof" that ridiculed antifederalists. He even dreamed up a "Grand Antifederalist Procession," an imaginary inversion of a federalist celebration of ratification. The antifederalists' ritual moved to the "Dead March" from Handel's oratorio *Saul* played on hurdy gurdies, Jew's harps, and banjo, an assemblage of folk and street instruments associated with the lower ranks, slaves, and free blacks. These instruments cast the antifederalists as ill-suited for leadership and the funereal music symbolized their downfall. Hopkinson had Eleazer Oswald, printer of the Philadelphia *Independent Gazetteer*, carry a banner marked with the "Demon of Defamation" while two "printers' devils" distributed the newspaper's ode mocking a federalist procession.[39]

Hopkinson elaborated ideas from his prose allegory "The New Roof" in "The Raising: A New Song for Federal Mechanicks" (see Figure 1.4). Hopkinson furthered the notion that the Articles of Confederation constituted a roof broken beyond repair. In Hopkinson's lyrics, mechanics, or craftsmen, constructed a new roof (the Constitution) to replace the failing one. This powerful image of a failed first national constitution not only obscured the fact that over half the Articles of Confederation had been retained in the Constitution but also justified the federalists' circumvention of the unanimous approval of amendments to the Articles of Confederation by specifying in Article VII of the Constitution that nine states' assent was sufficient for it to go into effect.[40]

Scholars have largely remained silent about Hopkinson's verse as music even though he designated it a song. Hopkinson's "The Raising" was printed in 1800 as a reworking of "Balance a Straw," a melody circulating in England before he arrived there in 1766. In the mid-1750s, "Balance a Straw" celebrated the performance of London slackwire performer Anthony Maddox, who kicked a straw up into a glass held in his mouth, tossed the straw out, and then caught and balanced the straw on the edge of the glass, all while balancing himself on a slackwire. Before Hopkinson arrived in England, David Garrick wrote new lyrics to "Balance a Straw" to be sung as the epilogue of Arthur Murray's comedy *All in the Wrong*. In the epilogue, Garrick

Come, up with the Plates, lay them firm on the Wall,  
Like the People at large, they're the Ground-work of all;  
Examine them well, and see that they're sound,  
Let no rotten Parts in our Building be found;  
For our Roof we will raise and our Song still shall be—  
Our Government firm, and our Citizens free.

Now hand up the Girders, lay each in his Place,  
Between them the Joists must divide all the Space;  
Like Assembly-men these should lye level along,  
Like Girders, our Senate prove loyal and strong;  
For our Roof we will raise, and our Song still shall be—  
A Government firm, over Citizens free.

The Rafters now frame—your King-Posts and Braces,  
And drive your Pins home, to keep all in their Places;  
Let Wisdom and Strength in the Fabric combine,  
And your Pins be all made of American Pine;  
For our Roof we will raise, and our Song still shall be—  
A Government firm, over Citizens free.

Our King-Posts are Judges---how upright they stand,  
Supporting the Braces, the Laws of the Land—  
The Law of the Land, which divide Right from Wrong,  
And strengthen the Weak, by weak'ning the Strong;  
For our Roof we will raise, and our Song still shall be—  
Laws equal and just, for a People that's free.

**Figure 1.4.** Francis Hopkinson's "The Raising" was first printed in 1788 with no tune indicated. The tune "Balance a Straw," used here, was indicated in an 1800 printing. New Haven *Connecticut Journal*, 20 February 1788. Readex/NewsBank.

Up! Up with the Rafters—each Frame is a State!
How nobly they rise! their Span, too, how great!
From the North to the South, o'er the Whole they extend
And rest on the Walls, while the Walls they defend!
For our Roof we will raise, and our Song still shall be—
Combined in Strength, yet as Citizens free.

Now enter the Purlins, and drive your Pins through,
And see that your Joints are drawn home, and all true;
The Purlins will bind all the Rafters together,
The Strength of the Whole shall defy Wind and Weather;
For our Roof we will raise, and our Song still shall be—
United as States, but as Citizens free.

Come, raise up the Turret—our Glory and Pride—
In the Centre it stands, o'er the Whole to preside;
The Sons of Columbia shall view with Delight
It's Pillars and Arches; and towering Height;
Our Roof is now rais'd, and our Song still shall be—
A Federal Head, o'er a People still free.

Huzza! my brave Boys, our Work is complete,
The World shall admire Columbia's fair Seat;
It's Strength against Tempest and Time shall be Proof,
And Thousands shall come to dwell under our ROOF
Whilst we drain the deep Bowl, our Toast still shall be—
Our Government firm, and our Citizens free.

**Figure 1.4.** Continued.

began each verse by addressing a different portion of the audience, much like Hopkinson began each verse of "The Raising" by naming a different element of the new roof.[41] The stepwise melody was easy to sing and remember, and its opening phrases used a modest range well-suited to amateur singers.

In addition to promoting the notion that the Constitution was a necessary, wholesale replacement of the Articles of Confederation, Hopkinson used "The Raising" to focus attention on the process of, and progress toward, ratification. Abandoning his allegory's attacks on antifederalists, and paralleling the structure of Garrick's epilogue to *All in the Wrong*, Hopkinson instead narrated, stanza by stanza, the process of constructing the new "roof" that symbolized the restructured government. By doing so, he lent ratification an air of inevitability. While the "Yankee" structured his song after the ideal thirteen-state union, Hopkinson, by limiting his song to nine verses (the length of Garrick's epilogue), highlighted the minimum ratification requirement for the Constitution to go into effect. His song, which was accompanied in the *Massachusetts Centinel* by an expanding series of pillars representing states that had ratified and were expected to do so next, focused attention on this critical point of ratification by a ninth state (which came in summer 1788). Well aware of this cumulative process, federalists sometimes delayed their states' proceedings to take advantage of the momentum provided by others' ratification; in New York, for example, federalists proposed a slow method for reviewing the document knowing that, as the ninth state ratified in the meantime, continued antifederalist opposition would appear "futile" and harmful to the inland portion of the state because it would encourage the economic center New York City to separate to join the union. New York ultimately ratified the Constitution even though antifederalist delegates had outnumbered federalists forty-six to nineteen.[42]

## "The People" and the Government

Hopkinson used "The Raising" to articulate the people's relationship to the Constitution and the new government created through it. Hopkinson's song had ordinary people—mechanics—constructing the new government. Such assertions of the people's role in "raising" the Constitution made a stronger centralized government seem less frightening and more like "the protector and direct agent of the people." This portrayal was significant as federalists sought to create a more powerful federal government amid long-standing popular fears of centralized government.[43] While Hopkinson's "mechanics" could be understood as the men responsible for writing, signing, and ratifying the Constitution, Schloss maintains that Hopkinson also intended the term to be understood literally. Hopkinson highlighted this literal interpretation in a massive procession he organized for Philadelphia's celebration of ratification by ten states on July 4, 1788: the position of hundreds of architects and carpenters was one of just two exceptions to the determination of the trades' positions by lot—they accompanied the "New Roof–Grand Federal Edifice" (a large dome supported by thirteen columns), reflecting the opening stanzas of his song.[44] ▶ Other songwriters, using less multivalent language, stressed that the Constitution was the people's choice, approved by the "people's voice," and adopted by each citizen. Along with publicized toasts and coverage of ratification celebrations, their lyrics portrayed the people as integral to the government's shaping—both vital to ratification and the source of sovereignty in the Constitution.[45]

While the Constitution's emphasis on the people did reflect a significant difference from the Articles of Confederation—the national government's new ability to pass laws impacting individual citizens directly—the similar emphasis in musical propaganda surrounding ratification was misleading. First, while songwriters' references to the people amplified the federalists' claim that sovereignty was derived from the people, those references also diverted attention from the Constitution's negative impact on states' rights and its failure to protect individuals' rights. As Patrick Henry and other opponents of ratification noted, the phrase "We the People" in the Constitution's preamble—instead of "We the States"—effectively destroyed states' rights and jeopardized those of individuals.[46]

Second, despite songwriters' emphasis on "the people," the Constitution was biased toward the interests and views of a subset of the people—the coastal mercantile elites—and was designed to curtail the masses' influence. The Constitution's content prioritized the legal and commercial needs of mercantile communities over the customs of small communities, and as news of ratification drove up securities prices, speculators—including those who lobbied for ratification across state lines—benefited. The reconstituted government—through its large legislative districts, longer terms, checks and balances, and two houses (only one of which had members chosen directly by the voters)—was designed to limit the influence of average Americans, influence decried by federalists as the tyranny of the majority. Even though "the people" loomed large in musical propaganda, ordinary people were deemed "very unequal to the task of forming a judgment upon the Constitution" and governing themselves. Proponents of the Constitution felt that restructuring the government would prevent the nation from degenerating into tyranny or anarchy as a result of excess democracy.[47]

Third, this Constitutional bias was problematic because of limitations on the people's role in the ratification process. Despite the prominence of Americans in lyrics like Hopkinson's "The Raising," the exact role of the people in ratification was unclear and contested. Citizens in Connecticut, for example, wondered if they were only to choose delegates, or also instruct delegates how to vote and represent them. Ratification was also marred by flawed representation. Non-proportional representation within some states gave added weight to eastern federalist elites. Delegates from fifty Shaysite towns in western Massachusetts could not make the costly and difficult trip to the Boston convention, and their absence made ratification possible.

Residents of some states complained of having to choose delegates to their conventions before they had seen or had time to consider the document to be ratified. Because of such limitations, Connecticut's ratification process was perceived as "another *artful maneuver*" designed "to hurry on matters before the people have a chance to understand [the Constitution] and so as to be able to make a judicious choice of delegates to act conformable to their own minds."[48]

Public celebrations of states' ratification, which included performance and distribution of music, first exposed and then obscured the people's limited role. Pennsylvania's ratification was marked by a procession of convention delegates, judges, university professors, and militia officers, joined by apparently few members of the public. One of Philadelphia's antifederalists drew attention to ordinary people's limited role in Pennsylvania's ratification by noting their scant interest and participation in the procession. He exclaimed, "O strange behavior! The people do not seem to know what grandeur is preparing for them and their posterity." Printed accounts show that the people were to take their place, last, as undistinguished "citizens," following twenty-eight groupings of government leaders and keepers of the peace.[49]

Organizers of subsequent celebrations portrayed the relationship between the people and Constitution differently. More inclusive celebrations were organized by committees in cities like Boston and New York, and in Philadelphia again after ratification by nine states ensured that the Constitution would go into effect. These celebrations obscured the limited role of ordinary people in the ratification process as they featured massive displays of the trades. These displays drew attention to artisans and their skills, promoted American goods, called for protection, and signified mechanics' support for ratification.

In the processions, music was used to stimulate a connection between the people and the Constitution. Printers, when representing and performing their trades in the processions, often issued verses to be distributed to the crowds. They distributed songs affirming ratification and inculcating allegiance to the new government. In Portsmouth's June 1788 celebration of ratification, local "pressmen" issued the "Federal Song," likely written by federalist lawyer Jonathan Mitchell Sewall. Once distributed to the crowds, Sewall's lyrics directed them, "See each industrious ART moves on/To ask protection, praise and fame." Sewall and local printers guided onlookers to see their community's artisans placing their faith in the Constitution rather than questioning it, and serving as models for the whole community.[50]

In reality, mechanics' support for ratification varied in inverse relation to states' existing protective legislation. While federalism was strong among mechanics in New York and Baltimore, it was weaker in Philadelphia and Boston. In Boston, newspaper printer Benjamin Russell and Paul Revere took swift action in early 1787 to voice and magnify the interests of federalist mechanics.[51] Some mechanics' displays and mottos—like the Philadelphia clockmakers' motto "Time rules all things"—made little reference to the ratification process or the Constitution. The artisans' realistic presentations—by deviating from the allegorical style of European processions—pointed to their conception of the nation as founded on "the people and their economic and occupational activities," rather than elitist politics, foreshadowing the Republican and Federalist parties. Federalist elites and artisans each claimed what they wanted from the celebrations. Tradesmen sought recognition—highlighted in the detailed accounts they gave newspaper printers to circulate about the processions. Federalists sought to project a unity of sentiment and confirm progress made on what Knott has called the "sentimental project" focused on the social reformation of the republic. In his public comments on Philadelphia's celebration of ratification by ten states, Benjamin Rush noted that "rank for a while forgot all its claims." Francis Hopkinson praised the procession's thousands of spectators for "exhibiting a spectacle truly magnificent and irresistibly animating" themselves, as "every countenance appeared to be the index of a heart glowing with urbanity and rational joy."[52]

As a result, even as tradesmen used the celebrations for their own ends, they bolstered federalists' assertions, including the notion that the Constitution was a product of the people's will. Such assertions were captured by a "Lady" in song on the occasion of Philadelphia's second procession celebrating ratification on July 4, 1788 (see Figure 1.5).[53] Among the leading Federalist women capable of writing such lyrics was Julia Stockton Rush, daughter of poet Annis Stockton and the wife of Dr. Benjamin Rush. Echoing Benjamin Rush's interpretation, the "Lady" marked the occasion of ratification as one "When all ranks of men in friendship should mix." Despite the relatively weak federalism among Philadelphia mechanics, she described the procession as a "glorious sight where thousands appear,/Assembled with emblems to shew/Their Union is firm, their rejoicing sincere."

Outside the processions, songwriters elaborated the people's proper place under this newly reconstituted federal government. Shortly after Massachusetts's ratification, a subscriber to the Boston *Independent Chronicle*

**Figure 1.5.** This song, "written by a LADY in Philadelphia, 4th July, 1788," proclaimed that year as the start of new era fated to ensure the ratification of the Constitution and the nation's bountiful future. Providence *United States Chronicle*, 28 August 1788. Readex/NewsBank.

writing under the pseudonym "SKNUG" chastised, "If common people all must fix,/To bear a part in politicks,/Confusion must ensue:—/Let each conduct his proper sphere,/Nor with each other interfere, /Mind what they have to do."[54] By articulating the "common people's" place outside government, such lyrics reflected a basic attitude of many federalists. As New Hampshire clergyman Jeremy Belknap bluntly asserted, "Let it stand as a principle that government originates from the people; but let the people be taught . . . that they are not able to govern themselves." Songwriters promised financial rewards if ordinary Americans focused on their own work, leaving the business of government to the elites. As the songwriter "Dr. S" commanded ordinary Americans with a biblical reference, "Bend your 'spears to pruning hooks'; break up the gen'rous soil,/While fruits of plenty round the land, reward the reapers toil." The message was tailored not only to encourage domestic production and strengthen the economy but also to keep the general public out of the business of government, end opposition to ratification, and promote allegiance to the new federal government.[55]

Clearer attributions illustrate how members of various ranks reinforced this message in Philadelphia, where the pace and initial celebration of ratification had drawn criticism. Local craftsman Andrew Adgate (1762–93) echoed the views of elite federalists Francis Hopkinson and Dr. Benjamin Rush. Born in Norwich, Connecticut, Adgate was well known in Philadelphia as a cardmaker and the city's "premier music teacher." As a mechanic, he produced cards, metal-toothed instruments used to smooth cotton or wool fibers. He was also a psalmodist, tunebook compiler, choir leader, and music instructor at the Young Ladies' Academy of Philadelphia. To improve choral singing, Adgate was determined in 1785 to found a free singing school funded by subscriptions to the pupils' concerts. This Uranian Society became the Uranian Academy and Philadelphia's leading musical institution. The sacred concerts were held at the College of Philadelphia (later the University of Pennsylvania) where Hopkinson was a trustee. Rush and Hopkinson, men who shared interests in free schooling and the importance of music education, were among the society's managers or patrons.[56]

Adgate's "Mechanic's Song" drew on his dual roles as musician and mechanic. Addressing his fellow artisans in his song, Adgate blended professional pride with a directive of obedient productivity to fuel the economy and prevent political dissent. He commanded his fellow mechanics, "Stick close to your looms and your wheels and your cards." Adgate echoed local federalist elites. His lyrics sustained a primary message of Hopkinson's "The Raising" and the ratification processions conducted as street theater. Published accounts of the processions—including an account submitted by Hopkinson—had noted how yeoman and artisan participants were "at work" or "occupied," "each with their proper implements," as the processions moved through the streets. Partway through Hopkinson's "The Raising," mechanics ceased being agents of the reconstituted national government and became subjects and spectators contemplating the "new roof." As mechanics and yeoman displayed their skills, they enacted an orderly, productive society submitting to a newly constituted government designed by nonlaboring elites. Adgate addressed members of each craft in turn, directing them to their work with genial humor and historical references bringing out the importance of their work. Adgate concluded with a collective command in the thirteenth verse, "Each *Tradesman* turn out with his tool in his hand,/To cherish the *Arts* and keep *Peace* through the land." Adgate's lyrics and repeated assurances, "You have nothing to fear," directed laborers' attention away from the postwar depression and from the uncertainties about the country's future under the reconstituted government.[57]

Hopkinson and Rush got help from other Philadelphians to promulgate federalists' views about the people's relationship to the Constitution. Committee members from the elites organized ratification processions and oversaw the division and arrangement of people based on occupation and, by extension, rank. Bands of musicians regulated the processions' temporal conduct and sustained the public display of the relationships among members of these "distinct orders." As a consequence, they reinforced hierarchical distinctions between plebeians who worked and patricians who governed.[58] In Philadelphia's procession held on July 4, 1788, to mark ratification by ten states, the arrangements committee demonstrated extraordinary attention to order: marshals with megaphones were assigned to groups of marchers to help regulate their movements. ▶ The "excellent" band was carefully located to highlight the Constitution and its creators, and the city's leading composer, Alexander Reinagle, composed a "Grand March" for it to play. The band was placed between marchers representing the convention that produced the Constitution and the display of the Constitution on a staff carefully marked in gold with the motto "The People." However, the ten men representing "Citizens at large" seated under Charles Wilson Peale's ten-foot diameter Constitutional dome called the "New Roof or Grand Federal Edifice" were ultimately displaced by ten men representing states that had ratified the Constitution.[59] Thus, music like Reinagle's and Adgate's embodied a contradiction in federalist propaganda: while federalists strove to portray the Constitution as a product of the people, they wanted the people to stay out of the business of government.

## Cultivating Allegiance

Despite federalists' efforts to showcase the Constitution as a product of the people, as Larkin has reminded us, the Constitution "was hardly an expression of a national will or a national consensus. Quite the contrary, the Constitution provoked passionate dissension and was only adopted thanks to a series of negotiations and public relations campaigns." Notwithstanding the impression of strong support conveyed through large ratification celebrations on the mercantile coast and rapid ratification by small states poised to benefit from federal trade regulation, the Constitution may have had the support of only half of the population.[60] Even after ratification by nine states, there were still uncertainties. Would all the remaining states ratify it, retaining the union of thirteen states, or would some hold out? Would the union survive ongoing sectionalism, provincialism, and states' desires for autonomy? Would antifederalists accept the Constitution or fight it, as their continued protests suggested? Would antifederalists in the new Congress hinder progress on important legislation? If such problems arose, would the Constitution itself be circumvented and replaced like the Articles of Confederation?[61]

These uncertainties meant that broader allegiance to the newly structured government was vital for its success. Federalists were eager to silence their opponents and gain adherents because in some states, ratification came through manipulation of timing, not strong support. For example, most delegates to the New Hampshire convention opposed the Constitution in February 1788. New Hampshire ultimately ratified the Constitution by only a narrow margin, and only after John Langdon's "masterstroke" of seeking adjournment in February. When delegates reconvened in June, not only had more states ratified, but Massachusetts's agreement to ratify now and amend later had provided a model for proceeding with ratification despite ongoing local debates. After disappointing leaders like Washington for not ratifying in February, in June New Hampshire had the opportunity for redemption by becoming the ninth and final state needed for the Constitution to go into effect. Six delegates' change of heart between February and June ensured that New Hampshire beat out Virginia for that honor.[62]

With this less-than-overwhelming victory, federalists feared sustained debate and called for broader support for the Constitution and an end to opposition. One song for the New Hampshire ratification celebrations in

Portsmouth, likely written by local lawyer and federalist Jonathan Mitchell Sewall "to a new tune nam'd Union," offered a hyperbolically optimistic view of the nation's future under the Constitution, a future filled with peace, thriving commerce, "wisdom, justice, harmony and love." His lyrics cast any continued opposition as an unacceptable block on the nation's progress: "Hence local Animosities shall cease,/Insurgency no more shall find a name,/Nor civil Discord interrupt our peace,/Nor check AMERICA! Thy rising fame." Sewall's chorus not only called people to sing in support of the new union under the Constitution but also noted the significance of that singing as a means of cultivating broader support. The chorus commanded, "In rapt'rous lays/Your voices raise/Columbia's song,/In accents strong,/Shall echo to our joys, and dwell on ev'ry tongue."[63] Another New Hampshire songwriter called the opponents of ratification to reflect on the harm they had done and seek pardon, promising that such political "converts" would be welcomed as the reconstituted government went into effect (see Figure 1.6). The songwriter targeted local antifederalist Joshua Atherton—whose legal background and acquisition of antifederalist propaganda from other states (through New Yorker John Lamb) made him the most effective opposition voice in the New Hampshire convention.[64] Any American involved in a British conspiracy to ruin the nation deserved hanging, charged the songwriter. This attack on Atherton provided both a rallying point for celebrating federalists—as the final two verses signaled with a standard toast to the ladies and three cheers—and a warning in print to anyone intending to persist in challenging them. The songwriter contextualized this personal attack to appeal to the reader, singer, or listener by accusing critics like Atherton of violating Washington's call for each man to do his part in rescuing the nation through ratification.

Songwriters cultivated allegiance to the restructured government by portraying the Constitution as the nation's savior and protector. They cast the Constitution as the sole guardian of freedom and the culmination of Revolutionary era sacrifices. Singers—the spectators—in Portsmouth's celebration of ratification explained that the Goddess of Peace had led Americans to set the nation's cornerstone in war and its top-stone through ratification. If, as songwriters suggested, the Constitution ensured the national independence gained through local efforts during the war, Americans had a duty to give allegiance to the government in support of their forefathers' sacrifices. Indeed, one versifier, possibly a Connecticut Wit, equated opposition to the Constitution with desecration of Revolutionary War heroes'

A FEDERAL SONG.

Tune *Bunker Hill.*

NOW, come ye federal ſons of fame,
And join your chearful voices,
And let your *Waſhing'on's* great name,
(In which good men rejoices,)
Be chorus'd THRICE, and THRICE the cauſe,
Which we have been contending,
The Conſtitution and the laws,
Are ſurely worth defending.
Fol lol lol lol lol.

II.

The CONSTITUTION's now got down,
In ſpite of oppoſition,
Since Waſhington of high renown,
Firſt made the propoſition ;
For one and all to—'VENTION call
To try to ſave the nation,
And every man do what he can,
According to his ſtation.
Fol lol lol lol lol.

III.

Some men of might with ranc'rous ſpite,
Have tri'd to raiſe commotions,
And ſcatter'd forth, from ſouth to north,
Their *Antifederal* notions :
Supported by ſome Britiſh ſpy,
Who ſecret ſpreads his money,
Which makes the Anti-Lawyers ſpeak
As ſmooth as any honey.
Fol lol lol lol lol.

IV.

Let A————n, that noted ſon
Of Antifederaliſm,
No longer plead, or ſow the ſeeds
Of anarchy and ſchiſm.
Let ev'ry one of ANARCH's ſons,
Be eaſy now and quiet,
Since the Conſtitution has gone down,
At the laſt gen'ral DIET.
Fol lol lol lol lol,

V.

Let all the ſons of bribery,
And ſuch rabſcallion fellows,
Like Britiſh ſpies, for their groſs lies,
Be hang'd upon the gallows,
Though they have try'd on every ſide
To ſcatter great confuſion ;
The WORK is DONE, let ev'ry one
Rejoice at the concluſion.
Fol lol lol lol lol,

VI.

And let all Anties have a care,
And think what they've been doing,
Since very ſoon they'l change their tune,
And be for pardons ſuing ;
Yet nevertheleſs, if they'l confeſs,
That they have been miſtaken,
They ſhall partake of our beef ſteak,
With PORTER, CHEESE and BACON,
Fol lol lol lul lol.

VII.

And let us drink to that dear laſs,
Who loves the man of *feeling*,
Come fill the bumper in the glaſs,
For ſure you muſt be willing ;
For if it was not for the fair,
What would become of man, ſirs,
They thread the needle to a hair,
And kiſs you when they can ſirs,
Fol lol lol lol lol.

VII.

I greet you all—ye ſons of mirth,
New-Hampſhire has compleated,
And brought the Fabrick into birth,
Which ſome would have defeated ;
Now let us give three hearty cheers,
To honor thoſe Conventions,
Whoſe noble deeds have quell'd our fears,
God bleſs their good intentions.
Fol lol lol lol lol.

**Figure 1.6.** One federalist songwriter called the opponents of ratification to reflect on the harm they had done and seek pardon. Exeter *Freeman's Oracle*, 11 July 1788. Readex/NewsBank.

graves.[65] Other songwriters called for quasi-religious reverence of the Constitution and the new federal government, ending lyrics with "Amen."[66]

Songwriters also cultivated allegiance to the Constitution by highlighting it as a transformative device in historical narratives of national development. In her reading of the Philadelphia ratification procession, the "Lady" marked the year 1788, not 1776, as the nation's critical birth. This year began a fated period of economic prosperity and federalism that would restore order and fulfill a heliotropic vision of America as the last and greatest empire.[67] The "Lady" underscored the import of this new federal era through the tune she reworked: George Alexander Stevens's "The Gods of the Greeks," also known as "The Origin of English of Liberty." Stevens's tune had already been used by Thomas Paine for his well-known 1775 song "Liberty Tree." ▶ Both Steven's and Paine's songs articulated a conceit of gods blessing a fated land with liberty, a conceit that the "Lady" maintained through "Old

Time" (see Figure 1.5). But by naming Stevens's song, rather than Paine's, the "Lady" invoked Paine's well-known song through melodic association but rejected the Revolutionary era as the nation's critical era. Instead, it was the Constitutional era that began a fated new empire.

In narrative structure and imagery, songwriters presented a Constitution that transformed the nation by confining the evils of contention, rage, discord, sectional jealousy, state-centric solutions, insurgency, and anarchy to its dark past and by initiating an enlightened "new era" of flourishing arts, science, commerce, manufacturing, agriculture, and peace.[68] "An ODE on the Anniversary of Independence, July 4, 1788," which fit the tune "The Watery God" or "Neptune's Resignation," offered a historical narrative through a parallel to the Israelites. ▶ The anonymous writer likened Washington to Moses and Joshua and reflected that after "wand'ring twelve long years/Thro' wilds of faction, fraud and fears,/We hail the promis'd land," thanks to the Constitution. This ode was circulated in the federalist *Newport Herald* amid a long fight for allegiance—Rhode Island did not ratify until 1790, under growing pressure of economic sanctions and federalist success in passing additional, unbearable commercial restrictions against the state.[69]

A highly respected individual could provide a powerful focal point and help transfer loyalty and allegiance to the restructured government. Federalist propaganda had already invoked founding father figures: "The Grand Constitution" (see Figure 1.2) repeatedly referred to Benjamin Franklin and George Washington to extend reverence for them to the document itself. Washington was ideal for cultivating allegiance. He was a trusted, heroic figure and a wartime icon whose standing transcended sectional or state loyalties and who represented key national values and ideals. He elicited veneration and provided a sense of stability in times of great change. Critically for proponents of the Constitution, in Schwartz's assessment "loyalty to Washington the individual held the government together until the people could learn to be loyal to the government itself."[70]

Songwriters and organizers of public celebrations invoked Washington to promote allegiance to the new government. Songwriters exaggerated Washington's participation in the federal convention to extend Americans' loyalty to the war-era hero to the document and the restructured government (see Figure 1.6). One songwriter equated the mere thought of dissent with opposition to Washington.[71] Songwriters commonly developed the trope that Washington was "the man of our hearts."[72] Once he became president, Washington prompted musical expressions of loyalty to the nation and the restructured union on his repeated visits to the theater in the nation's capital and his trips through the states that had ratified the Constitution.[73]

The power of publicly performed loyalty to Washington and the newly structured government was dramatically conveyed in Trenton, where women played prominent roles in the typically male-dominated practice of receiving Washington. When Washington passed under a triumphal arch, young girls strewed flowers in front of him and, along with several ladies of the community, sang his welcome to the music of "See the Conquering Hero Comes" from Handel's oratorio *Judas Maccabeus*. Washington validated their expression of loyalty when he responded with a note acknowledging their novel reception and "the exquisite sensations he experienced in that affecting moment" due to the ladies' tasteful reception, their innocent appearance, and the contrast between the site's contemporary condition and its sad state during the war. Washington's description of how he was moved highlighted the importance of sensibility to shaping the new nation. Circulation of Washington's response showcased the personal connection between the new president and the people and turned an expression of loyalty to an individual into a display of feelings about the nation and a commentary on its growth. ▶ The shared sentiment of ordinary Americans, in immense gratitude for Washington's contributions to the nation and its independence, provided an antidote to fears of sectional division and disunion. By the following year, Mercy Otis Warren could describe Washington as the "one who has united all hearts in the field of conquest, in the lap of peace, and at the head of the government of the United States."[74]

Performances like that at Trenton and accounts emphasizing sentimental connections to Washington as a focal point of loyalty to the nation and its restructured government paralleled the rhetorical shift from emphasis on the states in the Articles of Confederation to emphasis on the people in the Constitution's preamble. Moreover, they validated the notion that sovereignty came from the people. Given the purported efficacy of such performances, made possible after all by Washington's carefully conceived trips, perhaps it should not be surprising that the lyrics sung by the women and girls of Trenton were written by a well-connected politician, the Revolutionary War officer, lawyer, and later New Jersey governor, Richard Howell.

## Misgivings

Before Washington's first term, federalist propaganda had promoted the notion that the Articles of Confederation were broken beyond repair, diverted attention from the Constitution's reduction of state powers, and conjured an amalgamation of threatening forces that could only be subdued by restructuring the government. Washington's reputation, image, and position made him an ideal figure for fostering allegiance to the government. But they also fostered adulation, which for some betrayed the nation's republican principles. Songwriters regularly described Washington in king-like and godly terms. Washington reenacted the "royal progress" of ancient kings on his inaugural trip, and the water music played on his arrival at Charleston resembled that of English monarchs.[75] The republican government adopted the trappings and traditions of European monarchies and Vice President John Adams harangued the Senate on the importance of elevated titles, such as "His Excellency" and "His Highness the President." Monarchical connections were reinforced as songwriters often selected the tune "God Save the King" for their new songs lauding Washington with lines like "Hail Godlike Washington!/Fair Freedom's chosen son,/Born to command."[76]

The tendency to monarchical and quasi-religious reverence of the president of the republic concerned some Americans. Since the Revolutionary War's end, idolatry of Washington had disturbed those who considered it a violation of the first commandment, offensive to republican principles, and a threat to liberty. Concern with idolatry resurfaced at Washington's inauguration[77] and continued in Washington's second term, fueling Republican opposition to the incumbent Federalist administration. The Federalists' intolerance of political opposition—already seen in the trumpeting of unity during ratification debates—itself became intolerable. Washington's difficult political decisions drew criticism, and, despite the Federalists' insistence on unity, some printers dared to publish such criticism. Amid these changing political conditions, music was increasingly used for popular political expression and particularly political protest.

## Notes

1. Charleston *South Carolina Weekly Gazette*, 3 May 1783; Philadelphia *Independent Gazetteer*, 17 May 1783; *Providence Gazette*, 6 December 1783; Philadelphia *Pennsylvania Packet*, 13 July 1784, 29 July 1785; Charleston *Columbian Herald*, 17 July

1785; Newburyport *Essex Journal*, 10 August 1785; New York *Independent Journal*, 10 August 1785; *New York Journal*, 6 July 1786; Richard B. Morris, *The Forging of the Union, 1781–1789* (New York: Harper and Row, 1987), 130–61; *New York Daily Advertiser*, 4 July 1786.

2. Pasley, "*Tyranny of Printers*," 41; F. Humphreys, *Life and Times*, vol. 1, 426.
3. Onuf, *Origins*, xiii; R. F. Jones, "Economic Opportunism," 359.
4. Knott, *Sensibility*, 9–10, "Music Physically Considered," *Columbian Magazine* (February 1789): 90–93.
5. Woody Holton, "Did Democracy Cause the Recession That Led to the Constitution?" *Journal of American History* 92, no. 2 (September 2005): 445–6, 457, 461–3; Roger H. Brown, *Redeeming the Republic: Federalists, Taxation, and the Origins of the Constitution* (Baltimore: Johns Hopkins University Press, 1993), 3, 53–96, 108–9, 120–1, 155; Lynn Warren Turner, *The Ninth State: New Hampshire's Formative Years* (Chapel Hill: University of North Carolina Press, 1983), 44; Edwin J. Perkins, *American Public Finance and Financial Services, 1700–1815* (Columbus: Ohio State University Press, 1994), 173–4; Leonard Richards, *Shays's Rebellion: The American Revolution's Final Battle* (Philadelphia: University of Pennsylvania Press, 2002), 81–8; Woody Holton, *Unruly Americans and the Origins of the Constitution* (New York: Hill and Wang, 2007), 65–82, 148–52; Pauline Maier, *Ratification: The People Debate the Constitution, 1787–1788* (New York: Simon and Schuster, 2010), 15; J. M. Opal, "The Politics of 'Industry': Federalism in Concord and Exeter, New Hampshire, 1790–1805," *Journal of the Early Republic* 20, no. 4 (Winter 2000), 651.
6. Boston *Massachusetts Centinel*, 21 June 1786; Richards, *Shays's Rebellion*, 20–1, 53–5, 60, 63–8.
7. Northampton *Hampshire Gazette*, 17 January, 14 March 1787; Richards, *Shays's Rebellion*, 5, 7–8, 10, 23–5, 51, 59, 63, 68, 70–5, 78–9; David O. Szatmary, *Shays' Rebellion: The Making of an Agrarian Insurrection* (Amherst: University of Massachusetts Press, 1980), 69, 76, 83–7, 92–3, 98–9; Holton, *Unruly Americans*, 37–8, 66–8, 74–6, 133–4; Merrill and Sean Wilentz, eds., *Key of Liberty*, 22; Maier, *Ratification*, 16.
8. *The Lark: Containing a Collection of Above Four Hundred and Seventy Celebrated English and Scotch Songs* (London: John Osborn, 1740), 29.
9. Northampton *Hampshire Gazette*, 27 December 1786, 17 January, 28 February 1787; Boston *Massachusetts Centinel*, 17 January 1787, Szatmary, *Shays' Rebellion*, 83; Holton, "Democracy," 465; Holton, *Unruly Americans*, 22, 46–54, 169–70.
10. Turner, *Ninth State*, 52–6, 60–2, 65; Nick Nourse, "Australia's First (British) Musical Import: The 'Rogue's March,'" *CHOMBEC News* 1 (Summer 2012): 1–3, http://www.bristol/ac.uk/music/chombec (accessed January 1, 2015).
11. Boston *Massachusetts Centinel*, 19 May 1787; Portsmouth *New Hampshire Gazette*, 26 May 1787; Portsmouth *New Hampshire Spy*, 14 July 1787, reprinted from the *Albany Gazette*.
12. Szatmary, *Shays' Rebellion*, 72, 74, 92, 100, 103, 107–10, 115–17; Richards, *Shays's Rebellion*, 117, Maier, *Ratification*, 15–17, 72–3; *New Haven Gazette and Connecticut*

*Magazine*, 17 February 1787, 399; Andrew Kuntz, "Fiddle Tune History: The Black Sloven," *Fiddler Magazine* 15, no. 1 (Spring 2008): 34–7. "Come, come my bold boxers" was reprinted in Hartford *Connecticut Courant*, 26 February 1787; Middletown *Middlesex Gazette*, 5 March 1787; Boston *Massachusetts Centinel*, 7 March 1787; *Worcester Magazine*, 8 March 1787, 609; Exeter *Freeman's Oracle*, 24 March 1787.

13. "Ode for His Majesty's Birth-day, 1746," *Scots Magazine* (November 1746), 521; Dustin Griffin, *Patriotism and Poetry in Eighteenth-Century Britain* (Cambridge: Cambridge University Press, 2002), 40–1; Boston *Massachusetts Centinel*, 10 February 1787.
14. Between 1785 and 1787, protests occurred elsewhere in New England, Maryland, South Carolina, New Jersey, Virginia, and Pennsylvania. See Szatmary, *Shays' Rebellion*, 77–9, 124–6; Robert E. Shalhope, *Bennington and the Green Mountain Boys: The Emergence of Liberal Democracy in Vermont, 1760–1850* (Baltimore: Johns Hopkins University Press, 1996), 190.
15. Donald S. Lutz, "The Articles of Confederation as the Background to the Federal Republic," *Publius* 20, no. 1 (Winter 1990): 55; John A. Altman, "The Articles and Constitution: Similar in Nature, Different in Design," *Pennsylvania Legacies* 3, no. 1 (May 2003): 20–1; Maier, *Ratification*, 12, 19, 29; Morris, *Forging*, 253–7.
16. Maier, *Ratification*, 14–26; Holton, "Democracy," 444; Holton, *Unruly Americans*, 4–5, 37–8, 162–76, 230; Szatmary, *Shays' Rebellion*, 120–34; Richards, *Shays's Rebellion*, 129–35; Richard Hofstadter, *The American Political Tradition and the Men Who Made It* (New York: Alfred A. Knopf, 1948), 3–6, 9–11; William Hogeland, *Founding Finance: How Debt, Speculation, Foreclosures, Protests, and Crackdowns Made Us a Nation* (Austin: University of Texas Press, 2012), 75, 84, 86–7, 153, 160–5, 179–80; William G. Anderson, *The Price of Liberty: The Public Debt of the American Revolution* (Charlottesville: University Press of Virginia, 1983), 13–14, 18–19; R. Brown, *Redeeming*, 22–4, 172–4; Onuf, *Origins*, 174–9. Songs often referred to the United States as an empire. See Edward Larkin, "Nation and Empire in the Early U.S.," *American Literary History* 22, no. 3 (Fall 2010): 503, 508–11; *Litchfield Monitor*, 30 January 1787; Springfield *Hampshire Chronicle*, 28 August 1787; Boston *Massachusetts Centinel*, 6 October 1787.
17. New Haven *Connecticut Journal*, 4 October 1786; *New Haven Gazette*, 5 October 1786; J. K. Van Dover, "The Design of Anarchy: *The Anarchiad*, 1786–1787," *Early American Literature* 24, no. 3 (1989): 246.
18. Jackson Turner Main, *The Antifederalists: Critics of the Constitution, 1781–1788*, foreword by Edward Countryman (Chapel Hill: University of North Carolina Press, 2004), xxvi; Van Dover, "Design of Anarchy," 238–40; Riggs, ed., *The Anarchiad*, 4–7, 9–11, 22, 26–8; *New Haven Gazette*, 25 January 1787; David Humphreys, *The Miscellaneous Works of David Humphreys* (New York: T. and J. Swords, 1804), 225–6.
19. Szatmary, *Shays' Rebellion*, 85; Richards, *Shays's Rebellion*, 15; F. Humphreys, *Life and Times*, vol. 1, 373–4, 377–8, 380–1, 393–401.
20. John Bach McMaster and Frederick D. Stone, eds., *Pennsylvania and the Federal Constitution, 1787–1788* (Philadelphia: Historical Society of Pennsylvania, 1888), 212; Maier, *Ratification*, 100.

21. Saul Cornell, *The Other Founders: Anti-Federalism and the Dissenting Tradition in America, 1788–1828* (Chapel Hill: University of North Carolina Press, 1999), 37, 81–2, 84, 87, 89ff, 97–9; Main, *Antifederalists*, xxvi; Maier, *Ratification*, 74.
22. Philadelphia *Independent Gazetteer*, 5 October 1787; 24 April 1788; *New York Journal*, 2 May, 28 July 1788; Philadelphia *Freeman's Journal*, 16 April 1788; Maier, *Ratification*, 99–101, 120; Morris, *Forging*, 300; Richards, *Shays's Rebellion*, 141.
23. R. Brown, *Redeeming*, 180–3; Maier, *Ratification*, 17–26, 58; Philadelphia *Pennsylvania Packet*, 20 August 1787; New York *Daily Advertiser*, 5 July 1788; Joseph L. Davis, *Sectionalism in American Politics, 1774–1787* (Madison: University of Wisconsin Press, 1977), 148–9; Holton, *Unruly Americans*, 249–50.
24. Boston *Massachusetts Centinel*, 6 October 1787; Vera Brodsky Lawrence, *Music for Patriots, Politicians, and Presidents* (New York: Macmillan, 1975), 101; "The Grand Constitution" was reprinted as a broadside and in numerous newspapers in New Hampshire, Pennsylvania, Rhode Island, South Carolina, and Connecticut, as well as Benjamin West, *Bickerstaff's Boston Almanack* (Boston: E. Russell, 1787), 3.
25. Ian Bartlett, with Robert J. Bruce, *William Boyce: A Tercentenary Sourcebook and Compendium* (Newcastle upon Tyne, UK: Cambridge Scholars, 2011), 128–9; William A. Pencak, *Contested Commonwealths: Essays in American History* (Bethlehem, PA: Lehigh University Press, 2011), 108.
26. *Carlisle Gazette*, 14 May 1788; Hogeland, *Founding Finance*, 82–3, 91–4; R. Brown, *Redeeming*, 146, 176–9.
27. Maier, *Ratification*, 17; Main, *Antifederalists*, 177–9; R. Brown, *Redeeming*, 152–3, 172–4; Henry Cruger Van Schaack, *Memoirs of the Life of Henry Van Schaack* (Chicago: A. C. McClurg, 1892), 154; Richards, *Shays's Rebellion*, 131, 134; Szatmary, *Shays' Rebellion*, 127–8; Holton, *Unruly Americans*, 243; Onuf, *Origins*, 183; Davis, *Sectionalism*, 149; Perkins, *American Public Finance*, 173–4.
28. New York *Daily Advertiser*, 5 July 1788; Exeter *Freeman's Oracle*, 11 July 1788; Davis, *Sectionalism*, 155; Maier, *Ratification*, 16; Gordon S. Wood, "Conspiracy and the Paranoid Style: Causality and Deceit in the Eighteenth Century," *William and Mary Quarterly* 39, no. 3 (July 1982): 401–41; Onuf, *Origins*, 179–83.
29. Boston *Massachusetts Centinel*, 29 December 1787; Philadelphia *Pennsylvania Packet*, 10 January 1788; Maier, *Ratification*, 14, 17; Morris, *Forging*, 134–5, 139, 205; Davis, *Sectionalism*, 155; Hofstadter, *American Political Tradition*, 10–2; John Tasker Howard and Eleanor S. Bowen, eds., *Music Associated with the Period of the Formation of the Constitution and the Inauguration of George Washington* (Washington, DC: United States Sesquiscentennial Commission, n.d.), 17.
30. Boston *Massachusetts Centinel*, 12 December 1787; *New York Morning Post*, 21 December 1787; Davis, *Sectionalism*, 151; Don Higginbotham, *George Washington: Uniting a Nation* (Lanham, MD: Rowman and Littlefield, 2002), 52; Onuf, *Origins*, 184.
31. Main, *Antifederalists*, xxiii–xxv, 134–42; Philadelphia *Pennsylvania Mercury*, 21 February 1788; New York *Daily Advertiser*, 27 February 1788; Baltimore *Maryland Gazette*, 4 March 1788; Charleston *City Gazette*, 31 March 1788; P. Thompson, *Rum*

*Punch and Revolution*, 134–42; Stephen L. Schechter, "A Biographical Gazetteer of New York Federalists and Antifederalists," in *The Reluctant Pillar*, ed. Stephen L. Schechter (Troy, NY: Russell Sage College Press, 1985), 165.

32. F. Humphreys, *Life and Times*, vol. 1, 380; Maier, *Ratification*, 137; Christopher Collier, *All Politics Is Local: Family, Friends, and Provincial Interest in the Creation of the Constitution* (Hanover, NH: University Press of New England, 2003), 88; Hartford *Connecticut Courant*, 13 August 1787; Richards, *Shays's Rebellion*, 69; Van Dover, "Design of Anarchy," 242–4; *The Documentary History of the Ratification of the Constitution Digital Edition*, ed. John P. Kaminski, Gaspare J. Saladino, Richard Leffler, Charles H. Schoenleber and Margaret A. Hogan. Charlottesville: University of Virginia Press, 2009, http://rotunda.upress.virginia.edu/founders/RNCN-02-03-01-0004. Original source: Ratification by the States, Volume III: Delaware, New Jersey, Georgia, and Connecticut; Jon L. Wakelyn, *Birth of the Bill of Rights: Encyclopedia of the Antifederalists*, vol. 1 (Westport, CT: Greenwood, 2004), 215; *New Haven Gazette*, 20 March 1788; Boston *Massachusetts Gazette*, 28 March 1788; Portsmouth *New Hampshire Spy*, 1 April 1788; Philadelphia *Pennsylvania Packet*, 22 April 1788; Elizabethtown *New Jersey Journal*, 30 April 1788.
33. F. Humphreys, *Life and Times*, vol. 1, 426; Hartford *American Mercury*, 17 December 1787; Middletown *Middlesex Gazette*, 31 December 1787, Maier, *Ratification*, 123, 129, 324; Turner, *Ninth State*, 75; Onuf, *Origins*, 149–54.
34. Pasley, "*Tyranny of Printers*," 43, 45; Cornell, *Other Founders*, 37, 81–2, 84, 87, 89ff, 97–9, 104, 121–8; Maier, *Ratification*, 58; Holton, *Unruly Americans*, 249, 252; Onuf, *Origins*, 174–5, 183–5; Michael J. Klarman, *The Framers' Coup: The Making of the United States Constitution* (New York: Oxford University Press, 2016), 397–545.
35. Owen S. Ireland, *Religion, Ethnicity, and Politics: Ratifying the Constitution in Pennsylvania* (University Park: Pennsylvania State University Press, 1995), 130–2.
36. Philadelphia *Pennsylvania Mercury*, 21 February 1788. This song was reprinted in several states prior to their ratification, including New York, New Hampshire, South Carolina, Maryland, and Virginia. Other reprintings appeared in Connecticut, Massachusetts, New Jersey, Rhode Island, and Vermont newspapers.
37. Maier, *Ratification*, 122–4; Holton, *Unruly Americans*, 252; Morris, *Forging*, 302–3, 311–3, 315; Onuf, *Origins*, 181, 201.
38. Oscar Sonneck, *Francis Hopkinson and James Lyon* (New York: Da Capo Press, 1967, first printing 1905), ix, 29, 31–3, 40–6, 63–116; George Everett Hastings, *The Life and Works of Francis Hopkinson* (New York: Russell and Russell, 1968), 52–4, 70–4, 78, 80–3, 150, 153, 174, 295, 315–17, 367–9, 410, 436–45, 461–4; Paul M. Zall, ed., *Comical Spirit of Seventy-Six: The Humor of Francis Hopkinson* (San Marino, CA: Huntington Library, 1976), 3, 7–9, 11–15, 19–20, 33, 95–101.
39. Whitfield Bell, "The Federal Processions of 1788," *New York Historical Society Quarterly* 46, no. 1 (January 1962): 29.
40. Ireland, *Religion*, 126–7; Lutz, "Articles of Confederation," 65–6, 69–70; Philadelphia *Pennsylvania Packet*, 29 December 1787; Philadelphia *Pennsylvania Gazette*, 6 February 1788. Hopkinson's song was reprinted promptly in newspapers in Pennsylvania, Connecticut, Massachusetts, Rhode Island, South Carolina, and New

Hampshire, as well as Philadelphia *American Museum*, July 1788, 95; *Politics for the People; or, Salmagundy for Swine* (London: D. I. Eaton, 1794), 75–7; *The Columbian Songster, or Jovial Companion* (New York: Greenleaf's, 1797), 184–6; *Nightingale of Liberty: or Delights of Harmony. A Choice Collection of Patriotic, Masonic, & Entertaining Songs* (New York: Harrison, 1797), 31–3; *Otsego Herald*, 24 April 1800; *The Eagle and Harp* (Baltimore: Vance and Cole, 1812), 54–6; *A National Song-Book* (Trenton: James J. Wilson, 1813), 39–40.

41. London *Public Advertiser*, 17 September 1756; William John Pinks and Edward J. Wood, *The History of Clerkenwell*, 2nd ed. (London: Charles Herbert, 1881), 418–9; *London Magazine or Gentleman's Monthly Intelligencer* 30 (June 1761), 327; *Otsego Herald*, 24 April 1800.
42. Boston *Massachusetts Centinel*, 9, 27 February, 1 March, 2 July, 2 August 1788; Holton, *Unruly Americans*, 252; Morris, *Forging*, 312–3; John P. Kaminski, "New York: The Reluctant Pillar," in *The Reluctant Pillar*, ed. Stephen L. Schechter (Troy, NY: Russell Sage College, 1985), 79–101, 112–15.
43. Davis, *Sectionalism*, 148–50.
44. Laura Rigal, "'Raising the Roof': Authors, Spectators and Artisans in the Grand Federal Procession of 1788," *Theatre Journal* 48, no. 3 (1996): 261; Dietmar Schloss, "The Nation as Spectacle: The Grand Federal Procession in Philadelphia, 1788," in *Celebrating Ethnicity and Nation: American Festive Culture from the Revolution to the Early Twentieth* Century, ed. Geneviève Fabre, Jürgen Heideking, and Kai Dreisbach (New York: Berghahn Books, 2001), 53; Philadelphia *Pennsylvania Packet*, 9 July 1788.
45. *Albany Journal*, 4 August 1788; Boston *Massachusetts Gazette*, 4 July 1788; Baltimore *Maryland Journal*, 18 December 1787; Hartford *Connecticut Courant*, 31 December 1787.
46. Griffin, *Patriotism and Poetry*, 100. Most individuals' rights remained unaddressed until 1789, when ten amendments to the Constitution, comprising the Bill of Rights, were proposed by Congress and went into effect in 1791.
47. Lutz, "Articles of Confederation," 66, 69; Maier, *Ratification*, 99–100, 107, 327; Hogeland, *Founding Finance*, 75, 87, 146, 152–5; Szatmary, *Shays' Rebellion*, 133; Holton, *Unruly Americans*, 7, 187–212; Holton, "Democracy," 443, 445; Morris, *Forging*, 310; Hofstadter, *American Political Tradition*, 4–7, 9, 12–5; Richards, *Shays's Rebellion*, 135–6, 150; Hartford *Connecticut Courant*, 7 January 1788; Turner, *Ninth State*, 74–5; Willi Paul Adams, *The First American Constitutions: Republican Ideology and the Making of the State Constitutions in the Revolutionary Era*, trans. Rita and Robert Kimber (Chapel Hill: University of North Carolina Press, 1980), 113–14.
48. Holton, *Unruly Americans*, 249; Szatmary, *Shays' Rebellion*, 133; Maier, *Ratification*, 99–100, 134–6.
49. Baltimore *Maryland Journal*, 18 December 1787; Philadelphia *Independent Gazetteer*, 21 December 1787; Hartford *Connecticut Courant*, 31 December 1787.
50. Portsmouth *New Hampshire Spy*, 28 June 1788; Richard C. Spicer, "Popular Song for Public Celebration in Federal Portsmouth, New Hampshire," *Popular Music and Society* 25 (2001): 17.

51. Robert Martello, *Midnight Ride, Industrial Dawn: Paul Revere and the Growth of American Enterprise* (Baltimore: Johns Hopkins University Press, 2010), 101; *The Documentary History of the Ratification of the Constitution Digital Edition*, ed. John P. Kaminski, Gaspare J. Saladino, Richard Leffler, Charles H. Schoenleber and Margaret A. Hogan. Charlottesville: University of Virginia Press, 2009, http://rotunda.upress.virginia.edu/founders/RNCN-02-04-01-0011. Original source: Ratification by the States, Volume IV: Massachusetts, No. 1.
52. Lawrence A. Peskin, *Manufacturing Revolution: The Intellectual Origins of Early American Industry* (Baltimore: Johns Hopkins University Press, 2010), 84–6; Charles G. Steffen, *The Mechanics of Baltimore: Workers and Politics in the Age of Revolution 1763–1812* (Urbana: University of Illinois Press, 1984), 90–5; Paul A. Gilje, "The Common People and the Constitution: Popular Culture in New York City in the Late Eighteenth Century," in *New York in the Age of Constitution, 1775–1800*, ed. Paul A. Gilje and William Pencak (Rutherford, NJ: Fairleigh Dickinson University Press, 1992), 57–62; Schloss, "Nation as Spectacle," 54–9; Spicer, "Popular Song," 1–3, 11–17; Knott, *Sensibility*, 1–2; Francis Hopkinson, "Account of the Grand Federal Procession in Philadelphia," *American Museum*, July 1788, 62–3, 75–6; Benjamin Rush, "Observations on the Federal Procession, on the Fourth of July, 1788, in the City of Philadelphia," *American Museum*, July 1788, 76; Rigal, "'Raising the Roof,'" 254, 267; Philadelphia *Pennsylvania Packet*, 9 July 1788.
53. New York *Daily Advertiser*, 4 August 1788; Peskin, *Manufacturing Revolution*, 84–6. The Lady's song was reprinted in newspapers in South Carolina, Rhode Island, New Jersey, Pennsylvania, and New Hampshire.
54. Boston *Independent Chronicle*, 28 February 1788.
55. New York *Daily Advertiser*, 24 July 1788.
56. Harmon Dean Cummings, "Andrew Adgate: Philadelphia Psalmodist and Music Educator" (PhD diss., University of Rochester, 1975), 80, 91, 95, 138, 142, 148, 151, 159.
57. Rigal, "'Raising the Roof,'" 263–4; Hofstadter, *American Political Tradition*, 4–7; Harmon Cummings, "Andrew Adgate," 29, 91, 156, 298–305; John Ogasapian, *Music of the Colonial and Revolutionary Era* (Westport, CT: Greenwood Press, 2004), 142; Philadelphia *Independent Gazetteer*, 13 January 1789; *New York Packet*, 20 January 1789; Boston *Massachusetts Centinel*, 31 January 1789; Hartford *Connecticut Courant*, 2 February 1789; Keene *New Hampshire Recorder*, 19 March 1789; Portsmouth *New Hampshire Spy*, 28 June 1788; Andrew Adgate, *The Mechanic's Lecture: Showing the Usefulness of the Mechanic Arts* (Philadelphia: John McCulloch, 1789).
58. New York *Impartial Gazetteer*, 26 July 1788; *New York Packet*, 25 July 1788; Howard and Bowen, *Music*, 8, 13; Portsmouth *New Hampshire Spy*, 28 June 1788; Gilje, "Common People," 54–8; Worcester *Massachusetts Spy*, 29 May 1788; Gordon S. Wood, *Empire of Liberty: A History of the Early Republic, 1789–1815* (New York: Oxford University Press, 2009), 105–6.
59. Charles Biddle, *Autobiography of Charles Biddle, Vice-President of the Supreme Executive Council of Pennsylvania, 1745–1821* (Philadelphia: E. Claxton, 1883), 225–8; Philadelphia *Pennsylvania Packet*, 9 July 1788; Bell, "Federal Processions,"

18; Alexander Reinagle, *Federal March as Performed in the Grand Procession in Philadelphia the 4th of July 1788* (Philadelphia: n.p., 1788).

60. Larkin, "Nation and Empire," 513; Holton, *Unruly*, 249.
61. Barry Schwartz, *George Washington: The Making of an American Symbol* (New York: Free Press, 1987), 82; Simon P. Newman, "Principles or Men? George Washington and the Political Culture of National Leadership, 1776–1801," *Journal of the Early Republic* 12, no. 4 (Winter 1992): 480; Bell, "Federal Processions," 28–9.
62. Onuf, *Origins*, 207–8; Turner, *Ninth State*, 72–9; Merrill Jensen and Robert A. Becker, eds., *The Documentary History of the First Federal Elections, 1788–1790*, vol. 1 (Madison: University of Wisconsin Press, 1976), 769.
63. Portsmouth *New Hampshire Spy*, 28 June 1788; Spicer, "Popular Song," 17.
64. Turner, *Ninth State*, 32, 75–6; Portsmouth *New Hampshire Spy*, 15 February 1788; Portsmouth *New Hampshire Mercury*, 27 February 1788; Boston *Massachusetts Centinel*, 5 March 1788; Exeter *Freeman's Oracle*, 21 March 1788.
65. Philadelphia *Pennsylvania Packet*, 9 July 1788; Portsmouth *New Hampshire Spy*, 28 June 1788; Exeter *Freeman's Oracle*, 11 July 1788; New York *Daily Advertiser*, 24 July 1788; *Albany Journal*, 4 August 1788; "Union Our Only Hope: A Federal Poem," *American Museum* 4, no. 2 (1788): 193–5; Spicer, "Popular Song," 17.
66. Exeter *Freeman's Oracle*, 11 July 1788; Boston *Massachusetts Gazette*, 4 July 1788; Philadelphia *Pennsylvania Packet*, 17 July 1788; Boston *Massachusetts Centinel*, 6 October 1787; Jürgen Heideking, "Celebrating the Constitution: The Federal Processions of 1788 and the Emergence of a Republican Festive Culture in the United States," in *Celebrating Ethnicity and Nation: American Festive Culture from the Revolution to the Early Twentieth* Century, ed. Geneviève Fabre, Jürgen Heideking and Kai Dreisbach (New York: Berghahn Books, 2001), 37–8.
67. Richard M. Gamble, "'The Last and Brightest Empire of Time': Timothy Dwight and America as Voegelin's 'Authoritative Present,' 1771–1787," *Humanitas* 20, no. 1 (2007): 24–5, 33.
68. New York *Daily Advertiser*, 24 July 1788; Philadelphia *Pennsylvania Packet*, 17 July, 31 July, 5 August 1788; Portsmouth *New Hampshire Spy*, 28 June 1788; *Albany Journal*, 4 August 1788; Philadelphia *Federal Gazette*, 2 March 1791.
69. *Newport Herald*, 7 August 1788; *Political Sermons of the American Founding Era: 1730–1805*, vol. 1, 2nd ed. (Indianapolis: Liberty Fund, 1998), 604–62; *The Documentary History of the Ratification of the Constitution Digital Edition*, ed. John P. Kaminski, Gaspare J. Saladino, Richard Leffler, Charles H. Schoenleber and Margaret A. Hogan. Charlottesville: University of Virginia Press, 2009, http://rotunda.upress.virginia.edu/founders/RNCN-02-24-01-0012. Original source: Ratification by the States, Volume XXIV: Rhode Island, No. 1.
70. Schwartz, *George Washington*, 45, 87–8; Garry Wills, *Cincinnatus: George Washington and the Enlightenment* (Garden City, NY: Doubleday, 1984), xxi.
71. Exeter *Freeman's Oracle*, 11 July 1788; New York *Daily Advertiser*, 24 July 1788; John H. Aldrich and Ruth W. Grant, "The Antifederalists, the First Congress, and the First Parties," *Journal of Politics* 55, no. 2 (May 1993): 302; Philadelphia *Federal Gazette*, 4 July 1789.

72. Philadelphia *Freeman's Journal*, 29 April 1789; *New York Journal*, 6 July 1786; Boston *Massachusetts Magazine*, October 1789, 653–4; Portsmouth *New Hampshire Gazette*, 9 July 1789; Philadelphia *Gazette of the United States*, 1 June 1791; Portsmouth *New Hampshire Spy*, 7 July, 3 November 1789; Boston *Massachusetts Centinel*, 17 February 1790; *New York Morning Post*, 5 July 1790; Schwartz, *George Washington*, 81.
73. Boston *Massachusetts Centinel*, 4 July 1789; Schwartz, *George Washington*, 74–6; Thomas E. Baker, "Guilford Courthouse: George Washington's Visit—June 2, 1791" (National Park Service, US Department of the Interior, 1991); Nicholas Michael Butler, *Votaries of Apollo: The St. Cecilia Society and the Patronage of Concert Music in Charleston, South Carolina, 1766–1820* (Columbia: University of South Carolina Press, 2007), 55, 128–30; Philadelphia *Gazette of the United States*, 25 April 1789, 21 May 1791; Paul Leicester Ford, *Washington and the Theatre* (New York: Benjamin Blom, 1967), 43–5; Higginbotham, *George Washington*, 54; Providence *United States Chronicle*, 2 September 1790; Boston *Massachusetts Magazine*, October 1789, 653–4, 659–61.
74. Newman, "Principles or Men?" 484; *Washington's Reception by the Ladies of Trenton Together with the Chorus Sung as He Passed under the Triumphal Arch* (New York: Society of Iconophiles, 1903), 15–16; Howard and Bowen, *Music*, 15; Philadelphia *Freeman's Journal*, 29 April 1789; Boston *Massachusetts Centinel*, 29 April 1789; Richard Howell, *A Sonata, Sung by a Number of Young Girls... As General Washington Passed under the Triumphal Arch Raised on the Bridge at Trenton, April 21, 1789* [Trenton: Isaac Collins, 1789]; Knott, *Sensibility*, 234; Mercy Otis Warren, *Poems, Dramatic and Miscellaneous* (Boston: I. Thomas and E. T. Andrews, 1790), iv.
75. Maier, *Ratification*, 20–4; *The American Songster* (New York: Campbell, 1788), 1.
76. Lawrence, *Music*, 63; *Boston Gazette*, 1 August 1785; *New York Journal*, 6 July 1786; Philadelphia *Independent Gazetteer*, 5 March 1787; Worcester *American Herald*, 16 July 1789; Boston *Massachusetts Centinel*, 2 May 1789, 17 February 1790; Philadelphia *Gazette of the United States*, 25 April 1789; Portsmouth *New Hampshire Spy*, 7 July 1789, 3 November 1789; Boston *Massachusetts Magazine*, October 1789, 660–1; Ford, *Washington and the Theatre*, 35; Schwartz, *George Washington*, 60.
77. Schwartz, *George Washington*, 42–3, 50–1, 56, 61–3; Newman, "Principles or Men?" 485–7.

# 2

# Debating the Nature of the Young Republic in Song

"It is time to dismiss all those songs and toasts which are calculated to enslave, and operate to suffocate reflection." Thomas Paine's declaration, published in early 1792, presaged the direction of American political song during Washington's second term. Paine rejected songs and toasts to monarchical authority. Through a transatlantic practice encapsulated in guidebooks like *Pocock's Everlasting Songster*, songs and toasts expressing political allegiances were performed in a ritualized, predetermined fashion at gentlemen's convivial gatherings. While the United States had freed itself of monarchy, songwriters and singers expressed panegyric and hagiography of Washington. Moreover, as James Monroe and other Republican leaders had predicted, an American counterrevolution emerged; this paralleled British counterrevolutionary impulses and fueled concerns over American adoption of the trappings of aristocracy and monarchy. The unfolding French Revolution and broader transatlantic circulation of revolutionary texts accelerated Americans' engagement with what David Waldstreicher has called "the Age of Revolution's great social and political question: aristocracy versus equality."[1] Fulfilling Paine's declaration, Americans increasingly used music to voice their political opposition.

Americans' popular engagement in debates over aristocracy and equality was itself a political challenge to the young republic's Federalist leaders. In their view, Americans were to defer to elected representatives rather than participate directly in political debate. Federalists condoned limited direct political participation by property owners; these were to defer to elected representatives seen to possess greater capacity for virtue. The public's knowledge was to follow from the deliberation of those elite representatives, as disseminated in official publications and reinforced through official ritual acts. Expression of popular political opposition outside elections was seen as the unvirtuous product of self-interest, a challenge to the government, a threat to order, a sign of ruin, and an extra-legal activity that in Wood's words

*Hail Columbia*. Laura Lohman, Oxford University Press (2020). © Oxford University Press.
DOI: 10.1093/oso/9780190930615.001.0001

would "undermine the very idea of a legal representative government." As Massachusetts native Jonathan Jackson put it in 1788, "an excess of republicanism," which "might more properly be styled *unchecked* democracy, has threatened the ruin of our country."[2]

While Federalists perceived democracy as something to be curtailed, their emerging Republican opponents presented it as an ideal. Broad participation in the French Revolution and British revolutionaries' pursuit of universal male suffrage demonstrated alternatives to the Federalists' classical republicanism and prompted what Hale has called a "French-inspired democratic awakening." [3] Amid broad American interest in the unfolding French Revolution, Republicans articulated a democratic republican vision of public political participation. Challenging Federalist concepts and values, Americans advocated "universal principles" of liberty and equality. Through both prose and song, Americans voiced their political opposition through "a cosmopolitan, Painite language of natural rights. They measured federal policies not against past models of virtuous governance, but against the radical enlightenment abstractions of liberty, equality, and universal justice."[4]

This discourse of "popular cosmopolitanism" was fostered by the organization of political opposition, the transatlantic flow of people and culture, and the growth of oppositional newspapers. The "parties" that James Madison identified in late 1792 as divisions of opinion in Congress developed into a prominent part of American political culture. Federalist and Republican camps lacked the structure of later political parties, but their ideological divisions and prominence earned them contemporaneous designations of "factions" and "parties." Like their British counterparts, Americans also formed local oppositional political societies.[5] American opposition was fueled by a transatlantic flow of people, ideas, and cultural artifacts. Songs from Britain and France were reprinted and adapted in the United States, while American orations and lyrics were reprinted in England and Ireland.[6] Long-standing European rituals were adapted to New World contexts. Partisan dialogue was fueled by the transatlantic movement of people. In addition to Thomas Paine, who left America in 1787 for England and later France, these included Englishman William Cobbett and Ann Julia Hatton, a member of a prominent British theatrical family, who wrote the opera *Tammany; or the Indian Chief* for New York City Republicans.[7] Republican newspapers were instrumental to the spread of oppositional musical expression. While most newspapers echoed John Fenno's *Gazette of the United States* and Benjamin Russell's *Columbian Centinel* in publishing Federalist material in support of Washington's administration, a number joined Philip Freneau's *National Gazette* in printing oppositional material. Opposition editors used news from abroad to cast Federalists as "anti-democratic counterrevolutionaries" and address the multitudes, or " 'the people,' whose interests stood in opposition to the privileged 'few.' " Through these newspapers, Cotlar has argued, "American readers learned to weave local and international events into the coherent cosmopolitan narrative that, for many, motivated their political behaviors."[8]

Building on and extending the work of Cotlar, Mason, Horgan, and Hale, this chapter explores how Republicans used music to bring their compatriots into larger transatlantic struggles between "the people" and the "privileged orders" and advance a democratic republicanism that challenged Federalists' model of deferential republicanism. This oppositional project entailed reshaping perceptions of time and place. Federalists had proclaimed in song and with trumpet fanfares that the Constitution ushered in a "new era"; Republican songwriters responded with a millennial perspective that emphasized global, rather than national, progress. Republicans answered Federalists' street theater with processions of their own that placed America and Americans in the midst of a global rise of democratic republican principles. Americans used songs and symbolic occasions to profess their commitment to democratic principles and to wed the histories and ideals of the French and American republics. Capitalizing on French and British music circulating in a transatlantic context, writers, editors, and performers of music challenged a vision of the American republic based on deference to elites and British models. Although Federalists repeatedly denounced popular politics, they participated in it to mount a counterrevolutionary response that drew on and echoed that in Britain.[9]

## Sounding Popular Cosmopolitanism and Democratic Republicanism

For Americans, the early 1790s ushered in utopian aspirations and euphoric celebrations of worldwide transformation. In the unfolding French Revolution, Americans saw an expansion of republican government and growth of democracy. As Cotlar has explained, "It was with particular zeal that Americans celebrated the political transformations in France and gloated over the desperate fears that they provoked among Britain's ruling elite." In his assessment, the Revolutionary War had left "a visceral Anglophobia, and this combined with the memory of French generosity [during the war] to overdetermine the American response to the events of 1789. When Lafayette sent Washington the key to the Bastille in 1790, it cemented the perception that the French Revolution was a European manifestation of the same spirit" underlying the American revolution. Thomas Paine's *Rights of Man* solidified this American interpretation of wedded revolutionary fates. Writing from England, the pamphleteer of the American Revolution defended republican government and the French Revolution against the counterrevolutionary attacks published by Edmund Burke. Forcefully articulating the merits of republican government based on elected representation as opposed to monarchy based on hereditary succession, Paine's text spurred in America the greatest anti-aristocratic political discourse since the ratification of Constitution. Published in two parts in 1791 and 1792, *Rights of Man* sold between 50,000 and 100,000 copies in the United States, an impressive quantity when print runs rarely exceeded 2,000 copies. Americans quickly saw themselves as Painite "citizens of the world" who sought "utopian solutions for social problems" as "friends to humanity" or "friends of the people." This discourse of popular cosmopolitanism provided a broader framework for domestic political opposition. "By positioning themselves as advocates for universal political principles that transcended political boundaries," Cotlar has argued, Republicans framed their political opposition not as "narrow-minded party spirit" but rather an "egalitarian and oppositional force of cosmopolitanism."[10]

An early musical expression of this cosmopolitanism came through the circulation of Irish praise of the United States as a revolutionary model for Europe. At a Belfast dinner attended by over a hundred supporters of an independent Irish republic, America was celebrated as a model republic in song. The song, attributed to Thomas Stott of Dromore, cited American inspiration for revolutionary efforts in France and, by extension, Ireland: "May the spirit of Sparta her armies inspire/And the Star of America guide!/May a Washington's wisdom—a Mirabeau's fire—/In her camps and her councils preside!" While the United Irishmen's song would later become the basis of James Montgomery's seditious libel trial in counterrevolutionary Britain,[11] the lyrics' reprintings in American newspapers from Vermont to North Carolina portrayed the United States as part of, and an inspiration for, a broader revolution spreading across Europe with the potential to liberate "the world."[12]

This musical expression of popular cosmopolitanism became prominent in late 1792 and early 1793, when Americans learned of the abolition of the French monarchy and French military victories. They used songs to celebrate France's achievement and the anticipated spread of republican government throughout the world. Embedded in their celebrations was a rejection of American reversion into monarchy and establishment of a domestic aristocracy. As Waldstreicher has noted, as "the extent of America's democratic transformation remained unclear, the French Revolution addressed the insecure achievements of the American Revolution." Amid this uncertainty about the nation's future, Americans advocating greater democracy used the French Revolution to construct a compelling argument. As Benjamin Franklin Bache's *Aurora General Advertiser* put it, "Upon the establishment or overthrow of liberty in France probably will depend the permanency of the Republic in the new world." Made hopeful by the French Revolution's apparent successes, writers cited the United States as a model and echoed Paine's pride in the "rapid progress in the world" made by the principles of American government. Noting Columbia's peace and plenty, the "fruits of Bravery" gained through war, one songwriter urged, "From her example—Frenchmen, then/Persist—Support your Rights as Men;/And bravely, whilst you can,/My Standard plant in Galia's ground;/And *thunder* to the Nations round,/THE DIGNITY OF MAN!!!"[13] The debate over the shaping of the American republic through democratic or deferential republicanism and the corresponding prioritization of equality or aristocracy was well under way.

Americans took a position in this debate by integrating milestones of French revolutionary progress with the domestic celebratory calendar. In the dead of winter, Americans in dozens of communities from New Hampshire to Georgia and the Kentucky frontier organized celebrations of the French military victory at Valmy.[14] On the surface, the day's festivities celebrated the unexpected French victory on September 20, 1792, against the invading allied Austrian and Prussian armies. These allies sought to reverse or contain the spread of revolution in Europe. The French victory coincided with the French National Convention's establishment of the First Republic and abolishment of the monarchy, and it suggested a spreading revolt against European monarchies.

The most elaborate commemoration took place in Boston. Boston's Civic Feast—organized by a hatter and furrier, a merchant, and truckman, among others—offered a ritual spectacle of street theater that integrated music and other multisensory components in a highly symbolic, motivating statement of America's role in global democratization.[15] Answering the uncertainties about the American republic's future, the feast was a powerful complex of oppositional political expression fostered through the transatlantic circulation of ideas, texts, and practices. Bostonians, like Americans in other states, measured French revolutionary time in localized expressions of a popular cosmopolitanism that announced for a domestic audience momentous global revolutionary progress.[16] With colorful silk flags, rousing music, and the smell of roasted meat filling the streets, Bostonians designed the Civic Feast to titillate all their neighbors' senses. Organizers called for shopkeepers to close at noon to focus attention squarely on the street theater, which they made broadly available for members of the community—men and women, white and black, old and young, merchants and mechanics, sailors and schoolchildren. The festivities entailed no less than three processions and commemorative meals enjoyed across the town.[17] Songs were written for the local military companies, the band of singers, and the afternoon entertainment in Faneuil Hall. The day was filled with praises of liberty and equality and rejections of monarchy and aristocracy. Emulating the French, the organizers used the egalitarian term "citizen" to emphasize these themes, even when naming the governor and lieutenant governor, John Hancock and Samuel Adams.[18] Not surprisingly, the Federalist governor did not join the entertainment at Faneuil Hall, which the like-minded John Quincy Adams deemed an "anarchical dinner" and refused to attend.[19]

Bostonians used the celebration of the French military victory and republic to make powerful statements about their own nation, its political direction, and its place in the broader spread of republican government. The most public statement came in the town's 11 AM "Peace Offering to Liberty and Equality," when a band called townsfolk to attend the impending ritualized violence enacting aristocracy's global demise. Near the front of the procession, a group of citizens eight wide and eight deep were preceded by the band and followed by other citizens processing with "cleavers, knives, steels, etc." Behind them came the offering from the fifteen states in the union. Leading the decorated cart carrying the sacrificial offering were fifteen horses, guided by fifteen men dressed in white, each symbolizing an American state (Vermont and Kentucky had joined the original thirteen that ratified the Constitution). The sacrificial beast, an ox roasted the previous night, represented aristocracy. In preparation for the symbolic procession, the committee of nine men in charge of the ox had specifically requested that Boston mechanics turn in the "Colours of the Several Crafts used in the introduction of the President of the United States into this town" in October 1789 so they could decorate the sacrificial procession; these flags of white silk, painted with the arms and emblems of each craft, no longer welcomed a president but rejected monarchy and aristocracy. "He"—as newspaper accounts referred to the aristocratic carcass—was paraded in the streets with a "full band, with drums and fifes."[20]

Two local newspapers offered a dramatic account of the ritual climax:

> The OX, who personated ARISTOCRACY, and gawdy decorations, represented the Title of that political Hydra, was, consecrated as a "PEACE OFFERING to LIBERTY and EQUALITY." The moment for the sacrifice, was now at hand; the white rob'd Priests, (*Butchers*) began the duties of their office; and the surrounding multitudes, assisting in the Ceremony, immolated the victim on the Altar of DEMOCRACY. Reiterated applauses attended the process; and to render this Republican Exhibition complete, a Band of Musicians ascended the Balcony in front of the State-House, and played the National Carol "CA IRA," amid the continued shouts of enraptured "CITIZENS."[21]

The procession's organizers made the ritual's central tenet democracy—the force that Federalist leaders were determined to contain and check. The ritual reversed Federalists' efforts, destroying instead "aristocracy" and "titles."

For a Bostonian, "aristocracy" and "titles" referenced a growing pattern of assertions and actions by Federalist leaders that undercut the principles and purpose of the American revolution. Republicans noted with dismay that Federalists often voiced support for both monarchy and aristocracy. John Adams, in his "Discourse on Davila" series in the *Gazette of the United States*, wrote that although mankind "had tried all possible experiments of elections of Governors and Senates . . . they had almost unanimously been convinced that hereditary succession was attended with fewer evils than frequent elections" that promoted rivalries and divisions. The wealthy New York lawyer Governeur Morris declared, "There never was, and never will be a civilized Society without an Aristocracy." John Jay maintained that "those who own the country ought to govern it," and Alexander Hamilton declared that he had "long since . . . learnt to hold popular opinion of no value." Meanwhile, Republicans had noted the incursion of monarchical trappings, including Washington's levees, liveried servants attending Adams's carriage, and Adams's interest in elevated titles, such as "His Highness the President."

Moreover, the Order of the Cincinnati, with its hereditary officers' membership, seemed an effort to establish a nobility.[22]

The Civic Feast was part of a series of protests against a counterrevolutionary effort to centralize power within an elite few. Bostonians had rejected "aristocratic" efforts to limit popular participation in local town meetings in which many white males were accustomed to participating. While Thomas Paine had written nothing critical about the United States and its government in *Rights of Man*, his text's meaning had been shaped for Americans by Jefferson's supportive foreword in the Philadelphia reprinting by Samuel Harrison Smith and Benjamin Franklin Bache in May 1791. As Marcus Daniel has argued, Jefferson's commentary, taken as an attack on John Adams, "transformed Paine's *Rights of Man* from a critique of counterrevolutionary politics in Europe into a critique of American politics, encouraging Paine's readers and admirers to draw invidious parallels between the politics of the United States and of revolutionary Europe."[23]

Fearing the transformation of America's republican government into monarchy and aristocracy, Bostonians performed the song "Ça ira" at the climax of the Valmy celebration to sonically and publicly reject such relapse. Used by the French to commemorate the first anniversary of the taking of the Bastille, "Ça ira" had become in France "an emblem of revolutionary aspirations."[24] Bostonians brought "Ça ira" into this American ritual as a sonic denunciation of monarchy and aristocracy. A bright, energetic tune filled with whirlwind repetitions of short, rapid figures, "Ça ira" has been described as unsingable and more prone to rhythmic shouting than singing.[25] Whether sung or shouted by Bostonians, "Ça ira" put an exclamation point on the community's frenetic destruction of the symbol of aristocracy, the roasted ox. Not surprisingly, Federalists countered the Republicans' interpretation. Abigail Adams, for one, mocked the Republicans' calls for equality and denunciation of aristocracy by insisting on calling the ox "citizen ox" and the public "citizen Mobility."[26] The Civic Feast was particularly threatening because it had mobilized an inclusive community in a memorable commemoration that marked and made sacred French, if not global, revolutionary time, "setting it apart from ordinary life and dedicating it to the fulfillment of transcendent, divine purposes."[27] Bostonians' handling of the symbolic ox showcased this mobilization. Unlike Philadelphia's July 4, 1788, ratification procession in which two live oxen symbolizing "anarchy and confusion" were paraded but slaughtered several days *after* the procession, with the meat distributed to the poor,[28] organizers of the Boston procession paraded roasted meat ready for eating, and while the butchers began the carving, "surrounding multitudes, assisting in the Ceremony, immolated the victim on the Altar of DEMOCRACY." Consistent with their conceptions of the republic, federalists had prioritized order and control in their street theater, while Republicans prioritized broad and visible participation.

The day inspired local songwriters to offer new musical expressions of popular cosmopolitanism. Songwriters confirmed and elaborated Paine's contrast, in *Rights of Man*, between republican government and government based on conquest and priestcraft.[29] Writing a song for Boston's civic feast, and directing readers of the local *Massachusetts Mercury* to find an appropriate tune for his lyrics, "Horatio" rejected both secular and religious tyranny. Targeting European leaders, "Horatio" railed "Ye scourges, of earth, born the plagues of mankind/Vile diadem'd scoundrels, divested of mind!/The light'ning of Freedom shall sweep you from time,/And Man reign the Sov'reign of nature sublime.//No MONARCH henceforward shall guide the wild car,/Whose high mettled coursers stand panting for war;/No bigotted PRIEST shall enfetter the soul;/But REASON and FREEDOM embrace the vast whole."[30] "Horatio" articulated a view of Protestant America as a divinely chosen tool for defeating the Antichrist, understood to encompass the pope and princes as contemporary tyrants.[31] Such inflated rhetoric captured both imagery typical of the day and stark dualisms that would continue to shape domestic political discourse for years.

"Horatio" rejected religious tyranny, but that did not mean there was no place for religion in this discourse. In Plymouth, Joseph Croswell interpreted the French victory at Valmy as the beginning of the long-prophesied millennium. Croswell (b. 1742?) was the son of radical separatist minister and itinerant preacher Andrew Croswell. Joseph had witnessed the Boston Massacre and was a Plymouth shopkeeper. He wrote songs and poems of Republican conviction in the Boston press, as well as a five-act play, and would go on to protest the Jay Treaty.[32] His lyrics were sung by his Plymouth neighbors; were promptly printed, by their request, along with Reverend Chandler Robbins's address for the day; and were circulated in New England and mid-Atlantic newspapers.[33]

Like Robbins's address, Croswell's ode expressed a widely held millenialism (see Figure 2.1). Robbins and Croswell interpreted the French republic's establishment and the unexpected French defeat of the Austrian and Prussian armies as the unfolding of the battles prophesied in millennial scripture. In these battles, the forces of heaven would defeat those of the Antichrist to

A N

# O D E

## *TO LIBERTY.*

*Composed by Mr.* Joseph Croswell, *and sung at the Civic Feast at* Plymouth, *January* 24, 1793.

---

Hail glorious Liberty,
May all the world be free,
And live in peace;
Lo the great Æra's come,
When tyrants meet their doom,
And Monarchs cease.

Hark from the *Gallic* shore,
Hear the loud cannon roar,
Fame's trumpet sounds;
Despotic armies fly,
*France* gains the victory,
Freedom abounds.

See the bright flame arise,
In yonder eastern skies,
Spreading in veins;
'Tis pure Democracy,
Setting all nations free,
Melting their chains.

*Prophets* and *Seers* of old;
Such happy times foretold,
Halcyon days;
'Tis the world's *Jubilee,*
*And mankind must be free,*
Give GOD *the praise.*

**Figure 2.1.** Joseph Croswell, "Ode to Liberty," 1793. From Gale. Eighteenth Century Collections Online (ECCO). © 2011 Gale, a part of Cengage, Inc. Reproduced by permission. www.cengage.com/permissions.

begin a thousand years of peace before a final conflict between good and evil would usher in Judgment Day. Orations in New England had created "a popular public discourse in which millennialism and republicanism were almost indistinguishable."[34] Robbins framed his address with a quote from Daniel, "Blessed be the name of GOD for ever and ever; for wisdom and might are his—HE changeth the times and the seasons, HE REMOVETH KINGS." Croswell used his neighbors' voices to sound this millennial interpretation in the Court-House Chamber dinner and military exercises, for which nearly 150 inhabitants gathered.[35] Croswell anticipated worldwide freedom and the time when "MONARCH's cease." Croswell had his neighbors declare "Lo the great AERA's come," to herald the unfolding revolution as the millennium. Using multisensory imagery of light, heat, and trumpet blasts that were staples of American song following the French revolution,[36] Croswell had the choir bring the millennium to life by singing of democracy's flame coursing through the veins of those in the east and melting their chains of bondage. Croswell's neighbors connected the revolution to millennial scripture, concluding in song that "Prophets and Seers of old; Such happy times foretold; Halcyon days; 'Tis the world's *Jubilee*." In a town that he would later describe as being fully controlled by Federalists, Croswell's Plymouth neighbors gathered to sing his lyrics that espoused millennial principles flavored by transnational democratic egalitarianism. The unity and communal sentiment reflected in the performance and the printing of the sermon and ode by request stand in stark contrast to the partisan division and persecution that the sexagenarian Croswell would describe to Jefferson as hallmarks of Plymouth in the following decade when he pleaded for assistance in gaining a local political post and cited his Republican verses to make his case.[37]

Croswell's song is significant not simply as an expression of a widespread New England view of the French Revolution, attributable to one person and his local community. It is also significant because it prompted rare specific evidence of how new lyrics were adapted to melodies. Rightly noting the awkward lyrics of political songs written to existing tunes, Goodman has asserted that such songs were "rarely meant to be sung."[38] The Plymouth celebration illustrates not only that such political verses were sung but also how lyrics were adjusted to fit tunes in performance. While Croswell's lyrics were not printed with a tune indication, the Boston *Independent Chronicle* explained that "with the repetition of the fifth line, it suited the old tune of 'God save great George our King.' "[39] ▶ Such repetition turned Croswell's six-line verses into seven-line verses matching the poetic meter and verse length of the British song. Moreover, the fifth line of each of Croswell's verses addressed a key concept that merited repeating: tyrants' downfall, victorious France, and impending freedom. The melody's stepwise motion, narrow range, and repetitive, simple rhythms were ideal for communal performance.

As Boston newspapers pointed out, this tune provided an additional layer of meaning. As "a Plymouth wit," possibly Croswell himself, explained, "Pressing this boasted *loyal tune* into the service of Liberty, is like melting down the Statues of Kings into Artillery to fight the battles of Freedom." In this interpretation, music, the act of writing it and the act of singing, became means for Americans to participate in realizing the millennial prophecy. Such an interpretation suggests a mode of engagement far removed from the "passive mode of political engagement" Goodman noted when contemplating the silent singing of political lyrics in the young republic.[40] A melody that had been used to praise British kings and then George Washington was communally sung in Plymouth to praise democracy; sustaining this repurposing, in the coming years the melody would increasingly be circulated with new lyrics articulating a transatlantic commitment to democratic principles.

Although stylistically different, the odes of Croswell and "Horatio" and "Ça ira" expressed central tenets of popular cosmopolitanism in American celebrations. Prominent among these were the shift toward impersonality in political authority and an allegiance to universal principles rather than one nation or a "temporary set of leaders who claimed to speak for it." The American president was noticeably absent from many of the day's lyrics, including those of "Horatio" and Croswell. The toasts prepared for the Faneuil Hall entertainment were offered in the reverse of the usual order, beginning with a toast to "The People" and leaving a toast to Washington near the end. Outside Faneuil Hall, the Independent Fusileers toasted Washington, not as president but "as a CITIZEN of America." By lowering Washington to the level of "citizen," contravening the customary order of toasts, and omitting Washington from celebratory lyrics, celebrants rejected a classical notion of republicanism based on deference and carried out Paine's urge "to dismiss all those songs and toasts which are calculated to enslave, and operate to suffocate reflection." This allegiance to universal principles over a nation or its leader challenged Federalists who "thought that only substantial and spontaneous public veneration for the Constitution and its elected stewards could ensure the survival of the fragile new nation's republican experiment."[41]

As seen in commemorations of the French victory at Valmy and the French republic, Americans voiced a powerful transatlantic dialogue of popular cosmopolitanism through song. They sang the perceived ties and influence between the American and French republics and addressed their transatlantic brethren. From 1793 onward, tens of thousands of Americans commemorated the storming of the Bastille, marked France's constitutional reforms, and welcomed their diplomats. Responding to this interest, from the same year, English immigrant composer and music printer Benjamin Carr and other printers circulated French revolutionary songs as sheet music for domestic use.[42]⊙ Americans wedded French revolutionary successes with the domestic celebratory calendar and performed musical pronouncements of global revolutionary progress music on occasions of historical significance to the United States, including July 4, Evacuation Day, the anniversary of the Battle of Bunker Hill, and the anniversary of the Franco-American Alliance of 1778.[43] Celebrations and related songs challenged the Federalists' notion of deferential classical republicanism. The celebrations' inclusive nature—opening channels for political expression across ranks, genders, race, and generations—strengthened this fundamental challenge and showcased the domestic potential of a broader democratic republicanism. By celebrating a continued, global revolution envisioned through the discourse of popular cosmopolitanism, Americans defined a standard of democratic republicanism that Federalists feared and resisted in their own republic.

## Resisting British Influence

In addition to voicing tenets of popular cosmopolitanism, Americans used music to reject the modeling of America after Britain. Federalists sought to shape the nation in British fashion, and Alexander Hamilton, determined to create a strong national government and economy, launched federal programs that were dependent on alliance with, investment by, and commerce with Britain.[44] Republicans wanted a nation independent of the influence of Britain, which they saw as a threat to the spread and survival of republican governments. This domestic division was exacerbated by Britain's entry into the Wars of the First Coalition against France in February 1793. Washington's April 22, 1793, Proclamation of Neutrality did not resolve the domestic debate, for neutrality was understood by many Americans to be a failure to show reciprocity for French aid in the Revolutionary War and a betrayal of France.

Americans quickly challenged Washington's decision through their enthusiastic—and often musical—welcomes of French ambassador Edmond Genet. A music lover, harpsichordist, and singer with an ebullient personality, Genet was happily feted on his trip from Charleston to Philadelphia, where Republican printers like Benjamin Franklin Bache and Philip Freneau helped organize grand receptions in his honor. Despite Washington's proclamation, Philadelphians used Genet's visit to sing of the historical, ideological, and emotional ties between France and America.[45] As a reworking of Charles Wesley's hymn "The Jubilee," they sang "Hail, Hail! Columbia's sons,/ The cause of France is thine,/With you she fought and bled,/Those laurels to entwine,/Hence let our ev'ry action show;/We feel her joys, we see her woe." While singing the final verse, likely to the four-part psalm tune "Lenox," they joined hands around the liberty cap placed at the head of the table between the American and French flags.[46]

The connection of musical, religious, and political expression was also seen in Americans' circulation of European reworkings of "God Save the King." This eighteenth-century song of long-disputed authorship had expressed loyalty to British monarchs, was adapted to express loyalty to George Washington, and was reworked to support Republican principles. When reworking the song, songwriters often retained the opening reference to God. Using a European reworking of the song, Republican printer, poet, and songwriter Philip Freneau challenged Washington's Proclamation of Neutrality during Genet's visit to Philadelphia in June 1793. Freneau's reworking of the reworking was one of several songs incorporated into celebrations of Genet's visit held in the elegant Oeller's Hotel. Freneau extracted two verses from London Corresponding Society member Robert Thomson's "God Save 'The Rights of Man!' " and added four new verses. The result was sung after the celebrants toasted "The Spirit of Seventy Six and Ninety Two." Freneau took a tune that had honored a king and a president and accompanied British counterrevolutionary burnings of Paine's effigy, and he used it to defiantly urge the spread of republican government to Russia and Asia.[47] Appearing at the peak of American support for the French Revolution, Freneau's expression of unwavering commitment to the French cause became one of the most reprinted revolutionary songs in the United States.[48] Supported by songs like Freneau's, Americans' generous reception of Genet exposed the threat that popular cosmopolitanism posed to the domestic authority of national government and national security, for when Genet sought American aid in the war with Britain and Washington would not offer assistance, Genet threatened to take his case directly to the sympathetic American people.[49]

In addition to Freneau's reworking, Republicans circulated British radical and revolutionary reworkings of "God Save the King" to reject Anglophilic policies at home. One of these was Joseph Mather's "God Save Great Thomas Paine," written and performed as part of Sheffield's radical culture. To the melody of "God Save the King," Mather had written "Down aristocracy,/Set up democracy,/And from hypocrisy/Save us good Lord." Such lyrics were well aligned with Republican views across the Atlantic.[50] They were part of a larger body of British songs that denounced despotism and Edmund Burke's and William Pitt's efforts to suppress revolutionary actions and literature, efforts collectively known as "Pitt's reign of terror." One song circulated in the United States was John Taylor's "The Trumpet of Liberty," which rejected the possibility that "Britons the chorus of liberty hear/With a cold and insensible mind." Originally written to celebrate the storming of the Bastille, Taylor's lyrics calling for the broader fall of tyranny had longer-lasting value in transatlantic circulation: they surfaced four years later in the United States when they were brought over by an "English gentleman."[51]

While drawing on transatlantic texts, Republicans organized their domestic resistance. Fueling their concerns about increasing wealth inequality and homegrown aristocracy were many of Hamilton's economic plans, including the assumption of state debts, the national bank, and excise taxes, which created a more powerful federal government and emulated British models. From spring 1793, concerned Americans formed forty-one Democratic-Republican societies across twelve states. These paralleled the development of corresponding societies in London, Sheffield, Edinburgh, and other British centers of revolutionary and radical activity. Comprising mechanics, small merchants, tradesmen, professionals, political leaders, landowners, slave owners, seamen, and unskilled workers, the American societies challenged the Federalists' concept of classical republicanism based on deference to elites. Their members insisted on participatory democratic republicanism founded on "the right to freedom of speech, press, and assembly; the right to criticize governmental representatives and to demand of them an explanation of their public acts; and the right to publish their reactions in a free press." Societies exercised those rights with the support and membership of leading newspaper editors and printers like Thomas Greenleaf, Thomas Adams, and Benjamin Franklin Bache, who reported on British repression of revolutionary and radical political societies to paint, in Cotlar's words, "a nightmarish picture of a British politics that had essentially outlawed the Atlantic world's emerging practices of democratic self-rule."[52]

As tensions, frustration, and humiliation with British treatment increased, Americans used music, including both British and French music, to criticize the Federalists' apparent acceptance of British aggression and willingness to make the United States subject to Britain once again. Britain occupied western posts in violation of the Treaty of Paris of 1783 and was widely seen as supporting Native American attacks on the frontier and enabling Algerian pirates' capture of eleven American merchant vessels and enslavement of their crews. As the war with France escalated, Britain placed tighter restrictions on US shipping, and impressment and maritime spoliation increased. In February 1794, Americans learned of an additional 250 merchant vessels seized under Britain's secret and increasingly stringent Orders in Council targeting trade in the French West Indies.[53]

As the war unfolded, Americans linked French and American opposition to British military, political, and commercial dominance through song. They sang and published French revolutionary songs, such as "La Marseillaise," "La Carmagnole," and "Ça Ira," as they used the egalitarian title "citizen," tricolor cockades, and long pants in place of silk stockings to show their support for the French Revolution and its global potential.[54]▶ In Philadelphia, boys and girls processed and sang French revolutionary songs, with a hundred youths singing, dancing, and leaping around a liberty pole.[55] Such songs were an impactful and memorable part of Americans' experience of transatlantic revolutionary fervor and sympathy. Reflecting on these years in 1821, attorney general William Wirt confessed,

> Even at this moment my blood runs cold, my breast swells, my temples throb, and I find myself catching my breath, when I recall the ecstacy with which I used to join in that glorious apostrophe to Liberty in the Marseilles Hymn, "O Liberty! Can man resign thee, once having felt thy gen'rous flame." And then the glorious, magnificent triumphs of the arms of France, so every way worthy of her cause! O, how we used to hang over them, to devour them, to weep and sing, and pray over these more than human exertions and victories![56]

As the war's impacts on Americans intensified, New York Republicans protested British offenses and taunted local Federalists with French revolutionary music.[57] Americans also wrote, performed, and circulated new songs in English. While some artists capitalized on interest in the revolution for profit, others adopted an anti-British stance as they commemorated revolutionary progress and articulated their own political values and allegiances through reference to the revolution's key events.[58] As Cotlar has explained, "Framing France as a vanguard nation carrying on the political work of the American Revolution, opposition writers argued that America's current leaders were too admiring of Britain, too lukewarm in their support for France, and thus threatening to bring about a Burkean counterrevolution in America."[59]

In newspapers, theaters, and July 4 celebrations, Americans resisted British dominance through song. American songwriters praised a local voluntary embargo and a buildup of American coastal defenses, and they fiercely rejected British spoliation on the seas, occupation of western posts, and naval and political dominance. Songwriters used the public's efforts to highlight the administration's weakness. Adopting the British naval tune "Heart of Oak," one songwriter praised the coastal fortification efforts that illustrated Americans' determination: "Our *wrongs* to avenge, and our *rights* to defend."▶ Denied by Washington the opportunity to fight Britain alongside the French, Republicans used song to oppose British aggression. Battling the British navy through its trademark tune, the songwriter promised the destruction of its men-of-war: "Thence *Freedom* her thunders unerring shall aim; . . . And our foes see their black *floating hells* in a flame." The Republican songwriter deemed the members of Washington's administration capitulators to British aggression who let the nation down, the antithesis of the citizen volunteers who defended it by building coastal fortifications. The songwriter described the fortifications as "walls of defiance by *Citizens* built/There high shall the *standard of liberty* rise/Undisgraced by compulsion, untainted by guilt." Shamefully, in this account, members of Washington's administration turned out to be mere "vassals" willing to "be kidnap'd and press'd" by Britain.[60]

American frustration eventually turned to outrage over the Jay Treaty, an outrage expressed in song. Colloquially named after the envoy who negotiated it, Chief Justice John Jay, the "Treaty of Amity, Commerce and Navigation" was silent about British impressment of American seamen.

Britain's renewed promise to evacuate the western posts seemed empty given her failure to meet similar terms in the earlier Treaty of Paris. Terms for dealing with Britain's illegal ship seizures were so complicated that compensation seemed impossible. Discontent with the treaty was particularly strong in ports and slaveholding states, and it stimulated the activities of Democratic-Republican societies. The treaty was decried as "a surrender to Great Britain, a betrayal of France, an infringement upon congressional control of foreign trade, and an outright fixing of the United States within the British sphere" of commercial and political dominance. In sum, opponents felt that the treaty turned Americans into British subjects. Intensifying opposition to the treaty was its debate and ratification in the Senate in secrecy. The Senate ratified the treaty by a vote of 20 to 10, precisely the minimum vote required. Editor Benjamin Franklin Bache scooped the treaty in his *Aurora* in June 1795 and six months of public debate ensued. As Estes has stressed, "What the treaty actually said became, in the debate ahead, less important than what both sides thought it meant or said it meant."[61]

While Federalists benefited in this debate from the superior rhetorical abilities of Alexander Hamilton, Republicans outdid their opponents in promoting their position in verse. Transatlantic circulation of songs aided Republicans' attacks on British behavior and submissive Anglophilic American policies. New York Republicans at the Democratic, Tammany, Mechanic, and Military Societies' partisan July 4 celebration rejected British bondage and the growth of a domestic aristocracy by performing a British revolutionary song. The lyrics complained, "So much tribute we pay, that we scarcely can live;/For the Light of the Sun what a rent do we give?/To be told "*We are happy!*"—'Tis mere Gasconade;/For we're burden'd like Slaves, and like Packhorses made!"[62] London Corresponding Society member Robert Hawes had circulated these lyrics on tobacco papers so they could quickly be burned amid increasing government surveillance in London's taverns and public houses.[63] On the surface, Hawes's song, which referred to Pitt and to America from afar, seems an odd American musical utterance. But Hawes's lyrics provided American Republicans a means of protesting British abuses as part of larger transatlantic community. By singing the lyrics of Hawes and other British reformers and radicals, Republicans sustained the global community initiated through the rise of popular cosmopolitanism but shifted their focus as the French Revolution's growing violence made it more difficult for Americans to maintain enthusiasm for the French cause. Republicans performed British revolutionary and radical songs and circulated them in larger collections to protest American submission to Britain through the Jay Treaty, the British impressment of American seamen, and Hamilton's Anglophilic programs. Amid the outrage over the treaty, in 1795 New York printer Samuel Loudon reprinted Robert Thomson's 1793 songster *Tribute to Liberty* as *A Tribute to the Swinish Multitude*. Loudon put into American hands dozens of radical and revolutionary songs denouncing the British government under a title that lauded the very masses that conservative Edmund Burke had notoriously derided as pigs.

Along with reprints and performances of British radical songs, Republicans penned and sang new lyrics mocking and critiquing the treaty.[64] "M.H." offered new verses in traditional ballad meter (quatrains alternating lines of iambic tetrameter and iambic trimeter) that accused Federalists of having sold the United States to Britain with the treaty's ratification. One songwriter whose lyrics first appeared in the Baltimore *Telegraphe* sarcastically noted the treaty's "gains": "The Indians now are civil grown,/As many *Wise* ones say:/The Western Posts are *now* your own;/Huzza for Justice J!//Perhaps in *two*, or ten, years hence;/Or in *some future* day,/You'll man them for your own defence;/Huzza for Justice J." Expressing a Republican desire to end British commercial hegemony, the songwriter claimed that the treaty had secured British friendship—a key concept in the treaty's first article—in exchange for submission to British commercial dominance. Portraying the treaty as a literal reversal of the Boston Tea Party, the songwriter sarcastically predicted, "Then to oblige your British Friends,/You'll surely buy their—TEA!!!/His *Majesty* on you depends;/Huzza for Justice J!"[65] The songwriter cast the treaty as antithetical to and a betrayal of the American revolution.

Shortly after Washington signed the treaty, a Republican subscriber to *Greenleaf's New York Journal* recounted British offenses in song and took on not only Britain and Chief Justice "Johnny Jay," but also the Federalist and Anglophilic writers who had been cultivating public support for the treaty. In the fourth verse, the songwriter targeted prominent Federalists Alexander Hamilton, who authored pro-treaty editorials as "Camillus," and Noah Webster, who edited the *American Minerva*. But then the subscriber dwelled on William Cobbett, a notoriously vicious Anglophilic political writer.[66] After arriving in the United States from England in 1792, Cobbett shattered the ideals of impartiality and impersonality established in American newspapers. In particular, personal lives of leading figures had been off-limits in the press. Cobbett crossed these lines as he specialized in harsh, graphic attacks on the public and personal lives of leading American figures.[67] Responding to Cobbett's new tone in kind, the Republican subscriber penned attacks on Jay, Hamilton, and Cobbett far removed from the uplifting, idealistic, and noble lyrics of Croswell and Freneau. Setting the lyrics to a theater tune that had already been used for political purposes in Britain, the subscriber created an image of Federalist weakness and urged Republicans to persevere in criticizing government policy:

You all of you have heard how the British dogs did bite us,
Encouraging the Indian dogs to quarrel with and fight us,
And turn'd the Algerines, their bloodhounds, out of kennel,
With bull dogs, mongrel, mastiff, water dog, and spaniel
    Bow wow wow.

Americans are civil dogs, who never bite their neighbours,
But wish to see each quiet dog enjoy the fruit of labours:
But 'tis not so with British dogs, who seiz'd them by the throat, sir,
First choak'd them out of breath, and then trod them under foot, sir.
    Bow wow, &c.

Then J****y J**, a grave dog, was chosen from the kennel;
We took him for a mastiff—he prov'd to be a spaniel,
Who never growl'd nor bark'd once, but justice humbly begs, sir—
Not getting which, ran home with his tail between his legs, sir.
    Bow wow, &c.

Camillus is a cunning dog, who tries to make you easy;
Minerva is a surly dog, endeavoring to teaze you;
While little Billy Whiffet, the dog who barks so loud, sir,
Will hardly look at common dogs, he is so cursed proud, sir.
    Bow wow, &c.

Some little time ago, Billy barked like a sad dog,
He call'd the people jacobins, and said they were all mad dogs,
Who wish'd to see all government, good order, and propriety,
O'erturned by the Rabble, alias Democrat Society.
    Bow wow, &c.

But lately little Billy has been so very quiet,
Perhaps he'll bark no more, 'cause he gets no pudding by it;
Or, per adventure, took the scent, and very wisily gone to law,
For fear some noted Democrat should send him home a bone to gnaw
Bow wow, &c.

There's a good old maxim, I believe it to be right, you,
The dog that barks the loudest, is seldom known to bite you;
And so it is with Billy, the dog that lost his tail, sir;
He very fiercely barks, but to bite his heart doth fail, sir.
Bow wow, &c.

Cobbett's caustic and personal attacks had fueled what Daniel has called an "intrusive and interrogatory politics 'dedicated to the unmasking of hypocrisy.'" Republicans issued attacks in response as reworkings of darker tunes. A particularly attractive tune for this purpose was "Derry Down," a gloomy minor-mode melody with a long history of carrying political lyrics on both sides of the Atlantic.[68] It was readily singable, as it used a stepwise or scalar melody within an amateur singer's vocal range. With this melody, one Republican songwriter used the treaty's secrecy to highlight the Federalists' disdain for the public. Attributed to both Philip Freneau, editor of the *National Gazette*, and Anthony Haswell, editor of the Bennington *Vermont Gazette*, this reworking of "Derry Down" illustrated how poet-editor-printers advanced Republican views through music. As the songwriter stressed, the Federalists felt that "the rabble had nothing to hear or to view,/Say the *twenty*, the secret's too sacred for you,/Ye are down, down, down, keep ye down." The Republican songwriter praised Senator Stephens Thomson Mason for leaking the treaty to engage the public in the debate, framing the matter in stark dualisms of aristocracy versus equality and tyranny versus freedom. The songwriter declared, "'Twas the act of a freeman, who joined with the TEN,/To save us from tyranny, rank us with men." With "tyranny," the songwriter protested Americans being kept in ignorance by their elected representatives as the treaty was debated in secret and complained about British abuses against American commerce and Britain's continued impressment of American seamen. After invoking a phrase equating the people's voice with the voice of God, the songwriter challenged the Federalists' pursuit of a British alliance and their classical republicanism by turning the "Derry Down" refrain into a resolution to defeat their plans and ideology: "*Vox Dei, Vox Populi*, truly but one,/Shall tell dark designers—*our will shall be done.*/Till you're down, down, *twenty* times down."[69] Such lyrics bluntly conveyed Republican determination and defiance.

In 1795, July 4 was treated as a day of mourning for the loss of liberty. In anti-treaty demonstrations, music accompanied mourning processions with Jay's effigy in the nation's capital, Newport, Charleston, Boston, and other coastal towns. In Portsmouth, 300 to 400 people marched with effigies of John Jay and British Foreign Secretary Lord Grenville, accompanied by a fife-and-drum rendition of the minor-mode air-turned-death march "Roslin Castle," before the figures were burned at the local wharf. ▶ In Charleston, protesters "dragged a British flag through the dirt to the tune of 'Yankee Doodle.' "[70] When Pennsylvania governor Thomas Mifflin called the militia to observe July 4 in traditional fashion, one militia member objected, quickly citing the essential role of music in the envisioned protest:

> A procession on that day is highly necessary; but it ought to move to the tune of *Roslin Castle*, and you ought to be clad in *mourning*, to manifest your sorrow at the *last* anniversary of American *Independence*. The [Jay] Treaty has again made you the *colonies* of Great Britain, and if you consider this a subject of rejoicing, and your administration deserves homage for it, obey the orders which have been issued. . . . It can never be that the patriotic Militia of Philadelphia, who hazarded their fortunes and their lives against a British tyranny, will become a band of *parasites*, [and] rejoice at the establishment of *British policies* in our country. . . . [A]ssert the dignity of your characters, act as freemen, and rather than become the abject *machines* of government, array yourselves in *mourning*, and bewail the fallen state of your country.[71]

Despite Federalists' rejection of oppositional political expression outside elections as the unvirtuous product of self-interest, a threat to order, and an extra-legal activity, Republicans intensified their rhetoric. Republicans responded as members of a global community, singing, printing, and reworking songs selected from a broader, transatlantic, revolutionary repertoire. Republicans sang in antiphonal dialogue with their transatlantic brethren who stood up to British monarchical and counterrevolutionary forces. Republicans tapped into the transatlantic circulation of texts, ideas, and rituals to raise their oppositional voice as part of a larger community initially inspired by a Painite popular cosmopolitanism. As the Republicans' oppositional voice grew during Washington's second term, Federalists responded in kind, using music to denounce their challengers and to promulgate Federalist values.

## Defending Classical Republicanism

Federalists feared for their country's future as much as Republicans did. As John Quincy Adams described the oppositional tensions in early 1793, "The Situation of our affairs is such, and the passions and rivalry's of our most conspicuous characters assume an aspect so alarming, that we have indeed much to apprehend for the fate of the Country." These "conspicuous characters" included the country's most prominent Republican leaders and editors who challenged the Federalists' authority, claims, and values. Adams wrote these words after being pressured by Bostonians to subscribe to the Civic Feast celebrating the French victory at Valmy, the feast that culminated in aristocracy's sacrifice on the altar of democracy in a grand example of street theater. As Adams wrote to his father, "I persisted in refusing to appear at the anarchical dinner which was denominated a civic feast, though I was urged strongly by several of my friends to become a subscriber, upon principles of expediency. Those friends disliked the whole affair quite as much as I did, but thought it necessary to comply with the folly of the day."[72] Adams's letter is revealing, for it suggests that the enthusiasm for popular cosmopolitanism that followed the French Revolution was so strong that Federalists felt pressured to conform.

Amid this enthusiastic spread of contrary values, Federalists used music to undermine political challengers. At first, Federalists turned to long-standing traditions to reinforce their power. One tradition was the election-day sermon, which typically framed government within a larger agreement between God and people to provide for the common good, reminded people to follow their elected officials, and reminded those officials to work for the good of all citizens. A musical example of this melding of religious and political expression was psalmodist Timothy Olmsted's "Columbia. An Ode, sung at the General Election in Hartford, 1792." Olmsted's ode was likely sung on May 10, 1792, when the Connecticut General Assembly convened in Hartford. This election day was marked by elaborate military and religious exercises and a sermon.[73] Olmsted composed a graceful three-part setting for the lyrics, which were printed as a broadside (see Figure 2.2). Olmsted called on God not only to guide "Our Councils" to "truth" and prevent "vice, unruly voice," or "rebel route." In a reflexive commentary on the act of singing, Olmsted maintained that "While choral voices sound,/Hail! Columbia, happy land,/Here freedom takes her lasting stand." Olmsted's ode thus reinforced the key Federalist principle that freedom was dependent on order and submission.

To discredit challenges to Federalist policies, authority, and classical republicanism, songwriters quickly capitalized on the Whiskey Rebellion. Whiskey was used for barter and wages on the western frontier in the absence of specie. Frontiersmen who faced harsh living conditions, depredations by Native Americans, distant markets, and the increasing wealth of non-resident speculators therefore viewed as oppressive and unfair the 1791 federal excise placed on such distilled spirits. In Slaughter's summary of westerners' views, "The government heaped an ideologically, culturally, and economically repulsive tax on the very people least able and least willing to suffer the imposition." The tax was central to Hamilton's economic program for the federal assumption of state debts and the strengthening of a federal government through stable, centralized finances. Unwilling to remain the "economic captives of remote commercial and political overlords" in the east, residents in western portions of several states opposed the excise through both peaceful and violent means.[74] Washington's administration targeted western Pennsylvania to demonstrate the federal government's authority: nearly 13,000 militiamen and volunteers from Virginia, Maryland, Pennsylvania, and New Jersey marched west across the Allegheny and Appalachian mountains in the fall of 1794 under the leadership of Washington and Hamilton. By the time the forces reached western Pennsylvania in late October, the protestors had dispersed. The troops resorted to rounding up the few remaining suspects and marched them back to the nation's capital.[75]

Federalist songwriters exaggerated the threat of disorder and violence to increase fear of political opposition and defend classical republicanism. One gentleman songwriter from Colonel MacPherson's Blues, a predominantly Federalist Philadelphia volunteer battalion, portrayed the protestors as the enemies of "the Eagle of Freedom" and urged his men to "chace her fell fiends o'er the hills of the west." In the lyrics of the Blues' songwriter, such opposition was the product of "the serpent of anarchy."[76] One "Jersey volunteer" songwriter blamed the protesters for "murders" and "foul mis-rule and party rage" that threatened to infringe on "law and liberty." The songwriter charged protestors with "sedition," echoing British counterrevolutionary trials.

**Figure 2.2.** Timothy Olmsted, "Columbia. An Ode, sung at the General Election in Hartford, 1792." Connecticut Historical Society.

Despite Republican and French revolutionary songs emphasizing reason as the basis of liberty, and despite the efforts of Democratic-Republican Societies to distance themselves from the rebels, Federalists linked the rebels, Republicans, and the "friends of liberty," and portrayed them all as the antithesis of reason and governed by passion.[77]

Insistent on establishing a foil for their challengers, Federalist songwriters constructed idealized portrayals of the volunteers that contradicted their plundering, use of excessive force, hiring of substitutes to fill elites' places, and petty arguments over rank, command, and uniforms. In the words of one "Jersey volunteer," his comrades were "unstain'd with crimes" and willing to die "to save from spoil the virtuous few." Published lyrics exaggerated the difficult conditions of the march and magnified the volunteers' classical republican virtue through their self-sacrifice for the greater good. The reality was somewhat different, though. The "Jersey volunteer" songwriter was actually Governor Richard Howell. And he had been spurred to write the lyrics because his own troops' behavior had become intolerable. Reaching the mountains amid foul weather in late October, the men had begun to question the expedition's purpose. They were not ready to march in the mornings, and they were repeatedly chastised for stealing from inhabitants, including an impoverished man near the camp. Howell's lyrics therefore described how he *wished* his men to act: promptly "Rous'd at the call" and "Unstain'd with crimes" like stealing, for which they were repeatedly rebuked.[78]

A virtuous image of the volunteers was sustained by Susanna Rowson, the resourceful actress, playwright, and poet in Thomas Wignell's Philadelphia theater company who promptly capitalized on interest in the Whiskey Rebellion by writing the comic opera *The Volunteers* (see Figure 2.3).[79] Echoing other songs inspired by the rebellion, Rowson put in the mouth of the character Trueman the line "Where is the Soldier will complain," highlighting the resolve and virtuous self-sacrifice of the recently returned volunteers. Alexander Reinagle's expansive range and dotted rhythms helped convey the volunteers' determination to restore order. Building on these contrasts between the volunteers and the rebels, Rowson coopted a French revolutionary phrase that had been used to celebrate a king's execution, "Vive la liberte." Rowson placed the phrase in a new context of American rebellion and made Federalists seem like the trusted guardians of freedom rather than its foes. While Republicans used the word "liberty" to prioritize equality and individual freedoms, Federalists cast liberty as the maintenance of order. Lyrics like Rowson's effectively denied Republicans' claim to liberty

**Figure 2.3.** Alexander Reinagle and Susanna Rowson, *The Volunteers*, 1795. Library of Congress, Music Division.

and instilled a long-standing dualism between the "friends of order" and the "friends of liberty" that would shape partisan political discourse for years.

Critical to the Federalists' counterattack was connecting the Republicans to the Whiskey Rebellion. Gentlemen songwriters like Howell made this connection when they blamed the protesters for "foul mis-rule and party rage." To discredit the Democratic-Republican societies, Federalist critics and songwriters specifically associated them with the rebels' violent image.[80] Some went further, using the connection to expose Republican hypocrisy. One Federalist writer of a mock Democratic-Republican society song put in the "club" members' mouths the chorus, "Sing Whiskey, friskey, turn about then,/And we'll keep up a dust till we are Great Men." In the recitatives the songwriter undercut the common Republican labeling of Washington and Hamilton as a "king" and "tory," respectively, by portraying the Republicans as aspiring aristocrats who would only criticize the government until they secured power for themselves; then the Republicans would "laugh at the fool [*sic*] who have made us great men."[81] In this Federalist musical interpretation, if the society members were not violent criminals, then they were clever, untrustworthy, hypocritical schemers who were using the people instead of looking out for them.

Such mock songs emerged as an ideal form for Federalists' satire. The power of this satire was illustrated best in Federalist songs attacking the Republicans as "jacobins." The term instantly associated the domestic opposition with destruction and rule-breaking and roused fears through association with the French Revolution's increasing violence. The Federalists labeled the Democratic-Republican societies "Jacobin clubs," a powerful shorthand for a host of evil attributes that tapped into fears of the violence seen in the Reign of Terror. As Federalist US District Attorney Edward St. Loe Livermore later explained to his Portsmouth neighbors, "jacobin" referred to "a disorganizer and opposer of the government, and lover and favourer of the French, and tainted with their infidelity."[82] Satirical verses portrayed these American "Jacobin Club" members as murderers, arsonists, thieves, proponents of war, and threats to law, science, and the arts. A British counterrevolutionary song modified for the Federalist *Columbian Centinel* had the Republicans in their "Jacobin Club" idolizing Genet and purportedly toasting confusion and "perdition to Congress and laws!" Responding to the Democratic-Republican societies' criticism of the government, Federalist songs either mocked their goal of equality or portrayed it as the violent, lawless pursuit of economic redistribution. The refrain of one mock song painted Boston's "Jacobin Club" not as the friend of liberty, but its enemy, as the group supposedly chanted to the melody of "Rule Britannia," "Rule Confusion, rule the Free,/Order shall submit to thee."[83]

Mounting their counterattack, Federalists responded with even greater threats of violence, yet simultaneously claimed to be protectors of order.

The violent rhetoric can be seen as both parties capitalized on the transatlantic circulation of songs. From a July 4 celebration in Hamburg, Germany, Republicans printed a reworking of "God Save the King" that began "God save the Guillotine,/'Till England's King and Queen,/Her power shall prove." Later attributed to one of the leaders of the London Corresponding Society, John Thelwall, the graphic, direct, and widely reprinted musical call for the monarchs' execution was initially attributed to American Joel Barlow, who had left the Connecticut Wits in 1788 and eventually became a French citizen moving in revolutionary and diplomatic circles.[84] The Boston Federalist "C.H." responded almost instantly with another reworking beginning "God save all Guillotines,/Till all our Jacobins,/Their power shall prove."[85] "C.H." invoked Robespierre's execution, which had occurred just three weeks after the Hamburg July 4 celebration, to invalidate Barlow's (or Thelwall's) revolutionary verses and the associated domestic opposition. "C.H." predicted of the Federalists' domestic opponents that "The wild, unruly crew,/Will pay their homage due/The Guillotine." Writing these lyrics just as the militia were reaching western Pennsylvania with Washington personally checking on their progress, "C.H." presaged the trials for treason and death sentences of the protestors rounded up in western Pennsylvania by the militia. "C.H." ended by calling Americans to "Behold the happy day,/When Freedom we'll display,/In Order's bright array,/And peace begin."[86] Although the Federalists' direct link between the broad movement of the Democratic-Republican societies and the Whiskey Rebellion was unfounded, both phenomena were treated as unwanted expressions of opposition. They were denounced not only by the Federalist press but also by members of Washington's administration, including the president himself, who condemned "self-created societies" in November 1794.[87]

Despite Federalists' criticism and efforts to stifle such opposition, the Democratic-Republican societies continued to impact American politics. In several cities, they helped build the Republican base and had already begun to impact elections, such as the congressional elections of 1794.[88] Partisan songs and local electioneering songs increased, as did panegyrics and personal attacks.[89] As American political discourse became increasingly caustic and personal during public debates over the Jay Treaty, the sacrality of Washington's character was shattered.[90] The extent of this partisanship was illustrated in one song that captured Vice President John Adams's attention enough that he clipped it and sent it with a letter to his wife. In the Philadelphia *Aurora*'s song titled "Political Chess," Washington was the king convinced that he cannot be attacked and Hamilton the powerful queen. The songwriter portayed Federalist judges as untrustworthy and crooked, noting "The Knights who our pawns by their quirks circumvent,/By two chiefs of the law we might well represent,/To the views of your party their motions are true,/They the straight line of principle never pursue." Despite the songwriter's assurance in the final verse that "the pawns of Democracy give you check-mate," Republicans would have to wait another four years for a presidential victory, after Washington's heir apparent John Adams defeated Jefferson in the 1796 election.[91]

In her study of British political song, Kate Horgan asserted, "In Paine's view, songs operated outside of the sphere of rational enlightenment that was necessary to achieve the rights of man and they were designed with forethought, or 'calculated' to oppress the people by keeping them 'enslaved.'"[92] Yet American practice showed that this was only half the picture. Republicans capitalized on a growing body of music in transatlantic circulation, supplemented with homegrown songs, to vigorously advocate for democratic republicanism. They appealed to American audiences disturbed by their country's adoption of monarchical traditions and federal programs that benefited the elite few at the expense of the hard-working masses. Central to circulating this body of song were Republican printers who, even when their subscribers routinely failed to pay, were willing to live in precarious financial conditions in order to continue spreading oppositional values. Through music, Republicans challenged the Federalists' deferential politics, their authority, and their revered leaders, including Washington.

As the two parties debated politics through music, their adherents' desire to hear partisan tunes led to violence in streets and theaters. In theaters, clever addresses and patchwork compositions like Benjmain Carr's *Federal Overture* blended melodies with both Republican and Federalist associations in an effort to satisfy heterogeneous audiences and silence partisans' riot-inducing calls for their favored tunes. Such methods of appeasement would not work for long, as the theater would soon showcase the most partisan lyrics of the decade.[93]

## Notes

1. Thomas Paine, *Rights of Man* (Philadelphia: D. Webster, 1797), 21; Daniel, *Scandal and Civility*, 98–9; Glenda Goodman, "American Identities in an Atlantic Musical World: Transhistorical Case Studies" (PhD diss., Harvard University, 2012), 144–8; Waldstreicher, *Perpetual Fetes*, 128.

2. Albrecht Koschnik, *"Let a Common Interest Bind Us Together": Associations, Partisanship, and Culture in Philadelphia, 1775–1840* (Charlottesville: University of Virginia Press, 2007), 30–1; Thomas P. Slaughter, *The Whiskey Rebellion: Frontier Epilogue to the American Revolution* (New York: Oxford University Press, 1986), 133; Cornell, *Other Founders*, 151; Harvey J. Kaye, *Thomas Paine and the Promise of America* (New York: Hill and Wang, 2005), 72–3; Terry Bouton, *Taming Democracy: "The People," the Founders, and the Troubled Ending of the American Revolution* (New York: Oxford University Press, 2007), 178; G. Wood, *Empire of Liberty*, 163.
3. Matthew Rainbow Hale, "Regenerating the World: The French Revolution, Civic Festivals, and the Forging of Modern American Democracy, 1793–1795," *Journal of American History* 103, no. 4 (March 2017): 898.
4. Philip Sheldon Foner, *The Democratic-Republican Societies, 1790–1800: A Documentary Sourcebook of Constitutions, Declarations, Addresses, Resolutions, and Toasts* (Westport, CT: Greenwood Press, 1976), 37; Todd Estes, *The Jay Treaty Debate, Public Opinion, and the Evolution of Early American Political Culture* (Amherst: University of Massachusetts Press, 2006), 129; Cotlar, *Tom Paine's America*, 55, 67–9, 75.
5. Foner, *Democratic-Republican Societies*, 17, 40; Koschnik, *Common Interest*, 105; G. Wood, *Empire of Liberty*, 161–3; Estes, *Jay Treaty Debate*, 4; "From Thomas Jefferson to Francis Hopkinson, 13 March 1789," *Founders Online*, https://founders.archives.gov/documents/Jefferson/01-14-02-0402; James Madison, "Parties," Philadelphia *National Gazette*, 23 January 1792.
6. Cotlar, *Tom Paine's America*, 71; *Politics for the People*, 75–7; Reverend Thomas Dunn, *A Discourse Delivered in the New Dutch Church . . . before the New York Society for the Information and Assistance of Persons Emigrating from Foreign Countries* (London: Eaton, 1795).
7. Oscar Sonneck, *Miscellaneous Studies in the History of Music* (New York: Macmillan, 1921), 57–64; Andrew Luke Hargruder, "'A Circle Form'd of Friends:' Candor, Contentiousness, and the Democratic Clubs of the Early Republic" (MA thesis, Louisiana State University, 2015), 24–41.
8. Cotlar, *Tom Paine's America*, 33, 75; Pasley, *Tyranny of Printers*, 96, 108–9.
9. Estes, *Jay Treaty Debate*, 52, 55.
10. Cotlar, *Tom Paine's America*, 39, 50, 55, 70; Thomas Paine, *The Writings of Thomas Paine*, ed. Moncure Daniel Conway (New York: AMS Press, 1967), 382; Kaye, *Thomas Paine*, 98.
11. *Walker's Hibernian Magazine; or, Compendium of Entertaining Knowledge* (July 1792), 73–9; Samuel M'Skimin, *Annals of Ulster; or, Ireland Fifty Years Ago* (Belfast: John Henderson, 1849), 15–16; Kate Horgan, *The Politics of Songs in Eighteenth-Century Britain, 1723–1795* (London: Pickering & Chatto, 2014), 26–7, 130–1, 161–6; Michael Scrivener, *Poetry and Reform: Periodical Verse from the English Democratic Press, 1792–1824* (Detroit: Wayne State University Press, 1992), 50–1; James Montgomery, *The Poetical Works of James Montgomery* (Philadelphia: Lindsay and Blakiston, 1853), 168.

12. Philadelphia *Federal Gazette*, 13 September 1792; Philadelphia *General Advertiser*, 18 September 1792; *Baltimore Evening Post*, 19 September 1792; *New York Journal*, 26 September 1792; *Salem Gazette*, 2 October 1792; Halifax *North Carolina Journal*, 3 October 1792; New York *Diary*, 10 October 1792, 16 December 1793; Philadelphia *Independent Gazetteer*, 13 October 1792; Windsor *Spooner's Vermont Journal*, 29 October 1792; *American Museum or Universal Magazine* 12 (July 1792), 9; *Columbian Songster; or Jovial Companion*, 147–9.
13. Foner, *Democratic-Republican Societies*, 17; Philadelphia *Federal Gazette*, 25 March 1793; Boston *Massachusetts Mercury*, 2, 7 February 1793; New York *Diary*, 27 November 1793; G. Wood, *Empire of Liberty*, 7–8; Waldstreicher, *Perpetual Fetes*, 129; Kaye, *Thomas Paine*, 73; Philadelphia *Independent Gazetteer*, 5 January, 23 February 1793.
14. *Medley or New Bedford Marine Journal*, 2 February 1793; Warren *Herald of the United States*, 9 February 1793; Charleston *State Gazette*, 17 January 1793; *Essex Journal*, 6 February 1793; *New York Journal*, 29 December 1792, 6 February 1793; Charleston *City Gazette*, 21 February 1793; Newman, *Parades*, 137–8.
15. Newman, *Parades*, 122; *The Boston Directory* (Boston, 1789); *The Boston Directory* (Boston, 1796); *Society for the Information and Advice of Immigrants. Boston, December 30, 1793* (Boston: [1794]); Oliver Ayer Roberts, *History of the Military Company of Massachusetts, Now Called the Ancient and Honorable Military Company of Massachusetts*, vol. 2 (Boston: Alfred Mudge and Son, 1897), 161, 215; Boston *Columbian Centinel*, 19 January 1793; *Boston Gazette*, 21 January 1793; Lora Altine Woodbury Underhill, *Descendants of Edward Small of New England, and the Allied Families with Tracings of English Ancestry*, vol. 1 (Cambridge, MA: Riverside Press, 1910), 77; Boston *Massachusetts Mercury*, 26 January 1793; *Boston Directory* (Boston: Edward Cotton, 1805), 55; Edward Hartwell Savage, *Police Records and Recollections, or, Boston by Daylight and Gaslights* (Boston: John P. Dale, 1873), 43–4.
16. Matthew Rainbow Hale, "On Their Tiptoes: Political Time and Newspapers during the Advent of the Radicalized French Revolution, circa 1792–93," *Journal of the Early Republic* 29, no. 2 (Summer 2009): 195–200.
17. *Boston Gazette*, 14, 21 January 1793; Boston *Argus*, 22 February 1793; Boston *Massachusetts Mercury*, 26 January 1793; Boston *Columbian Centinel*, 26 January 1793; Boston *Independent Chronicle*, 31 January 1793, Newman, *Parades*, 123–6; Simon P. Newman and Marion Vaillant, "La Révolution française vue de loin: la celebration de Valmy à Boston, en janvier 1793," *Revue d'histoire moderne et contemporaine* 58, no. 1 (January–March 2011): 80–99.
18. *Boston Gazette*, 14 January 1793; Boston *Massachusetts Mercury*, 17 January 1793; Boston *Argus*, 22 February 1793.
19. "John Quincy Adams to John Adams, 10 February 1793," *Founders Online*, http://founders.archives.gov/documents/Adams/04-09-02-0230.
20. *Boston Gazette*, 21 January 1793; Boston *Massachusetts Mercury*, 26 January 1793; Boston *Columbian Centinel*, 26 January 1793; Boston *Independent Chronicle*, 29 October 1789, 31 January 1793; Boston *Herald of Freedom*, 27 October 1789.

21. Boston *Massachusetts Mercury*, 26 January 1793; Boston *Independent Chronicle*, 31 January 1793. The ox procession echoed both French and British rituals. Horgan, *Politics of Songs*, 141–2.
22. Hartford *American Mercury*, 4 February 1793; Philadelphia *Gazette of the United States*, 27 April 1791; Kaye, *Thomas Paine*, 68, 104; Walt Brown, *John Adams and the American Press: Politics and Journalism at the Birth of the Republic* (Jefferson, NC: McFarland, 1995), 51–7; Foner, *Democratic-Republican Societies*, 5, 6, 10–11, 413; Newman, *Parades*, 50–3; Schwartz, *George Washington*, 61–3, 66; G. Wood, *Empire of Liberty*, 74–85; Daniel, *Scandal and Civility*, 98–9; Richard H. Kohn, *Eagle and Sword: The Federalists and the Creation of the Military Establishment in America, 1783–1802* (New York: Free Press, 1975), 172; Waldstreicher, *Perpetual Fetes*, 132.
23. Newman, *Parades*, 126–9; Daniel, *Scandal and Civility*, 73–4, 98–9.
24. Laura Mason, *Singing the French Revolution: Popular Culture and Politics, 1787–1799* (Ithaca, NY: Cornell University Press, 1996), 40–5.
25. Myron Gray, "French Revolutionary Song for Federal Philadelphia: Benjamin Carr's Music Sheets," *Common-place* 13, no. 2 (Winter 2013). http://www.common-place-archives.org/vol-13/no-02/gray/.
26. Newman and Vaillant, "La Révolution française," 89–90; "Abigail Adams to John Adams, 1 February 1793," *Founders Online*, http://founders.archives.gov/documents/Adams/04-09-02-0225.
27. Hale, "On Their Tiptoes," 197.
28. Hopkinson, "Account," 66; Philadelphia *Independent Gazetteer*, 10 July 1788.
29. *Greenleaf's New York Journal*, 25 October 1794; Philadelphia *Federal Gazette*, 22 January 1793; Boston *Courier*, 23 September 1795; Paine, *Writings*, 308, 382.
30. Boston *Massachusetts Mercury*, 22 January 1793.
31. Richard M. Gamble, "'The Last and Brightest Empire of Time': Timothy Dwight and America as Voegelin's 'Authoritative Present,' 1771–1787," *Humanitas* 20, no. 1–2 (2007): 18, 27–8.
32. "To Thomas Jefferson from Joseph Croswell, February 1803," *Founders Online*, http://founders.archives.gov/documents/Jefferson/01-39-02-0511.
33. Boston *Massachusetts Mercury*, 22 January 1793; Boston *Independent Chronicle*, 24, 31 January 1793; Newburyport *Essex Journal*, 30 January 1793; Boston *Columbian Centinel*, 26 January 1793; Portland *Eastern Herald*, 31 January 1793; New York *Diary*, 4 February 1793; Philadelphia *Dunlap's American Daily Advertiser*, 5 February 1793; Philadelphia *Federal Gazette*, 5 February 1793; Springfield *Hampshire Chronicle*, 5 February 1793; *Albany Register*, 11 February 1793; Portsmouth *Osborne's New Hampshire Spy*, 23 February 1793; Chandler Robbins, *An Address, Delivered at Plymouth, on the 24th Day of January, 1793, to the Inhabitants of That Town* [Boston], [1793], 19–20.
34. Michael Lienesch, *New Order of the Ages: Time, the Constitution, and the Making of Modern American Political Thought* (Princeton, NJ: Princeton University Press, 2014), 185–9; Michael Lienesch, "The Role of Political Millennialism in Early American Nationalism," *Western Political Quarterly* 36, no. 3 (September 1983): 446–51.
35. Robbins, *Address*, 5, 16; Boston *Independent Chronicle*, 31 January 1793.

36. Boston *Independent Chronicle*, 24 January 1793; Newburyport *Essex Journal*, 30 January 1793.
37. "To Thomas Jefferson from Joseph Croswell, February 1803;" "To Thomas Jefferson from Joseph Croswell, July 1803," *Founders Online*, http://founders.archives.gov/documents/Jefferson/01-41-02-0027.
38. Goodman, "American Identities," 134, 136, 170, 173.
39. Boston *Independent Chronicle*, 31 January 1793.
40. Boston *American Apollo*, 1 February 1793; Boston *Independent Chronicle*, 31 January 1793; Goodman, "American Identities," 136.
41. Cotlar, *Tom Paine's America*, 51; Daniel, *Scandal and Civility*, 125–6; Newburyport *Essex Journal*, 30 January 1793; Newman, *Parades*, 94, 122–4; Philadelphia *Federal Gazette*, 25 January 1793; Elizabethtown *New-Jersey Journal*, 30 November 1793; Boston *Massachusetts Mercury*, 22, 26 January 1793; Albrecht Koschnik, *Common Interest*, 31; Boston *Independent Chronicle*, 24, 31 January 1793.
42. Gray, "French Revolutionary Song."
43. Newman, *Parades*, 131, 135, 145; *New York Weekly Museum*, 12 July 1794; *Greenleaf's New York Journal*, 5 July 1796; New York *Diary*, 27 November 1793; *New York Daily Gazette*, 26 February 1794; Philadelphia *Independent Gazetteer*, 9 July 1796; Matthew Rainbow Hale, "'Many Who Wandered in Darkness': The Contest over American National Identity, 1795–1798," *Early American Studies: An Interdisciplinary Journal* 1, no. 1 (Spring 2003): 127–75.
44. John Ferling, *Adams vs. Jefferson: The Tumultuous Election of 1800* (New York: Oxford University Press, 2004), 48–9; Christopher J. Young, "Connecting the President and the People: Washington's Neutrality, Genet's Challenge, and Hamilton's Fight for Public Support," *Journal of the Early Republic* 31, no. 3 (Fall 2011): 442.
45. M. E. Barnes-Ostrander, "Domestic Music Making in Early New York State: Music in the Lives of Three Amateurs," *Musical Quarterly* 68, no. 3 (July 1982), 364–8; Alfred F. Young, *The Democratic-Republicans of New York: The Origins, 1763–1797* (Chapel Hill: University of North Carolina Press, 2012), 353; Joseph Eckley, *A Sermon, Preached at the Request of the Ancient and Honourable Artillery Company, June 4, 1792* (Boston: Samuel Hall, 1792), 11.
46. New York *Diary*, 5 June 1793.
47. Jon Mee, *Print, Publicity, and Popular Radicalism in the 1790s: The Laurel of Liberty* (Cambridge: Cambridge University Press, 2016), 78–81; Kaye, *Thomas Paine*, 73–4; Paine, *Writings*, 267, 305, 385, 389, 398, 512; Philadelphia *Independent Gazetteer*, 5 January, 23 February 1793; Portsmouth *New Hampshire Gazette*, 6 February 1794; Judith R. Hiltner, *The Newspaper Verse of Philip Freneau: An Edition and Bibliographical Survey* (Troy, NY: Whitson, 1986), 528–30.
48. Philadelphia *Federal Gazette*, 3 June 1793; Philadelphia *National Gazette*, 5 June 1793; Philadelphia *Gazette of the United States*, 5 June 1793; Frederick *Bartgis's Maryland Gazette*, 13 June 1793; Boston *Argus*, 14 June 1793; *Albany Register*, 24 June 1793; Windsor *Spooner's Vermont Journal*, 5 August 1793; Northampton *Hampshire Gazette*, 14 August 1793; New York *Weekly Museum*, 9 November 1793. A similar perspective was expressed in song as late as 1796. See *Rutland Herald*, 27 June 1796.

49. Cotlar, *Tom Paine's America*, 86–8; Daniel, *Scandal and Civility*, 55; C. Young, "Connecting the President and the People," 445–52.
50. *Greenleaf's New York Journal*, 2 May 1796; Horgan, *Politics of Songs*, 134, 137–9, 143–4.
51. Ferling, *Adams vs. Jefferson*, 60–1; Boston *Massachusetts Mercury*, 28 March 1794; *Greenleaf's New York Journal*, 25 October 1794; Newburyport *Impartial Herald*, 21 November 1794; *Salem Gazette*, 9 December 1794; Concord *Mirrour*, 17 July 1795; *Jovial Songster: Containing a Variety of Patriotic and Humorous Songs* (New York: John Harrisson, 1794), 51; Edward Taylor, ed., *Hymns and Miscellaneous Poems of John Taylor of Norwich* (n.p.: n.p., 1863), xx–xxi.
52. W. Brown, *John Adams*, 19; Foner, *Democratic-Republican Societies*, 3–4, 6, 9–11, 13, 20–1, 413; Koschnik, *Common Interest*, 24, 32; Waldstreicher, *Perpetual Fetes*, 130, 132; Ferling, *Adams vs. Jefferson*, 48–9, 60–1; Cornell, *Other Founders*, 195–7; Kaye, *Thomas Paine*, 104; Roland M. Baumann, "Philadelphia's Manufacturers and the Excise Tax of 1794: The Forging of the Jeffersonian Coalition," in *The Whiskey Rebellion: Past and Present Perspectives*, ed. Steven R. Boyd (Westport, CT: Greenwood Press, 1985), 146; Matthew Schoenbachler, "Republicanism in the Age of Democratic Revolution: The Democratic-Republican Societies of the 1790s," *Journal of the Early Republic* 18, no. 2 (Summer 1998): 245–7; Kohn, *Eagle and Sword*, 172; G. Wood, *Empire of Liberty*, 163; Cotlar, *Tom Paine's America*, 78–9.
53. Slaughter, *Whiskey Rebellion*, 107–8; *New York Weekly Chronicle*, 3 September 1795; *Greenleaf's New York Journal*, 5 September 1795; Donald H. Stewart, *The Opposition Press of the Federalist Period* (Albany: State University of New York Press, 1969), 178–2; Norwich *Weekly Register*, 18 March 1794; A. B. C. Whipple, *To the Shores of Tripoli: The Birth of the U.S. Navy and Marines* (Annapolis, MD: Naval Institute Press, 1991), 36; H. G. Barnby, *The Prisoners of Algiers: An Account of the Forgotten American-Algerian War 1785–1797* (New York: Oxford University Press, 1966), 103; Lawrence A. Peskin, *Captives and Countrymen: Barbary Slavery and the American Public, 1785–1816* (Baltimore: Johns Hopkins University Press, 2009), 129; Hale, "'Many Who Wandered,'" 134–6.
54. Publications and performances included Mary Ann Pownall [Wrighten] and James Hewitt, *Six Songs; For the Harpsichord or Piano Forte* (New York: J. Hewitt, 1794); New York *Daily Advertiser*, 29 March 1794; *The Democratic Songster* (Baltimore: [Angell for] Keatinge, 1794), 25–36; *Tom Paine's Jests* (Philadelphia: Richard Folwell for Mathew Carey, 1794), 55–6; R. Thomson, *A Tribute to the Swinish Multitude, Being a Choice Collection of Patriotic Songs* (New York: Samuel Loudon, 1795), 61–2, 81–2; Charleston *City Gazette*, 15 February 1794; *Greenleaf's New York Journal*, 5, 12 March 1794; *New York Daily Gazette*, 26 February 1794; Norfolk *Virginia Chronicle*, 22 February 1794; Newman, *Parades*, 142; Philadelphia *National Gazette*, 25 May 1793; New York *Diary*, 22 May 1793.
55. John Fanning Watson, *Historic Tales of Olden Time, Concerning the Early Settlement and Progress of Philadelphia and Pennsylvania* (Philadelphia: E. Littell and T. Holden, 1833), 109–10.
56. John P. Kennedy, *Memoirs of the Life of William Wirt*, vol. 2 (Philadelphia: 1849), 122.
57. Heather Nathans, *Early American Theatre from the Revolution to Thomas Jefferson: Into the Hands of the People* (Cambridge: Cambridge University Press,

2003), 136; Paul A. Gilje, *The Road to Mobocracy: Popular Disorder in New York City, 1763–1834* (Chapel Hill: University of North Carolina Press, 1987), 101–2; New York *Columbian Gazetteer*, 27 February 1794; New York *Daily Advertiser*, 28 February 1794; *Greenleaf's New York Journal*, 12 March 1794; Horgan, *Politics of Songs*, 142.

58. Ezekial Forman, "Amusements and Politics in Philadelphia, 1794," *The Pennsylvania Magazine of History and Biography* 10, no. 2 (July 1886): 185; Philadelphia *General Advertiser*, 22 March 1794; New York *Daily Advertiser*, 6 August 1794; *New York Gazette*, 22 June 1795; George C. D. Odell, *Annals of the New York Stage*, vol. 1 (New York: Columbia University Press, 1927), 365–6, 394; Farnsworth, *Oration*, 22–3.
59. Cotlar, *Tom Paine's America*, 75; Daniel, *Scandal and Civility*, 98–9.
60. New York *Diary*, 26 April 1794; Philadelphia *Independent Gazetteer*, 31 May 1794; Philadelphia *Gazette of the United States*, 12 June 1794; George O. Seilhamer, *History of the American Theatre: New Foundations* (New York: Haskell House, 1969), 155–7; Norfolk *Virginia Chronicle*, 9, 21 July 1794; Stewart, *Opposition Press*, 186.
61. Foner, *Democratic-Republican Societies*, 36–7; Estes, *Jay Treaty Debate*, 29–31, 33–4, 71–103; Charles R. Ritcheson, "Thomas Pinckney's London Mission, 1792–1796, and the Impressment Issue," *International History Review* 2, no. 4 (October 1980): 531, 537.
62. *Greenleaf's New York Journal*, 8 July 1795, 2 May 1796; Foner, *Democratic-Republican Societies*, 223–4, 231; *Tom Paine's Jests*, 63–5; *New York Weekly Museum*, 15 March 1794.
63. David Worrall, "Robert Hawes and the Millennium Press: A Political Microculture of Late-Eighteenth-Century Spitalfields," in *Romanticism and Millenarianism*, ed. Tim Fulford (New York: Palgrave, 2002), 173–4; David Worrall, "Blake and the 1790s Plebeian Radical Culture," in *Blake in the Nineties*, ed. Steve Clark and David Worrall (New York: St. Martin's Press, 1999), 206; Mee, *Print*, 81.
64. *New York Weekly Museum*, 8 August 1795; Wilmington *Delaware Gazette*, 15 August 1795; Hartford *Connecticut Courant*, 17 August 1795; *Salem Gazette*, 25 August 1795; Halifax *North Carolina Journal*, 14 September 1795.
65. Estes, *Jay Treaty Debate*, 105–6; *Greenleaf's New York Journal*, 29 August 1795; Philadelphia *Independent Gazetteer*, 23 May 1795; Portsmouth *Oracle of the Day*, 9 June 1795; Wilmington *Delaware Gazette*, 13 June 1795; Philadelphia *Aurora*, 30 June 1795; G. Wood, *Empire of Liberty*, 192–3.
66. *Greenleaf's New York Journal*, 5 September 1795; Hannah Barker and David Vincent, eds., *Language, Print and Electoral Politics, 1790–1832* (Suffolk: Boydell Press, 2001), 17–9. "Another New Bow Wow" was likely inspired by and a response to one that had appeared in *New York Weekly Chronicle*, 3 September 1795.
67. Daniel, *Scandal and Civility*, 59, 187–229.
68. Goodman, "American Identities," 157–72.
69. Daniel, *Scandal and Civility*, 216; Hiltner, *Newspaper Verse*, 744; John Spargo, *Anthony Haswell, Printer-Patriot-Balladeer: A Biographical Study with a Selection of His Ballads and an Annotated Bibliographical List of His Imprints* (Rutland, VT: Tuttle, 1925), 150; Philadelphia *Aurora*, 22 September 1795; Philadelphia *National Gazette*, 19 December 1792.

70. Foner, *Democratic-Republican Societies*, 37; Estes, *Jay Treaty Debate*, 75; *Greenleaf's New York Journal*, 8 July 1795; New York *Argus*, 15 July 1795; Philadelphia *Independent Gazetteer*, 8 July 1795; Springfield *Hampshire and Berkshire Chronicle*, 7 September 1795; *Boston Gazette*, 14 September 1795; Philadelphia *Gazette of the United States*, 18, 19 September 1795; Waldstreicher, *Perpetual Fetes*, 138; W. Brown, *John Adams*, 20–1; Horgan, *Politics of Songs*, 141–2.
71. Koschnik, *Common Interest*, 104.
72. "John Quincy Adams to John Adams, 10 February 1793," *Founders Online*, http://founders.archives.gov/documents/Adams/04-09-02-0230.
73. Hartford *Connecticut Courant*, 14 May 1792; Timothy Stone, *A Sermon, Preached before His Excellency Samuel Huntington* (Hartford, CT: Hudson & Goodwin, 1792).
74. Slaughter, *Whiskey Rebellion*, 64–74, 88, 95; Cotlar, *Tom Paine's America*, 79; Jeffrey J. Crow, "The Whiskey Rebellion in North Carolina," *North Carolina Historical Review* 6, no. 1 (January 1989), 16–28; Andrew Shankman, "'A New Thing on Earth': Alexander Hamilton, Pro-Manufacturing Republicans, and the Democratization of American Political Economy," *Journal of the Early Republic* 23, no. 3 (Autumn 2003): 324–31.
75. Slaughter, *Whiskey Rebellion*, 118–21, 159–60, 213–19; Roger V. Gould, "Political Networks and the Local/National Boundary in the Whiskey Rebellion," in *Challenging Authority: The Historical Study of Contentious Politics*, ed. Michael P. Hanagan, Leslie Page Moch, and Wayne Te Brake (Minneapolis: University of Minnesota Press, 1998), 40.
76. *Greenleaf's New York Journal*, 14 February 1795; William W. Clapp Jr., *A Record of the Boston Stage* (New York: Greenwood, 1969), 41; *Philadelphia Gazette*, 27 January 1795; Slaughter, *Whiskey Rebellion*, 69–70, 73–4; Koschnik, *Common Interest*, 106–12; Concord *Mirrour*, 12 December 1794; *Carlisle Gazette*, 7 January 1795; Philadelphia *Gazette of the United States*, 26 November 1794; Nigel Little, *Transoceanic Radical, William Duane: National Identity and Empire, 1760–1835* (London: Pickering and Chatto, 2008), 142–4.
77. Philadelphia *Dunlap's American Daily Advertiser*, 7 November 1794; *Kline's Carlisle Weekly Gazette*, 19 November 1794; Concord *Mirrour*, 12 December 1794; *Collections of the New Jersey Historical Society*, vol. 7 (1872): 109–11; Philadelphia *Gazette of the United States*, 26 November 1794; Philadelphia *Claypoole's American Daily Advertiser*, 21 February 1795; *Philadelphia Gazette*, 18 February 1795; Slaughter, *Whiskey Rebellion*, 12–27; Estes, *Jay Treaty Debate*, 115.
78. "Journal of Major William Gould during an Expedition into Pennsylvania, 1849," *Proceedings of the New Jersey Historical* Society 3 (1849): 182–4, 189; Daniel Agnew and Richard Howell, "A Biographical Sketch of Governor Richard Howell, of New Jersey," *Pennsylvania Magazine of History and Biography* 22, no. 2 (1898): 228; *Philadelphia Gazette*, 18 February 1795; Koschnik, *Common Interest*, 108–9; G. Wood, *Empire of Liberty*, 7–8; Slaughter, *Whiskey Rebellion*, 213–14, 218; Concord *Mirrour*, 12 December 1794; *Carlisle Gazette*, 7 January, 18 February 1795; *Greenleaf's New York Journal*, 14 February 1795; Philadelphia *Gazette of the United States*, 26 November 1794.

79. Alexander Reinagle and Susanna Rowson, *The Volunteers: A Music Entertainment as Performed at the New Theatre* (n.p.: n.p., 1795), https://www.loc.gov/item/2015562334/; *Philadelphia Gazette*, 22 January 1795; Philadelphia *Aurora*, 26 January 1795.
80. Cotlar, *Tom Paine's America*, 79; Concord *The Mirrour*, 12 December 1794; Schoenbachler, "Republicanism," 254; Foner, *Democratic-Republican Societies*, 27, 29–30; Estes, *Jay Treaty Debate*, 64–5; Slaughter, *Whiskey Rebellion*, 163, 165; Ferling, *Adams vs. Jefferson*, 63–4; Philadelphia *Dunlap's American Daily Advertiser*, 21 February 1795.
81. Columbia *South Carolina State Gazette*, 2 October 1794.
82. Edward St. Loe Livermore, *An Oration, in Commemoration of the Dissolution of the Political Union between the United States of America and France* (Portsmouth, New-Hampshire: n.p. 1799), 28; Philadelphia *Aurora*, 23 September 1796.
83. Foner, *Democratic-Republican Societies*, 23, 27; Boston *Columbian Centinel*, 1, 3 March, 5 April 1794; Peter Pindar, Esq. [John Wolcot] *Odes to Mr. Paine, Author of "The Rights of Man," on the Intended Celebration of the Downfall of the French Empire, by a Set of British Democrates, on the Fourteenth of July* (London: J. Evans, 1791), 8–10; *The Anti-Levelling Songster* (London: J. Downes, 1793), 4.
84. Benjamin J. Lossing, *Lossing's Pictorial Field Book of the War of 1812*, vol. 1 (New York: Harper and Brothers, 1868), 94; Boston *Independent Chronicle*, 9 October 1794; *Greenleaf's New York Journal*, 18 October 1794; Philadelphia *Independent Gazetteer*, 18 October 1794; Wilmington *Delaware Gazette*, 25 October 1794; *Greenfield Gazette*, 30 October 1794; Hartford *Connecticut Courant*, 3 November 1794; Windsor *Spooner's Vermont Journal*, 17 November 1794; Rutland *Farmer's Library*, 18 November 1794; Walpole *New Hampshire Journal*, 21 November 1794; Cotlar, *Tom Paine's America*, 41.
85. Boston *Columbian Centinel*, 11 October 1794; Newburyport *Impartial Herald*, 18 October 1794; Hartford *American Mercury*, 20 October 1794; Hartford *Connecticut Courant*, 3 November 1794.
86. Ten men were tried, and two were sentenced to death by hanging. Those were pardoned by Washington.
87. Foner, *Democratic-Republican Societies*, 31, 33; Ferling, *Adams vs. Jefferson*, 64–5; Slaughter, *Whiskey Rebellion*, 1986, 221.
88. Baumann, "Philadelphia's Manufacturers," 148–52; Koschnik, *Common Interest*, 29–30; Ferling, *Adams vs. Jefferson*, 2004, 63; Foner, *Democratic-Republican Societies*, 38–9.
89. New York *Argus*, 13 July 1795; Newburyport *Impartial Herald*, 23 February 1796; Newman, *Parades*, 52–3, 83–104, 147, 149–50; Stewart, *Opposition Press*, 218; Travers, *Celebrating the Fourth*, 88–100; Waldstreicher, *Perpetual Fetes*, 129; Foner, *Democratic-Republican Societies*, 223–4; Koschnik, *Common Interest*, 104–5; Concord *Federal Mirror*, 26 July 1796; Keene *Rising Sun*, 2 August 1796.
90. Daniel, *Scandal and Civility*, 133.
91. Wilmington *Delaware Gazette*, 4 October 1794; "John Adams to Abigail Adams, 15 January 1796," *Founders Online*, http://founders.archives.gov/documents/Adams/

04-11-02-0065]; *Greenleaf's New York Journal*, 4 April 1795; Philadelphia *Aurora*, 15 January 1796.

92. Horgan, *Politics of Songs*, 131.
93. Clapp, *Record of the Boston Stage*, 26; Benjamin Carr and Irving Lowens, *Benjamin Carr's Federal Overture (1794)* (Philadelphia: Musical Americana, 1957), 8–10, 12, 14–15; Waldstreicher, *Perpetual Fetes*, 139; *Carlisle Gazette*, 19 August 1795; *Norwich Packet*, 2 September 1795; Newburyport *Impartial Herald*, 26 February 1796; Liam Riordan, "'O Dear, What Can the Matter Be?': The Urban Early Republic and the Politics of Popular Songs in Benjamin Carr's Federal Overture," *Journal of the Early Republic* 31, no. 2 (Summer 2011), 193–6.

# 3

# "A Glorious Opportunity to Destroy Faction"

In late 1797, "J.S. of Freeport" summarized the country's dilemma in song—the United States was an advancing nation, but threatened by partisan division. "J.S." argued that the nation could avoid being manipulated by world powers if Americans remained "firmly determined in a bond of friendship." But such political unity was not to be. During John Adams's presidency, described by Wood as one of the "most politically contentious" periods in US history, partisanship reached new heights.[1] And music became an even more prominent vehicle for articulating it.

Federalist partisanship was fueled by foreign affairs. When Adams assumed the presidency in 1797, he immediately faced deteriorating relations with France. As European wars dragged on, the United States sought to maintain neutral trade rights with both Britain and France. But French spoliation of US commerce escalated: in 1797 alone, approximately 300 American vessels were seized. Seizures were fueled by unrest in the French West Indies, stoppage of payments on the French loan for the American War of Independence, and French interpretation of the Jay Treaty as a violation of the Franco-American alliance of 1778 and an alliance with Britain.[2] Diplomatic relations stalled when the French Directory rejected the new American ambassador, and they reached a crisis point with the XYZ Affair, when French attempts to bribe US diplomats prompted public outrage and justified a defense of US rights in the Quasi War.

Despite—or rather, because of—these difficulties, the Federalists were able to reach new heights of popularity and pass aggressive legislation. Federalist Senate leader Theodore Sedgwick promptly identified the XYZ Affair as a "glorious opportunity to destroy faction."[3] Music, already a vehicle for partisan expression, took on a new role during this "opportunity": Federalist songwriters used it to incessantly reiterate a narrative of political dominance, a narrative so powerful that it shaped historical scholarship through the twentieth century.[4]

*Hail Columbia*. Laura Lohman, Oxford University Press (2020). © Oxford University Press.
DOI: 10.1093/oso/9780190930615.001.0001

Since their first circulation and performance through the twentieth century, the Federalist songs of this period have been characterized as patriotic effusions. Yet they were carefully constructed, performed, and circulated for partisan purposes. Extending the work of music scholars such as Gray, and early American historians such as William Coleman, Sarah Knott, and Kirsten Wood, this chapter situates these songs in their historical and performative contexts to clarify how they advanced a partisan narrative of legitimacy and a patriotism rooted in partisan conceptions of the nation and liberty. Featuring boldly contrasting bogeymen and heroes, this partisan narrative presented the Federalists as dauntless protectors of the nation from external and internal foes, and it defined the Republicans as the nation's destroyers and domestic enemies. Despite the Federalists' frequent calls for and claims of unity, music fostered stark and violent displays of divergent political views. Music was more than a "symbolic gesture" expressing anger with French aggression.[5] Rather, through music, Federalists articulated specific political priorities and sought to silence their opponents. Republican songwriters, undaunted by the prospect of arrest under the Federalists' Sedition Act, contested the Federalists' prevailing narrative. Refusing to be silenced, they used many of the Federalists' symbols, strategies, and tunes to prioritize different forms of "liberty," promote different causes, and inspire oppositional political action.

## The Year of Federalist Song

Tense diplomatic relations with France sparked a chain of political events that made 1798 the year of Federalist song. Early in Adams's term, American diplomacy hit an impasse as French spoliation of US commerce escalated. Adams explained to Congress in May 1797 that France, in rejecting the American ambassador, treated the United States "neither as allies, nor as friends, nor as a sovereign state." He would send two additional envoys but also called for defensive naval preparations in case they were turned away. This ended Adams's honeymoon period with the Republican press. At the Philadelphia *Aurora*, Benjamin Franklin Bache saw Adams's statement as abandoning the non-partisan elements of his inaugural speech and a militaristic response influenced by his Anglophilic Hamiltonian cabinet members. When the envoys were again rejected, Adams told Congress that he had no expectation of diplomatic success. In early April, Federalists in Congress joined suspicious Republicans in calling for the release of the envoys' dispatches detailing their reception. The dispatches, subsequently known as the XYZ papers, revealed that the envoys had been expected to pay a bribe and make a loan before negotiations could begin. Compounding this insulting and corrupt treatment of American diplomats were French communications intended to foster discord in US domestic politics.[6]

Once published, these dispatches prompted public outrage over the humiliating treatment of the nation and its diplomats. While the French Revolution had captured broad American interest in the early 1790s, to the point that Federalists had felt pressured to attend sympathetic celebrations, now French efforts to bribe and divide Americans fueled American anger to the point that public expression of such sympathy was unacceptable. Americans expressed their anger by joining volunteer militias, donning symbolic anti-French clothing, gathering to sign petitions, and writing songs. Between April 1798 and March 1799, Americans sent Adams hundreds of petitions expressing support for his administration. To deliver their address to Adams, 1,200 young men marched through Philadelphia accompanied by martial music. Petitioners stressed the hostility of French demands for tribute, the fairness of American diplomatic efforts, the dishonorable nature of further concessions, and the inseparability of Americans from their government. The petitions' common themes and broad geographic and demographic distribution allowed Adams to see them as "proof of a remarkable conformity in sentiment and feelings." After being criticized in the Republican press in May 1797, Adams and the Federalists enjoyed surging popularity in 1798.[7]

In Philadelphia, Federalists capitalized on the moment. Citing illegitimate votes and unauthorized voting locations, they had recently managed to reverse a state assembly election, electing Federalist Benjamin R. Morgan in late February. Once the French dispatches had become front page news, Federalists organized a celebration in the Southwark district that had previously supported Morgan's Republican opponent. With 32 toasts and nearly 300 huzzas, the Federalists gloated not simply over Morgan's victory but particularly over the absence of the French flag, which had been prominent years before in the very same location when Republicans had toasted "perpetual union between the two Republics of France and America." The Federalists made their point in the song composed for the occasion by French cellist and composer Henri Capron, who, by early 1785, had established himself in the United States and whose wife ran a boarding school and targeted Federalist clients. The lyrics, likely supplied by a local Federalist and set in a galant style by Capron, promised "From traitor friends with serpent smile/We'll rend the thin disguise" and rejoiced over the contrast with previous celebrations, "Here once by folly's son display'd/The Gallic standard shone/No ribband now our feasts invade/There waves our flag alone." Music printers capitalized on surging anti-French sentiment, selling the song as sheet music, "Come Genius of Our Happy Land," in Philadelphia, Baltimore, and New York.[8]

Americans expressed their support for the Federalist administration through music, often writing new lyrics for British tunes with military and political associations. Some Republican publications, facing strong anti-Republican sentiment and declining circulations, also voiced such messages. Through "American Union," a reworking of "Rule Britannia," *Greenleaf's New York Journal* emphasized unity and invoked the Revolutionary War as a call to arms against a new French despot. After linking America's fight for independence to France's struggles to throw off its monarchy, the songwriter scolded, "But France you now forget your friend,/Our amity is at an end./You rob our commerce, insult us on our coast,/*Divide and conquer* is your boast. . . . //Our fathers fought and so will we/. . . . Like them we'll conquer and be free." Republican outlets' printing of such material supported the Federalist *Newport Mercury*'s report that "from various parts of the country, we receive the pleasing intelligence of an encreasing [*sic*] harmony and union among the people. 'That we had better die all *freemen* than live all *slaves*,' seems to be one universal sentiment."[9] Such calls for and claims of political unity were a central part of the Federalists' narrative in both song and prose.[10]

Adams called for Americans to unite on May 9, 1798, in "a day of Solemn Humiliation, Fasting, and Prayer" to acknowledge their sins and those of the nation. But the fast day fueled opposition.[11] Republican newspapers rejected the fast, seeing it as "part of a Hamilton-inspired Federalist campaign to eradicate the Jeffersonian opposition." Their rejection extended to verse once Suffield, Connecticut, resident Benjamin Tappan submitted to the Republican press a "parody" on Isaac Watts's Psalm 148 ("Ye tribes of Adam, join"); Watts's psalm was commonly sung to Lewis Edson's four-voice psalm tune "Lenox." In Tappan's words, his " 'Psalm' accused the Federalists of wishing, not so much to worship the Almighty, as to excite the people into a war against France."[12] Tappan blasted Federalists as hypocritical Anglophilic warmongers, attacked their leaders, and denounced the anticipated fast day sermons and measures to fund war. Federalists responded in kind, producing both a "Federal Psalm" and "The Jacobin's Psalm" as their own parodies of Watts's psalm. The parodic verses answered Tappan's accusations of Federalist religious hypocrisy by accusing the Republicans of atheism. The Federalist psalms predicted the Republicans' downfall with crude but typical imagery and attacked national Republican leaders, including Vice President Thomas Jefferson.[13]

As these psalm parodies demonstrated, Federalist songwriters were quick to highlight the heroes and villains in what would become the prevailing political narrative of Adams's term. An account of July 4 celebrations in Newport, Rhode Island, presented the cast of characters:

> The various and multiplying Dangers with which our Independence is threatened, the restless Intrigues of foreign and internal Foes, the Solicitude of all true Patriots to preserve, and the ferocious Eagerness of the Anarchists to Destroy, our Constitution and Government; together with those Doubts of ultimate Success inseparable from the Prospect of every Contest, all contributed to characterize this Anniversary with an Anxiety and an Interest never before experienced on a similar Occasion.[14]

In even bolder language, Federalist songwriters portrayed the French as villains, Federalists as heroes, and Republicans as domestic bogeymen conspiring with French government officials and emigrés to subvert the US government and turn the country into a French province. Federalist songwriters called the French "butchers" and "pickpockets" and Foreign Minister Talleyrand "a cloven foot Reptile." As July 4 festivities became increasingly partisan, Federalist celebrations in Newport featured a comical song written to "Yankee Doodle" that cast the French as inept fighters who joined the American War of Independence for selfish reasons.[15] Such lyrics undermined Republican claims that the United States owed the French for their previous support in a critical time of need. Francophobic immigrant William Cobbett aided the Federalists' cause in another colorful reworking of "Yankee Doodle." Of Cobbett's pseudonymous character Peter Porcupine, Abigail Adams had noted that he "says many good things. . . . I have a great curiosity to see the Creature. . . . He can write very handsomely, and he can descend & be as low, and vulgar as a fish woman." True to Adams's assessment, in his chorus Cobbett had Americans crudely pun the literal meaning of "Sans Culottes" (the lower-class laborers driving the French Revolution), "If Frenchmen come with naked bum,/We'll *spank* 'em hard and handy." Switching to biblical references, Cobbett likened the French Directory expecting the three US envoys to pay bribes to Nebuchadnezzar expecting three steadfast monotheists to bow in homage to his golden image.[16]

Federalist songwriters honed their portrayals of American heroes to advocate a military buildup modeled after European powers. Federalists had already learned to influence public opinion through the press during French ambassador Edmond Genet's visit. In spring 1798, Alexander Hamilton pseudonymously lobbied for a large army and warned of an impending French invasion. Legislation paved the way for the standing army that Republicans despised as a debt- and tax-producing catalyst for war. The Federalist-dominated Congress appropriated millions of dollars for national defense and levied a new property tax—the nation's first direct tax—to fund this growing military.[17] Heroes were easily constructed. Songs performed from July 4 presented George Washington—appointed by Adams to command the expanding army—as a heroic leader capable of guarding the nation against French aggression.[18] With Adams represented as the captain of the nation-as-ship, songwriters promoted the two presidents as complementary heroic military figures.[19]

Along with these heroes and villains, Federalists wrote the average American into this prevailing narrative. From Providence, the *United States Chronicle* commanded Americans through song, "Take the brown musket" to "Defend your rights, your country's laws" against the false French proponents of freedom. Robert Treat Paine wrote the American yeoman into the Federalists' narrative in "The Green Mountain Farmer."▶ In a pastoral-patriotic-partisan synthesis fit to music by British opera composer William Shield, Paine portrayed the title character as a faithful patriot defending the nation against anarchy, homegrown traitors, and foreign invasion. Referencing the strong wood used for shipbuilding, Paine declared, "The hardy yeoman, like the oak. . . . /Would baffle Anarch's vengefull stroke,/And shelter law and order. . . . //Should hostile fleets our shores assail,/By home-bred traitors aided,/No free-born hand would till the vale,/By slavery degraded." Through his varied choruses, Paine stressed a Federalist conception of liberty that prioritized not individuals' rights but rather the need to protect the nation's neutral trade rights, treaties, and autonomy from French aggression and invasion.[20] Such partisan rhetoric was integrated in American communities' rituals of commemoration and celebration.

In a song for July 4 celebrations in Meredith, New Hampshire, Reverend Simon Finley Williams warned that the French would "traverse lawless o'er the coast" and called his community to support the Federalists' expanded army by declaring "We'll fight and conquer by [Washington's] side." In his ode and oration for July 4 festivities in Hanover, New Hampshire, twenty-nine-year old Dartmouth graduate Josiah Dunham not only foregrounded the villains and heroes of the Federalists' narrative but also used the War of Independence to portray military preparation as Americans' obligation to their ancestors. Dunham's rhetoric was designed to invoke feelings of moral inferiority, guilt, and shame. After reviewing France's conquests that had "extended her empire round half the globe," Dunham fumed, "She now crosses the ocean, plunders our commerce, insults our nation, abuses our government, violates our treaties, robs, murders, and enslaves our citizens! Good GOD! Where is the spirit of '76? Where are our fathers who led the way to freedom?" After describing how France "plundered," "butchered," and "annihilated" Europe, Dunham challenged his listeners to defy pro-peace Republicans. "Shall we become the prey and the sport of pretended patriots?" he asked. "Pretended patriots! who would sell their country, as JUDAS sold his master, for *thirty pieces of silver*!" He called Americans to rouse, unite, and "unsheath the sword of vengeance." Dunham's song reminded Americans that they had long been able to "Enjoy the smiles of *Peace*" but now must "Swear to avenge [their] country's wrong." His lyrics praised both Washington and Adams, portraying the latter as steady as a rock. Using a common phrase, he presented Americans just two choices as his chorus commanded them "UNITE—LIVE FREE-OR DIE!" Dunham promptly sent his oration to George Washington as a "fellow citizen" and received the president's grateful acknowledgment of honor and flattery in return.[21]

As the XYZ Affair unfolded, Federalist songwriters added Republican villains to this prevailing narrative. In Federalist publications like Joseph Dennie's *Farmer's Weekly Museum*, moderate calls for unity were soon overshadowed by direct attacks on Republicans, demands for "no faction," and accusations of Republican conspiracy to destroy the nation. Adams, in response to petitions, had been careful to acknowledge Republicans' fidelity to their country. Yet lyrics circulated through William Cobbett's vitriolic *Porcupine's Gazette* and sung at the Federalists' celebratory dinner in Southwark claimed that Republicans lacked patriotism and blamed the "Jacobin breed" for the "nation's undoing" through their promotion of "civil wars" and "sedition." Federalist songwriters portrayed Republicans as hypocrites and cowards who weakened the country and "dross" that had to be separated—by Americans themselves—from "pure" patriotism and

Americanism. The songwriter "P. Pencil," in the chorus of "The Farmer's Patriotic Ode," had American yeomen declare, "From Gallic weeds, we'll purge our land,/And crush the reptile faction." Casting farmers' tools as weapons, "P. Pencil" called for ordinary Americans to unite under the first president as their leader in battle. Portraying an entire nation intent on defeating the French and their allies, the last verse painted a melodramatic scene of children and wives who would "brave each sad disaster" to "spurn a Gallic master." "P. Pencil" was not alone in using gender to highlight Republican deficiency. Using a female character to criticize an opponent, a song in the *Gazette of the United States* portrayed a pacifist Republican judge as his wife's punching bag, a "coward" who would " 'bow at the feet'/Of his foes and entreat them to spare him" rather than fight to defend his country and its women.[22]

Partisanship intensified as Federalist songwriters vilified prominent Republicans by name. Reflecting the influence of William Cobbett's personal attacks, Federalist songwriters claimed that John Randolph and James Monroe would have to be "purged of their crimes" and "Reform'd from their damn'd machinations" before the world would "be at peace."[23] One of the Federalist songwriters who attacked leading Republican printer Benjamin Franklin Bache explained that his "Democrat's Education" in France had turned him into a liar, atheist, and promoter of war and murder. Another included Vice President Jefferson among the destroyers of the nation and its laws. Referring to Jefferson's harsh criticism of Federalists in a letter to his friend and former neighbor Philip Mazzei, the song's final verse commanded Americans, "Rise Then, ye sons of freedom, rise! . . . Lest, while you doubt, some Gallic slave,/Some 'Mazzai's friend' prepare a grave,/For Adams and our laws."[24]

Perhaps the Federalists' clearest musical portrayal of Republicans as destroyers and enemies of the nation came from the 1798 battle to represent Maryland's 5th Congressional District. Attorney James Winchester sought to unseat Republican Samuel Smith, a wealthy Revolutionary War hero who had served as the district's representative in Congress since 1793. Electioneering was so heated that it was reported in New York, Massachusetts, and New Hampshire.[25] Winchester's campaign shifted from attacks on Smith's record to character assaults that marked "a new low in scurrility and abuse" for Baltimore. Local coverage focused on Smith's purportedly telling Adams that the American envoys should have paid the bribes demanded by the French in the XYZ Affair as a cheaper alternative to war. Federalist accounts went further, accusing Smith of arranging French protection for his own shipping and denouncing the militia. Smith responded by drumming up support among mechanics through the local militia, of which he was brigadier general. Volunteer militia companies paraded to his home in shows of support and mechanics came forward to accuse Winchester's backer, the merchant John O'Donnell, of refusing to hire them unless they voted for Winchester, a powerful intimidation tactic in a state that voted by voice until 1803. Mechanics assembled in one of the city's largest gatherings and issued a denouncement of such intimidation and "corrupted aristocracy." The charge was not inaccurate; as the *Federal Gazette* later acknowledged, Winchester's supporters held four-fifths of the city's wealth.

Winchester's camp responded with fearmongering lyrics to rally Federalist support. Enhancing the sense of danger, the lyrics were fit to the tune of "Cease Rude Boreas," a British song about a ship's crew fighting to save their vessel as it took on water in a sea storm. A Baltimore songwriter reminded his neighbors of the "wicked schemes" that the French used "'Gainst your *wise administration*" and counseled, "Remember too, they boast insulting,/ They've here a PARTY at command/Of JACOBINS, who're now consulting/ To bring *French* armies to our land." To urge voters to support Winchester, the final hyperbolic verse painted a horrid scene of French invasion spurred by infidel Republicans, "When you see the *French* ships pouring,/Brutal armies on our shore;/See your *sisters, wives* imploring,/*Babes* and *parents* stretched in gore./Too late in fruitless lamentation/You'll curse the *authors* of your woes;/The vile adherents of a nation/Who to *God and Man are foes*."[26] Days before voting began, the candidates' supporters paraded through town. As the two groups came together, Smith's men plowed into Winchester's and dispersed them. Following the electioneering practices of the day, Smith made sure the local taverns were ready to host his supporters with free libations when the polls opened. Smith won a resounding victory.[27]

Such lyrics were important not for aesthetic reasons but for their responsiveness to a specific political need. Election-related lyrics, written both before and after elections, were penned quickly and promptly abandoned. Many were likely never circulated in print at all (the Baltimore lyrics only appeared in the city's *Federal Gazette* a month after the election amid a dearth of interesting news). Instead, they were simply written and sung on the spot in a tavern, home, or political meeting and discarded. As songwriters continued to turn out such verses, they made 1798 the year of Federalist song. They supplied a continuous stream of support for Adams's administration and offered starkly contrasting portrayals of Federalist heroes and French and Republican villains that reduced the nation's foreign conflicts and domestic political division to one simple battle between good and evil.

## "Patriotic" Hits as Propaganda

Of the many Federalist songs prompted by the XYZ Affair, several escaped the fate of ephemera. Performed and reprinted across many states, these hits promoted the Federalists' narrative among a broad audience. Then, as now, they were frequently described as "patriotic." But they were used in highly partisan ways to intimidate, humiliate, undermine, silence, or eliminate the Republican opposition. Through these songs, Federalists promoted a partisan conception of liberty, touted starkly contrasting national heroes and political villains, and called ordinary Americans to play their appropriate role in the ongoing struggle between them.

The most prominent of these hit songs was "Hail Columbia." Written in April 1798 by Philadelphia's Federalist lawyer Joseph Hopkinson (son of Francis), the song quickly captured attention in Philadelphia, New York, Providence, Alexandria, Baltimore, and Boston. Theater performers capitalized on its popularity for benefit concerts, musicians used it to honor President Adams at receptions, and community organizers made it a centerpiece of their July 4 celebrations.[28] With a particularly well-documented and widespread reception, "Hail Columbia" illustrates the many ways in which one song could be understood and used for political purposes in both performance and print.

According to the standard account, actor and singer Gilbert Fox had asked his former schoolmate Hopkinson to write a song that he could perform in Philadelphia's Chestnut Street Theatre to boost ticket sales on his benefit night. Hopkinson wrote the lyrics just a few blocks from the theater at his family's extant Spruce Street home. Hopkinson's account, written four decades later, suggests that Fox's desperation for a good audience on his benefit night drove the song's production. But this "commission" also responded to a broader Federalist interest in unifying Americans in the nation's capital during the XYZ crisis. As Abigail Adams explained to her sister and son after the song's premiere, the XYZ dispatches had prompted conflicting calls in the theater in the previous weeks for "Ça ira" from one "party" and "Yankee Doodle" and Philip Phile's "President's March" from the other. One night, the orchestra was "driven off" by the audience after refusing to play the march to counter those who had called for "Ça ira." Theater managers had blamed this conflict on the lack of words for the march. Hopkinson's song, written at Fox's request, quickly addressed this problem.[29]

To ensure the ample attendance of staunch Federalists at the premiere of "Hail Columbia," the plan for the performance was given to a local, supportive journalist. The journalist was not a moderate Federalist but rather the Federalists' most vituperative journalist, immigrant Francophobe William Cobbett. Along with the evening's program, Cobbett ran an editorial approving the song and making clear that its purpose was to end the calls for French revolutionary song in the theater, thereby silencing the opposition in public.[30] Not surprisingly, then, when Abigail Adams went to the theater, she went to see the song's "Effect"—not to hear it. That relished effect was to drown out the opposition. She promptly reported, "The song by the manner in which it is received, is death to their Party."[31]

In writing words to the "President's March," Hopkinson capitalized on the French desire to divide Americans to make partisan division seem untenable. While he drew on common vocabulary and phraseology,[32] Hopkinson achieved a dramatic effect in the theater by combining elevated but simple, direct language of moderate tone with widely recognized references to the War of Independence and powerful symbols like Washington (see Figure 3.1). ▶ The melody was already a physical call to action—it was a bright, memorable march based on short, crisp dotted figures. To target listeners' emotions, Hopkinson had these figures carry a series of commands to defend the nation but avoided mentioning either Britain or France. And he took advantage of the march's generic presidential association to invoke both Washington and Adams as heroic figures. In the third verse, Hopkinson's clever invocation of Washington practically demanded audiences to respond with applause. Building such signals for participation, Hopkinson opened his recurring chorus with an even more emphatic and self-referential command, "Firm, united let us be." Abigail Adams reported that "the whole Audience broke forth in the Chorus whilst the thunder of their Hands was incessant, and at the close they arose, gave 3 Huzzas, that you might have heard a mile. My Head aches in consequence of it."[33] Hopkinson's chorus had the audience call their compatriots to join them in unity. With a strong contingent of Federalists in the audience ensured by Cobbett's advance plug for the song, Hopkinson achieved a nearly unanimous public expression of loyalty to the president and his party at the premiere.

Figure 3.1. Joseph Hopkinson and Philip Phile, "Hail Columbia." From the New York Public Library. https://digitalcollections.nypl.org/items/9b2975d0-a2c1-0134-359d-00505686a51c.

The song's initial performance produced exactly what Hopkinson, the first lady, and the first president valued—a display of unity approaching unanimity. After the conclusion of the contentious 1796 presidential election, which awkwardly put John Adams's opponent, Thomas Jefferson, in the vice

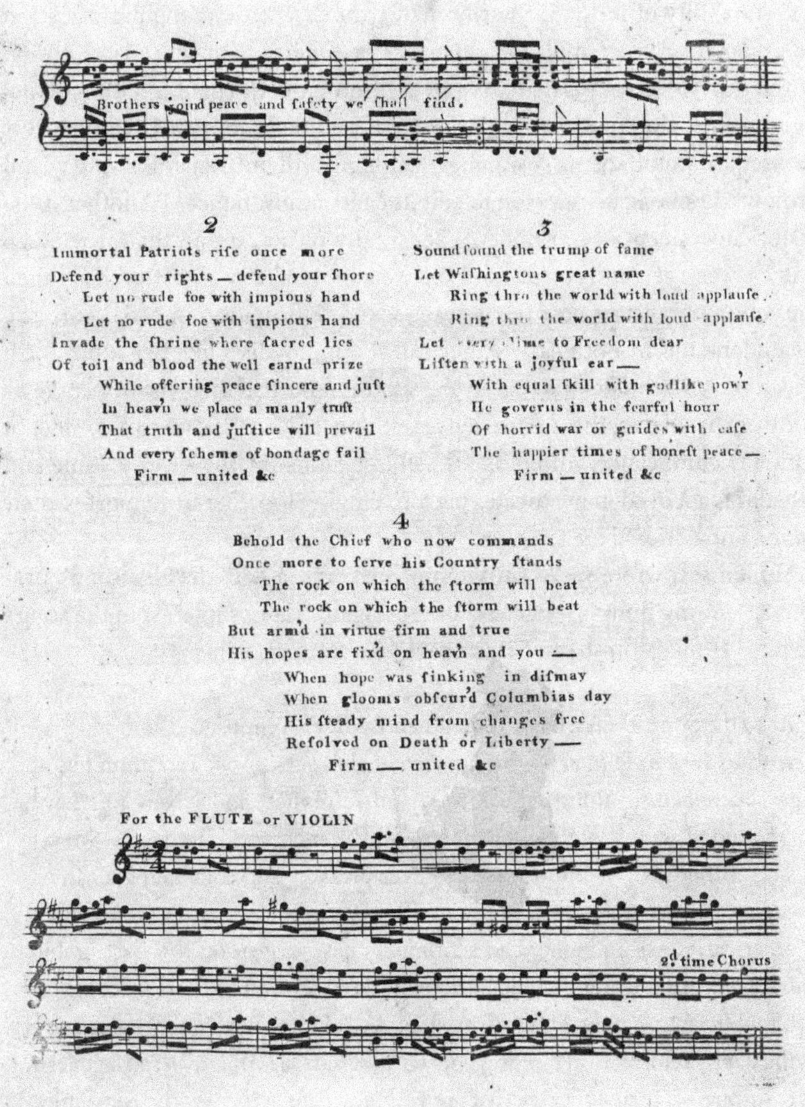


**Figure 3.1.** Continued.

presidential chair, Abigail Adams had assured her husband, "I have not a Doubt but all the Discords may be tuned to harmony, by the Hand of a skillful Artist."[34] While at the time she may not have envisioned that artistry being in musical form, her comments made clear her hope and help explain her interest in personally seeing the "effect" of Hopkinson's song in the theater.

The suitability of music for harmonizing the discords among partisans can be understood from multiple perspectives. One is a transhistorical notion of the experience of participating in communal performance with national significance. The emotional and stirring sensations of unity with compatriots aroused by simultaneously singing a national anthem are familiar today and prompted Benedict Anderson to coin the term unisonance.[35] Another is the historical concept of sensibility, a sensitivity of perception that provided a link between self and society and that was integral to what Knott has called the sentimentalist project focused on social reformation in early America. As understood by both early American sentimentalists like Benjamin Rush and modern scholars like Mestyan, singing and listening move people as bodily experiences; those experiences, connected in this case to a conflict of national significance, would have been intensified by the sheer volume and visual impact of so many theater patrons singing together in support of their nation and national leader.[36]

Hopkinson wrote to Washington a week and a half after his song's premiere, sending him the song. Echoing Abigail Adams's interest in the song's "Effect," Hopkinson stressed its impact—its extrinsic value.

> As to the Song it was a hasty thought and a hasty composition, and can pretend to very little *intrinsic* merit—Yet I beleive it's public reception has at least equalled any thing of the kind. The theatres here and at New York have resounded with it night after night, and the men and boys in the Streets sing as they go. I mention these things as pleasing and convincing testimonies of the great change that has taken place in the *american* mind, when american tunes and american sentiments have driven off those execrable french murder shouts—which not long since tortured our ears in all places of public amusement, and in every lane and alley in the United States. May the happy reformation rapidly proceed, and the true *American spirit* govern & inspire us. I trust that we that are young will keep in view the constancy, the courage and the invincible patriotism of our fathers, and prove ourselves worthy of the rich inheritance they have atchieved for us—May God preserve you once more to animate your Country to a just defence of their Independence and unalienable rights, once more to bind us in the irrefragable bands of firmness & unanimity.[37]

With this final sentence, Hopkinson alluded to what Abigail Adams had made explicit when writing to her son about the song's reception—the imminent plans to raise a defense through both a national navy and an army, the latter which Washington would be tasked to lead in the summer.[38]

Washington, after thanking Hopkinson for sending him the song and expressing other "favourable sentiments," commiserated,

> To expect that all men should think alike upon political, more than on Religious, or other subjects, would be to look for a change in the order of nature; but at so dangerous a crisis as the present, when every thing dear to Independence is at stake, the well disposed part of them might, one would think, act more alike; opposition therefore to the Major will, and to that Self respect which is due to the National character, cannot but seem strange!
>
> But I will unite with you in a fervent wish, and hope, that greater unanimity than heretofore, will prevail; for enough, I think we have seen, to remove the mist entirely; and that, the young men of the present day, will not suffer the liberty for which their forefathers fought—bled—died—and obtained—be lost by them: either by supineness, or divisions among themselves, disgraceful to the Country.[39]

Hopkinson's exchange with the first president and the first lady's detailed commentary on "Hail Columbia" only strengthen Myron Gray's corrective to Oscar Sonneck's interpretation of "Hail Columbia" as a "non-partisan" song.[40]

At the same time, Hopkinson's and Washington's comments indicate that "Hail Columbia" and its reception expressed a developing American nationalism. The XYZ Affair prompted the divorce of a nascent nationalism from the transcendent transnationalism that had fueled such powerful notions of Franco-American interdependence during the early 1790s. Abigail Adams quickly deemed Hopkinson's lyrics a "National song." And as Hopkinson later explained, his intent "was to get up an American spirit which should be independent of, and above the interests, passion and policy of both belligerents [Britain and France], and look and feel exclusively for our honour and rights. . . . Of course the song found favour with both parties, for both were American, at least neither could disown the sentiments and feelings it indicated."[41] Hopkinson's account and its claims of bipartisan appeal obscured the intentional partisan work behind the song's creation, premiere, and reception.

Despite Hopkinson's claims of bipartisan appeal, "Hail Columbia" was used and represented as a tool of intimidation to vilify, bully, and silence

Republican opposition from its first performances. Consistent with practices of the time, Chestnut Street theatergoers asked the orchestra to play another song after "Hail Columbia," one favored by Republicans, but the bulk of the audience denounced those making the request and the song went unheard. Intimidation efforts continued in print the morning after the premiere. As the Federalist *Gazette of United States* explained, "It is hoped the Ladies will practice the music and accompany the words at its next repetition—the two or three French Americans that remain will then feel the charm of patriotism, and join the chorus *'Firm—united—let us be.'*" While many songs presented unity as an ideal, Federalist publications used "Hail Columbia" and its reception to call for complete political unanimity.[42] The Boston *Columbian Centinel's* colorful account from Philadelphia explained that "the few insignificant jacobins, who were present, hung their lanthorn jaws in despair, and one or two of them, having the impudence to call for the cut-throat tune of *Ca-ira*, a universal hiss proclaimed the sovereign detestation of the audience." With "lanthorn jaws," the Federalist critic intensified his Francophobic account by invoking British language popularized by David Garrick during the Seven Years' War. The effusive account by "Philo-Laertes" in the *Philadelphia Gazette* portrayed the "rotten" Republicans in the theater as no match for the zealously patriotic audience. Adding moral judgment to Abigail Adams's observation of the song's reception being "death to their Party," "Philo-Laertes" acknowledged that "a solitary spark from the dying embers of opposition found its way into some dark corner of the house; but the rottenness of its source, could not withstand the fervid attack of patriotic fire—it evaporated in the sacred flame of enthusiasm that followed, or was crushed into its original nothingness."[43]

Performances of "Hail Columbia" provided a pretext for Federalists to circulate a powerful caricature of Republicans that capitalized on growing xenophobia following the XYZ Affair. When young Federalists sang "Hail Columbia" at the New York battery later in the summer, Republicans responded with "Ça ira," and the encounter escalated from a musical duel to blows. Federalist newspapers seized on the altercation to portray the Republicans as deceitful, treasonous, un-American would-be murderers and co-conspirators with the French. To undermine the political legitimacy of the singers of "Ça ira" and, by extension, Republicans in general, a widely reprinted report from the New York *Daily Advertiser* used labels of foreignness, rank, occupation, character, and criminality. While the "young men" walking on the battery sang "Hail Columbia," the "boatmen and low fellows from the wharves and docks" who responded in song were "instigated by the deluding demon of French Jacobinism, and no doubt by some of its mad or corrupted votaries." Describing the musical duel, the writer exclaimed, "Heavens, what a contrast! How honorable to those who wore the badge of Americanism—How degrading and traitorous in the others." Having a "National song" available as an alternative to the leading musical symbol of enlightenment cosmopolitanism, transnationalism, and democratic egalitarianism intensified the Federalists' caricature of republicans as dangerous and "deviant foreign disorganizers" in an increasingly xenophobic environment.[44]

Republican newspapers used "Hail Columbia" to challenge the Federalists' political narrative. One tactic was charging the Federalists with idolatry. In the *Aurora*, Bache described the song as "a badge of devotion to the executive" containing "more of idolatry than of patriotism." The description was not unfounded: newspaper accounts cast the song's reception as an expression of public support for Adams himself, and Philadelphia youths sang "Hail Columbia" as a midnight serenade under the president and first lady's window. Hopkinson's lyrics had reinstated individual leaders as objects of devotion after songs inspired by the French Revolution had focused on abstract political principles. Music publishers James Hewitt and Benjamin Carr reinforced Adams's heroic status in American homes by adding "an elegant likeness of the President" when selling the song as sheet music (see Figure 3.1).[45] Underscoring the *Aurora's* accusation, in one of several editorials featuring "Hail Columbia" *Carey's United States Recorder* quoted its chorus to criticize "his Serene Highness John Adams" and portray the hero of the Federalists' narrative as a leader intolerant of opposition.[46] This Republican backlash, particularly in Philadelphia, may have prompted Carr to print a version of the sheet music with an eagle rather than a portrait.[47]

Bache was determined to use "Hail Columbia's" reception to undermine the Federalists' prevailing narrative of political legitimacy and dominance. Fundamental to the Federalists' narrative was what Roth has called a "tight and effective" syllogism: "Government equals order: faction destroys order: therefore faction (Jeffersonianism and democracy) destroys government."[48] Bache used "Hail Columbia" to challenge this syllogism's core. He portrayed the Federalists not as "friends of order" but as irrational, dangerous, aggressive leaders who would drive the nation back to monarchy or incite civil war. In his account, the Federalists were driven out of control and beyond rationality by the song's premiere:

> When the wished-for song came,—amidst the most ridiculous bombast, the vilest adulation to the Anglo-Monarchical Party, and the two Presidents, the extacy of the party knew no bounds, they encored, they shouted, they became—Mad as the Priestess of the Delphic God, And in the fury of their exultation threatened to throw over, or otherwise, ill treat every person who did not join heartily in the applause. The rapture of the moment was as great, as if Louis the 18th had actually been seated on the throne of France, or John Adams had been proclaimed king of America.

With this comparison, Bache undermined the Federalists' common Francophilic portrayal of Republicans and focused on the danger of counterrevolutionary reversion into monarchy, a danger he reinforced by noting recent performances of "God Save Great George Our King." Describing the New York battery altercation, the *Aurora* stressed the hypocrisy of the Federalists' calls for unity amid their divisive and destructive bullying. Bache's newspaper noted that the "governmental Party. . . chuse to consider an unqualified approbation of all the measures of the Executive, a servile devotion to the person of the President as the only criterion of love of country. A man must sing 'Hail Columbia' and wear a black cockade, or he is called by them a disorganizer, a Jacobin, a pensioned tool of the French."[49]

As Bache rightly pointed out, the Federalists used "Hail Columbia" and other cultural symbols as propaganda, relying on common techniques of fearmongering, exaggeration, and name-calling to construct what Cotlar has called a powerful "caricature of the dangerous democrat." Elaborating on their partisan use of "Hail Columbia" and other symbols, the *Aurora* declared, "It would seem really the view of some of the lowdest vociferators for union to excite a civil war in our country; they cannot expect, that by their denunciations, their insults & their abuse they can bully the republicans into silence or an acquiescence in their sentiments or measures."[50] Through such rhetoric, Republican writers like Bache offered a counternarrative of Federalist partisanship and shifted the blame for destroying the country from Republicans to Federalists themselves.

"Hail Columbia," which was known as the "Philadelphia Patriotic Song," was soon joined by "The New York Patriotic Song," the "Boston Patriotic Song," the "Portsmouth Song,"[51] and the "Worcester Patriotic Song."[52] All were circulated across state lines. Most were written or requested by men with theater connections. Through a mutually beneficial relationship, theaters and artists who commissioned, created, and performed such songs assisted

Federalists in promulgating their dominant political narrative while songs drew much-needed theater audiences during challenging economic times with displays of national determination.[53] Like petitions sent to Adams, these songs became symbols of locally held patriotism and, when circulated more broadly, illustrated widespread support for the Federalist administration.

Yet the "patriotism" showcased and cultivated through these songs cannot be taken at face value. Republicans did not reject patriotism—the minutes of the Tammany Society regularly noted that brothers sang "patriotic" songs.[54] Rather, Federalists defined patriotism to exclude Republicans. During the early 1790s, at popular cosmopolitanism's height, Federalists Noah Webster and David Osgood labored to define—in contrast to localism and allegiance to universal principles that transcended national boundaries—"a viable anti-French conception of virtuous patriotic American citizenship."[55] In the Federalists' prevailing narrative, patriotism meant passion for one's nation, expressed through fidelity to the federal government. That government being under attack through French efforts to divide American opinion provided a powerful pretext to advance this concept of patriotism. Those who refused to demonstrate allegiance to Federalist leaders like Adams were deemed by Federalists like Josiah Dunham as lacking in patriotism or vilified as "pretended patriots."

Despite the label "patriotic," the various "city" songs were partisan expressions and encapsulated Federalist values. This was particularly clear in "The New York Patriotic Song," titled "Federal Constitution Boys and Liberty Forever" and written by teacher, schoolmaster, and dramatist William Milns.[56] In lyrics like Milns's, "freedom," "liberty," and "rights" were not general concepts or references to individuals' rights but rather shorthand for communal rights such as "free navigation, commerce, and trade." In these songwriters' work, the defense of the nation's rights to trade took precedence over individuals' rights championed by Republicans.

These "patriotic" songs, like black and tricolor cockades, were signs of partisan affiliation used to intimidate, shame, and silence political opponents. Recognizing the value of such musical emblems, the *New York Gazette* urged Americans to continue singing songs like "Hail Columbia" to display their support for the Federalist government and heroes Adams and Washington and expose the country's internal foes. Once opponents were identified, the intimidation could proceed. As *Porcupine's Gazette* reported, in Mount Holly, New Jersey, when thirty members of Captain Mahlon Budd's military company arrived wearing the tricolor French cockade, the company voted to remove and burn their comrades' emblems, and they sang "Hail Columbia" as they carried out the act. The song accompanied the ritualized "death" not only of the cockade but also of what it symbolized—American support for the French Revolution, transnational values, Republican opposition, and disunity.[57]

The "Philadelphia Patriotic Song" was also performed to intimidate Republican House leader Albert Gallatin as part of an elaborate battle to control the local soundscape in Reading, Pennsylvania. In July 1798, Gallatin spoke against the Federalists' Sedition Act, which violated the first amendment of the Constitution. When Gallatin spent a night in Reading on his way home to western Pennsylvania, local Republicans welcomed him with cannon fire and the ringing of the town's church and courthouse bells for nearly thirty minutes. In the early American soundscape, bells were sounded to receive dignitaries and were associated with freedom. Local Federalists, seeing Gallatin as anything but a dignitary and prioritizing communal and national rights over individuals' freedoms, sought to wrest control of these sounds from Republicans and sonically reshape the meaning of Gallatin's visit. Federalists responded by having the Volunteer Blues march into town with a drum-and-fife rendition of "The Rogue's March" to shame Gallatin and his supporters and mark their political views as illegitimate. ▶ The Blues ignored the Republican sheriff John Christ's order to silence "The Rogue's March." Instead, they overturned the Republicans' celebratory cannon and threatened to break the church windows if the bell-ringers did not silence the bells. The Blues continued "huzzaing for Adams, Washington and the Federal Government, to the utter dismay of a petty knot of Democrats, who hung their heavy heads in silent sorrow." Yet silencing the Republicans was not enough. Intent on intimidating the outspoken Republican senator, the Blues spent the night "singing Hail Columbia and other good patriotic songs, for the purpose of serenading Gallatin." They burned his effigy in front of him the next morning as he helped his wife and sister into their carriage to leave. Yet ultimately, Gallatin was the one who silenced the Blues—while they waited for him at the inn's entrance, he sneaked out the back to foil their plans to beat him out of town with another rendition of "The Rogue's March."[58]

Along with "Hail Columbia," Boston's "patriotic song" became a national hit that ultimately spawned new verses of its own. "Adams and Liberty" was penned by Robert Treat Paine Jr. (1773–1811). He was the second son of Robert Treat Paine, a Massachusetts lawyer, politician, and signer of the Declaration of Independence. Robert Treat Paine Jr. was born Thomas Paine and known in print as "Thomas Paine of Boston" (distinguishing him from the similarly named author of *Rights of Man*) until he adopted the name of his deceased older brother in 1801. He graduated from Harvard; wrote poetry; dabbled in running a newspaper, the Boston *Federal Orrery* (1794–96); and then gravitated toward the theater. He married an actress and was appointed Master of Ceremonies at the Boston theater. Paine was frequently asked to write verse and deliver orations, and he earned income from his songs before he practiced law. In verse, Paine drew his metaphors, similes, and allegories from everyday scenes and conversations. Singled out for praise were his "exact rhymes, happy allusions, his brilliant imagery." An ardent Federalist, Paine corresponded with Washington and John Adams and defended the repressive Alien and Sedition Acts that targeted outspoken Republicans and their supporters. In reply, John Adams described Paine as "a pregnant and prolific Genius," praised his "talents and character," and invited Paine to visit him in Quincy.[59]

"Adams and Liberty" was one of several songs that Paine wrote at the Massachusetts Charitable Fire Society's request to aid fundraising; for it he reportedly received $750. While Washington Irving would later criticize Paine's poetry for its excessive and "far-fetched metaphors" that strained the ear, "Adams and Liberty" gained immediate praise and wide circulation. Heard in theater and concert performances in Boston, New York, Philadelphia, and Chambersburg, Pennsylvania, and sung on July 4 (see Figures 3.2 and 3.3), "Adams and Liberty" became one of the most widely circulated sets of new lyrics written to the melody "Anacreon in Heaven," familiar to readers as the melody of "The Star-Spangled Banner."[60]▶

Praised by the Boston *Columbian Centinel* for their "energy of sentiment, and ardency of patriotism," Paine's lyrics firmly articulated the Federalists' narrative by weaving into one song its heroes, its foreign and domestic villains, its prioritization of commercial rights, its growing militarism, and its intolerance of opposition. Unlike Hopkinson's "Hail Columbia," which was written in a moderate tone but used in highly partisan ways, Paine's lyrics took strong aim at Republicans and supported the Federalists' military expansion. To justify the expansion of armed defense, including the navy, Paine used a vague reference to "pirates" that encompassed numerous threats, including British impressment, French spoliation, and Algerian piracy, while countering Republican charges by asserting that the navy's role was not to instigate war. At the suggestion of Benjamin Russell, editor of the *Centinel*, Paine added a verse invoking Washington as the nation's faithful military commander. Reversing the imagery of French revolutionary songs,

**Figure 3.2.** John Stafford Smith and Robert Treat Paine Jr., "Adams and Liberty." *The American Musical Miscellany* (1798). Library of Congress, Music Division.

which had associated "light" with popular cosmopolitanism, democracy, and reason, and "darkness" with tyranny, monarchy, and aristocracy, Paine blamed Republicans for instigating the "dark clouds of Faction" and spoiling the nation's rapid development and growing reputation, the "sun of American glory." Confirming Republicans' charges of idolatry, Paine's lauding of Adams as hero in the final verse was transformed into a "token of veneration, love and respect" as the audience joined in the chorus when the president attended a Boston performance in 1799.[61]

These hit songs were quickly reworked themselves—often in more strongly partisan terms—to acclaim political developments like the Federalists' growing navy, their desired national army, and Washington's "unretirement" to serve as its commander in chief.[62] An example was William Charles White's "Worcester Patriotic Song," performed at central Massachusetts July

**Figure 3.2.** Continued.

4 celebrations. For the occasion, the twenty-two-year-old playwright, actor, and gentleman son of a Boston merchant wrote new lyrics for "Adams and Liberty" that hyperbolically portrayed Adams and Washington as heroic warriors fighting off anarchy and treason. In his fourth verse, White turned Adams into a soldier and cast the Federalist administration that generated the repressive Alien and Sedition Acts as the epitome of justice. White portrayed Republican disloyalty in frightening terms, "Should the grim monster TREASON Columbia invade/And scream her dire orgies through all its vast region,/Our ADAMS in armor of Justice array'd/Would prostrate the night fiend and seal her extinction./His prudence well tried,/Our freedom shall guide,/And in his great virtue we'll ever confide,/Who nobly disdaining with chains to agree,/Has spurn'd at all bondage and dar'd to be free."[63] Such fearmongering was an important ingredient in propaganda supporting the Federalists' military buildup.

ADAMS AND LIBERTY.

*THE BOSTON PATRIOTIC SONG.*
*Written by* THOMAS PAINE, A. M.

YE ſons of *Columbia*, who bravely have fought,
For thoſe rights, which unſtain'd from your Sires had deſcended,
May you long taſte the bleſſings your valor has bought,
And your ſons reap the ſoil, which their fathers defended.
'Mid the reign of mild peace,
May your nation increaſe,
With the glory of *Rome*, and the wiſdom of *Greece*;
*And ne'er may the ſons of* Columbia *be ſlaves,*
*While the earth bears a plant, or the ſea rolls its waves.*

In a clime, whoſe rich vales feed the marts of the world,
Whoſe ſhores are unſhaken by *Europe's* commotion,
The *Trident* of Commerce ſhould never be hurl'd,
To incenſe the *legitimate* powers of the ocean.
But ſhould *Pirates* invade,
Though in thunder array'd,
Let your *cannon* declare the *free charter* of TRADE.
*For ne'er ſhall, &c.*

The fame of our arms, of our laws the mild ſway,
Had juſtly ennobled our nation in ſtory,
'Till the dark clouds of *Faction* obſcur'd our young day,
And envelop'd the ſun of American glory.
But let TRAITORS be told,
Who their *Country* have ſold,
And barter'd their *God*, for his image in *gold*—
*That ne'er ſhall, &c.*

While *France* her huge limbs bathes recumbent in *blood*,
And *ſociety's baſe* threats with wide diſſolution;
May PEACE, like the *Dove*, who return'd from the flood,
Find an *Ark* of abode in our mild CONSTITUTION!
But though PEACE is our aim,
Yet the boon we diſclaim,
If bought by our SOV'REIGNTY, JUSTICE, or FAME.
*For ne'er ſhall, &c.*

**Figure 3.3.** Robert Treat Paine Jr., "Adams and Liberty." Boston *Columbian Centinel*, 9 June 1798. Readex/NewsBank.

Indeed, the entire group of patriotic "city" songs so effectively articulated the surge of federalism, nationalism, and militarism that a single line from "Hail Columbia" could symbolize the nation's militant spirit. Using Philadelphia as a metonym for the nation, the first lady wrote to John Quincy Adams, "This City, which was formerly torpid with indolence, and fettered with Quakerism; has become *one* Military School, and every morning, the Sound of the drum and fife, lead forth 'A Band of Brothers joind.' The Martial Spirit resounds from one end of the Country, to the other."[64] While these hit songs were described as patriotic, they used fundamental techniques of propaganda, articulated partisan values, and were performed in violent acts of partisan intimidation. While the songs often centered on "liberty," Federalists used the term not to

'Tis the fire of the *flint*, each American warms;
Let *Rome's* haughty victors beware of *collision*
Let them bring all the vassals of *Europe* in arms,
WE'RE A WORLD BY OURSELVES, and disdain a *division*!
While, with patriot pride,
To our laws we're allied,
No foe can subdue us—no faction divide.
*For ne'er shall, &c.*

Our mountains are crown'd with imperial *Oak*,
Whose *roots*, like our *Liberties*, ages have nourish'd;
But long ere our nation submits to the yoke,
Not a *tree* shall be left on the field where it flourish'd.
Should *invasion* impend,
Every *grove* would descend
From the *hill-tops* they shaded, our *shores* to defend.
*For ne'er shall, &c.*

Let our Patriots destroy *Anarch's* pestilent *worm*,
Lest our Liberty's *growth* should be check'd by *corrosion*;
Then let clouds thicken round us, we heed not the storm;
Our realm fears no *shock*, but the earth's own explosion.
*Foes* assail us in vain,
Though their FLEETS *bridge* the main,
For our *altars* and *laws* with our lives we'll maintain!
*And ne'er shall, &c.*

Should the TEMPEST OF WAR overshadow our land,
Its bolts could ne'er rend FREEDOM'S *temple* asunder;
For, unmov'd, at its *portal*, would WASHINGTON stand,
*And repulse, with his* BREAST, *the assault of the* THUNDER!
His *sword* from the sleep
Of its *scabbard*, would leap,
And conduct, with its *point*, every *flash* to the deep.
*For ne'er shall, &c.*

Let FAME to the world sound AMERICA'S voice;
*No* INTRIGUE *can her sons from their* GOVERNMENT *sever*;
*Her* PRIDE *is her* ADAMS—*his* LAWS *are her* CHOICE,
*And shall flourish, till* LIBERTY *slumber forever*!
Then unite, heart and hand
Like *Leonidas'* band,
And swear to the GOD of the ocean and land,
*That ne'er shall the sons of* COLUMBIA *be slaves*,
*While the earth bears a plant, or the sea rolls its waves.*

**Figure 3.3.** Continued.

refer to individuals' rights, which were championed by their Republican rivals, but rather rights of the nation. This partial and partisan prioritization of rights and the intimidation tactics voiced through these songs would be taken to an extreme when Federalists prosecuted Republicans under the Sedition Act. Yet before that would happen, Federalists pursued another legislative path that would garner them greater public support and celebration through song.

## "Millions for Defense"

As Republican newspapers railed against Federalists' intimidation tactics and intolerance of opposition, Federalists attracted further public support through naval expansion. Along with the army, Federalists sought to expand the navy into a respectable institution in emulation of and capable of squaring off against European fleets. The Department of the Navy was created in July 1797, and in the same year three frigates authorized by the 1794 Naval Act—the USS *United States, Constellation*, and *Constitution*—were completed and launched. Spurred by French spoliation and diplomatic failures, Federalists pursued naval expansion in spring of 1798. The secretary of the navy planned for a permanent peacetime navy, and legislation authorized constructing three additional frigates, acquiring more warships through gift or purchase, arming merchantmen, and establishing the marines. The public aided this expansion: motivated by outrage over the XYZ Affair, skyrocketing shipping insurance rates, and commercial losses, residents of coastal mercantile cities began subscription efforts to build and purchase warships for the navy. In May 1798, US warships were authorized to take armed French vessels that waited in US coastal waters to strike unarmed vessels leaving port. At a Federalist dinner honoring envoy John Marshall, South Carolina congressman Robert Goodloe Harper famously captured this rapidly growing militarism in the toast "Millions for defense, but not one cent for tribute."[65]

After the undeclared Quasi-War with France began in 1798, musical and multimedia performances defined the navy, its vessels, and officers as protectors of the nation's neutral trade rights and added engaging heroes to the Federalists' narrative of political dominance. Naval growth enabled writers to sustain this narrative despite a rift between the High Federalists intent on declaring war against France and moderate Federalists like Adams who stopped at undeclared war and preferred diplomacy. As the expanding army, the High Federalists' priority, disintegrated in 1799 due to organizational, legislative, and communication difficulties, the navy, the moderate Federalists' priority, grew and demonstrated national might in the undeclared Quasi-War.[66]

In eastern cities, theaters broadcast updates on Federalists' naval expansion. Theater managers' interest in broadly appealing productions intensified from the mid-1790s, when deadly yellow fever, a devastating fire, and increasing competition from new entertainment venues challenged theaters' profitability in Philadelphia and Boston.[67] Lavish, multimedia displays of naval expansion targeted broad audiences of elites, merchants, tradesmen, and sailors. Theater companies celebrated the construction and launching of frigates by joining rousing music and representations of warships with elaborate machinery simulating moving water and vessels passing through local ports. On September 20, 1797, the designated day for launching the frigate *Constitution* in Boston, the city's Haymarket Theatre staged the event in John Hodgkinson's farce *The Launch, or Huzza for the Constitution*.[68] To the tune "Arethusa," the sailor Constant praised the Federalists' navy as the protector of the nation's neutral trade rights, a protector that would respect other nations' rights and avoid instigating war. Hodgkinson's farce was later performed in the Newport Theatre and adapted to the launching of the frigate *President* in New York as warship celebrations continued through 1800.[69] While these performances were designed to appeal to broad audiences, address theaters' financial difficulties, and enhance actors' benefit nights, they simultaneously supported the Federalists' expanding military, reinforced the Federalists' self-portrayal as defenders of the nation, and extolled partisan values, such as the primacy of communal rights over individuals' rights. Theaters' naval productions cleverly focused on evidence of national growth that most Americans could take pride in, a far more difficult task with the High Federalists' army, which, in a nation so distant from Europe, easily roused fears of its use against the domestic population. In contrast, the navy could be explained, accepted, and celebrated by a broad public as national defense.[70]

Musical performances showcased popular support for Federalists' naval expansion by marking the construction and completion of warships funded by public subscription.[71] During Newburyport, Massachusetts's construction of the USS *Merrimack*, a July 4 procession, headed by a "band" or ensemble of musicians, addressed the shipbuilders at the Federal Ship Yard and marched by the houses of the ship's subscribers, who had given over $40,000 to fund the twenty-gun warship. The musical procession highlighted community members' devotion to their nation and federal government and their continued willingness to make sacrifices for the greater good of the community and nation (notwithstanding merchants' need for naval protection for their own continued profit). When a ball and concert commemorated the *Merrimack*'s launch in October, the *Newburyport Herald* called "all friends to their country and government" to show their support by joining "to swell the chorus of the Patriotic Songs."[72] In "The Launch, a Federal Song," a "young gentleman" songwriter described the *Merrimack*'s launch as an occasion for "true Federal spirit" and aggression toward domestic opposition. He urged, "Let true Federal mirth be seen in each face,/No *Jacobin* or *Traitor* your country disgrace;/But shew your dislike to such characters as these." His lyrics sustained emphasis on visible, perceptible signs of feelings and sentiments and leveraged them as tools of intimidation and discovery.

Articulating a common Federalist theme, he accused Republicans of false patriotism and equated their lack of allegiance to the Federalist cause with lack of national allegiance. This "young gentleman" believed so resolutely in Federalist concepts of republican deference and limited popular political participation that he had his fellow Americans sing, "While ADAMS and WASHINGTON stands at the helm,/We'll mind our own business, and leave their's to them." Distributed as a broadside for communal singing and circulated in Boston's influential Federalist *Columbian Centinel*, his lyrics capitalized on the launch to promote partisan values that extended far beyond the navy.[73]

The construction and launching of warships was one thing Americans could be proud of, but a naval victory was another. And Thomas Truxton quickly produced a victory with the USS *Constellation*, one of six frigates authorized by the Naval Act of 1794. His was a victory that even the staunchest Republicans would have had difficulty criticizing. In early February 1799 off the Caribbean island of Nevis, Truxton defeated *L'Insurgente*, France's fastest frigate. Truxton's crew left seventy Frenchmen injured and twenty-nine killed, while just one American was killed and five were wounded.[74] Through broadsides, songsters, newspapers, and theater performances, Americans enjoyed dozens of songs touting Truxton's victory as a national accomplishment.[75]

Theaters promptly offered multimedia representations of Truxton's victory featuring naval songs. This was a wise tactic for both theaters and Federalists: rousing songs of naval prowess drew sailors, mechanics, and merchants to theaters to boost sales, and they voiced support for the nation's expanding defenses while reinforcing the Federalists' narrative of political dominance. While sailors were normally derided in theaters as rowdy "gallery gods" lacking virtue, they were now lauded as national heroes and courted by theaters with songs like "Huzza for the Constellation!"[76] In Philadelphia and Baltimore, theater audiences enjoyed the dramatic sketch *The Constellation; or, A Wreath for American Tars*, in which Alexander Reinagle's incidental music animated a "representation of the Chase and Action" between the two frigates. Combining song, dialogue, and dance, *American True Blue* showcased "a grand naval procession" with "the admired glee of 'Our Country's Like a Ship of War.'" Elaborating this commonly used simile, the glee not only validated the Federalists' naval project but also reinforced the notion of deference—just as every man had his station on a ship, every citizen had his proper role, including deference to appointed leaders.[77] Celebrations of Truxton's victory continued in theaters through 1800 to the benefit of theaters, actors, and Federalists, and beyond the major cities, Portland and Portsmouth held balls honoring Truxton's victory.[78]

Quick to capitalize on current events, Susanna Rowson presented the navy as an institution of protection, benefit, and pride for the entire nation in "Truxton's Victory." To reinforce the significance and potential of the navy as a national institution, Rowson wrote her new lyrics to the British tune "Heart of Oak," a theatrical song that celebrated the end of Britain's Seven Years' War with France and achieved the status of a national song. In reworking this tune, Rowson stressed America's growing naval prowess in emulation of Britain's feared fleet. Rowson promised "From our young rising NAVY our thunders shall roar,/And our Commerce extend to the earth's utmost shore."[79]

Rowson's reference to commerce was indicative of how songwriters used Truxton's victory to prioritize a Federalist conception of freedom. As Marc Lendler has summarized, the Federalists saw their Republican "opposition as advocating a destructive primacy of rights over obligation, individual liberty over community." Truxton's victory offered Federalist songwriters the ideal opportunity to assert the primacy of communal rights. Reworking "Adams and Liberty," one anonymous songwriter promised that through such naval prowess "Fair Freedom shall reign,/And Columbia's sons ever scorn subjugation" to foreign foes. The songwriter's claim that "In America Freedom unsully'd shall flow" extolled the nation's right to free trade and ignored the violations of individual rights carried out through the Sedition Act, which made it illegal to criticize the government or its officials and enabled arrests of vocal Republicans.[80]

Truxton's victory provided additional fuel for increasingly bombastic and partisan expressions of Federalist dominance in the summer of 1799. An example was Royall Tyler's "Convivial Song," sung at a Federalist July 4 gathering in Windsor, Vermont. Tyler roused his Federalist neighbors with a drinking song toasting Washington, American sailors, Truxton, the ladies of Vermont, and finally, Adams, before concluding with a nod to their "next Fed'ral meeting."[81] Some of the most intensely partisan lyrics were written by Portsmouth's Federalist lawyer Jonathan Mitchell Sewall. Sewall's lyrics illustrated New England Federalists' growing sense of invincibility and intolerance of Republican opposition. This was most apparent in his "Festival Song" for July 4, a reworking of "The Gods of the Greeks" (the same melody often designated through references to "In a Mouldering Cave" and "The Death of General Wolfe"). ▶ Sewall portrayed the nation as so invincible that it did not even need divine assistance. As he explained, "The aid of the Gods, Columbia declines, Tho' assail'd from *within* and *abroad.*/Her arms and her Counsels shall blast their designs,/And rebels subdue with her rod./Her *Tars* are all Truxton's, Her *Soldiers* ne'er fly,/Her *Fleets* shall invincible prove;/Sage Adams for wisdom, with Pallas may vie,/Whilst Washington equals a Jove!"[82] Once Federalists passed the repressive Alien and Sedition Acts, which they would use to target, arrest, and silence their Republican opponents, such bombastic musical expressions of invincibility became more common.[83]

## Republicans Battle Back in Song

Despite the Federalists' most extreme efforts, they failed to destroy faction. As Federalists adopted more vitriolic language in song, Republicans responded with increasing opposition before the 1800 presidential election. Republican songwriters challenged the Federalists' values, their self-portrayals as the nation's protectors, and the foundation of their prevailing narrative of political legitimacy.[84] They did so by directing similar language, imagery, rhetoric, and melody to very different ends. They prioritized different forms of "liberty," called Americans to stand firm like "hearts of oak" for different causes, and invoked the Revolutionary War to motivate Americans to take oppositional political action. In ritual and print, musical battles continued well after the New York battery duel between "Hail Columbia" and "Ça ira."

Republicans challenged Federalist values and self-portrayals despite being targeted by the Alien and Sedition Acts. This legislation made it illegal to make false or libelous statements about, or to fuel sedition or public animosity against, the government or its officers. It also required immigrants to reside in the United States for fourteen years, rather than the previous five years, before they could vote. This legislation targeted Republican editors, printers, politicians, and immigrants, who were among the Republicans' strongest supporters in the 1796 elections.[85] Republican songwriters highlighted the legislation's partisan purposes. Lyrics in the *Aurora* (under William Duane's editorship following Bache's death of yellow fever) charged, "Why the laws were ne'er meant for us all,/But those of a CERTAIN persuasion,/But most damnably hard do they fall/On the Demo—who speaks truth and reason." Indeed, both Republicans and prominent Federalists Abigail Adams and Noah Webster acknowledged that Federalists were guilty of harsh rhetoric and defamation that could have been prosecuted under the Sedition Act.[86]

Republicans battled Federalists by co-opting their rhetoric and turning the Federalists' accusations back against them. Republicans labeled the Alien and Sedition Acts a system of terror and Jacobinism, warned that Federalists' partisan cockades foretold of murder and civil war, and, redirecting the Federalists' xenophobia, attacked the Federalists' most vituperative journalist, William Cobbett, as a dangerous British influence.[87] Republican songwriters similarly turned the Federalists' charge of Republican infidelity to revolutionary principles back on their opponents. Federalist songwriters regularly invoked the war and Americans' moral debt to their forefathers to garner public support.[88] As French revolutionary politics lost appeal, Republicans emphasized "constitutional orthodoxy" to portray the Federalists as betrayers of the principles of the War of Independence. As a Brooklyn song printed in the *Centinel of Freedom* put it, "The Alien Law curtails that Freedom,/For which our fathers bled so free." Such lyrics, along with popular protests like Fries's Rebellion in 1799, accused the federal government of undermining revolutionary gains.[89] In the lyrical battles that ensued, each party claimed that the other had failed to fulfill its obligation to those who had fought for independence.

Republican songwriters took the oak, the symbol of sturdiness and steadfastness used in so many Federalist songs, particularly in the wake of Truxton's victory, and reinterpreted it as a symbol of opposition. While Federalists used the symbolic oak to prioritize neutral trade rights, the enforcement of treaties, and national autonomy, Republicans used it to prioritize individual rights guaranteed in the Constitution, such as the freedoms of speech and the press.[90] The Brooklyn song printed in the *Centinel of Freedom* used the oak to call Americans to oppose the Alien and Sedition Acts, commanding them "Stand to your rights, ye hearts of oak,/For now has come the *trying hour*." A subsequent verse concluded, "Preserve the Tree of Liberty." By connecting the phrase "hearts of oak" to the "Tree of Liberty," the songwriter legitimized the ongoing raising of liberty poles from locally felled trees in protest of Federalists' excessive legislation.[91] With this image, and the definition of liberty that it represented, Republicans countered Federalist songs, including "Adams and Liberty," which depicted trees being felled to build the US naval fleet and defend the nation's shores. Instead of warships defending the nation's autonomy against a hypothetical French invasion, the oak represented individual Americans' power in defending their individual rights against a repressive federal government. By reclaiming and repurposing this naval symbol, Republican songwriters challenged the way in which Federalists had based their entire legislative program and narrative of political dominance on the need to defend the nation's autonomy against imminent French invasion.

These musical battles over the meaning of symbols and the nature of Americans' historical debts to their forefathers resounded in American communities and their local celebrations. Colorful accounts of musical contests survived from Vermont, the home of the most notorious Republican congressman of the day, Matthew Lyon, and a prolific Republican songwriter and newspaper printer, Anthony Haswell. Born in Portsmouth, England, Haswell (1756–1816) was a cousin of Susanna Haswell Rowson. After his mother died, his father brought Haswell and his older brother to Boston, apprenticed them, and promptly returned to England to remarry. At the pottery where Haswell was apprenticed, he was surrounded by Loyalists who expressed their political views in song. Haswell had a knack for songwriting and supported the American cause. His master potter knew the value of Haswell's expressive talents for the American cause and let him be apprenticed to the printer Isaiah Thomas. After briefly serving in the army, Haswell began a long printing career and accepted an invitation to establish a newspaper and printing office in Bennington, Vermont. An ardent Republican and fixture in Bennington's celebrations, Haswell wrote many songs supporting Republican causes and commemorating local events. He was motivated to write particularly pointed songs after Federalists prosecuted Lyon under the Sedition Act.

After the Sedition Act was passed on July 14, 1798, it was no accident that Lyon, one of its staunchest opponents, was one of the first arrested under it. When Lyon had arrived in New York about thirty years earlier as a teen fleeing Ireland, he had already developed a hatred for corrupt authority, a disdain for gentlemanly affectations, and a determination to advocate for common folk. After moving to New England in 1774, Lyon lobbied for full political participation by ordinary Americans. He became a champion for equal rights and took Paine's *Rights of Man* as a foundational text.[92] In late January 1798, he fueled partisan debate in the House of Representatives, and Connecticut's Federalist congressman Roger Griswold responded by attacking Lyon's war record. In turn, Lyon spit tobacco juice in Griswold's eye. When the Federalists could not expel Lyon from Congress, Griswold beat him with a hickory walking stick. Lyon fought back with a pair of fireplace tongs. By mid-year, the Federalists had the Sedition Act in place of walking sticks to quiet their critics. But even the Sedition Act could not deter Lyon and Haswell from expressing criticism. While Haswell printed the *Vermont Gazette*, Lyon began *The Scourge of Aristocracy* from October 1 as an outlet for his views. The same month, under the Sedition Act, Lyon was arrested for his political criticism and was subsequently sentenced to six months in prison and a $1,000 fine. The sentence backfired. While in prison his letters circulated in the Republican press, and he was reelected to Congress. He emerged from prison in February 1799 a hero and was welcomed by crowds on his way back to Congress in Philadelphia.

When Lyon arrived at the State Arms Tavern in Bennington, local Republicans greeted him with two of Haswell's songs that used most of the Republicans' rhetorical strategies.[93] In song, Benningtonians challenged the Federalists' interpretation of freedom, their self-portrayal as defenders of freedom, and their imposition of economic measures that burdened laborers of the land to enrich coastal mercantile elites. To the tune "Black Sloven," Haswell had his neighbors attack the Federalists' violation of constitutional freedoms, singing "The freedom of speech to discuss and debate,/On the deeds of our servants who govern the state,/We'll never resign to the sticklers for power." Through Haswell's new lyrics set to the English melody "Joys of Scolding," Benningtonians declared themselves defenders of the freedoms of speech and press in the face of Federalist "foes of Freedom" (see Figure 3.4 and Figure 3.5). This uncommon choice of tune invited multiple interpretations.[94] Haswell's neighbors could have heard the melody's scolding wife, unrelenting in her criticism, transformed into the Republicans with their untiring commitment to criticizing the Federalists' violation of the Constitution, a commitment that Haswell himself called for in his final lines. Or they could have heard the wife as a mockery of the Federalists, who were constantly complaining about and attacking their Republican opponents. Most accurate in this hearing was the wife's admission, "I always am a chiding,/And still find Fault with every Dish, Though of my own providing," for the growing Republican opposition that the Federalists decried was fueled by their own efforts to silence it.

Bennington's ritual marking of Lyon's release with communal song and powerful oration was not just a celebration of an individual's triumph over persecution but a display of a larger Republican persistence in challenging the Federalists' narrative of legitimacy and unjust legislation. Haswell predicted the Federalist administration's downfall in song and captured it in a powerful image—one that again reversed Federalists' charges against the Republicans: Haswell called the Vergennes prison in which Lyon was held the "Federal Bastille."[95] Meanwhile, in neighboring New Hampshire, Haswell's

The liberty of speech and press,
Our sacred right by charter,
Our constitution shall express,
When Jacks are at low water.

Tho Wanton knaves and Blinking fools*
Make stallion stalls and Halls ring,
We scorn both principals and tools,
And soon shall of their falls sing.

To face the truth in fair debate,
They dread like pains of dying,
This sacred truth will bear its weight,
They rose and throve by lying.

Come take the glass, and drink his health,
Who is a friend to LYON,
First martyr under federal Law,
The junto dared to try on.

And may a conscious virtue bless,
His hours of meditation,
And give him language to express,
The truths must save the nation.

**Alluding to certain miscreants.*

**Figure 3.4.** Anthony Haswell, "Patriotic Exultation on Lyon's Release from the Federal Bastille, in Vergennes, Sung at Bennington, the third day of release, February 12, 1799." Bennington *Vermont Gazette*, 14 February 1799. Readex/NewsBank. Haswell's lyrics are set to the melody of "Joys of Scolding" or "The Scolding Wife," as it was printed in *The Vocal Magazine, Containing a Selection of the Most Esteemed English, Scots, and Irish* Songs, vol. 1 (Edinburgh: C. Stewart, 1797), 212–3.

Parnassus.

THE SCOLDING WIFE.

SOME women take Delight in Dreſs,
And ſome in Cards take Pleaſure;
While others place their Happineſs,
In heaping Hoards of Treaſure.
And ſome there are whoſe chief Delight
In Secrets is unfolding;
But my chief Joy, from morn to night,
Conſiſteth all in ſcolding.
In th' Morning when I ope mine Eyes,
I drive away all Silence;
Before my Huſband can ariſe,
You'll hear my Clack a Mile hence.
And when I ſit down at my Meat,
You've one continual Riot;
I eat and ſcold, and ſcold and eat,
My Clack is never quiet.
Too fat, too lean, too raw, too roaſt,
I always am a chiding;
And ſtill find Fault with every Diſh,
Though of my own providing.
And when I go to bed at Night,
I ſurely fall a weeping;
For then I loſe my Soul's Delight
I cannot ſcold when ſleeping.
But this my Pain doth mitigate,
And drives away all Sorrow;
For though I cannot ſcold to Night,
I'll make it up to Morrow.

**Figure 3.5.** "The Scolding Wife." Windsor *Spooner's Vermont Journal*, 11 March 1793. Readex/NewsBank.

Federalist counterpart Jonathan Mitchell Sewall clung to faith in the power of "upright Judges, Patriots true,/With juries, fines, chains, prisons, too" to restrain the likes of Lyon.[96]

Songwriters like Sewall were determined to realize the potential that Federalist Senate leader Theodore Sedgwick had seen when he called the XYZ Affair a "glorious opportunity to destroy faction." Writing from Portsmouth, where Federalists faced emerging Republican opposition, Sewall called his neighbors to expel Republicans in his "Ode to Independence." On July 4, he had his fellow townsmen command, "Columbia rise! Be firm, be free!/ The friends of France are foes to Thee!/Detest the tools of Talleyrand,/And spurn each Traitor from the land!" Responding to Republican attacks on the Alien and Sedition Acts, Sewall not only defended the legislation but threatened that far worse punishment would come. Using a common formulation of gender roles that would remain active through the War of 1812, women could inspire men to defend the nation and rebuke those who failed to do so. Drawing on this formulation in his final verse, Sewall invoked the convention of a concluding toast to the country's fair to mark Republican men as outsiders unworthy of even "one smile" from American women. The antithesis of broad communal celebration of an anniversary of national significance, lyrics like Sewall's instead promoted increasingly strident rhetoric and partisan rituals that separated neighbors and attacked opponents' political legitimacy.[97] "Faction" continued as the presidential election neared and both parties' well-honed rhetorical strategies found new use in election songs. "Jefferson and Slavery, or, Federalism Triumphant, a new patriotic song" painted the French and the Republicans—including Vice President Jefferson—as untrustworthy, irreligious schemers intent on destroying and "enslaving" the nation. Republican songwriters cast the Federalists as Tories working to restore "king-craft" and enslave the people.[98] The two sides became more entrenched and extreme in their rhetoric. The more Republicans blasted the Federalists' violations of the Constitution through the Sedition Act, the more steadfastly Federalist songwriters maintained that the nation's leaders made no such violation.[99]

In the hands of Federalists like Sewall, music articulated ever more extreme portrayals of Federalist heroes and domestic and foreign villains. And it supported more intense intimidation tactics designed to exclude, convert, or silence Republican opposition. An unending stream of songs continuously articulated this Federalist narrative of political legitimacy. While most were ephemeral, a few were crafted carefully enough to achieve lasting circulation and not only gained widespread attention but spurred new lyrics of their own. Despite the Federalists' efforts to destroy political opposition through music and other forms of propaganda and intimidation, Republicans persisted in their resistance. Through music, they turned nearly every Federalist accusation back on the Federalists and reinterpreted powerful symbols, melodies, and rhetorical strategies to highlight the Federalists' betrayals of the Constitution and the principles on which the Revolutionary

War was fought. Although Republicans failed to repeal the Alien and Sedition Acts, they strengthened their organization and communication, leading to gains in Congress, and ultimately, to Adams's defeat. Federalist popularity was so thoroughly tied up with the crisis with France that once peace seemed possible, it rapidly weakened as Republican popular support grew.[100] With Jefferson's election, it was the Republicans' turn to craft a new narrative of political dominance, articulated as forcefully and humorously as ever in song.

## Notes

1. Newburyport *Impartial Herald*, 26 September 1797; G. Wood, *Empire of Liberty*, 208.
2. James Morton Smith, "Background for Repression: America's Half-War with France and the Internal Security Legislation of 1798," *Huntington Library Quarterly* 18, no. 1 (November 1954): 39; Bouton, *Taming Democracy*, 245; Stanley M. Elkins and Eric McKitrick, *The Age of Federalism* (New York: Oxford University Press, 1993), 647–9; Alexander DeConde, *The Quasi-War: The Politics and Diplomacy of the Undeclared War with France, 1797–1801* (New York: Charles Scribner's Sons, 1966), 9–10; Frederick C. Leiner, "The Subscription Warships of 1798," *American Neptune* 46 (Summer 1986): 142.
3. Marc Lendler, "Equally Proper at All Times and at All Times Necessary": Civility, Bad Tendency, and the Sedition Act," *Journal of the Early Republic* 24, no. 3 (Autumn 2004): 426.
4. Douglas Bradburn, "A Clamor in the Public Mind: Opposition to the Alien and Seditions Acts," *William and Mary Quarterly* 65, no. 3 (July 2008): 566, 595–600.
5. Thomas M. Ray, "'Not One Cent for Tribute': The Public Addresses and American Popular Reaction to the XYZ Affair, 1798–1799," *Journal of the Early Republic* 3, no. 4 (Winter 1983): 392.
6. J. Smith, "Background for Repression," 40; W. Brown, *John Adams*, 88–93; Arthur Scherr, "Inventing the Patriot President: Bache's 'Aurora' and John Adams," *Pennsylvania Magazine of History and Biography* 119, no. 4 (October 1995): 378–91; DeConde, *Quasi-War*, 57; G. Wood, *Empire of Liberty*, 243.
7. Koschnik, *Common Interest*, 115; Ray, "Not One Cent," 391, 393–9, 400–2, 405, 410; W. Brown, *John Adams*, 88–97; Philadelphia *Gazette of the United States*, 20 October 1798; Scherr, "Inventing the Patriot President," 389–92; Bennington *Vermont Gazette*, 13 March 1798.
8. Philadelphia *Gazette of the United States*, 23 April 1798; Philadelphia *Carey's United States Recorder*, 1 May 1798; Myron Gray, "Musical Politics in French Philadelphia, 1781–1801" (PhD diss., University of Pennsylvania, 2014), 220–2; Philadelphia *General Advertiser* 22 April 1794; Philadelphia *Dunlap's American Daily Advertiser*, 12 May 1794; Philadelphia *Porcupine's Gazette*, 30 August, 3 September 1798; H[enri] C[apron], "Come Genius of Our Happy Land" (Philadelphia: B. Carr, [1798]).
9. Boston *Massachusetts Mercury*, 20 April 1798; Portsmouth *Oracle of the Day*, 7, 10 July 1798; Ray, "'Not One Cent,'" 394, 398–9; Philadelphia *Gazette of the United States*,

6 July 1798; *Philadelphia Minerva*, 31 March 1798; *Greenleaf's New York Journal*, 6 June 1798; *Newport Mercury*, 10 July 1798; Newark *Centinel of Freedom*, 29 May 1798; DeConde, *Quasi-War*, 79, 84–5.

10. Philadelphia *Porcupine's Gazette*, 1 August 1798; *Alexandria Times*, 4 July 1798; Baltimore *Federal Gazette*, 25 June 1798; Dover *Sun*, 22 August 1798; *The Federal Songster, Being a Collection of the Most Celebrated Patriotic Songs* (New London, CT: James Springer, 1800), 6–10.
11. Philadelphia *Gazette of the United States*, 27 March 1798; Charles Ellis Dickson, "Jeremiads in the New American Republic: The Case of National Fasts in the John Adams Administration," *New England Quarterly* 60, no. 2 (June 1987): 193, 195–6.
12. Boston *Independent Chronicle*, 30 April 1798; Donald J. Ratcliffe, ed., "The Autobiography of Benjamin Tappan," *Ohio History* 85 (Spring 1976), 121–2.
13. Boston *Independent Chronicle*, 30 April 1798; Newark *Centinel of Freedom*, 23 April 1799; Philadelphia *Carey's United States Recorder*, 8 May 1798; New York *Time Piece*, 11 May 1798; New London *Bee*, 16 May 1798; Suffield *Impartial Herald*, 16 May 1798; Boston *Columbian Centinel*, 12 May 1798.
14. *Newport Mercury*, 10 July 1798.
15. Newport *Companion*, 7 July 1798; Philadelphia *Porcupine's Gazette*, 1 August 1798.
16. Stewart Mitchell, ed., "New Letters of Abigail Adams," *Proceedings of the American Antiquarian Society* (October 1945): 321–2; Marshall Smelser, "George Washington and the Alien and Sedition Acts," *American Historical Review* 59, no. 2 (January 1954): 323, 331; DeConde, *Quasi-War*, 93, 98–9; *Newport Mercury*, 14 August 1798; *Federal Songster*, 10–12, 18–20; *The Columbian Songster*, no. 1 (Nathaniel Heaton Jr., 1799), 10–13; Philadelphia *Gazette of the United States*, 26 June 1798; Susan Branson, *These Fiery Frenchified Dames: Women and Political Culture in Early National Philadelphia* (Philadelphia: University of Pennsylvania Press, 2010), 90.
17. C. Young, "Connecting the President and the People," 465; Aaron N. Coleman, "A Second Bounaparty?" A Reexamination of Alexander Hamilton during the Franco-American Crisis, 1796–1801," *Journal of the Early Republic* 28, no. 2 (Summer 2008): 204; William J. Murphy Jr., "John Adams: The Politics of the Additional Army, 1798–1800," *New England Quarterly* 52, no. 2 (June 1979): 236–9; DeConde, *Quasi-War*, 90–2, 96, 191; Bouton, *Taming Democracy*, 245.
18. Newport *Companion*, 7 July 1798; *Rutland Herald*, 9 July 1798; Thomas Green Fessenden, *Original Poems* (Philadelphia: E. Bronson, 1806), 1–5; Baltimore *Federal Gazette*, 30 July 1798; Philadelphia *Gazette of the United States*, 13 August 1798; Robert Treat Paine, *The Works in Verse and Prose of the Late Robert Treat Paine, Jun. Esq.* (Boston: J. Belcher, 1812), 267; William C. Foster, *Poetry on Different Subjects Written under the Signature of Timothy Spectacles* (Salem, NY: John M. Looker, 1805), 113–14.
19. *Newport Mercury*, 14 August 1798; *Federal Songster*, 3–4, 10–12; New York *Daily Advertiser*, 23 May 1798; *Norwich Packet*, 24 July 1798; Peter Albrecht Von Hagen, "Adams and Washington: A New Patriotic Song" (Boston: P. A. von Hagen, 1798); Providence *United States Chronicle*, 11 April 1799; Walpole *Farmers Weekly Museum*, 22 July 1799; *Columbian Songster*, no. 4, 19; Francis Hopkinson, "Brother Soldiers All Hail!" (Philadelphia: B. Carr, 1799); Fessenden, *Original Poems*, 1–5.

20. Providence *United States Chronicle*, 12 July, 30 November 1798.
21. Dover *Sun*, 22 August 1798; *Salem Gazette*, 10 July 1798; Josiah Dunham, *An Oration, for the Fourth of July, 1798* (Hanover, NH: Benjamin True, [1798]), 12–3; Boston *Massachusetts Mercury*, 20 July 1798; "To George Washington from Josiah Dunham, 13 July 1798," *Founders Online*, http://founders.archives.gov/documents/Washington/06-02-02-0315.
22. Philadelphia *Porcupine's Gazette*, 25 April 1798; *Albany Gazette*, 6 July 1798; *Federal Songster*, 22–5, 59–60, 74–6; *Columbian Songster*, no. 4, 20–2, 24–5; Ray, "Not One Cent," 395; *Norwich Packet*, 24 July 1798; Philadelphia *Gazette of the United States*, 4 August 1798; Brookfield *Political Repository*, 11 September 1798; Peacham *Green Mountain Patriot*, 16 November 1798.
23. Walpole *Farmer's Weekly Museum*, 10 July 1798; Philadelphia *Porcupine's Gazette*, 25 April 1798; DeConde, *Quasi-War*, 85–6; Philadelphia *Gazette of the United States*, 4 August 1798.
24. Philadelphia *Gazette of the United States*, 7 May 1798; *New York Gazette*, 2 August 1798.
25. *New York Daily Advertiser*, 11 September, 5 October 1798; Hanover *Eagle*, 16 October 1798; Boston *Massachusetts Mercury*, 19 October 1798.
26. Baltimore *Federal Gazette*, 5 October, 6 November 1798; *The American Songster; or, Federal Museum of Melody and Wit* (Baltimore: Warner and Hanna, 1799), 26–7.
27. Steffen, *Mechanics of Baltimore*, 157–66; A. Taylor, "'The Art of Hook & Snivey,'" 1388, 1392.
28. Philadelphia *Gazette of the United States*, 26 April 1798; *Philadelphia Gazette*, 26 April 1798; New York *Weekly Museum*, 5 May 1798; *Providence Gazette*, 5 May 1798; *Alexandria Times*, 5 May 1798; David Ritchey, *A Guide to the Baltimore Stage in the Eighteenth Century* (Westport, CT: Greenwood Press, 1982), 226–7; Boston *Massachusetts Mercury*, 25 May 1798; New York *Spectator*, 11 July 1798; Philadelphia *Aurora*, 2 August 1798; Worcester *Massachusetts Spy*, 8 August 1798; Elizabethtown *New Jersey Journal*, 3 July 1798; *Albany Gazette*, 6 July 1798; *Newburyport Herald*, 18, 21 September 1798; *Columbian Songster*, no. 1, 1–2; *Federal Songster*, 21–2 (mistitled "Adams and Liberty"); James R. Heintze, *Music of the Fourth of July: A Year-by-Year Chronicle of Performances and Works Composed for the Occasion, 1777–2008* (Jefferson, NC: McFarland, 2009), 29–37.
29. Oscar Sonneck, *Report on "The Star-Spangled Banner" "Hail Columbia" "America" "Yankee Doodle"* (New York: Dover, 1972. First published 1909), 43, 69; Philadelphia *Porcupine's Gazette*, 24 April 1798; Riordan, "'O Dear,'" 222; "From Abigail Adams to Mary Smith Cranch, 26 April 1798," *Founders Online*, https://founders.archives.gov/documents/Adams/04-12-02-0273; "From Abigail Smith Adams to Thomas Boylston Adams, 1 May 1798," *Founders Online*, http://founders.archives.gov/documents/Adams/99-03-02-0001.
30. Myron Gray, "A Partisan National Song: The Politics of 'Hail Columbia' Reconsidered," *Music & Politics* 11, no. 2 (Summer 2017). DOI: http://dx.doi.org/10.3998/mp.9460447.0011.201.
31. Gray, "A Partisan National Song"; "From Abigail Adams to Mary Smith Cranch, 26 April 1798," *Founders Online*, https://founders.archives.gov/documents/Adams/04-12-02-0273.

32. New York *Gazette of the United States*, 20 June 1789; *Ode for Election-Day, 1792.*
33. J. Smith, "Background for Repression," 43; Philadelphia *Gazette of United States*, 26 April 1798; "From Abigail Adams to Mary Smith Cranch, 26 April 1798," *Founders Online*; "From Abigail Smith Adams to Thomas Boylston Adams, 1 May 1798," *Founders Online*, https://founders.archives.gov/documents/Adams/99-03-02-0001
34. "Abigail Adams to John Adams, 15 January 1797," *Founders Online*, http://founders.archives.gov/documents/Adams/04-11-02-0259.]
35. B. Anderson, *Imagined Communities*, 145.
36. Adam Mestyan, *Arab Patriotism: The Ideology and Culture of Power in Late Ottoman Egypt* (Princeton, NJ: Princeton University Press, 2017), 3; "Music Physically Considered."
37. Joseph Hopkinson to George Washington, 9 May 1798, *Founders Online*, https://founders.archives.gov/documents/Washington/06-02-02-0191.
38. "From Abigail Smith Adams to Thomas Boylston Adams, 1 May 1798," *Founders Online*, https://founders.archives.gov/documents/Adams/99-03-02-0001.
39. George Washington to Joseph Hopkinson, 27 May 1798, *Founders Online*, https://founders.archives.gov/documents/Washington/06-02-02-0227.
40. Gray, "A Partisan National Song."
41. Hale, "'Many Who Wandered,'" 132, 168; Sonneck, *Report*, 43.
42. Philadelphia *Gazette of the United* States, 26 April, 2 May 1798; Philadelphia *Porcupine's Gazette*, 28 April 1798.
43. Boston *Columbian Centinel*, 5 May 1798; *Philadelphia Gazette*, 28 April 1798; Paul F. Rice, *British Music and the French Revolution* (Newcastle: Cambridge Scholars Publishing, 2010), 4; Todd Gilman, *The Theatre Career of Thomas Arne* (Newark: University of Delaware Press, 2013), 303.
44. New York *Daily Advertiser*, 30 July 1798; Cotlar, *Tom Paine's America*, 82, 99–100. Alternative accounts of the battery incident were offered in Philadelphia *Aurora*, 1 August 1798; *Greenleaf's New York Journal*, 1 August 1798.
45. Philadelphia *Aurora*, 1, 2 August 1798; Philadelphia *Porcupine's Gazette*, 28 April 1798; Philadelphia *Gazette of the United States*, 2 May 1798; New York *Daily Advertiser*, 5 May 1798; New York *Commercial Advertiser*, 5, 18 May 1798; Worcester *Massachusetts Spy*, 8 August 1798; Mitchell, ed., "New Letters of Abigail Adams," 349; Sonneck, *Report*, 46; Joseph Hopkinson, "Hail Columbia, the Favorite New Federal Song," retrieved from the Library of Congress, https://www.loc.gov/item/ihas.100010486/.
46. Philadelphia *Carey's United States' Recorder*, 12, 30 June, 24 July 1798.
47. Gray, "A Partisan National Song."
48. George L. Roth, "Verse Satire on 'Faction' 1790–1815," *William and Mary Quarterly* 17, no. 4 (October 1960): 475.
49. Philadelphia *Aurora*, 27 April, 1 August 1798.
50. Cotlar, *Tom Paine's America*, 82; Philadelphia *Aurora*, 1 August 1798.
51. Portsmouth *Oracle of the Day*, 20 October 1798; Portland *Eastern Herald*, 29 October 1798; Philadelphia *Gazette of the United States*, 3 November 1798; Baltimore *Federal Gazette*, 7 November 1798; Boston *Columbian Centinel*, 17 November 1798; Carlisle

*Gazette*, 21 November 1798; *Vergennes Gazette*, 29 November 1798; Jonathan Mitchell Sewall, *Miscellaneous Poems, with Several Specimens from the Author's Manuscript Version of the Poems of Ossian* (Portsmouth: William Treadwell, 1801), 155–8.

52. Boston *Columbian Centinel*, 26 May, 9 June 1798; Portsmouth *New Hampshire Gazette*, 26 June 1798; Portland *Eastern Herald*, 29 October 1798; *Vergennes Gazette*, 8 August 1799; *Federal Songster*, 62–4; *Columbian Songster*, no. 1, 3–4.
53. *Boston Gazette*, 4 June 1798; *Providence Gazette*, 30 June 1798; *Salem Gazette*, 12 June 1798; Heintze, *Music*, 31; Nathans, *Early American Theatre*, 119–21, 157; John Alden, "A Season in Federal Street: J. B. Williamson and the Boston Theatre, 1796–1797," *Proceedings of the American Antiquarian Society* (April 1955): 16.
54. Tammany Society, or Columbian Order, "Committee of Amusement Minutes," New York Public Library Digital Collections. http://digitalcollections.nypl.org/items/0b59d950-ab40-0133-3b9c-00505686d14e.
55. Cotlar, *Tom Paine's America*, 88–93.
56. New York *Daily Advertiser*, 23 May 1798; Boston *Massachusetts Mercury*, 25 May 1798; Providence *United States Chronicle*, 31 May 1798; Suffield *Impartial Herald*, 25 June 1798; Augusta *Herald*, 23 July 1800.
57. Koschnik, *Common Interest*, 105, 115–17; *New York Gazette*, 30 July 1798; Philadelphia *Porcupine's Gazette*, 24 May 1798.
58. *Albany Centinel*, 21 September 1798; Richard N. Rosenfeld, *American Aurora: A Democratic-Republican Returns* (New York: St. Martin's Press, 2014), 229–30; M. Smith, *Listening*, 10–12.
59. R. Paine, *Works*, xxx, xxxvii–xliii, xlvi, xlix–li, lix, lxvii, lxx–lxxi, lxxvii, lxxx; "From George Washington to Thomas (Robert Treat) Paine, 1 September 1799," *Founders Online*, http://founders.archives.gov/documents/Washington/06-04-02-0235; "To John Adams from Robert Treat Paine, 27 July 1799," *Founders Online*, http://founders.archives.gov/documents/Adams/99-02-02-3813; "From John Adams to Robert Treat Paine, 4 August 1799," *Founders Online*, http://founders.archives.gov/documents/Adams/99-02-02-3844.
60. R. Paine, *Works*, xlvi; Washington Irving, *The Works of Washington Irving in Twelve Volumes*, vol. 8 (New York: G. P. Putnam's Sons, 1881), 320–1; John Stafford Smith and Robert Treat Paine Jr., "Adams and Liberty" (A. Wright, for D. Wright and Company, Northampton, MA, 1798). Retrieved from the Library of Congress, https://www.loc.gov/item/ihas.100010461/; Richards, *Shays's Rebellion*, 33; R. Paine, *Works*, xlv–xlvi, 243–55; Boston *Columbian Centinel*, 6, 9 June 1798; *Boston Gazette*, 4 June 1798; New York *Commercial Advertiser*, 7 June 1798; Philadelphia *Gazette of the United States*, 14 June 1798; Chambersburg *Farmers' Register*, 17 October 1798; Boston *Massachusetts Mercury*, 22 February, 7 June 1799; Clapp, *Record of the Boston Stage*, 68–9; New York *Mercantile Advertiser*, 18 June 1799; *Providence Gazette*, 30 June 1798; *Salem Gazette*, 3 July 1798; *Greenfield Gazette*, 9 July 1798; Portland *Gazette*, 9 July 1798; Baltimore *Federal Gazette*, 22 June 1798; Norwich *Courier*, 12 July 1798; *Columbian Songster*, no. 3, 31–5; James B. Hosmer, *Music Book*, Connecticut Historical Society, Manuscript 38923.
61. Boston *Columbian Centinel*, 26 May 1798, 8 June 1799; R. Paine, *Works*, xlv–xlvi.

62. New York *Spectator*, 11 July 1798; *Kline's Carlisle Weekly Gazette*, 22 August, 5 September 1798; Baltimore *Federal Gazette*, 4 August 1798; Cooperstown *Otsego Herald*, 7 November 1799.
63. Nathans, *Early American Theatre*, 114–17; *Vergennes Gazette*, 8 August 1799; *Federal Songster*, 62–4, 74–6.
64. "From Abigail Smith Adams to John Quincy Adams, 12 June 1798," *Founders Online*, http://founders.archives.gov/documents/Adams/99-03-02-0076.
65. Elkins and McKitrick, *Age of Federalism*, 643, 645; DeConde, *Quasi-War*, 93; Leiner, "Subscription Warships," 142, 148–9, 155.
66. DeConde, *Quasi-War*, 104–5, 112–13, 115, 169, 178, 180, 182, 185, 188; William H. Gaines Jr., "The Forgotten Army: Recruiting for a National Emergency (1799–1800)," *Virginia Magazine of History and Biography* 56, no. 3 (July 1948): 273–6; Murphy, "John Adams," 243–9.
67. Nathans, *Early American Theatre*, 155–8; Alden, "A Season in Federal Street," 24, 27–8.
68. Nathans, *Early American Theatre*, 120–1, 150; Clapp, *Record of the Boston Stage*, 56–57. On the first launch attempt, attended by President Adams, the *Constitution* only moved about 20 feet; it was successfully launched on the third attempt on October 21, 1797. See John S. Barrows, "The Beginning and Launching of the United States Frigate Constitution," *Proceedings of the Bostonian Society* 9 (January 1925): 22–37.
69. *New York Gazette*, 28 September 1797, 19 May 1798, 12 April 1800; Daniel Ebsworth, *Republican Harmonist*, 2nd ed. (Boston: n.p., 1801), 91–2. See *Newport Mercury*, 24 September 1799; New York *Daily Advertiser*, 23 May 1798, 10, 11 April 1800, 17 September 1800; *Philadelphia Gazette*, 28 June 1800.
70. This broader appeal can be seen, for example, in the printing of naval lyrics in Ebsworth, *Republican Harmonist* (1801), 91–2.
71. Ritchey, *Guide*, 261; Philadelphia *Aurora*, 28 November 1799.
72. *Salem Gazette*, 10 July 1798; *Newburyport Herald*, 9, 12, 16 October 1798; Leiner, "Subscription Warships," 157.
73. Boston *Columbian Centinel*, 20 October 1798; *The Launch, a Federal Song* ([Boston]: n.p., [1798]).
74. Elkins and McKitrick, *Age of Federalism*, 652.
75. Baltimore *Federal Gazette*, 16 March 1799; Portland *Eastern Herald*, 8 July 1799; Savannah *Columbian Museum*, 28 May 1799; *Federal Songster*, 15–17, 27–9, 44–6, 84–5; Walpole *Farmers Weekly Museum*, 22 July 1799; Portsmouth *Federal Observer*, 25 July 1799; Boston *Columbian Centinel*, 1 June 1799; Windsor *Spooner's Vermont Journal*, 16 July 1799; Georgetown *Washington Federalist*, 11 December 1800; Charleston *City Gazette*, 12 March 1800; New York *Commercial Advertiser*, 4, 5 June 1799; New York *Daily Advertiser*, 20 May 1799; Providence *United States Chronicle*, 4 July 1799.
76. Paul A. Gilje, "The Meaning of Freedom for Waterfront Workers," in *Devising Liberty: Preserving and Creating Freedom in the New American Republic*, ed. David Thomas Konig (Stanford, CA: Stanford University Press, 1995), 110; "Huzza for the Constellation" (Philadelphia: B. Carr, 1799).

77. *Philadelphia Gazette*, 30 March 1799; Providence *United States Chronicle*, 4 July 1799; Thomas Clark Pollock, *The Philadelphia Theatre in the Eighteenth Century* (New York: Greenwood Press, 1968), 384–7, 390, 395; Ritchey, *Guide*, 41, 260, 262, 266, 274; Eola Willis, *The Charleston Stage in the XVIII Century* (New York: Benjamin Blom, 1968), 463. Reinagle's music was published in *Mr. Francis's Ballroom Assistant*, no. 2 (Philadelphia: G. Willig, n.d.); DeConde, *Quasi-War*, 57; Wood, *Empire of Liberty*, 243; Boston *Massachusetts Mercury*, 20 April 1798.
78. Ritchey, *Guide*, 41, 266, 274; Reese Davis James, *Cradle of Culture, 1800–1810: The Philadelphia Stage* (Philadelphia: University of Pennsylvania Press, 1957), 17; Willis, *Charleston Stage*, 463–4; Portland *Gazette*, 1 April 1799; Boston *Columbian Centinel*, 20 March 1799.
79. Susanna Rowson, "Truxton's Victory," (N.l.: n.p., 1799); *American Songster* (1799), 20–2; Kate Van Winkle Keller, *Music of the War of 1812 in America* (Annapolis: Colonial Music Institute, 2011), 24–6.
80. Lendler, "Equally Proper," 434; *Otsego Herald*, 7 November 1799.
81. Brattleboro *Federal Galaxy*, 22 July 1799; *Federal Songster*, 44–6.
82. *Philadelphia Gazette*, 17 July 1799; *Federal Songster*, 66–7; Sewall, *Miscellaneous Poems*, 169–71.
83. Boston *Columbian Centinel*, 20 October 1798.
84. Newark *Centinel of Freedom*, 18 September, 13, 20 November 1798, 16 July 1799; Philadelphia *Aurora*, 24 May 1799; New London *Bee*, 21 March 1798; Bouton, *Taming Democracy*, 246–8; DeConde, *Quasi-War*, 102; Daniel, *Scandal and Civility*, 90; Merrill and Wilentz, eds. *Key of Liberty*, 32–6.
85. James Morton Smith, "The Enforcement of the Alien Friends Act of 1798," *Mississippi Valley Historical Review* 41, no. 1 (June 1954): 86; Smelser, "George Washington," 323, 331; Manning J. Dauer, *The Adams Federalists* (Baltimore: Johns Hopkins University Press, 1953), 163–6, 206; DeConde, *Quasi-War*, 94, 99–101; Bouton, *Taming Democracy*, 250.
86. Lendler, "Equally Proper," 435; Daniel, *Scandal and Civility*, 256; Philadelphia *Aurora*, 24 May 1799.
87. Daniel, *Scandal and Civility*, 255–6, 264–7.
88. *Boston Gazette*, 11 June 1798; *Greenfield Gazette*, 9 July, 20 August, 6 October 1798; Portland *Eastern Herald*, 8 July 1799; Heintze, *Music*, 30–35.
89. New London *Bee*, 8 August 1798; Boston *Constitutional Telegraph*, 29 October 1800; Bouton, *Taming Democracy*, 245; Newark *Centinel of Freedom*, 16 July 1799.
90. New London *Weekly Oracle*, 27 August 1798; Providence *United States Chronicle*, 30 November 1798; *New Hampshire Gazette*, 9 July 1799; Sewall, *Miscellaneous Poems*, 172–4.
91. Newark *Centinel of Freedom*, 16 July 1799.
92. Robert E. Shalhope, *Bennington and the Green Mountain Boys: The Emergence of Liberal Democracy in Vermont, 1760–1850* (Baltimore: Johns Hopkins University Press, 1996), 153–60, 201–3; Richard J. Purcell, "An Irish Crusader for American Democracy: Matthew Lyon, 1750–1822," *Studies: An Irish Quarterly Review* 25, no. 97 (March 1936): 47–64.

93. Spargo, *Anthony Haswell*, 49–56, 233–4; Bennington *Vermont Gazette*, 14 February 1799; Newark *Centinel of Freedom*, 26 February, 5 March 1799.
94. Various printings of the song include Windsor *Spooner's Vermont Journal*, 11 March 1793; *The Vocal Magazine Containing a Selection of the Most Esteemed English, Scots, and Irish Songs, Ancient and Modern: Adapted for the Harpsichord or Violin*, vol. 1 (Edinburgh: C. Stewart, 1797); *Columbian Songster*, no. 2, 4–5; *Federal Songster*, 39–40; Philadelphia *Constitutional Diary*, 27 January 1800; *Philadelphia Repository*, 10 July 1802.
95. Spargo, *Anthony Haswell*, 54–6; Bennington *Vermont Gazette*, 14 February 1799; Newark *Centinel of Freedom*, 26 February, 5 March 1799.
96. Portsmouth *New Hampshire Gazette*, 9 July 1799; Sewall, *Miscellaneous Poems*, 172–4.
97. Portsmouth *New Hampshire Gazette*, 2 July 1799; *Federal Songster*, 69–71; Sewall, *Miscellaneous Poems*, 172–4; "The Ladies Patriotic Song" (Boston: P. A. von Hagen, [1798]); Heintze, *Music*, 34; Newman, *Parades*, 104–13.
98. Boston *Russell's Gazette*, 2 September 1799, 17 March 1800; *Greenleaf's New York Journal*, 20 April 1799; Boston *Constitutional Telegraph*, 14 June 1800.
99. Walpole *Farmers Weekly Museum*, 22 July 1799.
100. Bradburn, "Clamor," 567, 574, 593; DeConde, *Quasi-War*, 264–6.

# 4
# Singing Republican Ascendance

In early March 1801, music punctuated a dramatic change in the political direction of the nation. An elaborate pageant in Virginia presented the recent presidential election as a battle in which evildoing Federalists attacked Liberty, constructed as a symbol of all things Republican. Federalists, portrayed by a king, bishop, soldier, orator, and statesman—the latter carrying papers marked Sedition Act, Alien Act, monarchy, army, navy, bankruptcy, and so on—harassed Liberty and incited a mob to join in her demise. With her death imminent, a trumpet miraculously announced that Thomas Jefferson was to be president. The public rallied around Liberty. She destroyed the Federalists' weapons, and sixteen women representing the states declared that "Union can only be maintained by preserving Liberty."[1]

This tidy presentation counteracted, rather than reflected, the electoral process. Filled with intrigue and protracted—the outcome remained unclear through much of February—the 1800 presidential election was not a revolution, as commonly claimed. In many states, John Adams fared better than in the 1796 election, and with only an additional 250 votes in New York City, he would have won the electoral college outright.[2] Once the electoral votes were counted, Jefferson and fellow Republican Aaron Burr tied with 73 votes and the outcome was left to the House of Representatives. Federalists explored options such as invalidating a few electoral college votes to make Adams victorious and exploiting rules of succession to put a Federalist senator or representative in the executive. After two months of maneuvering and deal-making by both Republicans and Federalists—accompanied by rumors of armed force and secession—the outcome was finally determined by the House. Representatives began voting on February 11 and, after thirty-five inconclusive votes, determined the outcome nearly a week later on the thirty-sixth vote. Ultimately, enough Federalists agreed to cast blank ballots, likely in response to Jefferson's perceived acceptance of one of their colleague's conditions, and by doing so, gave the victory to Jefferson over Burr.[3]

Erasing this ambiguity and intrigue, the Virginia pageant's dramatic narrative of Republican ascendance quickly took root. Songwriters elaborated

*Hail Columbia*. Laura Lohman, Oxford University Press (2020). © Oxford University Press.
DOI: 10.1093/oso/9780190930615.001.0001

the pageant's claims into historical narratives that magnified the importance of Republican ascendance and articulated the legitimacy of Republican leadership. Songwriters reworked musical symbols of Federalist power and legitimacy, including "Hail Columbia" and "Adams and Liberty," using fundamental propaganda techniques and adapting specific rhetorical and narrative techniques from Federalist precedents. Republicans claimed the concept of liberty for themselves, detailed a litany of Federalist wrongs, and portrayed Jefferson as a savior. Counteracting years of Federalist assaults and their caricature of the "dangerous Democrat," the Republicans' primary narrative foregrounded a new image of Jefferson, cast the Federalists as evildoers, and stressed the Republican party's laudable priorities and values. Immigrants not only expanded the Republicans' musical narrative but also drew Federalist critiques. Despairing of their marginalized status, Federalists leveraged immigrant and African American characters to contest the Republicans' narrative with personal attacks, cutting satire, and sectional views. Leading political voices turned to music, and new periodicals such as Joseph Dennie's *Port Folio* and Levi Lincoln's *National Aegis* provided outlets for escalating dialogues of punch and counterpunch in song and musical commentary.[4] Through such outlets and community celebrations, Republican songwriters persisted in circulating creative narratives of political ascendance and legitimacy across state lines and solidified lasting themes in the recollection of the Jeffersonian era.

## Repurposing Federalist Songs

As the presidential election's resolution remained unclear, Republicans began crafting their narrative of ascendance by touting their congressional gains. Republicans gained twenty-two seats in the House of Representatives, leaving Federalists outnumbered thirty-eight to sixty-eight. This reversal was fueled by significant shifts in Rhode Island, South Carolina, Massachusetts, and New Jersey.

In New Jersey, Republican gains in Congress followed months of persistent and innovative organizational efforts. New Jersey Republicans engaged in pamphleteering and held two novel statewide conventions in 1800 leading up to the congressional, state legislative, and presidential elections. They sought control of the state legislature to select presidential electors who would vote for Jefferson. While they failed at these aims, Republicans pursued a final aim of winning the state's five seats in the House of Representatives. Federalists, unwilling to lose two or three seats in Republican-dominated districts, legislated an at-large district to determine all the state's congressmen through statewide voting. Republicans dominated only three of thirteen counties, but Republican leaders carefully selected a slate of five popular candidates and used a statewide convention and expanding party organization to woo more voters. Republican leaders from Philadelphia helped by circulating campaign literature. With a 71 percent voter turnout and the parties' circulation of pre-filled ballots as was common at the time, the entire Republican slate was narrowly elected in late December.[5]

"Republicanus" promptly celebrated the Republican victory in song, reveling in the complete takeover of the state's congressional seats. The Newark songwriter placed the election's outcome in a longer historical narrative by writing new verses to the 1794 song "Jersey Blues." "Republicanus" appropriated the energetic, determined tone of the Federalist lyrics celebrating armed suppression of the Whiskey Rebellion and used that tone to amplify the Republican triumph. As one of the original Federalist verses had portrayed the rebels,

> Since proud ambition rears its head,
> And murders rage, and discords spread;
> To save from spoil the virtuous few,
> Dash over the mountains, Jersey Blue.

But now votes were the ammunition, and New Jersey Republicans constituted a voting militia that chased away "The lordly crew."[6] "Republicanus" summarized the election results, noting that Federalists would have to "bid adieu" to the material rewards that often followed from carrying their leaders into office:

> The *would-be* lords, that Federal swarm,
> In *dust* and *ashes* now may mourn,
> To *loaves and fishes* bid adieu,
> And dread the strength of *Jersey Blue.*

In the new lyrics, "Republicanus" proudly named each elected Republican representative—several with far more modest backgrounds than their opponents' Princeton pedigree—and dismissed the Federalists' Trenton

"Address" that had been intended to assure their victory. "Republicanus" put an exclamation point on the Republican takeover by reworking a song that had been written by the state's Federalist governor, Richard Howell. Howell, who had organized Trenton's reception of Washington in 1789, wrote "Jersey Blues" when he was commanding the New Jersey militia and the northern wing of the army sent to suppress the Whiskey Rebellion. Howell wrote the song in October 1794 at Bedford, Pennsylvania, to motivate the soldiers to march on through the Allegheny Mountains when foul weather and bad conditions combined with unrest in the camp to border on insurrection.[7] Now "Republicanus" silenced Howell's accusations of Republicans' "foul misrule and party rage" and instead asserted the party's political legitimacy and integrity through the final verse's proclamation "We'll by our CONSTITUTION stand."

While "Republicanus" focused on New Jersey Republicans' congressional gains, many Americans focused on the presidential election. Despite the election's closeness and its protracted resolution far from the public, Republican songwriters stressed that Jefferson's election was "America's choice" and reflected the "nation's voice." Inaugural celebrations were widespread. The Federalist *Gazette of the United States* promptly dismissed such celebration, claiming of one event that "the sentiments expressed in the toasts were truly Jacobinical, and such as might be relished by any United Irishmen, French Jacobins, and fugitive members of the English Corresponding Society. Their music was Ca ira, The Rights of Man, Marseilles hymn, &c."[8]

Americans' use of music in inaugural celebrations was far more complicated than the *Gazette* claimed. For Plymouth celebrations of Jefferson's inauguration, Joseph Croswell penned new lyrics to Henry Carey's "He comes, the conquering hero comes," from the masque *Britannia* (1734).[9] An intriguing example was the reworking of the English song "Lilies of France" as "A Song to Freedom" by Paterson, New Jersey, Republican Abraham Godwin. Godwin had been a fife-major in the Revolutionary War when he was barely thirteen years old. Despite having little education, he developed many talents, including writing, painting, sketching, and engraving. He played several instruments, was a talented singer, and a convivial host, and he was soon elected a Republican member of the New Jersey Assembly.[10] Shortly before Jefferson's election was decided, Godwin wrote new lyrics for "Lilies of France," a song written by David Garrick in 1756 at the beginning of the

Seven Years' War and then repurposed in the Revolutionary War. Garrick's song had predicted that in the Seven Years' War England would prevail. As the final verse commanded Britons,

> Let us take up our muskets, and gird on our swords,
> And monscieurs, ye'll find us as good as our words;
> Beat drums, trumpets sound, and huzza for our king,
> Then welcome, *Belleisle*, with what troops thou can'st bring.
> Huzza for *Old England*, whose strong-pointed lance
> Shall humble the pride and the glory of *France*.

Godwin's tune choice was anything but Francophilic, as the *Gazette* suggested of Republican celebratory song. To portray the promise of Jefferson's administration, Godwin transformed both the French "lilies" and British "roses" that had represented two warring European nations in Garrick's original into symbols of American freedom. And he replaced Garrick's war-laden imagery with naturalistic imagery. With gentle evocations of "zephyr" and "perfume," Godwin conjured a pristine state of freedom that had been destroyed in the colonial era when "to tyrant oppression thy sons all had stoop'd" and later when men (Federalists) in positions of power corrupted the nation and betrayed the principles of the Revolutionary War by making Americans "slaves to a crown" (see Figure 4.1). Freedom's flowers had become "withered" and "droop'd," but with Jefferson's election, those flowers—not accidentally the "lilies"—were "once more into bloom." Godwin's reworking both conjured the naturalistic imagery of Thomas Paine's Revolutionary era song "Liberty Tree" and foreshadowed the *Aurora*'s exuberant description of the "days of regeneration" when it celebrated the Louisiana Purchase. Godwin's lyrics, set to cheerful and confident triadic melodic figures, were sung to celebrate Jefferson's inauguration at a key Republican election organizing site.[11]

The *Gazette*'s tying of inaugural celebrations to French revolutionary songs was misleading in another respect, for Republicans celebrated their ascendance by appropriating Federalist symbols, including the best-known Federalist songs. Confidently presenting the tie between Jefferson and Aaron Burr as assurance of a Republican presidency (despite Federalists' efforts to obtain a different outcome), the editor of the Washington, Pennsylvania *Herald of Liberty* used "Hail Columbia" to articulate the significance of

Thy garden, O Freedom hath once been assail'd,
By a despotic blast and O! had it prevail'd,
Thy Lilies had withered; thy roses had droop'd,
And to tyrant oppression thy sons all had stoop'd,
　　But as one they determined the rights to maintain,
　　Thus came Britain's disgrace and America's fame.

The conquest thus lost, they with shame bore away;
Then thy radiance and lustre illumin'd our day,
Thy sons fill'd with transport, proclaim'd the decree:
They would doubtless for ages live happy and free,
　　For they fought and they conquer'd, their rights to maintain,
　　To establish thy blessing and America's fame.

**Figure 4.1.** Abraham Godwin, "A Song to Freedom." Newark *Centinel of Freedom*, 3 February 1801. Readex/NewsBank.

But our prospect how chang'd, how strange to relate
That corruption so soon should have crept in our state,
That the men we've exalted, plac'd high in renown,
Our cause should desert, and turn slaves to a crown,
While their honor they plighted our rights to maintain,
With delusions are striving to lead us in chains.

O! how alter'd the picture, how dire to unfold,
That attempts should be made thus to barter for gold;
Those high prized blessings, we bought with our blood,
And our men in high stations approv'd the deed good,
But we will go on still our rights to maintain,
And such wolves in sheep's cloathing we'll mark with disdain.

Yet O Goddess forsake not the land of thy love,
Tho the slaves of oppression with virtue have strove.
To fair virtue the palm, those deluders must yield;
Yet the transcendent virtues of JEFFERSON wield;
Our affections he merits, our rights he'll maintain,
And with BURR, our lost credit once more will regain.

**Figure 4.1.** Continued.

Republican ascendance. An early "political professional," editor John Israel had managed the western Pennsylvania campaigns of the state's leading Republicans and printed a wide range of creative and highly partisan material since founding his newspaper in 1798. He deployed through music, verse, and prose the skills he had learned from Benjamin Franklin Bache, who his father had financially supported. Recalling the frequent singing of "Hail Columbia" during the apogee of Federalist power, Israel's editorial proclaimed,

> The serenading of the Federalists which used to be heard in the summer of '98 and '99 is now turned into sighs and hollow groans, their bursts of laughter and the looks of scorn, are metamorphosed into lamentations and dejected phizes [facial expressions]; the patriotic song of "Hail Columbia, happy Land" is paraphrased by them thus, "Damn Columbia, cursed land," and "The rock on which the storm shall beat," is changed to "The shoal on which our ship has beat."

Israel made public the frustration and dejection expressed by leading Federalists like Timothy Pickering, who in early 1801 admitted that "the federal cause" was "almost crushed." Emphasizing the Federalists' fate, Israel offered new Republican lyrics for "Hail Columbia" and trumpeted Republican ascendance by noting that "the President's March," the melody to which "Hail Columbia" was sung, "is no longer considered as the true standard of Federalism."[12]

Israel circulated just one of many Republican reworkings of the most widely recognized musical expressions of Federalist dominance. Among the many songs written for Jefferson's inauguration in 1801 were several reworkings of "Hail Columbia."[13] One was by William C. Foster, an uneducated mechanic in Elizabethtown, New Jersey, who later in Jefferson's first term established himself with a cabinetmaker near Albany, New York. Foster not only wrote poetry and songs for his local New Jersey and New York newspapers but also collected them for publication in 1802, 1803, and 1805 along with other political material originally addressed to his fellow mechanics. As relatively few songs with clear attributions to mechanics have survived, Foster's work provides important insight into their production and appreciation of song.[14] In addition to reworking "Hail Columbia" as an inauguration song, Foster reworked "Adams and Liberty." Foster's new version, "Jefferson and Liberty," which had first been published in mid-1800 to motivate voters in presidential and other elections, was recirculated the next February soon after the House of Representatives resolved the electoral tie for the presidency. Writing the song from Elizabethtown in 1800 amid growing Republican organizational efforts, Foster maintained that despite the efforts of opponents and critics, "Jefferson still is America's choice,/And he will her liberties guard from invasion." Shifting to Federalists the damaging labels they had assigned to Republicans, Foster chastised the Federalists as "internal foes" and "agents of Britain" and blamed them for "kindling the fire of faction." Having reversed the Federalists' charges, Foster declared that their "calumny and falsehood" against Republicans were in vain. Advocating the Republican cause, Foster stressed the priority of peace. While in "Adams and Liberty," Robert Treat Paine had stressed war imagery and the threat of European invasion, Foster placed such wartime "gore" far away with the Roman god Mars and wished that "peace bless our dear native shore."[15]

Written to urge votes for Jefferson, Foster's reworking of "Adams and Liberty" had a continuing impact after the election's resolution. Republican songwriters soon created from Foster's "Jefferson and Liberty" new lyrics articulating similar themes using similar techniques. By the anniversary of Jefferson's inauguration, songwriters had reworked Foster's (and Paine's) lyrics to stress Jefferson's legitimacy through a lineage from Washington. In a later reworking's simplified chronology, when Washington died (in late 1799) Columbia wept, but archangels in heaven assured her "Jefferson lives!" The writer of this "New Jefferson and Liberty" used the timing of Washington's death late in Adams's term to forge Jefferson's connection to the first president and establish Jefferson as "freedom's salvation," while erasing Adams's presidency—of which Jefferson had been a part—from its historical account.[16] With such cleverly constructed historical narratives, songwriters articulated Republican ascendancy as a fated, assured development rather than a choice left to legislative intrigue.

This erasure of Adams from the presidential lineage and linkage of Washington and Jefferson became common tactics regardless of songwriters' tune choice. A New York songwriter had Washington smile from heaven and point to his apparent successor Jefferson. A New Hampshire songwriter declared, "The genius of our Washington/Revives and shines in Jefferson." Sustaining the theme through Jefferson's second term, one songwriter addressed the first president directly, reporting with pride, "Great WASHINGTON, altho' no more,/Thy virtues shine in JEFFERSON;/This Godlike son, thy chosen heir,/Protects the rights your valour won."[17] Notably, songwriters readily adopted the same vocabulary that Bache and other early vocal Republicans had decried as monarchical adulation.

Foster's reassignment and reversal of damaging labels was another staple technique used by Republican songwriters to reshape understanding of American political history. Thus one songwriter took "Anarch's storm"—a label that federalists had assigned to antifederalists in the late 1780s and that Federalists had subsequently assigned to Republicans in the 1790s—and reassigned it to the pre-Revolutionary era as a label for British oppression.[18] Perhaps the most powerful of the Republicans' many reversals of Federalists' past charges was labeling the years of extreme Federalist rhetoric and legislation the "reign of terror." In the mid-1790s, Federalists had applied this description of the French Revolution's increasing violence to the Republicans to conjure the anarchy, violence, and lawlessness that Federalists maintained would lead to the nation's demise. Republican songwriters now used "reign of terror" to encapsulate the legal violence wrought on Americans' freedoms by excessive Federalist legislation, the Alien and Sedition Acts. Republican songwriters used this phrase not only to highlight their party's triumph on anniversaries of Jefferson's inauguration and July 4 but also to demonize Federalists during election seasons to boost voter turnout in local and statewide elections. Republican editors in the mid-Atlantic states were particularly diligent in reprinting such songs as part of their effort to expand their base.[19]

## Wilson's "Jefferson and Liberty"

Of these songs claiming the end of the Federalists' "reign of terror," the most widely circulated and performed was written by the "Father of American Ornithology," Alexander Wilson. A weaver, poet, violinist, and flutist, Wilson fled his native Scotland after getting into legal trouble for circulating verses critical of the Industrial Revolution's impact on weavers. He arrived in the United States in 1794 at the age of twenty-eight, resumed weaving, and then became a schoolmaster, settling about twenty miles outside Philadelphia. For his Milestown community, he gave an oration to celebrate Jefferson's inauguration. An admirer of Jefferson, Wilson later corresponded with the president, focusing on their shared ornithological interests.[20] Back in 1800, though, Wilson focused on celebrating in song the apparent Republican triumph in the presidential election. Confidently offering a periodization of his new nation's history, he proclaimed the end of the "reign of terror" at the opening and close of his reworking of the Scottish song "Willy Was a Wanton Wag." First printed in the *Aurora*, Wilson's reworking appeared under the title "Jefferson and Liberty" and several other titles before the electoral tie was broken, and it continued to circulate into Jefferson's second term (see Figure 4.2).[21]

Wilson chose to rework a song written by the Scottish soldier and poet William Hamilton (1665? –1751). ▶ Hamilton's song, itself written to a much older tune, had appeared in multiple Scottish editions in the early eighteenth century, including Allan Ramsay's *Tea-Table Miscellany*. Hamilton signed his song with the initials W.W., standing for both the song's title character and Hamilton himself, as Hamilton had previously adopted this nickname in his correspondence with Ramsay. Hamilton's highly descriptive song painted an amusing and titillating picture of a wedding celebration where Willy, a joyous, brave, reckless, and boastful youth, steals the show. Donning a rough Shetland wool doublet, adorned with a "tag" (tassel or leather strap) at the shoulder, he impresses the ladies with his kissing and "dancing" and wins the "gree," or first place prize (see Figure 4.3). With this song choice, Wilson thus underscored the Republicans' gaining of more electoral votes and Jefferson's anticipated presidency. It also reflected a larger trend of immigrants using Scottish and Irish melodies to carry their political lyrics.[22]

PATRIOTIC SONG.

*Sung at* WALLINGFORD, *at the Republican Thankſgiving on the 11th inſt.*

TRIUMPH OF LIBERTY.

THE gloomy night before us flies,
The reign of Terror now is o'er;
Its Gags inquiſitors and Spies,
Its hords of Harpies are no more!
*Rejoice! Columbia's Sons, rejoice!*
*To tyrants never bend the knee,*
*But join with heart and ſoul and voice,*
*For* Jefferſon *and* Liberty.

O'er vaſt Columbia's varied clime,
Her Cities, Foreſts, Shores and Dales,
In riſing majeſty ſublime,
Immortal *Liberty* prevails.
*Rejoice! Columbia's Sons, rejoice, &c.*

Hail! long expected glorious day!
Illuſtrious Memorable Morn!
That Freedom's Fabric from decay,
Rebuilds—for Millions yet unborn.
*Rejoice! Columbia's Sons, &c.*

His Country's Glory, Hope and Stay,
In Virtue and in Talents try'd,
Now riſes to aſſume the ſway,
O'er Freedom's Temple to preſide.
*Rejoice! Columbia's Sons, &c.*

Within its hallow'd walls, immenſe,
No hireling hands ſhall e'er ariſe,
Array'd in Tyranny's defence,
To cruſh an injur'd People's cries,
*Rejoice! Columbia's Sons, &c.*

No Lordling here with gorging jaws
Shall wring from Induſtry the food,
Nor fiery *Bigot's* holy Laws,
Lay waſte our fields and ſtreets in blood.
*Rejoice! Columbia's Sons, &c.*

Here ſtrangers from a thouſand ſhores,
Compell'd by tyranny to roam,
Shall find amidſt abundant ſtores,
A nobler and a happier home.
*Rejoice! Columbia's Sons, &c.*

Here Art ſhall lift her laurel'd head,
Wealth, Induſtry and Peace divine,
And where dark pathleſs Foreſts ſpread,
Rich Fields and lofty Cities ſhine.
*Rejoice! Columbia's Sons, &c.*

From Europe's wants and woes remote,
A dreary waſte of waves between,
Here Plenty cheers the humble Cot,
And ſmiles on every village-green.
*Rejoice! Columbia's Sons, &c.*

Here free as Air's expanded ſpace,
To every ſoul and ſect ſhall be,
That ſacred privilege of our race,
The *Worſhip* of the *Deity*.
*Rejoice! Columbia's Sons, &c.*

Theſe Gifts great Liberty! are thine;
Ten thouſand more we owe to thee;
Immortal may their Mem'ries ſhine,
Who fought and dy'd for Liberty.
*Rejoice! Columbia's Sons, &c.*

What heart but hails a ſcene ſo bright,
What ſoul but inſpiration draws,
Who would not guard ſo dear a right,
Or die in ſuch a glorious cauſe.
*Rejoice! Columbia's Sons, &c.*

Let foes to freedom dread the name,
But ſhould they touch the ſacred Tree,
Twice fifty thouſand ſwords ſhall flame,
For JEFFERSON and LIBERTY.
*Rejoice! Columbia's Sons, &c.*

From Georgia to Lake Champlain,
From Seas to Miſſiſippi's Shore,
Ye Sons of Freedom loud proclaim
THE REIGN OF TERROR IS NO MORE.
*Rejoice! Columbia's Sons rejoice!*
*To Tyrants never bend the knee,*
*But join with heart and ſoul and voice,*
*For* JEFFERSON *and* LIBERTY.

**Figure 4.2.** Alexander Wilson, "Jefferson and Liberty." Hartford *American Mercury*, 19 March 1801. Readex/NewsBank.

In addition to bookending his song with strong declarations that the Federalists' "reign of terror" was over, Wilson foregrounded many of the keywords that the *Aurora* and other Republican newspapers had circulated to paint in stark terms the contrasting choice of virtues and vices offered by

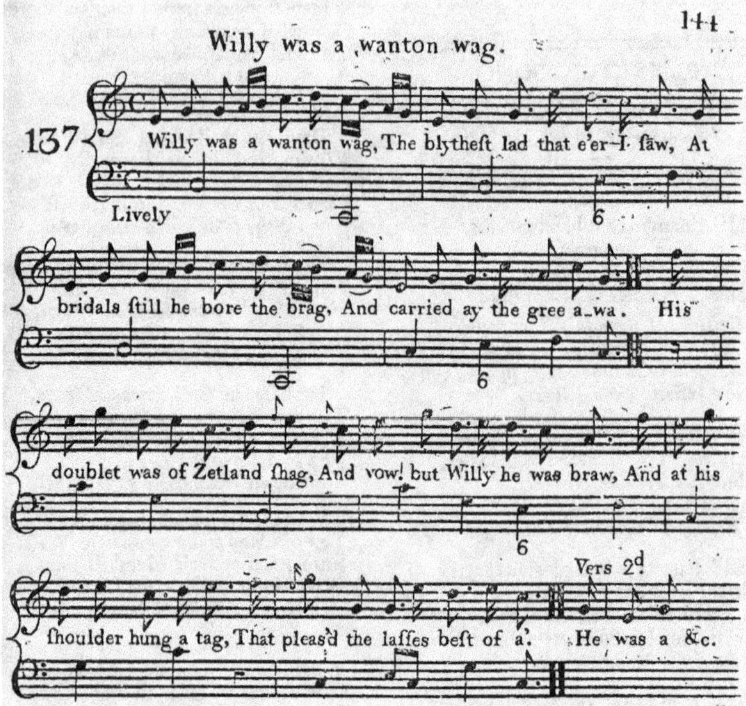


He was a man without a clag,
  His heart was frank without a flaw;
And ay whatever Willy ſaid,
  It was ſtill hadden as a law.
His boots they were made of the jag,
  When he went to the weapon-ſhaw;
Upon the green nane durſt him brag,
  The fiend a ane amang them a'.

And was not Willy well worth gowd?
  He wan the love of great and ſma';
For after he the bride had kiſs'd,
  He kiſs'd the laſſes hale-ſale a'.
Sae merrily round the ring they row'd,
  When by the hand he led them a',
And ſmack on ſmack on them beſtow'd,
  By virtue of a ſtanding law.

And was na Willy a great lown,
  As ſhyre a lick as e'er was ſeen,
When he danc'd with the laſſes round,
  The bridegroom ſpeer'd where he had been?

Quoth Willy, I've been at the ring,
  With bobbing, faith, my ſhanks are ſair:
Gae ca' your bride and maidens in,
  For Willy he dow do nae mair.

Then reſt ye, Willy, I'll gae out,
  And for a wee fill up the ring;
But ſhame light on his ſouple ſnout,
  He wanted Willy's wanton fling.
Then ſtraight he to the bride did fare,
  Says, Well's me on your bonny face;
With bobbing, Willy's ſhanks are ſair,
  And I'm come out to fill his place.

Bridegroom, ſhe ſays, you'll ſpoil the dance,
  And at the ring you'll ay be lag,
Unleſs like Willy ye advance;
  (O! Willy has a wanton leg:)
For wi't he learns us a' to ſteer,
  And formaſt ay bears up the ring:
We will find nae ſic dancing here,
  If we want Willy's wanton fling.

**Figure 4.3.** William Hamilton, "Willy Was a Wanton Wag." *The Scots Musical Museum*, vol. 2, printed in Edinburgh by James Johnson in 1788.

Republican and Federalist candidates. They had declared, "Our Country and our government are rescued from the talons of Monarchists" at a time when

An association of all that is bad in human
nature
*Leagued*
Against all that was Good.

| | | |
|---|---|---|
| Vice | | Virtue |
| Ignorance | | Learning |
| Dullness | | Talents |
| Stupidity | | Genius |
| Egotism | | Candor |
| Sophistry | | Reason |
| Declamation | | Eloquence |
| Falsehood | against | Truth |
| Vanity | | Modesty |
| Selfishness | | Liberality |
| Bigotry | | Toleration |
| Priestcraft | | Philosophy |
| Faction | | Justice |
| Monarchy | | Democracy |
| Tyranny | | Liberty |

In spite of all these
The public voice of America and of virtue
Prevails.[23]

While the *Aurora* offered blunt, unadorned dualisms in isolation, Wilson's song incorporated them in a clever, positive, engaging narrative inspired by his personal story as an immigrant. With a series of joyous exclamations and frequent alliteration, Wilson evoked the nation's potential and expressed a hopeful outlook that contrasted with the Federalist "reign of terror." His musical narrative foregrounded an idealistic America, at once pastoral and progressing, that offered religious tolerance, protection of individual freedoms, and an asylum for all kinds of immigrants. Wilson's America was a special, protected, and vast place, and his song underscored common notions of American exceptionalism and expansionism. Wilson concluded by delineating the expanse of American territory, illustrating an important shift from the global republican territory envisioned in the mid-1790s. In his version of "God Save 'The Rights of Man!' " Freneau had urged the spread of republican government to Russia and Asia, and Ann Julia Hatton, in both song and her opera *Tammany; or the Indian Chief*, described the republican expanse as reaching "From INDUS to the POLE."[24] Wilson focused instead on his new home, which had already expanded to the Mississippi and would soon stretch farther west as a long-envisioned "empire of liberty."[25]

This immigrant's song, based on an immigrant song tradition, was quickly woven into the growing tradition of American political song. By foregrounding general concepts, expressing optimism and idealism, and avoiding excessive topical or time-specific detail, Wilson wrote an enduring and popular song that had appeal across many states. His approach proved useful for several different purposes, including enhancing celebrations and motivating voters. One purpose was marking Jefferson's inauguration. Republican residents of Connecticut enjoyed and joined in performances of Wilson's song with instrumental accompaniment in inaugural celebrations held in Wallingford on March 11, 1801. This performance may have been to the jig "The Gobbio," a tune written in many American manuscripts, such as those of Marcus T. Hitchcock and Elijah Welles, under the title "Jefferson and Liberty." "The Gobbio" was the melody of an Irish song that described the sexual encounters of a promiscuous young woman in a military camp.[26] Regardless of the melody used, the local renaming of Wilson's song as the "Triumph of Liberty" captured his lyrics' value for celebrating Republican ascendance in a predominantly Federalist state. In ritual and symbolic importance, Jefferson's inauguration replaced the president's birthday celebrated during Washington's and Adams's terms. This shift represented a break from emulation of British monarchical birthday celebrations and reinforced Republicans' self-positioning as defenders of the nation against monarchical incursions. In 1805, Stanley Griswold, the editor of Walpole, New Hampshire's *Political Observatory*, reprinted Wilson's song for Jefferson's second inauguration because it was "calculated to animate the Republican, to excite his abhorrence of the evils escaped, and to remind him of the blessings obtained, by a distinguished event"—Jefferson's defeat of Adams four years earlier. Griswold would remember Wilson's song well, for he had given the sermon at Wallingford's inaugural celebration in 1801.[27] Capitalizing on the popularity of Wilson's song, other songwriters reworked "Jefferson and

Liberty" to commemorate Jefferson's inauguration and it was parodied by both Federalist and Republican songwriters.[28]

Wilson's song proved useful in elections as well. Griswold reprinted Wilson's song not only to shape perceptions of the president but also to motivate voters in upcoming elections. He exhorted his New Hampshire readers, "Rouse, freemen, rouse! and with the song of liberty in your mouth, repair to the election" for the governor's chair and Senate seats. The race gained attention across state lines and William Butler, a Republican congressman representing South Carolina, reworked Wilson's "Jefferson and Liberty" to motivate New Hampshire voters to support Langdon. Indeed, the 1805 race for governor between John Taylor Gilman and John Langdon proved to be a critical turning point for Republicans. After several years of eroding the long-serving Federalist's lead in the annual race for governor, Langdon finally defeated Gilman in 1805.[29]

Wilson's song also became a favorite for Republican celebrations of July 4. Anticipating the anniversary of independence in 1802, the Hartford *American Mercury* reprinted Wilson's "celebrated and much admired song" at its subscribers' request. In 1805, the Hudson *Bee* recorded and furthered the song's continuing popularity, explaining "As the 4th of July is approaching we anticipate the request of subscribers by giving a fourth edition of a favourite song generally sung on the occasion." Indicating that Wilson's song was to be sung "to its own tune" (whether that be the jig, the Scottish melody Wilson originally had in mind, or another tune locally known), the *Bee* demonstrated that a song known to one immigrant community could take on new life and become fully integrated into a larger political culture that had expanded to encompass numerous communities.[30]

Wilson's idealistic "Jefferson and Liberty" so aptly captured the import of Republican ascendance that it opened Jefferson's scrapbook of songs clipped from American newspapers. Although studies of Jefferson's interest in music have focused on his violin playing and sheet music collection, Jefferson, an avid newspaper reader, also preserved political songs in one of the four books of newspaper clippings from his presidency.[31] Wilson's song not only offered a strong statement of Republican ascendance but also expressed an idealistic, hopeful vision for the realization of America's potential. The placement of Wilson's song at the outset of Jefferson's political song collection provided a powerful narrative framework for a larger body of songs chronicling his presidency, with emphasis on his second term.

Beyond capturing the president's attention, Wilson's song proves that such music, often thought of as short-lived or circulated in ephemeral media, could have a remarkably long life. Wilson's "Jefferson and Liberty," written as a reworking of "Willy Was a Wanton Wag," was itself reworked by William C. Foster (relocated to Waterford, New York) in time for anniversary celebrations of Jefferson's inauguration in March 1803. Reprintings of Foster's song not only appeared in other states but also specified Wilson's intended tune. Outlasting the Jeffersonian era, Foster's reworking was itself reworked and circulated in 1828 to commemorate Andrew Jackson's inauguration on March 4, 1829.[32]

## Expanding the Historical Narrative in Song

In addition to commenting on Jefferson's election and inauguration, songwriters and song compilers offered longer historical narratives. These often conveyed the significance of Republican leadership by placing it in historical contexts extending back as far as the Revolutionary War. Both retrospective and forward-looking accounts circulated as individual songs and through expansive song collections.

Central to many of these accounts was the portrayal of Jefferson as the nation's "savior." To set up this portrayal, Republican songwriters persistently offered litanies of Federalist wrongs, such as their "gag law," fondness of armies, raising of taxes, and slave-like treatment of citizens.[33] In early 1801, a Pennsylvania songwriter chose the popular tune "Vicar and Moses" about a drunk parson and his clerk to emphatically narrate Adams's offenses in fourteen new, comical verses sarcastically titled "Adams and Liberty." The songwriter called the Republicans' defeat of Adams in the electoral college a "rout," playing on the word's dual meanings of rabble and sound defeat to emphasize how the Federalists' demise was brought about by those they considered the Democratic "rabble."[34] In the context of these Federalist offenses, Jefferson was, after Washington, the nation's "second savior" who would rescue "the sinking nation" and a "God-like" and "immortal" leader who would spread the message of freedom throughout the world. These songwriters took the technique of presidential apotheosis already applied to Washington and Adams and rooted in representations of the British monarchy and used it to valorize not monarchy or aristocracy but rather democratic egalitarianism and individual freedoms. Such representations of Jefferson as savior persisted for years in commemorations of his inauguration and July 4.[35]

Supporting this narrative, songwriters provided steady updates measuring Republicans' progress in righting Federalist offenses. Jefferson himself saved a musical marker of his administration's and party's success first published in the Wilmington, Delaware, *Mirror*. In "The Progress of Federalism," a songwriter from nearby New Castle celebrated the Republican-led repeal of the Judiciary Act of 1801. Linking the federal decision to Delaware's history, the songwriter humorously narrated the fate of Richard Bassett, a Revolutionary War veteran, former Delaware governor, and senator whom Adams had appointed as a "midnight judge" on the eve of Jefferson's inauguration. Bassett, along with Adams's other last-minute Federalist judicial appointments, was subsequently removed in 1802 when the act was repealed during a period of strong cooperation between Jefferson and the Congress.[36] Songs responding immediately to such political moments may seem to be of fleeting interest, yet they were captured and preserved in song collections, like Jefferson's clippings books, that incorporated them in a larger historical statement.

Two such song collections were created by committed Republican activists in Philadelphia whose use of music has been largely overlooked: Daniel Ebsworth and William Duane. Ebsworth was an auctioneer. He was derided by Federalists as a "drunken bell-ringer" who was known for "writing doggerel ballads for the crowd." The 1800 census put his residence between Spruce and South Streets, where he was likely supporting his wife, two young sons, and at least four daughters. As an Irish immigrant's newspaper reported, in December 1801 Ebsworth's wife gave birth to twin boys, named in celebratory verse "Jefferson" and "Aaron" after the president and vice president.[37] Much more is known of William Duane. Duane was born in 1760 in Newfoundland to Irish parents; after traveling for a period in North America, his widowed mother then raised him in Ireland amid growing resistance to British rule. Duane began his journalistic career in London and then immigrated to India, where his outspoken editorial style got him arrested, imprisoned, and placed in solitary confinement. He returned to London where he became the editor of the London Corresponding Society's journal. With a mindset shaped by Painite democratic egalitarianism, Duane immigrated to the United States in 1796. Almost penniless, he settled his family in Philadelphia, where he joined Republican activists centered at Benjamin Franklin Bache's *Aurora* and the American Society of the United Irishmen.

When Bache's chief editorial writer James Callender fled to Richmond to escape the Sedition Act, Duane replaced him. Then Duane became the newspaper's editor when Bache died just over a year later. Duane quickly became a powerful Republican printer and activist and is often credited with facilitating Jefferson's rise to the presidency. Disappointingly, Duane received no political patronage in return for his helping Republicans win elections.[38] Nevertheless, both Duane and Ebsworth remained active in Philadelphia politics and sustained a Republican musical voice.

Ebsworth was responsible for two important Republican song collections: his non-extant *The Republican Harmonist* of May 1800 and a second edition that was printed in Boston in 1801 and sold and advertised in Philadelphia and New York.[39] This 141-page collection featured songs written by Ebsworth and others; many lack attribution. Ebsworth's intent to use songs and song collections to craft a historical narrative can be seen in his introduction to his 1801 collection. Ebsworth noted the "historical and narrative" nature of his own songs and implied their intended use when he admitted that in length they exceeded "the bounds usually prescribed to convivial compositions."[40] He established a strong historical perspective by beginning the collection with about nineteen of his own songs that ranged from general historical narratives of the nation to accounts of the Federalists' fall and their eclipse by leading Republicans at both the state and federal levels. Ebsworth's collection gathered individual musical accounts of the Revolutionary era, the XYZ era, and the Republican ascent as recounted in the election and inauguration of Thomas Jefferson and Pennsylvania governor Thomas McKean. He established through song a longer narrative of Republican triumph that was rooted in the nation's early revolutionary trials and that overcame Federalist vices to lead the nation on a proper path of reason and virtue, echoing the dualisms made so clear in the *Aurora*.

William Duane sustained this historical narrative when he updated and reorganized Ebsworth's *The Republican Harmonist* in 1803 as the 130-page collection *The American Republican Harmonist*. Duane preserved from Ebsworth's collection the individual musical accounts of the Revolutionary era, the XYZ era, and the Republicans' ascent. Elaborating this historical arc, Duane also preserved from Ebsworth's collection many detailed and lengthy accounts of political episodes that would otherwise be of fleeting interest, including detailed ballad-like accounts of the intrigues and activities surrounding individual elections. To these Duane added detailed accounts of recent election battles and political debates through October 1803.

Duane lengthened his narrative of Republican triumph by adding many songs written and performed for July 1803 celebrations. In several of these songs, songwriters creatively erased John Adams from American history by highlighting Jefferson's early role in gaining the nation's independence, followed by Washington.[41]

The months following Duane's collection solidified a lasting component of the Republicans' historical narrative: peace. While Federalists like Joseph Dennie stubbornly circulated the stereotypical portrayal of Republicans as anarchical, lawless creators of violent conditions,[42] Republican songwriters foregrounded their role in maintaining peace and avoiding embroilment in war. A New Hampshire songwriter reworking Wilson's "Jefferson and Liberty" mentioned "peace" no less than six times, and in the final verse said of the warring European nations, "Let them contend who'll rule the sea,/Our Glory's Jefferson and Peace." Republicans sounded this theme in political organizations, such as the New York Tammany Society, and during spring elections for governorships and Senate seats.[43]

From 1803, Republicans magnified this prioritization of peace through the Louisiana Purchase. American leaders, including Federalists, had long been attentive to the value of this territory. When Americans learned in early July 1803 of a treaty arranging for the acquisition of the immense territory by purchase, it was quickly hailed in song as an exemplar of Republican efforts to avoid war. After Spain had ceded Louisiana to France in 1802 and prohibited the deposit of US goods in New Orleans for export, Federalists and westerners had fueled war rhetoric, and Americans feared that Napoleon would use Saint-Domingue (present-day Haiti) to establish an empire in North America. A slave revolt in Saint-Domingue and the escalating American war rhetoric ultimately resulted in Napoleon's offer to sell Louisiana by the time American diplomats arrived in France.[44]

The "peaceful acquisition" of Louisiana was a major occasion for celebration and was widely seen as providing a buffer zone between the United States and external forces. With the acquisition, the values stressed in song by Alexander Wilson when Jefferson assumed the presidency were amplified and quickly became part of an extended and lasting narrative about Jefferson's impact on America's future. These values included the intertwined importance of diplomacy, the avoidance of war, geographic expansion, plenty, peace, and a boundless future. Songwriters detailed the efforts of the administration to stay out of European conflict, stressing that its diplomatic skill even lessened domestic rivalry and preserved the union while expanding the nation's territory.[45] In a song called "Louisiana," Andrew Selden, a Massachusetts native who became a Vermont lawyer and justice of the peace, lavished praise on Jefferson.[46] Selden explained, "While the despots of Europe run mad from their birth,/Give rivers of blood for a hillock of earth;/Thy chieftain, Columbia, unpractis'd in spoil,/Gains realms for thy sons, without bloodshed or toil." Selden looked forward to the economic gains from acquiring territory that Federalists had intended to be a battlefield, effusing "Now down the broad river rich commerce shall roll,/ Where lawless invaders ungovern'd did stroll;/And temples of liberty rise and enchant,/Where late the wild war whoop rung dire in the haunt." Selden challenged European and Federalist inclinations to war through his choice of melody. He set his verses to "Black Sloven," a British tune that Americans had frequently used as a marching air in the Revolutionary War, turning it into a celebration of peace. ▶ As Selden also invoked a long-standing association of monarchy and war, he reinforced Republicans' commitment to a republican government based on the active participation of the people.[47] This was significant given that the Louisiana Purchase stokked long-standing concerns about the fragility of republics and the idea that the "centrifugal forces" unleashed in a large state could only be counteracted through a strong central government inclining toward despotism.[48]

Once the purchase was finalized, music was part of large celebrations in New Orleans and Washington as well as other celebrations across the country. Music praising the acquisition repeatedly stressed Jefferson's pursuit of peace, effective use of negotiations, establishment of friendly relations with European nations, and avoidance of bloodshed, glorifying the fact that war had been "banished from our frontiers." But the Republicans' emphasis on peace through this narrative was selective; the nation was actually embroiled in the Tripolitan War. The North African states of Tripoli, Tunis, Algeria, and Morocco fostered piracy and privateering, which yielded proceeds from vessels, goods, and slaves and pressured other nations to pay annual tribute as protection from future attacks. Dissatisfied with the United States' handling of its tribute agreements, in May 1801 the Bashaw of Tripoli declared war. Calculating annual tribute as costlier than a display of naval strength to force favorable negotiations, Jefferson led the United States into a five-year war. So while the narrative of Republican ascendance gained influence through repetition, it was a selective and constructed account. Meanwhile, through the *Aurora*, William Duane exuberantly announced a National Jubilee to celebrate the acquisition of Louisiana, to be held on May

12, 1804, the anniversary of the Republican Tammany Society. Holding a "national" celebration on a historically Republican day, particularly in the year of a presidential election, Duane reveled in the party's near-thorough dominance of the country.[49]

## Contesting the Narrative

Federalists quickly lost ground and became concentrated in New England, with other significant groups remaining in New York, Maryland, and South Carolina. Throughout Jefferson's first term, Federalists suffered further Republican inroads in New England, where Attorney General Levi Lincoln and Postmaster Gideon Granger helped strengthen the region's Republican press. Republican election organization and mobilization efforts continued in New England, often featuring music. By 1804, Republicans could narrate their regional gains in song, including Senate and House seats representing New Hampshire and Massachusetts, respectively.[50] Federalists used a multifaceted approach to challenge their opponents and their narrative of Republican ascendance in song. Federalists protested the Republicans' account of history, penned stinging satires, and launched vitriolic attacks as they celebrated key anniversaries and contested elections. Periodicals such as Joseph Dennie's Federalist *Port Folio* and Levi Lincoln's Republican Worcester *National Aegis* were among the important outlets for escalating partisan exchanges in song and musical commentary.

Republican success in marginalizing Federalists and its impact on musical rhetoric can be seen in Portsmouth, New Hampshire, where at an annual town meeting just weeks after Jefferson's inauguration, residents voted to rename "the Town Hall" above the market "Jefferson Hall." Local Republicans continued to gain sway later that year, and by the following July 4, Republicans were celebrating in Jefferson Hall and Federalists were celebrating separately.[51] Local Federalists sang a vitriolic ode by Jonathan Mitchell Sewall that rejected both the Republicans' assertions of political legitimacy and the transformation and dedication of the town's public space to the Republican cause. Sewall challenged his Republican counterparts' efforts to boost Jefferson's legitimacy by positing a direct lineage with Washington. Sewall declared, "The diff'rence how vast! In sense, genius, and worth,/ 'Twixt Vernon's great Chief, and his present successor!" Although he was reworking "Adams and Liberty," Sewall made no reference to Adams and instead, through forced rhetoric, called Portsmouth Federalists to look back to Washington and the values that he represented. In doing so, Sewall presaged the tactics of the Washington Benevolent Societies, which Federalists would form in future years. Denying historical facts and his party's own status as a national minority, Sewall claimed that "No dire factions" had spoiled Washington's era and accused Republicans of fueling contemporary faction. His backward-looking and revisionist narrative encapsulated the futility of the Federalists' cause and their inability to appeal to voters.[52]

While some Federalists rewrote history, others resorted to personal attacks and harsh satire. In their intensifying personal attacks, Federalists emulated William Cobbett, whose influence persisted after he returned to England. Although they had fiercely objected to the publication of slanderous writings by Republicans in the late 1790s, Federalists relied on character attacks to challenge their opponents' dominant narrative. In fact, as Pasley has stressed, in their newspapers Federalists "far outdid their Republican opponents in scurrilous and viciously personal defamation." Federalists sustained Cobbett's lurid language and attacks on politicians' personal lives and character. A repeated target was John Dawson of Virginia. To paint the Republican congressman as a lazy diplomat neglecting his duties and comparing him to a naïve, superficial young woman mesmerized by Parisian fashions, fine food, and gifts, Federalist songwriters reworked the eponymous air "Nancy Dawson," which had been popularized by an eighteenth-century Covent Garden dancer. Emily Mifflin, the wife of Joseph Hopkinson and daughter of Pennsylvania governor Thomas Mifflin, penned "Nancy Dawson's Return," casting the congressman on his return from carrying John Adams's dispatches to France as an expert in wigs, dresses, and lace.[53]

Women were not only writers and means of such attacks but also objects of them. One target was a Massachusetts woman who dared to write political verse and put her name on it. This "Sutton Songstress" wrote "Stanzas to Thomas Jefferson" predicting that his name would rival Washington's. Joseph Dennie instantly seized on this transgressive act of political publication by a woman, much like William Cobbett had attacked Susanna Rowson years earlier when she presented her play *Slaves in Algiers*. Dennie's target, "Rosanna Maria of Sutton," had transgressed twice before, asserting in an editorial that women were men's equals and singling out several Federalist newspapers for impinging on the rights of both. Attaching a woman's name to political "stanzas," Rosanna Maria defied the expectation that a woman, if she wrote verse, should adopt a pseudonym or remain an anonymous "lady," as Emily Mifflin had done when she mocked John Dawson in song. Joseph Dennie, writing as "Oliver Oldschool," promptly critiqued the versification skills of the "Sutton Songstress" and chastised Francis Blake, one of the editors of the *National Aegis*, for publishing such poor material. In the *Aegis*, "P. Prosody" responded with a line-by-line comparison of verses published in the *Port Folio* with verses from "Sternhold and Hopkins," the long-ridiculed sixteenth-century collection of English metrical settings of the Hebrew psalms. Turning the discussion back to the partisan heart of the conflict, "P. Prosody" sarcastically declared that to satisfy the likes of Oldschool, the "Sutton Songstress" would have to sing praises to King George III.[54]

Working with Levi Lincoln to advance the Republican cause in traditionally Federalist New England, Francis Blake became a common target of Federalists' attacks. Blake effusively praised William C. White's song for Worcester anniversary celebrations of Jefferson's inauguration in 1803. Levi Lincoln regarded White's "Patriotic Ode" as "one of the most animating and best composed songs" he had encountered on such an occasion. Lincoln's assessment drew on "feeling" rather than "judgment or taste," and it reflected music's relevance for the sensibility that Knott has shown to be intimately tied up with the Revolution and founders' efforts to shape the nation.[55] Federalist Charles Prentiss, a Massachusetts native and editor of the Baltimore *Republican or Anti-Democrat*, mocked Francis Blake's praise of the song and analyzed its poetical weaknesses in the manner of "Oldschool." Expanding his attack to encompass Jefferson's character, Prentiss stressed the song's "imbecility" and the "immorality" of singing Jefferson's praises in a house of worship given his character. Men would only write such uninformed praise if they were seeking an office, Prentiss argued. Exacerbating the attack was White's turncoat status: White had previously written Federalist verse and was accused of conveniently switching allegiances in sync with the Republicans' ascendance to gain a political appointment.[56]

To escalate the partisan ruckus over White's song, both Prentiss and his Republican parodist "Roderick Rhymeall" of Sutton, Massachusetts, used African American musical characters and music-making. Prentiss's parody of White's song cast an African American fiddler as the muse to mock White, while "Rhymeall" replaced the fiddler with a jew's harp player, joined by Cato and Quash, to parody Prentiss's parody. Prentiss filled his parody with "grunts," "squeals," and "yelps," drawing on the contemporary association of animals, slaves, and criminals as makers of noise, in contrast to free people who make sounds. Prentiss outdid White's original in sensory imagery by featuring the black fiddler's teeth-baring smile, the Republicans' "screaking howls," and Jefferson's "flatt'rers" licking his "great toes."[57]

Taking inspiration from William C. White's awkward commanding of the Muse to "sweep the thrilling chords of joy," one Massachusetts Federalist turned to other African American characters and penned the parody "The Master Sweep to His Apprentice." By referencing the familiar street cries and songs of chimney sweeps, the parodist tied the new verses to White's song while leveraging the stark contrast between Republicans' overblown ebullience and the black chimney sweeps' dangerous and lethal work to highlight Republican hypocrisy and bombast. White's command to "Fling, fling" the song "to the echoing sky" became the master sweep's ordering of a young black boy to "Fling, fling, your soot on all around." In a parody inflected by class and race, the Federalist used a child commanded to "sweep with joy" when laboring in unbearable conditions to highlight the hypocrisy of Republicans' praise for slave-owning Jefferson as the sage of liberty and freedom.[58]

The effect of these parodic techniques was to portray Republicans as incompetent leaders and highlight the hypocrisy of Republican claims to be champions of liberty while sustaining and benefiting from slavery. Using African American characters to criticize political opponents was not new. Francis Hopkinson did it when sketching his imaginary antifederal procession that moved to the "Dead March" from Handel's oratorio *Saul* played on hurdy-gurdy, jew's harp, and banjo. But now such material was being published. Such musical publications appeared after Jefferson's election amid increasing Republican organization in New England and the exposure of Jefferson's interracial sexual relationship with his slave Sally Hemings in 1802.[59]

Federalist songwriters featured another character, the Irish "alien," to attack the Republican editors who worked closely with party organizers. Extending the xenophobia that had become so prominent in the late 1790s, most notably through the Alien Acts, Alexander Hamilton's *New York Evening Post* circulated new lyrics fitted to the Irish tune "Ally Croker" that portrayed a "Larry O'Shanahan" recruiting more "patriotic aliens"—described as the filth and murderers of Europe—to be editors under Jefferson's patronage.[60] Such lyrics publicly circulated criticism expressed in private correspondence by leading Federalists such as Abigail Adams. After reading an account of a Republican celebration in Kentucky, she declared, "Hence, wretches, to your native dens—the bogs of Ireland, the dens of Scotland, and the outcasts of Britain."[61]

The real target of such attacks was William Duane. Federalists took Duane as a metonym for their Republican challengers and the inspiration for characters like "Larry O'Shanahan." A peripatetic "Citizen of the World," Duane became a US citizen in 1802 and worked hard to shape and defend his persona against xenophobia.[62] Duane's response to the Federalists' xenophobic attacks can be seen in his song collection *The American Republican Harmonist*, an updated and reorganized version of Daniel Ebsworth's *The Republican Harmonist.* But while Ebsworth had subtitled his collection "*a Select Collection of Republican, Patriotic, and Sentimental Songs, Odes, Sonnets &c. American and European*," Duane eliminated the reference to Europe and emphatically offered his collection of songs and odes as "*Written in America, on American Subjects and Principles*." By doing so he stressed that Republican principles were truly integral to the American nation. Responding further to the Federalists' long-standing attacks against French and Irish immigrants, Duane included a song that highlighted the hypocrisy of the Federalists' xenophobia. The song began "An American born, I all foreigners hate," but as it went on, it became clear that this Federalist xenophobia was in fact a selective one stemming from loyalty to England.[63]

Along with rewriting history and attacking opponents' character, another essential part of the Federalists' musical arsenal was satire. Satire was particularly relished by those Kerber dubbed "articulate Federalists," who used satire to reach the middling ranks who were less likely to be influenced by serious rhetoric. Satire provided an ideal vehicle for expressing Federalists' resentment, jealousy, and bitterness over the Republicans' ascendance and their dismay at seeing America develop in ways they did not understand or approve. Common targets of Federalist satire included Jefferson's love of experimentation, invention, and natural history and his many "projects."[64]

One of these "projects" was Jefferson's naval plans. Proponents of a large, European-style offensive navy, Federalists mocked Jefferson's redirection of the navy around the construction of gunboats and a dry dock. Gunboats were floating, single-cannon batteries intended to make the navy a defensive institution for US coastal waters; the dry dock was designed to preserve in peacetime the sizable investment already made in frigates.[65] Challenging this small, defensive, peace-oriented navy, Federalist songwriters used musical humor to portray the gunboats and dry dock as incapable of dealing with European fleets.

One song, titled "The Pride of the Navy; or, Gun-Boat No. One," placed the diminutive single-gun vessel in a comical battle with a seventy-four-gun ship of the line (see Figure 4.4). Gunboat No. 1 was ideal for ridiculing Jefferson's naval plans because shortly after going into commission it was blown seven miles inland by a hurricane and left stranded in a Georgia cornfield. The anonymous Federalist songwriter took inspiration from Charles Dibdin's "Poor Jack," a song from his 1788 musical London entertainment *The Whim of the Moment.* ▶ This was just one of Dibdin's many popular songs about the sea that quickly became part of British naval and national musical traditions and circulated in the United States. Imitating Dibdin's clever use of nautical terms and slang, the Federalist songwriter criticized not only Jefferson's plans for a defensive navy but also his administration's emphasis—as touted through Republican discourse—on maintaining peace through diplomacy and payment. The songwriter portrayed Jefferson as an admiral happier to "palaver" and "patter" (fuss and talk) about combat than to conduct it. Eager to avoid conflict altogether, the admiral promised that the gunboat could "scud" or sail quickly out of trouble should a warship appear; the final verse sarcastically lauded the dry dock as the ultimate goal—a safe escape from open-water combat. The admiral was the antithesis of Dibdin's original "Poor Jack," who feared nothing that the sea might bring. With such satire, Federalists made an about-face, replacing their 1790s caricature of the dangerous democrat with an exaggerated and simplified image of the Republican as a peace-loving wimp. In doing so, they capitalized on the Republicans' own narrative that tied Jefferson to peace. Federalists cast Jefferson's gunboat and dry dock plans as further proof of a misguided sense of economy that would cost the nation more in the long run than it saved. In the blunt words of an often-reprinted song performed at Salem July 4 celebrations, the Federalists maintained, "For still 'tis Our song, that they calculate wrong,/Who save at the spigot, and spend at the bung."[66] Songs like "The Pride of the Navy" cast Republican leadership as profoundly misguided.

Another target of Federalist satire was Republican electioneering and organizational efforts. Song had already been tied up with electioneering, as Republicans used songs to carry out, promote, and recount their electioneering efforts.[67] Jefferson's victory and Levi Lincoln's activism had prompted more Republicans in Essex County, Massachusetts, to transform the *Salem Register* into a partisan paper, increase their organizational efforts in advance of elections, and engage in electioneering. In 1802, campaigning rose "above blood heat" and congressional elections included a particularly "violent contest" in which Republicans defeated prominent Federalists John Quincy Adams and former secretary of state Timothy Pickering. These were

FROM THE UTICA PATRIOT.

*THE PRIDE OF THE NAVY;*
OR,
GUN-BOAT NO, ONE.

(Parodied; and to the tune of "Go patter to lubbers.")

You may laugh ye *land lubbers*, and joke d'ye see,
'Bout BOAT *number* ONE of the Navy;
A "*whirligig gun*" in a *shallop* give me
To blow *British ships* to Old Davy.
Should John Bull's *seventy-fours* dare hazard a fight,
By my soul, we will shew them what's civil,
Hoist boom—fire away—then *scud* right and tight,
And *frighten* them all to the d***l.
What then! avast sniv'ling! my lads never fear,
Our Adm'ral will keep us from harm,
On the banks of Potomac, high and dry, free and clear,
Is a DRY DOCK——a birth snug and warm.

I heard our *brave* Adm'ral palaver one day,
'Bout "BLOODY ARENAS" and such,
But he might full as well have had nothing to say,
"For 'twas just all as one, as high-dutch:"
Yet he said, how a *gun-boat* might *scud* d'ye see,
Should a *big man-of-war* heave in sight,
And many such things, that prov'd clearly to me,
He had much rather *patter* than *fight*.
What cheer then my lads, you have nothing to fear,
Our Adm'ral to danger's a foe,
On the banks of Potomac, high and dry, free and clear,
In a DRY DOCK—he'll take us in tow.

Figure 4.4. "The Pride of the Navy; or, Gun-Boat No. One." New York *Commercial Advertiser*, 23 October 1804. Readex/NewsBank.

I said to the FEDS—for you see they look'd queer,
  When we first put our *gun-boat* to sea,
What argufies tossing your heads with a sneer,
  Why what *swabs* and *land-lubbers* you be;
Don't you see in *shoal* water, we *safely* can ride,
  'Tis as good as a CAVE on the shore;
And if we *should* happen to get a *broad side*,
  Why, *you never will hear of us, more!*
What then, all's a hazard;—gi' us none of your fun,
  Our Adm'ral's the lad yet for me,
We'll *scare* off the DONS, with his whirligig gun,
  Then to DRY DOCK—as snug as a flea.

A *gun-boat* d'ye mind me, all danger can shun,
  'Tis the *trim* of its "*trimming*" projector;
Not a skiff on th' ocean, d'ye see, can *outrun*,
  This *skiff* of our NAVAL DIRECTOR.
Come then, my brave tars, let us man right and tight,
  We have *no* naval tactics to learn;
Should we meet an *arm'd* ship 'twould be *folly* to fight,
  Veer about then—and leave her *a-stern*.
Huzza'! who's afraid! when there's nothing to fear,
  *Keep well from the clutches of Davy!*
To the banks of Potomac, for a DRY DOCK quick steer,
  Your *gun boat*—the *pride* of the *navy*.

Figure 4.4. Continued.

dire developments in the stronghold of Federalist leadership known as the Essex Junto.[68]

Local Federalist anger over the 1802 election results surfaced in a vicious satirical musical attack on Republicans and their electioneering practices—a cantata called *The Caucus, with the Standard of Faction*. Multimovement cantatas had been written on political topics throughout the early national period, and they were typically circulated in newspapers with indications such as "recitative," "air," "chorus," and "grand chorus" but with no musical notation and sometimes no indications of tunes. *The Caucus* cast local Republican spokesmen as drunk, inconstant, deceitful, self-interested, and untrustworthy immigrants who were "pretenders to freedom." It specifically targeted prominent Salem Republicans such as lawyer and future Supreme Court justice Joseph Story and Unitarian minister and polymath William Bentley, both of whom wrote for the *Salem Register*. The final air, a reworking of the English song "Derry Down"—long used for American partisan political debate—featured a faithful, undaunted Federalist who emerged from the "bellowing band" of voters to warn of the Republicans' true character. The Federalist songwriter turned the Republicans' favored symbol, the liberty pole, against them:

> Its bottom, so artfully fix'd under ground,
> Resembles their scheming so low & profound
> The dark underminings and base dirty ends
> On which the success of the faction depends.
> *Derry Down.*[69]

Such songs mocking Republican electioneering and organizational efforts allowed Federalists to attack their opponents while presenting themselves as above the act of electioneering. When Republicans organized a festival in 1803 in New Haven marking the anniversary of Jefferson's inauguration, the Federalist press exposed a letter circulated among Republicans making clear that the festival was intended to organize support for the April elections for governor and the lower house.[70] In this event, Republicans were building on the successful precedent established at Wallingford in 1801, which had gathered a large contingent of Republicans from various parts of the state before spring elections. Two years later, Federalists penned mock odes for the New Haven festival that not only ridiculed Republican party activists but also challenged Republicans on issues of national scope where they had reversed Federalist policies and appointments by repealing internal taxes, diminishing the size of the navy, and terminating judicial appointments.

One mock ode by Theodore Dwight captured the Federalists' desperation in shocking terms. Dwight, recalled as an "amiable," "disinterested" man who possessed an "almost womanly sensibility to human suffering," produced cutting political satire. To attack Republican organizational efforts, Dwight parodied Isaac Watts's 148th Psalm ("Ye tribes of Adam join"), which

Connecticut Republicans planned to sing at their festivities. This psalm was often sung to Lewis Edson's "Lenox." Dwight's verses pretended to be an ode sung at the end of the day's festivities as Republicans retired for their evening enjoyments. In the lyrics he portrayed the festival as overtaken by Moll Carey, the proprietress of a notorious New York brothel. Dwight ridiculed a dozen local Republican leaders by last name or nickname—including those who organized the festival—and portrayed one "panting" after coming under Carey's spell.[71]

Dwight's satire illustrated local Federalist hypocrisy. Despite Dwight's and other Federalists' dismissals of electioneering, New England Federalists actually adopted many of the Republicans' strategies.[72] And while Federalist newspapers in the state had decried the organizers' design of the festival to attract both sexes, Dwight's song stooped far lower with its explicit imagery. The Republican *American Mercury* responded at length with charges of hypocrisy, blasphemy, and obscenity in two separate editorials, specifically noting the inappropriateness of such content in newspapers that circulated in families to wives and children. Commenting on Dwight's act of parodying the song, one editorialist asked, "Is there a man or woman in Connecticut, who in their sense, will justify the substitution of Moll Carey in place of the one infinite God?" Making the impact of Dwight's writing seem even more offensive, one writer reported that the daughter of a local Federalist councillor had already memorized the lyrics and sung them "in company." After commenting on the hypocrisy of New England Federalists' moral righteousness and pretense of piety, one Republican editorialist concluded that "federalists, finding that their cause is sinking, are desirous to tear down the whole fabric of society, and to expire in the general wreck of delicacy, modesty, morals, civil rights and religion." Designed to arouse strong emotions like contempt, the crudeness and punch of Dwight's satire were effective counterweights to the bombastic rhetoric and elaborate, at times far-fetched imagery used by Federalists Jonathan Mitchell Sewall and Robert Treat Paine. Dwight's parody captured enough attention to be referenced in Federalist newscarrier's addresses for two more years and was reportedly recalled for decades.[73]

## Counternarrative

While Republicans reiterated and refined their narrative of national ascent and legitimacy, Federalists offered a counternarrative. New England

Federalists adopted an increasingly regional outlook. This regional perspective can be seen in their deeming Republicans a faction, a perspective at odds with Republican dominance on a national scale. This regional outlook also manifested as expressions of regional supremacy and secessionist visions. An early and controversial musical expression of a regional supremacist view was "Rule New England," Robert Treat Paine's 1802 ode for the Massachusetts Charitable Fire Society.[74] Paine regularly wrote songs for the society's meetings to elect their officers and raise funds; an earlier example was "Adams and Liberty." Through the voice of the Boston singer and composer of the musical setting of "Rule New England," Francis Mallet, Paine declared "New England rules and saves."[75] To create a compelling account of this regional supremacy, Paine used some of the same narrative and rhetorical techniques that Republicans used. To motivate Massachusetts Federalists, Paine hyperbolically portrayed the nation as being in dire danger and needing rescue. He cast Liberty as the victim, as Virginia Republicans had in their 1801 inauguration pageant. In Paine's version, though, Liberty points to New England as her savior, rather than Jefferson. Paine declared New England the first part of the nation to "toil and bleed" for freedom. Invoking an outmoded concept of exclusionary classical republicanism, Paine touted New England as "Still true to virtue." To establish foils for the stalwart New England Federalists, he used the tired catchwords "Faction" and "Anarch," labels for political opposition since the late 1780s, but he instantly brought the Federalists' opponents to life in his fourth verse with a vivid image of demons in a graveyard. Paine quickly moved from vivid imagery to fantasy, claiming that democracy was doomed to disappear and Federalists were destined to enjoy a resurgence, alluding to the annual reelection of Federalist Caleb Strong as Massachusetts governor over Republican Elbridge Gerry.

"Rule New England" quickly sparked criticism. While often ephemeral, songs were analyzed as literature, at least when politically convenient. The *National Aegis* attacked the literary quality of Paine's song, and one of his friends defended it, quoting Milton and Shakespeare to deflate the accusation of plagiarism and "monstrous and misshapen" imagery. Interpreting and defending Paine's imagery by stressing the accuracy of his portrayal, his friend explained that one "figure thus presents Delusion in the shape of a Necromancer, infecting a nation's veins with her poisonous drugs, till Truth, overcome by her 'brew'd enchantments,' sleeps in chains. This we think too is not the less fine poetry because no fiction."[76] A Massachusetts Charitable Fire Society member complained in print about the imposition of such songs on the society, while the charitable donations had been "taxed" to pay Paine. In Boston, the *Independent Chronicle* mocked Paine's song as a sign of the Federalists' demise. The controversy was picked up by editors as far south as Charleston, attracted the notice of Jefferson, and was relished by Federalists outside New England for the upset Paine had caused among Republicans.[77]

New England Federalists' fundamental concerns were made explicit when a Republican from Salem promptly penned a reworking of "Rule New England" called "Let Congress Rule." As the song argued, "patriot statesmen" in congress, "unaw'd by faction" would set the nation on the right course. However, New England Federalists felt that they were outvoiced by southern Republicans. As "A Federalist" detailed in a commentary on "Rule New England," the five New England states had a larger free population but eleven fewer Representatives than four southern states.[78] This was due to the three-fifths compromise, an agreement reached in forming the Constitution in 1787 that each slave as would be counted as three-fifths of a person when determining a state's population for the purposes of apportioning representatives, presidential electors, and taxes.

Elaborating this complaint, New England Federalists supported Paine's argument of sectional supremacy and elaborated it into a secessionist vision. Their defense made clear why Congress's rule was unacceptable. Quoting Paine's lyrics, the *Boston Gazette* used a medical analogy to advocate secession and declared:

> "New England first in freedom's van"; the first to quell insurrection, and establish order, is not to be nosed about, and subjected to the visionary philosophiste of bloated and besotted Virginia and her satellites. It is better to apply the amputating knife at once, than to tamper with probes and plasters when the morbid member has become incureable.—The steady habits, moral energies, and physical force of New England must 'Rule,' or they will be subdued into Liberty by the logic of gunpowder, and the persuasion of the bayonet.[79]

As the *Gazette* explained, Virginia and the rest of the southern states were bloated with representation in the House of Representatives and the electoral college. New England Federalists refused to submit to the "tyranny" of a dissipated, autocratic Virginia that empowered Republican hypocrisy. And the "visionary philosophiste," the president mocked by Federalists for experimental, speculative reforms that they considered unsound and impractical, was an unacceptable leader.[80] With New England cast as the moral center of the nation, it was time to amputate the corrupted South. Amid recurring concerns of disunion, "Rule New England" prompted early expressions of secessionism before a series of Republican actions in 1803 would catalyze a formal secession plot.[81]

Federalists increasingly articulated their counternarrative through satire and crude, explicit character attacks. Key material came from the Scottish immigrant editor James Callender, who had turned on Jefferson and aided Federalists after not receiving the Richmond postmaster appointment as a reward for his previous efforts in support of the Republican cause. Callender's polemics in the Federalist Richmond *Recorder* had far-reaching effects, for as Pasley notes, Federalists "eagerly disseminated and embellished Callender's various aspersions on President Jefferson's personal and political morality," including his 1802 accounts of Jefferson's extended interracial sexual relationship with Sally Hemings, who was his slave and his deceased wife's half-sister.[82] In New England, the mid-Atlantic, and the South, Federalists elaborated the political significance of their relationship in verse. Among those Federalist versifiers was the newly elected Massachusetts state senator (and future senator and president) John Quincy Adams, whose work appeared in the *Port Folio* along with that of a sympathetic English gentleman A. Skelton.[83]

Federalist songwriters penned lurid and racist attacks to challenge the legitimacy of the Republicans' continued ascendance. The *New York Evening Post* crudely referred in song to Jefferson's long-standing relationship with Hemings and their children as evidence of Jefferson's insistence on economy and a means of avoiding having to purchase additional slaves.[84] To make such points, songwriters often wrote lyrics in Jefferson's voice, having him make blunt confessions like "For still I find to breed my kind,/A negro-wench the dandy!" Jefferson became the vehicle of writers' racist views and their desire, in Pasley's words, "to equate Republicans with what they imagined to be the lowest order of humanity."[85] Songwriters added Hemings to a growing list of women, including a London dancer and a New York madam, who proved useful characters for attacking an opponent. All were used to demean, ridicule, and undercut prominent Republicans at the national and local levels.

The multiple layers of Federalists' arguments were highlighted in satirical accounts that elaborated Jefferson's relationship with Hemings. With musical satires, Federalists highlighted the hypocrisy of Jefferson's and southern Republicans' emphasis on individual freedoms while holding slaves and undermined a claim at the heart of the Republicans' narrative of ascendance, their protection of the "rights of man." To craft these satires, Federalists juxtaposed a wide range of tones, registers, and symbolic references. Explanatory footnotes appended to a version of "Yankee Doodle" and Latin introductions to colloquial verses reinforced the gap between Jefferson's high office and the actions and base motivations attributed to him. A particularly valuable genre for creating such registral contrast was opera. In one pun-filled operatic scene a songwriter had Jefferson, the modern philosopher, singing a drinking song to a room full of his slaves and maligned partisans.[86]

An elaborate example in Joseph Dennie's *Port Folio* narrated Jefferson's personal development through his relationships with slaves like Hemings. "A Piece of an Ode to Jefferson" pretended to be a multimovement ode by William Duane to be performed on March 4. The ode's author heightened the satire's impact by following operatic conventions. He narrated Jefferson's life in recitatives and paused the narration to let characters express feelings in airs. The writer implied Jefferson's ineptitude for leadership in his being lulled to sleep with a banjo, an instrument that later in life "sooth'd his soul to pleasures." By having Jefferson schooled by slaves like Mungo who taught him "the sacred *rights of man*," the ode writer highlighted the hypocrisy of southern slaveholding Republicans' claims to be guardians of liberty. By playing on the famous phrase from Jefferson's first inaugural speech "we are all republicans, we are all federalists," the writer at once highlighted the falseness of Jefferson's claim and invoked his sexual relationship with Hemings. In the air "Poor negro hoe tobacco-hill," Mungo sang "Though you born here, and white as snow,/Poor Mungo black, from Guinea shore;/ Yet both alike—for Mungo know,/All white mans are all blackamoor." In the final air, Jefferson confirms the allusion to Hemings when, surrounded by his slaves, he confesses "Their glances from all sides my passion confound." The *Port Folio's* treatment confirms Gibbs's assertion that Mungo, Quashee, Pompey, and Caesar "were multivalent characters whose meaning was contingent on context and in whom cultural producers fused discourses of antislavery, racism, and partisan satire."[87]

Federalist editors synthesized the revelation of Jefferson's relationship with Hemings with their sectionalist rhetoric and other tactics in a mock song for Salem Republicans' March 4 celebrations of the anniversary of Jefferson's inauguration. From authorship to content, the song cleverly referenced plebeian and refined traditions to portray Republicans as pretenders to political leadership and elite culture. The song, penned by "Willy Sam Scarecrow, Esq.," set a series of toasts, typical of elite urban convivial gatherings, to the tune of "Yankee Doodle." After toasts to the Greatest Man, The Day, and Tom Paine, a toast to Madam Sally introduced a synthesis of objections to the three-fifths provision and personal attacks to charge the president himself with boosting Republican votes: "Three votes she'll give with every five/ She brings into the nation,/And once 'tis done by J-------n,/We trust he'll keep his station." Such lyrics challenged both the organizational means and constitutional basis for the Republicans' ascendance and growing influence. Federalists were devastated at the thought of being further marginalized by the expanding representation of the slave-holding South. Indeed, 1804 witnessed the "most devastating" elections for Federalists.[88]

Meanwhile, the secession argument that had surfaced in discussion of Paine's "Rule New England" developed into a full-fledged secession attempt by the end of 1803.[89] Timothy Pickering hatched a plot to unite New York and New England in seceding from the union and use the commercial center of New York City to force New Jersey to join the effort.[90] Although the plot failed, sectional and secessionist sentiments remained. Through 1805, July 4 celebrations by New England Federalists claimed regional superiority based on their foundational fight for the nation's independence, rejected political marginalization through the three-fifths compromise, and invoked the possibility of secession.[91]

Through 1805, the Federalist press synthesized the rewriting of history, personal attacks, sectionalism, and satire to express increasing resentment over the party's political marginalization. A particularly clever example came from the annual tradition of the newscarrier's address. Akin to the modern-day New Year's Eve television montage of the year in review, the newscarrier's address was usually a lengthy poem recounting in humorous fashion the events of the past year. The address was commonly printed as a broadside and presented to subscribers on New Year's Day by the carriers in exchange for tips for their year of delivery service. The address was then included in the first issue of the year. Local poets, newspaper editors, and carriers wrote addresses in varied poetic forms. For 1805, the *Courier of New Hampshire* offered as the newscarrier's address an ode to be sung alternately to the tunes "Yankee Doodle" and "Windham Bull-Frogs."▶ Reflecting on the year past, the ode mocked Republicans' prioritization of economy, the avoidance of war, and a gunboat-based navy; the purported riches of Louisiana; and the growing power of the South.[92]

The second tune indicated was critical to the humorous commentary on the past year's political events. The song "Windham Bull-Frogs" memorialized an embellished version of a 1754 incident in Windham County, Connecticut. Two lawyers and militia leaders roused their neighbors one night after hearing Native American war cries. The lawyers led their neighbors on a frenzied nighttime chase to defend the town against the invasion. By the light of dawn the real source of the frightening noises became clear. Bull-frogs were discovered in the hundreds, lying belly-up in a small, evaporating pond near one of the lawyers' homes; their death cries had sent the lawyers and, in turn, the town, on a frenzied, misguided, and useless chase.[93] Specifying the tune "Windham Bull-Frogs" instantly focused attention on the many false tales and other things "out of place" in a Federalist recollection of the year past. Much like the frogs that died in the dried-up pond, "Gun-Boat number one," the ode recounted, "took a sudden fright, and run/Right into Georgia's clover."[94] The tune helped the writer lampoon Jefferson's claims of natural wealth in the Louisiana territory and the hypocrisy in celebrating its chimerical riches—like the infamous "mountain of salt"—while criticizing clerics for preaching superstition. Evoking the colloquial language and wide-eyed observational stance of "Yankee Doodle," the ode mockingly recounted that Louisiana contained "Great heaps of clean Turk's Island salt/And swamps of hasty pudding//Moreover, it is shrewdly said,/And eke for truth it passes,/That there are monstrous quags of lead,/And lakes of pure molasses." Extending its account of fantastical tales, the ode noted "'Tis also said, that civil laws . . . Spontaneous grow among the Squaws."[95]

The songwriter could not skip over the "mammoth" events of the year past. "Mammoth" foods had followed Charles Wilson Peale's discovery in 1801 of a mammoth skeleton in New York, a discovery that Jefferson, as a natural historian and paleontologist, supported and relished. Jefferson was relentlessly mocked for maintaining that the animal still existed on the continent. The next year, a western Massachusetts Baptist preacher personally presented Jefferson a 1,235-pound "mammoth cheese" created by his community in appreciation of Republican support of religious tolerance. Then in 1804, as the songwriter recounted, the baker of the US Navy produced a twelve-foot-long "mammoth loaf" of bread. Jefferson himself joined in as the bread and accompanying meat were distributed among the people's representatives and ordinary citizens in the capitol as "Jefferson's March" was played. As the newscarrier's ode illustrated, Federalists simultaneously mocked the ostentatious "mammoth" displays of public support and Jefferson's fascination with scientific discoveries.[96]

As the newscarrier's address humorously conveyed, New England Federalists were fighting a losing battle. There were few national issues that Federalists could succeed with, and as their desperation increased, their measures were often self-defeating. Only Connecticut, aided by measures such as the public "stand-up vote," remained Federalist in 1807. It was not until the Republicans' failed embargo that Federalists enjoyed a brief, broader resurgence in the years leading up to the War of 1812.[97]

By early 1805, members of both parties synthesized the many strategies that they had honed over the previous four years to create imaginative narratives in response to Jefferson's landslide reelection. Depending on the affiliation of a given songwriter, Jefferson was either the nation's savior or the target of slander. In a song celebrating his second inauguration, an "Old Rhymer" in Richmond, New Hampshire, painted Jefferson's Federalist predecessor as a betrayer of Washington's values, linked Jefferson to the first president, and praised Jefferson's many achievements. Noting that Americans enjoyed a time of "plenty, peace, safety and liberty," the "Old Rhymer" effused about Jefferson's near miraculous quelling of Native American conflicts, avoidance of strife through the Louisiana Purchase, use of the navy to protect the nation's merchants in North Africa, preservation of free speech and religion, repeal of heavy taxes, reduction of the national debt, and rejection of a standing army.[98] Writing from a long-contested New England, the "Old Rhymer" took the core narrative of the Virginia pageant that had marked Jefferson's first inauguration and expanded it into a creative account of Jefferson's accomplishments and his place in the nation's history. An unnamed writer combined nearly all the Federalists' strategies to blast Jefferson in what reads like a parody of "Old Rhymer's" verses. In addition to recounting the Hemings affair and mocking Jefferson's dry dock and gun boat plans, "A Philosophic Song to celebrate the sublime virtues of Thomas Jefferson" repeated old accusations of his hasty flight to Carter's Mountain during the War of Independence and undermined the purchase of the Louisiana Territory as the irresponsible product of cowardice and an unwillingness to fight in defense of the nation. For the final punch, the Federalist songwriter put the president's theme song in the mouths of animals. Insulting the vast majority of the public that had supported Jefferson's reelection, the final verse cast his supporters as little more than rude animals singing his praise. The Federalist had Republicans singing "'Till asses bray the tuneful note/Swine grunting join the general cry—/And dunghill warblers pour their throats/To Jefferson and Liberty!"[99]

By this point, though, such Federalist attacks were futile. They could compete in almost no elections, and Republicans had persistently articulated their narrative tracing the party's political ascent and legitimacy. They had done so by reworking the best-known Federalist hits from Adams's presidency and adapting immigrant song traditions, integrating them into the fabric of American musical, political, and celebratory culture. They adopted well-worn rhetorical and narrative techniques, even applying the most damaging labels that the Federalists themselves had once wielded. The key themes of the Republicans' narrative had been so thoroughly established that they profoundly impacted the way Jefferson was remembered at his death. Despite the challenges that he would face in his second term, his reputation as the "Apostle of Liberty" and the reformer who "overturned the Federalist system" was already set.[100]

## Notes

1. Washington *National Intelligencer*, 6 March 1801.
2. David McCullough, *John Adams* (New York: Simon & Schuster, 2008), 556; DeConde, *Quasi-War*, 285.
3. Ferling, *Adams vs. Jefferson*, 177–96.
4. Pasley, *Tyranny of Printers*, 206–7.
5. Carl E. Prince, *New Jersey's Jeffersonian Republicans: The Genesis of an Early Party Machine* (Chapel Hill: University of North Carolina Press, 1967), 41–68; Benjamin W. Labaree, *Patriots and Partisans: The Merchants of Newburyport* (Cambridge, MA: Harvard University Press, 1962), 130; Andrew W. Robertson, "Voting Rites and Voting Acts: Electioneering Ritual, 1790–1820," in *Beyond the Founders: New Approaches to the Political History of the Early American Republic*, ed. Jeffrey L. Pasley, Answer W. Robertson, and David Waldstreicher (Chapel Hill: University of North Carolina Press, 2009), 60.
6. Newark *Centinel of Freedom*, 13 January 1801.
7. Philadelphia *Dunlap's American Daily Advertiser*, 7 November 1794; *Kline's Carlisle Weekly Gazette*, 19 November 1794; Concord *The Mirrour*, 12 December 1794; Suffield *Impartial Herald*, 9 May 1798; "Journal of Major William Gould," 182–4, 189, 191; Agnew and Howell, "Biographical Sketch," 228.
8. Morristown *Genius of Liberty*, 26 February 1801; Foster, *Poetry*, 122–4; Philadelphia *Gazette of the United States*, 9 March 1801.
9. Boston *Independent Chronicle*, 19 March 1801; "To Thomas Jefferson from Joseph Croswell, 15 July 1803," *Founders Online*, http://founders.archives.gov/documents/Jefferson/01-41-02-0027.

10. William Nelson and Charles A. Shriner, *History of Paterson and Its Environs*, vol. 1 (Paterson: Lewis Historical Publishing Company, 1920), 282–5.
11. New York *American Citizen*, 3 March, 10 June 1801; *The Poetical Works of David Garrick, Esq.*, vol. 2 (London: George Kearsley, 1785), 374–5; Philadelphia *Aurora*, 1 February 1804; Ronald L. Byrnside, *Music in Eighteenth-Century Georgia* (Athens: University of Georgia Press, 1997), 44; Rice, *British Music*, 13–5.
12. Pasley, *Tyranny of Printers*, 112–6; Washington *Herald of Liberty*, 5 January 1801; Kevin M. Gannon, "Escaping 'Mr. Jefferson's Plan of Destruction': New England Federalists and the Idea of a Northern Confederacy, 1803–1804," *Journal of the Early Republic* 21, no. 3 (Autumn 2001): 421.
13. *Alexandria Times*, 18 February 1801; Hartford *American Mercury*, 5 March 1801; Jared Potter Kirtland, "History," in *Song of Jefferson and Liberty, 1874*, in *American Poetry, 1609–1900: Segment II* (New Haven, CT: Research Publications, 1975), 3; *Alexandria Expositor*, 11 March 1803.
14. Elizabethtown *New Jersey Journal*, 3 March 1801; *Waterford Gazette*, 7 September 1802; *Albany Register*, 7 January 1803; Hartford *American Mercury*, 14 July 1803; *New York Evening Post*, 17 July 1805; Foster, *Poetry*, vii, 120–2, 131–7; Newark *Centinel of Freedom*, 27 January 1801.
15. Boston *Constitutional Telegraphe*, 20 August 1800; Boston *Independent Chronicle*, 21 August 1800; Wilmington *Mirror of the Times*, 17 September 1800; Morristown *Genius of Liberty*, 26 February 1801; William Duane, *The American Republican Harmonist* (Philadelphia: William Duane, 1803), 30–1; Foster, *Poetry*, 115–17.
16. Trenton *True American*, 9 March 1802; Boston *Constitutional Telegraphe*, 17 March 1802; Gross, *Jefferson's Scrapbooks*, 128–9.
17. Duane, *American Republican Harmonist*, 2–4, 9–11; Hudson *Bee*, 21 June 1803; Hartford *American Mercury*, 14 July 1803; Walpole *Political Observatory*, 7 April 1804; Portsmouth *New Hampshire Gazette*, 16 July 1805.
18. Hartford *American Mercury*, 14 July 1803.
19. Newark *Centinel of Freedom*, 27 January 1801, 15 March 1803; Boston *Constitutional Telegraphe*, 19 August 1801; Windsor *Spooner's Vermont Journal*, 1 March 1803; *Salem Register*, 1 November 1802, 3 March 1803; Frederick *Republican Gazette and General Advertiser*, 11 March 1803; Easton *Republican Star*, 15 March 1803; *Kline's Carlisle Weekly Gazette*, 24 December 1800, 23 March 1803; Frederick *Hornet*, 5 April 1803; *Alexandria Expositor*, 1 December 1803; Hudson *Bee*, 4 June 1805; Portland *Eastern Argus*, 28 June 1805; Gross, ed. *Jefferson's Scrapbooks*, 35–6.
20. Clark Hunter, ed., *The Life and Letters of Alexander Wilson*, vol. 154 (Philadelphia: American Philosophical Society, 1983), 3, 43, 48–70, 86, 92, 233, 238, 292.
21. Boston *Constitutional Telegraphe*, 4 February 1801; Newport *Guardian of Liberty*, 21 February 1801; Washington *Herald of Liberty*, 23 February 1801; New York *American Citizen*, 25 February 1801; Hartford *American Mercury*, 19 March 1801, 28 January 1802; *Kline's Carlisle Weekly Gazette*, 24 June 1801; *Waterford Gazette*, 16 February 1802; Peacham *Green Mountain Patriot*, 3 July 1802; Randolph *Weekly Wanderer*, 3 July 1802; Hudson *Bee*, 4 June 1805; Ebsworth, *Republican Harmonist*, 59–62, Duane, *American Republican Harmonist*, 78–81; Gross, *Jefferson's Scrapbooks*, 20; *Salem*

*Register*, 3 March 1803; Portsmouth *New Hampshire Gazette*, 26 February 1805; Portland *Eastern Argus*, 28 June 1805; Walpole *Political Observatory*, 2 March 1805. In addition to the songs by William C. Foster and Alexander Wilson, the title "Jefferson and Liberty" was used for a song by Michael Fortune and a jig, "The Gobbio," as notated in Elijah Welles, *Music Book*, Connecticut Historical Society manuscript 90474.

22. John Ross, ed., *The Book of Scottish Poems: Ancient and Modern* (Edinburgh: Edinburgh Publishing Company, 1878), 427; Baltimore *Republican; or Anti-Democrat*, 14 February 1803; Newark *Centinel of Freedom*, 18 October 1803; *Republican Watchtower*, 13 June 1804; *Alexandria Advertiser*, 2 October 1804.
23. *Kline's Carlisle Weekly Gazette*, 24 December 1800.
24. Philadelphia *Independent Gazetteer*, 5 January, 23 February 1793; Portsmouth *New Hampshire Gazette*, 6 February 1794; Hiltner, *Newspaper Verse*, 528–30; Boston *Massachusetts Mercury*, 7 February 1793; New York *Columbian Gazetteer*, 10 March 1794; Hatton, *Songs of Tammany*; Sonneck, *Miscellaneous Studies*, 57–64; Hargruder, "'A Circle Form'd of Friends,'" 24–41.
25. John M. Murrin, "The Jeffersonian Triumph and American Exceptionalism," *Journal of the Early Republic* 20, no. 1 (Spring 2000): 1–11, 15; Peter J. Kastor, "What Are the Advantages of the Acquisition?": Inventing Expansion in the Early American Republic," *American Quarterly* 60, no. 4 (December 2008): 1003–35; John L. Allen, "Thomas Jefferson and the Mountain of Salt: Presidential Image of Louisiana Territory," *Historical Geography* 31 (2003): 9–13.
26. Kirtland, "History," 3; Reflecting American repurposing and retitling of European tunes, Hitchcock's manuscript contains the melody of "Willy Was a Wanton Wag" under the title "Constitution March" and the tune of "The Gobbio" under the title "Jefferson and Liberty."
27. Hartford *American Mercury*, 19 March 1801; New London *Bee*, 24 March 1802; Walpole *Political Observatory*, 2 March 1805.
28. Utica *Patriot*, 2 May 1803; Boston *New England Palladium*, 23 July 1802; Worcester *National Aegis*, 21 December 1803.
29. Walpole *Political Observatory*, 2 March 1805; Donald B. Cole, *Jacksonian Democracy in New Hampshire, 1800–1851* (Cambridge, MA: Harvard University Press, 1970), 21; David Hackett Fischer, *The Revolution of American Conservativism: The Federalist Party in the Era of Jeffersonian Democracy* (New York: Harper and Row, 1965), 202–24; Gross, *Jefferson's Scrapbooks*, 507.
30. Hartford *American Mercury*, 1 July 1802; Hudson *Bee*, 4 June 1805; Welles, *Music Book*.
31. Helen Cripe, *Thomas Jefferson and Music* (Charlottesville: University Press of Virginia, 1974); Annette Gordon-Reed and Peter S. Onuf, *"Most Blessed of the Patriarchs": Thomas Jefferson and the Empire of the Imagination* (New York: W. W. Norton, 2016), 211–35. The complete Jefferson clippings books are maintained by the University of Virginia. Some of their contents are available in a contemporary edition. See Gross, *Jefferson's Scrapbooks*.
32. *Salem Register*, 3 March 1803; *Providence Phenix*, 23 February 1805; Sag Harbor *Suffolk Gazette*, 4 March 1805; Foster, *Poetry*, 122–4; *New Hampshire Gazette*, 16 December 1828.

33. Fredericksburg *Political Intelligencer*, 8 April 1801; Dover *Sun*, 12 June 1802; Foster, *Poetry*, 122–4; Boston *Independent Chronicle*, 19 March 1801; Hudson *Bee*, 14 December 1802; *Alexandria Expositor*, 18 March 1803; *Providence Phoenix*, 23 February 1805.
34. *Kline's Carlisle Weekly Gazette*, 18 February 1801.
35. Newark *Centinel of Freedom*, 27 January 1801; Newport *Guardian of Liberty*, July 11, 1801; Sewall, *Miscellaneous Poems*, 215–17; Goodman, "American Identities," 144–5; *Massachusetts Mercury*, 29 October 1799; *Federal Songster*, 76–8; Mitchell, ed., "New Letters of Abigail Adams," 406–7; Foster, *Poetry*, 122–4; Portland *Eastern Argus*, 1 March 1805; Worcester *National Aegis*, 13 March 1805; Portsmouth *New Hampshire Gazette*, 16 July 1805.
36. Gross, *Jefferson's Scrapbooks*, 35–6; *Salem Register*, 1 November 1802; *Alexandria Expositor*, 1 December 1803; Portland *Eastern Argus*, 28 June 1805; Lexington *Stewart Kentucky Herald*, 16 June 1801.
37. James Robinson, *Philadelphia Directory, City and County Register for 1803* (Philadelphia: William W. Woodward, 1802), 79; Philadelphia *Tickler*, 25 January 1809; Philadelphia *Temple of Reason*, 9 December 1801; Philadelphia *The Spirit of the Press*, 1 January, 1 December 1807.
38. Daniel, *Scandal and Civility*, 231–74, 281–3; Little, *Transoceanic Radical*, 18–119, 138, 156–7.
39. James Gilreath, ed., and Elizabeth Carter Wills, comp., *Federal Copyright Records, 1790–1800* (Washington, DC: Library of Congress, 1987), 70; New York *Commercial Advertiser*, 9 October 1801.
40. Ebsworth, *Republican Harmonist* (1801), 3.
41. Duane, *American Republican Harmonist*, 2–4, 9–11.
42. *Port Folio*, 10 July, 7 August 1802. For a rare example of a Republican song opposing peace, see Dover *Sun*, 27 March 1802; Gross, *Jefferson's Scrapbooks*, 128–9.
43. New York *American Citizen*, 4 July 1803; *Albany Register*, 22 May 1804; Walpole *Political Observatory*, 7 April 1804.
44. Donald E. Heidenrich Jr., "U.S. National Security and Party Politics: The Consensus on Louisiana, 1789–1803," *Arkansas Historical Quarterly* 62, no. 4 (Winter 2003): 370–85; Kastor, "What Are the Advantages of the Acquisition?" 1003–35; Peter S. Onuf, "The Revolution of 1803," *Wilson Quarterly* 27, no. 1 (Winter 2003): 22–9; Sean M. Theriault, "Party Politics during the Louisiana Purchase," *Social Science History* 30, no. 2 (Summer 2006): 297, 302, 308–9.
45. Thomas Fleming, *The Louisiana Purchase* (Hoboken, NJ: John Wiley, 2003), 57–9, 62–5, 73–7, 132, 135–7, 174–5; Bennington *Vermont Gazette*, 19 July 1803; William A. Robinson, *Jeffersonian Democracy in New England* (New York: Greenwood Press, 1968), 50; Pasley, *Tyranny of Printers*, 214.
46. Isaac Jennings, *Memorials of a Century: Embracing a Record of Individuals and Events, Chiefly in the Early History of Bennington, Vt., and Its First Church* (Bennington: Gould and Lincoln, 1869): 323; *Records of the Grand Lodge of Free and Accepted Masons of the State of Vermont* (Free Press Association, 1879), 39.
47. Newark *Centinel of Freedom*, 28 February 1804; Bennington *Vermont Gazette*, 17 July 1804; Kuntz, "The Black Sloven"; G. Wood, *Empire of Liberty*, 189.

48. Onuf, "The Revolution of 1803," 25; Kastor, "What Are the Advantages of the Acquisition?" 1014.
49. Philadelphia *Aurora*, 1 February 1804; *Pittsfield Sun*, 19 March 1804; Bennington *Vermont Gazette*, 8, 15 May 1804; Walpole *Political Observatory*, 26 May 1804; Michael Fortune, "The Acquisition of Louisiana: A National Song" (Philadelphia: G. Willig, 1804); Whipple, *To the Shores of Tripoli*, 20–1, 54, 63–4, 68; Frank Lambert, *The Barbary Wars: American Independence in the Atlantic World* (New York: Hill and Wang, 2005), 101–2, 124–5; Malone, *Jefferson the President: First Term*, 99.
50. Pasley, *Tyranny of Printers*, 203–11; W. Robinson, *Jeffersonian Democracy*, 31–51, 68–9; Bennington *Vermont Gazette*, 17 July 1804; Marcus Wilson Jernegan, *The Tammany Societies of Rhode Island* (Providence: Preston and Rounds, 1897), 8; New Haven *Connecticut Journal*, 24 February, 3 March 1803.
51. Charles W. Brewster, *Rambles about Portsmouth*, vol. 2 (Portsmouth: New Hampshire Publishing, 1972), 28–30; William Bentley, *The Diary of William Bentley, D.D., Pastor of the East Church, Salem, Massachusetts*, vol. 2 (Salem: Essex Institute, 1907), 389.
52. Boston *Mercury and New England Palladium*, 9 July 1802; Portsmouth *United States Oracle*, 10 July 1802; *Newport Mercury*, 20 July 1802; Providence *United States Chronicle*, 15 July 1802; *New York Herald*, 17 July 1802; Baltimore *Republican or Anti-Democrat*, 19 July 1802; Keene *New Hampshire Sentinel*, 24 July 1802; Augusta *Kennebec Gazette*, 30 July 1802.
53. Fischer, *Revolution of American Conservativism*, 150; Pasley, *Tyranny of Printers*, 255; Malone, *Jefferson the President: First Term*, 37, 95; *Port Folio*, 1 August 1801, 6 February 1802; Boston *Columbian Centinel*, 23 September 1801; Georgetown *Washington Federalist*, 25 September 1801; Linda K. Kerber, *Federalists in Dissent: Imagery and Ideology in Jeffersonian America* (Ithaca, NY: Cornell University Press, 1970), 11–4; Randolph Randall, "Authors of the Port Folio Revealed by the Hall Files," *American Literature* 11, no. 4 (January 1940): 401, http://www.jstor.org/stable/2920854.
54. Worcester *National Aegis*, 28 July, 25 August, 8 December 1802; 26 January 1803; Boston *Independent Chronicle*, 13 December 1802; Norwalk *Independent Republican*, 29 December 1802; *Port Folio*, 18 December 1802, 398; Horgan, *Politics of Songs*, 61–92.
55. "To Thomas Jefferson from Levi Lincoln, 15 March 1803," *Founders Online*, http://founders.archives.gov/documents/Jefferson/01-40-02-0052.
56. Baltimore *Republican or Anti-Democrat*, 23 March 1803; Worcester *Massachusetts Spy*, 13 April 1803.
57. Worcester *National Aegis*, 9 March, 27 April 1803; Baltimore *Republican or Anti-Democrat*, 23 March 1803; Worcester *Massachusetts Spy*, 13 April 1803; M. Smith, *Listening*, 11–12.
58. *Boston Gazette*, 17 March 1803; Paul A. Gilje and Howard B. Rock, "'Sweep O! Sweep O!': African-American Chimney Sweeps and Citizenship in the New Nation," *William and Mary Quarterly* 1, no. 3 (July 1994): 507–9, 512, 516–17.
59. *Port Folio*, 10 July, 2 October, 6 November 1802; Walpole *Farmer's Weekly Museum*, 10 May 1803.

60. Pasley, *Tyranny of Printers*, 144–5, 203–5, 253–4; *Port Folio*, 28 August, 11 December 1802; *Utica Patriot*, 23 May 1803; *New York Herald*, 31 July 1802; *New York Evening Post*, 17 August 1802, 28 October 1802, 7 June 1803; *New York Spectator*, 8 June 1803; Hudson *Wasp*, 7 July, 23 August 1802; *Kline's Carlisle Weekly Gazette*, 23 March 1803.
61. Mitchell, ed., "New Letters of Abigail Adams," 394, 415.
62. Little, *Transoceanic Radical*, 129–30, 132–3, 146–7, 154.
63. Duane, *American Republican Harmonist*, 59–60.
64. Kerber, *Federalists in Dissent*, x, 4, 11, 19–21, 67–72, 75–6.
65. Gene A. Smith, *"For the Purposes of Defense": The Politics of the Jeffersonian Gunboat Program* (Newark: University of Delaware Press, 1995), 15–22, 58–65, 74–5.
66. *New York Gazette*, 12 January 1805; *New York Evening Post*, 10 July 1805; Concord *Courier of New Hampshire*, 2 January 1805; Hudson *Balance*, 30 October 1804; New York *Commercial Advertiser*, 23 December 1805; *Newport Mercury*, 10 May 1803; *Salem Gazette*, 6 July 1804; Boston *Repertory*, 10 July 1804; *Greenfield Gazette*, 6 August 1804.
67. Pasley, *Tyranny of Printers*, 7–8, 255; Robinson, *Jeffersonian Democracy*, 57; Washington *Herald of Liberty*, 5 January 1801; Newark *Centinel of Freedom*, 20 October 1801; Boston *Columbian Centinel*, 30 October 1802; Hartford *American Mercury*, 17 March 1803; Duane, *American Republican Harmonist*, 32–4.
68. Pasley, *Tyranny of Printers*, 210–1; Bentley, vol. 2, 423, 456; Duane Hamilton Hurd, *History of Essex County, Massachusetts, with Biographical Sketches of Many of Its Pioneers and Prominent Men* (Philadelphia: J. W. Lewis, 1888), 120.
69. *Salem Gazette*, 5 November 1802; Goodman, "American Identities," 133–4, 156–61.
70. New London *Connecticut Gazette*, 2 March 1803.
71. Samuel Griswold Goodrich, *Recollections of a Lifetime*, vol. 2, (Ridgefield, CT: Miller, Orton, and Mulligan, 1856), 23, 119; Hartford *Connecticut Courant*, 2 March 1803; Norwich *Connecticut Centinel*, 15 March 1803; Baltimore *Republican or Anti-Democrat*, 16 March 1803; Hartford *American Mercury*, 17 March 1803; Kirtland, "History," 5, 8–16; Richard Crawford, ed., *The Core Repertory of Early American Psalmody*, vol. 11–12 (Madison: A-R Editions, 1984), xli; Kerber, *Federalists in Dissent*, 14.
72. *Greenfield Gazette*, 6 June 1803; Boston *Democrat*, 3 March 1804; Boston *Repertory*, 9 July 1805; New York *Commercial Advertiser*, 21 July 1804, 12 July 1805; *Kennebec Gazette*, 9 August 1804; Boston *New England Palladium*, 2 July 1805; *Portland Gazette*, 1 April 1805; *Providence Phoenix*, 6 April 1805.
73. Hartford *American Mercury*, 17 March 1803; *Newburyport Herald*, 14 January 1804; Stockbridge *Western Star*, 21 January 1804; Danbury *Republican Farmer*, 2 January 1805; Kerber, *Federalists in Dissent*, 14; *Papers of the New Haven Colony Historical Society*, vol. 2 (New Haven, 1877), 305, 325, 328.
74. Boston *Massachusetts Mercury*, 1 June 1802; Worcester *National Aegis*, 2 June 1802; R. Paine, *Works*, 252–3; Henry Harrison Sprague, *An Old Boston Institution: A Brief History of the Massachusetts Charitable Fire Society* (Boston: Little, Brown, 1893), 69–70; Robert Treat Paine, "Rule New England" (Boston: Mallet and Graupner, 1802).
75. Oscar Sonneck, *Early Concert-Life in America (1731–1800)* (Leipzig: Breitkopf & Härtel, 1907), 291.

76. Worcester *National Aegis*, 2 June 1802; Boston *Commercial Gazette*, 17 June 1802.
77. Boston *Commercial Gazette*, 3, 17, 21 June 1802; *Salem Register*, 3 June 1802; Boston *Independent Chronicle*, 7, 14 June, 19 July 1802; *New York Herald*, 12 June 1802; Charleston *City Gazette*, 26 June 1802; Charleston *Carolina Gazette*, 1 July 1802; Baltimore *Republican or Anti-Democrat*, 14 June 1802; Gross, *Jefferson's Scrapbooks*, 55.
78. Dover *Sun*, 12 June 1802; *Albany Gazette*, 21 June 1802.
79. *Boston Gazette*, 31 May 1802.
80. Kerber, *Federalists in Dissent*, 19–21, 23–66.
81. Daniel Corbett Wewers, "The Specter of Disunion in the Early American Republic, 1783–1815" (PhD diss., Harvard University, 2008).
82. Michael Durey, *"With the Hammer of Truth": James Thomson Callender and America's Early National Heroes* (Charlottesville: University of Virginia Press, 1990), 143–68.
83. Annette Gordon-Reed, *The Hemingses of Monticello: An American Family* (New York: W. W. Norton, 2008), 583; Fawn M. Brodie, *Thomas Jefferson: An Intimate History* (New York: W. W. Norton, 1974), 347–63, 370; Randall, "Authors," 408.
84. *New York Evening Post*, 28 October 1802. Italics in original.
85. Pasley, *Tyranny of Printers*, 255–7, 260; *Port Folio*, 2 October 1802, 6, 13 November 1802; *Boston Gazette Commercial and Political*, 11 October 1802; Joshua D. Rothman, "James Callender and Social Knowledge of Interracial Sex in Antebellum Virginia," in *Sally Hemings and Thomas Jefferson: History, Memory, and Civic Culture*, ed. Jan Ellen Lewis and Peter S. Onuf (Charlottesville: University of Virginia Press, 1999), 92–5.
86. Pasley, *Tyranny of Printers*, 253; *Port Folio*, 2 October, 13 November 1802, 19 March 1803; *Boston Gazette Commercial and Political*, 11 October 1802; Malone, *Jefferson the President: First Term*, 214 n. 22.
87. *Port Folio*, 19 March 1803; Jenna M. Gibbs, *Performing the Temple of Liberty: Slavery, Theater, and Popular Culture in London and Philadelphia, 1760–1850* (Baltimore: Johns Hopkins University Press, 2014), 45.
88. *Salem Gazette*, 11 March 1803; Theriault, "Party Politics," 309.
89. Mitchell, ed., "New Letters of Abigail Adams," 429–30; Pasley, *Tyranny of Printers*, 214, 255.
90. Gannon, "Escaping 'Mr. Jefferson's Plan of Destruction,'" 413–43.
91. *Salem Gazette*, 6 July 1804; Boston *Repertory*, 10 July 1804; Hudson *Balance*, 10 July 1804; *Haverhill Museum*, 23 July 1805.
92. Gerald D. McDonald, Stuart C. Sherman, and Mary T. Russo. *A Checklist of American Newspaper Carrier's Addresses, 1720–1820* (Worcester, MA: American Antiquarian Society, 2000); Concord *Courier of New Hampshire*, 2 January 1805.
93. "Lawyers and Bullfrogs," *Isaiah Thomas Broadside Ballads Project*, http://www.americanantiquarian.org/thomasballads/items/show/145; Oscar Jewell Harvey and Ernest Gray Smith, *A History of Wilkes-Barré, Luzerne County, Pennsylvania*, vol. 1 (Wilkes-Barre: Raeder Press, 1909), 464.
94. A similar comparison was made in the *Providence Gazette*, 16 February 1805.
95. *Salem Gazette*, 6 July 1804; Allen, "Thomas Jefferson and the Mountain of Salt," 9–13.

96. Jeffrey L. Pasley, "The Cheese and the Words: Popular Political Culture and Participatory Democracy in the Early American Republic," in *Beyond the Founders: New Approaches to the Political History of the Early American Republic*, ed. Jeffrey L. Pasley, Andrew Whitmore Robertson, and David Waldstreicher (Chapel Hill: University of North Carolina Press, 2004), 31–7, 44–6; Kerber, *Federalists in Dissent*, 67–72, 75–6; *Albany Centinel*, 10 April 1804.
97. Kerber, *Federalists in Dissent*, vii, 9; W. Robinson, *Jeffersonian Democracy*, 50, 74.
98. Walpole *Political Observatory*, 6 April 1805.
99. Northampton *Hive*, 8 January 1805.
100. Merrill D. Peterson, *The Jefferson Image in the American Mind* (Charlottesville: University of Virginia Press, 1960), 9–10.

# 5
# Debating the Embargo in Song

Among the many political songs that Jefferson clipped from newspapers during his presidency were lyrics debating the embargo, a controversial collection of legislation restricting international trade. Jefferson's placement of such songs in a volume separate from poetry suggests there was something peculiar about song and its potential impact that made it different from poetry. Not only could song be performed communally, but it could also enhance its impact by making reference to other familiar songs. Although conceived and collected as music, this body of song has been overlooked in studies of Jefferson's interest in music.[1] Jefferson's collection illustrates varied ways that songs were created—some were written to commonly reworked melodies while other lyrics were written and set to newly composed music. Jefferson clipped many embargo songs from the Trenton *True American*, edited by powerful New Jersey Republican James Jefferson Wilson.[2] Yet newspapers across the country printed such lyrics, and many local songwriters contributed verses, typically anonymously, to debate the embargo.

The embargo was a controversial response to consequences of the Napoleonic Wars. Britain and France pressed American seamen into naval service, seized ships, and tightened commercial restrictions. To maintain its neutral trade, a small nation needed strong treaties, a strong navy, or both. The United States had neither, and its neutral shipping rights were instead eroded through the Jay Treaty, the British *Essex* decision of 1805, and British orders in council. Jefferson's administration pursued diplomacy, but these efforts were hindered by impressment.[3] British "press gangs" forced men from other nations' merchant vessels into naval service to replace deserters fleeing the Royal Navy's notoriously harsh conditions and to maintain Britain's status as the ruler of the seas. British deserters constituted half the American merchant marine and were essential to American profit from the neutral carrying trade, trade that Jefferson saw as key to boosting the nation's economic power.[4] Consequently, US diplomats would not agree to Britain's stipulation that the American hiring of deserters cease.

*Hail Columbia*. Laura Lohman, Oxford University Press (2020). © Oxford University Press.
DOI: 10.1093/oso/9780190930615.001.0001

This troubled diplomacy transformed into calls for war in June 1807 when the HMS *Leopard* fired on the USS *Chesapeake* off the Virginia coast. Commodore James Barron had refused the British order to muster his crew to search for deserters. The *Leopard* responded with broadsides. Three of Barron's men were killed, eighteen were injured, and four men—including two African Americans and one US-born white man—were removed for suspicion of desertion. British impressment had now extended from merchant vessels to a warship. Public outrage crossed party lines and fueled resolutions calling for war.[5]

Amid intensifying commercial restrictions, depredations, and erosions of neutral trade rights during the Napoleonic Wars, through the embargo the United States struggled with what Sofka has called its "most critical foreign policy problem" after independence—self-preservation.[6] Americans regularly used music to debate how to achieve self-preservation and what had to be sacrificed to do it. The question, as Secretary of the Treasury Albert Gallatin put it, was whether it was better "to preserve a pacific and temporizing system, and to tolerate those injuries and insults" from other nations, "than to be prepared, like the great European nations, to repel every injury by the sword." There were only bad options: protracted diplomacy amid continued depredations, economic warfare, submission to the belligerents' commercial restrictions, or war. Each option entailed a sacrifice—either the sacrifice of an ideal, such as peace, honor, or independence, or the sacrifice of trade, profit, and material goods impacting the nation's economic power and its prosperity as well as the prosperity of its sections and citizens.[7]

In this context, Americans used music to address several critical political questions: What should the makeup and purpose of the navy be? How should the nation form an alliance among the major powers of Europe? Could the nation avoid embroilment in a large-scale European war? While these questions were not new, they stimulated increasing debate amid sustained depredations, failed diplomacy, and economic devastation at home. While Americans still used music to spread partisan character attacks and aid electioneering, they also used it to debate crucial foreign policy issues that would impact the nation's unity and the financial well-being of its communities.

The large body of embargo songs through which Americans debated these questions illustrates several trends in political expression through music. While political songwriters continued to draw on a sizable group of melodies in transatlantic circulation, they increasingly turned to two tunes,

"Yankee Doodle" and "Anacreon in Heaven." These tune choices commonly shaped how a songwriter made a political point. At the same time, editors and compilers adapted songs from the Revolutionary era and the XYZ Affair to the crisis at hand, reprinting older songs as a commentary on the present and fashioning them into larger satirical statements through mock ritual. Additionally, songwriters wrote lyrics that were intended not to be performed but rather to be enjoyed as satire. Finally, this body of songs illustrates an emerging interest in American productions, an interest that would swell in the coming years. Created in all these ways, music provided an engaging medium not only to debate complex, interrelated questions surrounding the embargo in the framework of the first party system but also to prioritize the sometime conflicting values of the nation, including peace, prosperity, and isolationism.

## Embargo and War

From July 4, 1807, shortly after the *Chesapeake* incident, songwriters and celebrants stressed the necessity of war preparations to defend the nation's rights and avenge the deaths of "our seamen." Celebrants toasted "the American Navy" vowing that "the late outrage on the frigate Chesapeake, be the last British lesson on our national rights." To articulate this sentiment in song, they repurposed Francophobic lyrics written by a Salem gentleman during the XYZ period. Likely replacing his references to the "French bear" with ones to the "British lion," they declared that "his hugs and his blows we will meet them like men,/And the Eagle shall drive the beast back to his den."[8] In New York, the front page of the Troy *Farmers' Register* carried William C. Foster's "War Song." Foster used the tune "Rule Britannia" to challenge British aggression and exhort readers, "Rise, sons of Freedom (patriot throng,)/Whose fathers fought for liberty;/*Advance, avenge!*—avenge your country's wrong,/Repulse the tyrants of the sea."[9] Following the administration's call for governors to organize and equip their quotas of the 100,000-man militia, songwriters issued war calls from summer through winter. As late as March 1808, a widely reprinted reworking of "Yankee Doodle" clipped by Jefferson in his scrapbook commanded in plain language, "Jersey Boys—Make ready then/Your Muskets, Pikes and Rifles."▶ Songwriters delineated a British enemy with propagandist language and falsely characterized the *Chesapeake* as "unarm'd" to exaggerate British wrongs.[10]

Extending initial American reaction to the *Chesapeake* incident, writers and songwriters also encouraged an embargo, one of several measures intended to cause hardship and apply financial pressure to Britain and the British West Indies. "Uncle Jonathan" made this argument on the front page of the Trenton *True American* in "Hetty's Hymn," one of many songs Jefferson saved from this newspaper edited by James Jefferson Wilson.[11]⯈ Hetty reflected on her beloved Jemmy going off to fight "in so glorious a cause" as that of avenging Britain's "demanding, and killing, American tars." Hetty not only predicted war but also envisioned the embargo's creation, in the meantime, of British famine, disease, and dismay that would "break all their merchants and ruin their banks."[12]

"Uncle Jonathan" extrapolated on a Republican belief that higher prices and shortages in Europe and the West Indies would force a repeal of severe European restrictions on neutral trade.[13] Yet for five years Britain and France would wage a war of economic sanctions and commercial restrictions that practically eliminated the neutral trade that was central to America's northern ports. In late 1806, Napoleon's Berlin Decree declared British goods forfeit, even when found on neutral ships, to exclude them from the European continent. In 1807, Britain responded with Orders in Council prohibiting neutral trade with France and its allies and requiring neutrals to first stop at British ports. Unlike France, Britain, with its enormous navy, could enforce the Orders in Council, making it the greater threat to US commercial interests.

Concerned that the United States would ultimately be hurt by a British maritime monopoly if it remained on the sidelines of the European war, Jefferson made a strong case for war against Britain as he drafted his October 1807 message to Congress. But his cabinet members wanted to avoid war, and at their urging, he revised his message: his account of British oppression and malice over American commercial aspirations was replaced with emphasis on the *Chesapeake* incident. In reality, concern over American competition in the Indian Ocean and China trade led several British constituents, including merchants and shipowners, to desire war with the United States. Congress, with its fear of war outweighing its concerns about commercial restrictions and merchant impressments, contemplated diplomatic responses.[14]

Meanwhile, not unlike the dual measures of war and embargo promoted in "Hetty's Hymn," Jefferson pursued an embargo and other preparations in anticipation of increased European hostility. Because American merchants had stopped shipping after the *Chesapeake* incident out of fear, Jefferson thought the public would support a temporary defensive embargo. He initially conceived such an embargo as a means of preparing for war by providing time for seamen and ships—the "maritime resources of war"—to come home and prevent a run on insurance that would stop banks from lending to the government in wartime. The embargo would also give Britain time either to make reparations for the *Chesapeake* incident and honor American neutral rights, or to clearly refuse to do so; such refusal was necessary, in Jefferson's eyes, to engender northeastern support for war. Jefferson therefore requested from Congress both an embargo prohibiting American vessels from leaving US ports and "every preparation for whatever events may grow out of the present crisis." Embargo legislation began in late 1807 and was later expanded. American foreign shipping was banned, foreign vessels were prohibited from taking cargo at American ports, and, consequently, foreign imports largely ended. Subsequent legislation banned US exports by land and expanded requirements to vessels in rivers, lakes, and bays to address smuggling, loopholes, and issues unrelated to the embargo's original defensive purposes. Jefferson anticipated the necessity or avoidance of war becoming clear and the embargo's repeal by the end of 1808.[15]

Ensuing debates over the embargo increasingly addressed complex, interrelated issues of foreign policy and domestic prosperity. Along with the embargo cartoons and anagrams that have often captured historians' attention, Americans used the extended medium and complex lyrical networks of song to make their cases for and against the embargo in a time of crisis. Through song, Americans debated the prospect of alliance with one of the European belligerents, the basis and breadth of prosperity, the purpose of the embargo, and the makeup and function of the navy. The embargo discourse was intimately connected with election cycles, fueling the rhetoric and sustaining the debates in song.[16]

Of the two melodies selected most often, "Yankee Doodle" was an attractive choice for those who wanted to present their arguments about the embargo legislation to newspaper readers regardless of whether the lyrics were read silently, read aloud and discussed with company, or sung among like-minded political company in an election season. The other, "Anacreon in Heaven," was a suitable choice for Americans who wanted to engage and coordinate community members in shared expression through song.[17] Each of these melodies shaped how the songwriter expressed a political view in words. The melody chosen not only shaped the verse structure, line length, and poetic meter but also typically the rhyme scheme, tone, vocabulary, and imagery. Widely circulated songs often remained faithful to the melody's earlier lyrics in as many of these dimensions as possible. Thus when writing a Federalist reworking of "Yankee Doodle" that was widely reprinted from the Chambersburg, Pennsylvania, *Franklin Repository*, "a sailor" complained about the effects of the embargo using colloquial language and yeoman imagery. The songwriter lamented in a combination of farmer's and sailor's vernacular, "With legs as small as marlin spikes,/I'm wasted to a scare-crow;/ No meat to eat, no grog to drink—/All by this damn'd embargo." Echoing the melody's earlier lyrics, other songwriters debating the embargo effectively incorporated references to pork, beef, "'lasses," and "pumpkin pye."[18] In dozens of new political songs, Republicans and Federalists capitalized on characters, concepts, and expressions associated with "Yankee Doodle" and "Anacreon in Heaven" to take their stands in debates over the embargo and the interrelated questions of European alliances, prosperity, isolationism, and peace.

## "Entangling Alliances with None"

Through embargo songs, Americans debated the concept and consequences of an alliance with one of the belligerents. On paper, the embargo laws applied to both belligerents. Nevertheless, partisan songwriters used wide-ranging propaganda techniques to cast support for or opposition to the legislation as a form of favoritism, alliance, or subservience to either belligerent and to reject such notions altogether.

Federalists, reluctant to break relations with Britain and fearful of Britain's fate in the Napoleonic Wars, promptly challenged the embargo as an alliance with France. Federalist fears of such an alliance had surfaced earlier in Jefferson's second term, and the embargo, contextualized by the war calls that followed the *Chesapeake* incident, strengthened expression of these fears.[19] Federalists used well-known melodies, such as "The Entered Apprentice" and "Yankee Doodle," to cast the embargo and its implementation as partial to France. In crafting these lyrics, Federalist songwriters tapped into earlier Republican interests in discriminating against British commerce and diversifying markets to free American exporters, especially in the agrarian South, from dependence on British financiers and merchants. Federalist songwriters did not simply assert that the embargo was intended to destroy the "British mercantile monopoly" but claimed that it had been "dictated by Napoleon."[20]

Using the common nation-as-ship metaphor and invoking the venerated first president, one songwriter rejected the embargo as blind, foolish, and cowardly subservience to a scheming plunderer. With matter-of-fact language set to "Yankee Doodle," New York and New England newspapers asked through these lyrics, "Had Captain WASHINGTON been found/Upon the quarter-deck, sir/D'ye think he'd run the ship aground/At BONAPARTE's beck sir?/Yankee doodle—no, not he—/Had such a pirate chas'd him/He'd quickly put the helm-a-lee,/And boldly turn'd and laced him."[21]

Federalist songwriters called instead for alliance with Britain. Such calls extended earlier Anglophilic views, as captured in the declaration of Massachusetts Federalist Fisher Ames that Britain "has a better right to exist, than neutrals have to trade." Adhering to a vision of an American nation shaped after British models and in "ideological and cultural affinity" with Britain, Federalists opposed war with Britain and championed instead the defeat of France. Federalists presented Britain as the last defense against French radicalism. Federalist newspaper editors reached across the Atlantic to strengthen their argument. By reprinting Irish poet Thomas Stott's March 1808 "Ode to Columbia," Federalists called on the United States to ally with Britain and warned that if Britain fell to France, the United States would be next. In Stott's words, "'Tis Britain's interest—and 'tis thine,/The bond of friendship to renew,/When Europe's tyrants all combine/Freedom's last refuge to subdue.//Were Britain once put down by France,/And sunk among her list of slaves,/Would not fell Gallia soon advance,/To SHACKLE THEE, across the waves?"[22]

A more complicated view was expressed in song by Michael Fortune. Variously described as an African American, a Catholic, and an immigrant arriving from northern Ireland around 1790, Fortune was a Philadelphia storekeeper and seller of lottery tickets who wrote to and shared with President Jefferson his songs "Jefferson and Liberty" and "The Acquisition of Louisiana." Fortune also used his musical talents to help black activists in Philadelphia celebrate the end of the international slave trade. In writing a "New Year's Anthem" sung in the African Episcopal Church in Philadelphia, Fortune focused on the commonalities binding the United States and Britain. Addressing the two nations that had legislated the end of the international slave trade, Fortune had his fellow Philadelphians sing, "From one parental stream ye spring,/A kindred blood your bosoms own" and asked the nations to "beg forgiveness" and "your mutual wrongs forgive/Unlock your hearts to social love."[23]

Prompted by a community's focus on abolition, such an emphasis on British and American bonds was not commonly expressed by Republicans. Republicans not only charged Federalists with pursuing an alliance with Britain but rejected the notion of an alliance altogether. Rejection was consistent with Washington's and Jefferson's past declarations. In his 1796 Farewell Address, Washington had stressed the dangers of "permanent alliances," while Jefferson, in his first inaugural address, had reiterated the importance of "peace, commerce, and honest friendship with all nations—entangling alliances with none." Their comments had not promoted isolationism but rather rejected "direct or *exclusive* alliance" that would make the United States a pawn in a two-state power struggle and expose the nation to invasion or reprisals. Such warnings and lyrical rejections of alliance sustained what Bukovansky has described as the "Founders' vision of America as a free and expansionary republic, unencumbered by military alliances and aloof from the machinations of European power politics."[24] One songwriter—possibly Edward Dillingham Bangs (1790–1838) who wrote for the Worcester *National Aegis*—rejected surrender, tribute, and subservience in a reworking of "Anacreon in Heaven." The songwriter countered Federalists' accusations of an alliance with France by stressing that Americans were "Both too wise to be trapp'd, and too strong to be bound." The songwriter rejected British alliance and blasted the Federalist "traitors" who "Talk of yielding our honor to *Englishmen's* sway." In a later, much-reprinted reworking of "Adams and Liberty" that shared a key line with the 1808 song, Bangs noted Britain's jealousy of American commerce and vowed that Americans would not "bend to Britain's control."[25] Skirting historical Anglophilic and Francophilic orientations associated with the two parties, songwriters asserted that the embargo saved Americans from depredations by *both* belligerents. Such lyrics reinforced a common perception that both European powers were trying to take over the world, either by conquest in the case of France, or by maritime monopoly in the case of Britain.[26]

Songwriters on both sides of this debate expressed fears of subservience and submission to a European power. America's independence required economic power, which required both trade and access to markets overseas. But an increasingly complex web of British and French commercial restrictions ultimately made neutral trade illegal and submission to one power's restrictions amounted to colonial status.[27] Jefferson leveraged this perspective inclusively when writing to the citizens of Beverly, Massachusetts, who petitioned for the embargo's end. As Jefferson explained, "To have submitted our rightful commerce to prohibitions and tributary exactions from others, would have been to surrender our independence." American independence in this conception was based on neutral trade. But withdrawing from trade to maintain the principle of neutral trade prompted a much larger debate over the nation's prosperity.

## "Nothing but Wreck and Starvation"

In debating the embargo, Americans addressed key questions of how the nation should achieve prosperity and who should have it. Members of both parties and all sections used song to debate the source and relative importance of the prosperity of the nation and its sections. Federalists went on the offensive. Federalist songwriters criticized the embargo as a Republican effort to ruin merchants and commerce. Responding to a Republican coalition that had merged rural agrarian and urban pro-manufacturing interests to fuel the election of Jefferson and Republicans at federal, state, and local levels, Federalist songwriters variously characterized the effort as a pro-manufacturing conspiracy or an agrarian agenda of turning merchants into manufacturers or farmers.[28]

The Federalists' charges were only partly true. Their portrayal ignored the fact that Republican diplomacy had sought to protect commerce and that the embargo included a ban on American exports in foreign vessels, which prevented farmers from flourishing while merchants suffered. The commercial sanctions also prompted an increase in domestic trade. Republicans did worry about the nation's heavy reliance on foreign trade and on people, such as merchants in the carrying trade, who profited from others without producing anything of their own. Republican newspapers not only highlighted how the embargo aided manufacturing, which was growing particularly in the mid-Atlantic, but also stressed more broadly the importance of the country's agricultural bounty, manufacturing, commerce, and arts.[29]

Intersecting with this partisan debate were charges of sectional bias. Northeastern merchants claimed economic martyrdom under biased southern Republican leaders. In New York and other middle states, discontented Republicans who opposed Virginian James Madison as Jefferson's successor challenged the embargo as a southern measure intended to hurt the rest of the country. Southerners claimed they were hurt more than northerners, as they lost the ability to export their goods while the northerners just lost profits, and they felt that they suffered for an interest largely outside the South—maritime rights for the northerners' carrying trade.[30] Such debate strained the Republican coalition that had expanded an old Republican agrarian vision into a broader conception of productive labor encompassing manufacturing, commerce, and navigation as the basis of the nation's prosperity. While those in the Northwest and South blamed European restrictions for their economic difficulties, northeasterners blamed the embargo. As their responses indicate, one of the embargo's challenges was that it did not call for equal opportunity for all but rather equal suffering. And as national commitment was defined in terms of sacrifice, sections vied to see who could claim to have suffered the most.[31]

Northeastern Federalists were particularly vocal in claiming the greatest suffering at the hands of southern and western leaders. For the *Portland Gazette*, one Federalist songwriter portrayed New England as the victim in an anti-embargo song written in the style of Charles Dibdin's theatrical sea songs. Supposedly sung by "Tom Loveall, an American Tar," the lyrics melodramatically blamed landlocked Kentuckians for creating "nothing but wreck and starvation."[32] Sectional suffering and superiority were intertwined. Bartholomew Brown's regional praise "New England," written for July 4, not only lauded the region as the nation's source of liberty but also singled out the South for wanting to keep its sailors locked up on land. A songwriter penning new lyrics to "Yankee Doodle" wedded sectional claims of superiority to the rejection of a French alliance. The tune, with its best-known lyrics being told from a New England perspective, reinforced claims of northern suffering. The songwriter declared, "Whatever Southern men may be,/New-England's sons are hearty;/They'll ne'er submit to bow the knee,/Nor crouch to Bonaparte."[33] Such claims of sectional suffering made for effective election-season rhetoric, and frustration with the embargo fueled a Federalist resurgence; in 1808 Federalists gained House seats in New Hampshire, Massachusetts, New York, Vermont, and Rhode Island and won control of the Massachusetts state legislature.

It was not that the Northeast was targeted for more harm than other regions but rather that key groups in the Northeast had thrived so greatly in previous years under British restrictions. They had prospered because more risk meant more profit. The carrying trade of West Indian raw materials to European ports had grown unnaturally in wartime and benefited merchants and elites in a few cities, especially Boston, Baltimore, New York, and Philadelphia.[34] Wealthy northeasterners had profited handsomely while European commercial restrictions remained in place.

Debating the necessity and unfairness of sectional and individual sacrifice for the nation's good resurrected a conflict between individual rights and community needs that was rooted in a classical concept of republicanism.[35] This conflict emerged in lyrics that circulated from Boston into other northeastern states and were scrapbooked by Jefferson himself. In a "song of spunky Jonathan," one songwriter adopted the voice of an idealized, faithful American republican: a resolute Revolutionary War veteran. The songwriter adopted a voice from the past to articulate moral expectations of Americans in the present, including the expectation of individual sacrifice for the community's good. Stressing that the embargo actually served the long-term benefit of all, "Jonathan" explained that in the ocean's tempests, "'Tis better in port to make sure of the whole,/Tho' we lose, for a while a proportion." As the veteran suggested, the prioritization required by the embargo was not only individual and sectional sacrifice for the greater good, but also short-term suffering for the long-term gain of European abandonment of commercial restrictions. The veteran put the embargo in perspective, recalling how he fought when hungry and worked when naked to ensure the nation's freedom. This veteran who knew how to do without then asked if he (and Americans) should now complain about "light burthens" like the embargo. While minimizing the embargo's negative impacts, the songwriter portrayed the opposition as self-interested whiners who would readily sell the nation's freedom to improve their own personal and sectional finances.[36] By issuing the lyrics from a veteran of the Battle of Lexington, the songwriter invoked the common Republican portrayal of Massachusetts Senator Timothy Pickering, who led strong attacks on the Republicans in New England, as a coward at the Battle of Lexington who refused to make a personal sacrifice for the good of the whole. ▶

In response, Federalists highlighted the hypocrisy of Republican claims that sacrifice was required for the greater good. Songwriters invoked Jefferson's first inaugural address, in which he had stressed that "a wise and frugal government" would leave citizens "free to regulate their own pursuits of industry and improvement," and would not "take from the mouth of labor the bread it has earned." Writing new lyrics to "Yankee Doodle," a Boston songwriter capitalized on the exposure of Republican hypocrisy to launch an elaborate narrative of partisan disarray. To set up the fifteen-verse narrative of Napoleon's and Republicans' wrongs, the lyrics reflexively commented on the tavern settings in which such songs would have often been read and shared. Featured above the fold of the first page of the *Boston Gazette*, the New England character promised, "I'll tell you Sam, how all this came,/ If you will sit awhile, sir;/And let us drink the other can,/An hour to beguile, sir." By engaging Jefferson's address, songwriters in Boston and Long Island portrayed the embargo as a hypocritical policy that restrained its citizens' work, reduced their income, and ruined the nation's agriculture, arts, and commerce. Such accusations were strengthened by the fourth and fifth embargo acts, which violated the fourth and fifth amendments to the Constitution by enabling search and seizure based on suspicion of illegal activity without warrants or due process.[37]

Despite claims of sectional suffering, the embargo's economic impacts were widespread. Both planters and merchants faced difficulties under the nation's self-imposed economic sanctions. Southern planters could not profit given high insurance rates, glutted markets, and low prices overseas. While growing manufacturing tempered the blow for the mid-Atlantic states, New England fishermen instantly lost their income and Massachusetts residents depended on soup houses for food. The embargo also deprived the federal government of tax revenues on imports, 90 percent of which were from the British Empire.[38]

Contestation over the embargo, the prosperity of the nation and its sections, and the risk of subservience to a European power reached a climax in the summer of 1808. New Jersey editor James Jefferson Wilson defended the legislation by portraying incessant Federalist complaints as illogical. In a reworking of "Yankee Doodle" clipped by Jefferson, "Jersey Blue" mocked Federalists for blaming everything on the embargo: the Federalists would even blame the legislation for grain-destroying weevils, ship-sinking waves and winds, and bankruptcy-inducing laziness and vice.[39]▶ This humorous defense could not stop frustration, though. In Massachusetts, which was responsible for over one-third of the nation's foreign trade in tonnage, Federalists mounted a petition campaign to repeal the embargo in August; Republican state conventions organized counterstatements. While citizens' correspondence with Jefferson showed general support for the embargo through the first half of the summer, by July, attitudes had shifted to increasing frustration with the entire complex of commercial restrictions.[40]

## "Embargo and Peace"

As supplemental embargo legislation addressed loopholes and issues unrelated to European belligerents' impressment and violations of neutrality on the high seas, the embargo's purpose was muddled. Carrying the embargo debates, music contributed to a fundamental change in the conception of the legislation as a tool of foreign policy. Republican songwriters increasingly defended the embargo in contradiction to Jefferson's original conception of it as a preparatory step for war—they stressed how the embargo preserved the nation's peace.[41] One Republican songwriter, possibly Edward Dillingham Bangs, conveyed this in the final verse of a reworking of "Anacreon in Heaven" that Jefferson preserved in his clippings book. Maintaining the moderate tone and language that were commonly used in American reworkings of this British gentleman's club song, the songwriter explained, "From the deep we withdraw till the tempest be past,/Till our flag can protect each American cargo,/While British ambition's dominion shall last,/Let us join heart and hand to support the EMBARGO,/For EMBARGO and peace/Will promote our increase!" Jefferson himself portrayed the embargo as a way to avoid war when defending the legislation to petitioners calling for its repeal. ⊙ As Jefferson explained to citizens of Beverly, Massachusetts, "the belligerent Powers have beset the highway of commercial intercourse with edicts which, taken together, expose our commerce and mariners, under almost every destination, a prey to their fleets & armies. Each party indeed would admit our commerce with themselves, with the view of associating us in their war against the other. But we have wished war with neither. Under these circumstances were passed the laws of which you complain."[42]

So determined were Republican songwriters to defend the legislation as a peaceful measure that they resorted to the same techniques Federalists had used in the heady days of intolerance following the XYZ Affair. In an item from Jefferson's clippings book, one Republican defender of the embargo warned, "Yankee doodle—look about—/Conspiracy and Treason,/With all their rascal rebel rout,/Should be suppress'd in season." Other lyrics saved by Jefferson declared, "Resistance to law is high treason in fact,/Then let us who cherish a system so free,/Make imps of sedition whoever they be." Resistance included smuggling in flagrant violation of the embargo, strong Federalist opposition organized by Pickering in Massachusetts, and ultimately talk of New England secession. As Federalists had done a decade before, Republicans accused their opponents, the Federalists, of wildness and ignorance and claimed for themselves the virtue of "reason and peace."[43]

Songwriters defended the embargo as an isolationist means of preserving the peace, avoiding entanglement in the European power struggle, and rejecting submission to either power.[44] This argument was made, soon after the legislation was passed in January, in a reworking of "Yankee Doodle" circulated from Philadelphia to New York (see Figure 5.1). The songwriter leveraged the older song's associations with the Revolutionary War to establish a context for a different type of independence, one gained through self-sufficiency and rational control rather than violence. The songwriter structured the song's verses to make self-sufficiency seem like a logical and appropriate action. The first verse opened by commanding Americans to don their moccasins and leggings, emblems of Native American attire that here served as markers of cultural difference from Britons. The chorus and the next five verses roused pride by recounting Americans' victories in the Revolutionary War and succinctly established Britain as a tyrannical foe. With Americans' ability to best Britain in battle well established, the seventh verse then performed a critical function, directing readers to go ahead and serve their country before orders to fight were given. But the way to serve the country, as the next five verses explained, was through self-reliance.[45] As other Republican versifiers did in the subsequent months, the songwriter effusively touted America's agricultural bounty, natural resources, manufacturing, commerce, and arts as the basis of the nation's freedom from European war. Evoking the country bumpkin popularized through the older "Yankee Doodle," the songwriter proudly maintained "Fine *dittany* our woods adorn,/The girls can cut and dry it" as a substitute for imported tea. Such lyrics promoted a broad notion of native productivity that not only defended the embargo but also appealed to a coalition of rural agrarian and urban pro-manufacturing Republicans, a coalition that had been strained by the embargo controversy and was vulnerable to third parties that developed in Pennsylvania and New York.[46] Unsurprisingly, the songwriter ended "A New Yankee Song" with a common call to unite, a call prepared by a reminder that the Revolutionary War victories had been gained by a collection of "mechanics, farmers, [and] jobbers."

Despite Jefferson's initial conception of the embargo as preparation for war and repeated statements explaining its defensive nature, in 1808 the embargo was conceived in more coercive terms and seen as a substitute for

Mount Helicon.

*From the (Phil.) Democratic Preſs.*

A NEW YANKEE SONG.

Tune—" Yankee Doodle."

Gird on your hunting ſhirts with ſpeed,
Your moccaſins and leggings,
And march to meet the red-coat breed,
And tories with them leaguing.

CHORUS.

Yankee doodle beat them now,
As Yankees did before us,
They made the generals Gage and Howe,
Deſert the Yankee ſtore-houſe.*

At Bunker's hill they worſted them,
Altho' but badly armed;
John Bull unuſed to ſuch a game,
Was very much alarmed.
Yankee doodle, &c.

The army was compoſed of
Mechanics, Farmers, Jobbers,
Yet bravely they diſpoſed of
The hoſt of Britiſh robbers.
Yankee doodle, &c.

The lords of England did declare
The Yankees dare not fight them;
But when the Yankees took them here,
It did moſt darn'dly ſpite them.
Yankee doodle, &c.

Burgoyne declar'd 4000 troops
Would penetrate the ſtates thro',
At Saratoga he had hopes
Of beating gen. Gates too.
Yankee doodle, &c.

George Waſhington and La Fayette
Coop'd up the earl Cornwallis;
His ſword he yielded with regret,
And curs'd his former follies.
Yankee doodle, &c.

Tho' you can fight them man for man
And drive them from our borders,
Purſue your Yankee fathers' plan,
Who waited not for orders.
Yankee doodle, &c.

If *tea* ye have not now to burn,
You may refuſe to buy it,
Fine *dittany* our woods adorn,
The girls can cut and dry it.
Yankee doodle, &c.

Hemp, cotton, flax, at home we have,
And wool for winter garment,
And if a penny we can ſave,
I wonder where's the harm in't.
Yankee doodle, &c.

America is a reſource
Exhauſtleſs as the ocean,
To home-made goods let's have recourſe—
*That there's a Yankee notion.*
Yankee doodle, &c.

Our mines and, mountains will produce
Materials for building,
And in a well conſtructed houſe,
Pray what's the uſe of guilding?
Yankee doodle, &c.

We've artiſans of ev'ry kind,
Great Britain has no better;
Her *toys* perhaps are more refin'd,
But Yankee *goods* are *better.*
Yankee doodle, &c.

Congreſs may inſtantly enact
A *Lex non-importation,*
To which you'll find none to object,
Except the Britiſh nation.
Yankee doodle, &c.

Let George and Alexander deal
Like amicable neighbors,
The poor of Britain then will feel
Suſpenſion from their labors.
Yankee doodle, &c.

Now let us ſtill united be,
And live within our income,
Then all our enemies will ſee
How Yankee boys can clink 'em.
Yankee doodle, &c.

* *Boſton.*

Figure 5.1. "A New Yankee Song." Sherburne *Olive Branch*, 30 January 1808. Readex/NewsBank.

war. Jefferson began transforming the embargo into an "economic weapon of war" rather than simply a means of protecting property. Considering US commerce as valuable to European powers, especially in wartime, Jefferson saw American neutrality as a way to bargain with the belligerents over access to markets and motivate them to treat the nation with justice. This coercive concept of the embargo received propagandist support from songwriters who maintained that the embargo "punished" the belligerents.[47]

Nearly all these Republican arguments were synthesized by Scottish immigrant Alexander Wilson in the frequently reprinted song, "Freedom and Peace; or, the Voice of America" (see Figure 5.2).[48] Wilson, who urged and celebrated Jefferson's election in song years before, had remained a dedicated Republican supporter and corresponded with the president on their mutual interest in ornithology. Having previously written song lyrics and political poetry, Wilson readily captured in verse moderate Republican arguments elaborating and justifying the embargo.[49]

Through the title and chorus, Wilson repeatedly stressed the importance of maintaining peace. Wilson portrayed the embargo as a noble and wise means of withdrawal rather than a cowardly act. In his third verse, Wilson justified the administration's method of avoiding the war-torn oceans by declaring that "From scenes so atrocious of blood and commotion/'Tis great—it is godlike—a while to withdraw!" Wilson responded to Federalists' rejection of the embargo as a "terrapin policy" resembling a turtle withdrawing into its shell.[50] Wilson gave his propagandist defense greater weight by claiming both justice and reason for Republican leadership. From his fourth verse, Wilson stressed the nation's self-reliance and ability to survive in isolation. He emphasized the importance of fostering native industry and arts as opposed to building a navy to engage in war and conquest. Wilson argued, "Far nobler the ARTS of our country to nourish,/Its *true* independence and powers to increase/And with our resource of industry flourish,/To hail the glad blessings of FREEDOM and PEACE." Wilson maintained that Americans should remain firm and "unmov'd" if European powers would not give the nation justice, having confidence that "*in ourselves we're a world!*" To make his case, in his fifth, seventh, and eighth verses Wilson touted the nation's riches and asked, "Is one human blessing or luxury wanted,/That flows not amongst us unmeasured and free?" At the same time, Wilson resolutely maintained in the third verse that the embargo would damage Britain through commercial deprivation.

Wilson's song entailed major contradictions. His inflated and idealistic account contrasted sharply with the recession that the embargo ultimately caused at home. More immediately, though, his message of peace and defense of the embargo contradicted the martial inclinations of radical Republican William Duane and others who had prompted the song's

TO THE FOLLOWING SONG

HAS BEEN AWARDED THE PRIZE MEDAL OFFERED BY THE

PHILADELPHIA MILITARY ASSOCIATION.

*Freedom and Peace; or, The Voice of America.*

A NATIONAL SONG.

I.

While Europe's mad powers o'er creation are ranging,
Regardless of right, with their bloodhounds of war;
Their kingdoms—their empires distracted and changing,
Their murders and ruins resounding afar—
Lo! *Freedom* and *Peace*, fair descendants of Heaven!
Of all our companions the noblest and best,
From dark eastern regions by anarchy driven,
Have found a retreat in the climes of the *West*.

Chorus—Then Freedom and Peace we will cherish together,
We'll guard them with valor—we'll crown them with art!
Nor ever resign up the one or the other,
For all that ambition's proud pomp can impart.

II.

Here dwell the blest cherubs so dear to our wishes!
Here thron'd in our hearts, they inspire all our themes!
They sport round each cottage with smiles and with blushes;
They glide through our cities—they sail down our streams;
The shades of our heroes, immortal, delighted;
Look down from the radiant mansions of day,
"Be firm!" they exclaim, "Be forever *united*!
"And nations may threaten; but *cannot* dismay!"

Chorus—For Freedom and Peace, &c.

III.

The demons of discord are roaming the ocean,
*Their* insult and rapine and murder are law!
From scenes so atrocious of blood and commotion,
'Tis great—it is Godlike—awhile to withdraw!
Perhaps when the hand that hath fed, is suspended,
When famine's pale spectres their steps overtake,
The firm voice of Truth may at last be attended,
And Justice and Reason once more re-awake.

Chorus—But Freedom, &c.

IV.

Away with the vultures of War and Ambition,
That headlong to rearing of Navies would run,
Those *cancers* of nations—those pits of perdition,
Where Britain and France will alike be undone!
Far nobler the Arts of our country to nourish,
Its *true* Independence and powers to increase;
And while our resources of industry flourish,
To hail the glad blessings of Freedom and Peace.

Chorus—Then Freedom, &c.

V.

The storm we defy—it may roar at a distance,
Unmov'd and impregnable here we remain;
We ask not of Europe for *gifts* or *assistance*;
But Justice, Good Faith, and the Rights of the Main;
Should these be refus'd, *in ourselves we're a world!*
And those who may dare its domain to invade,
To death and destruction at once shall be hurl'd,
For freedom hath sworn it, and shall be obeyed!

Chorus—Then Freedom, &c.

VI.

We want neither Emperor, King, Prince, nor Marshal,
No Navies, to plunder—nor Indies to fleece;
Our honest Decrees, are, "To all be impartial;"
Our Orders of Council, are Freedom and Peace:
But Commerce assail'd by each vile depredator,
Our country has will'd for a while to restrain,
And infamy light on the head of the traitor
Who tramples her laws for ambition or gain.

Chorus—Then Freedom, &c.

VII.

Look round on your country, Columbians! undaunted,
From Georgia to Maine—from the Lakes to the Sea,
Is one human blessing or luxury wanted,
That flows not amongst us unmeasured and free?
Our harvests sustain half the wide eastern world;
Our mines and our forests exhaustless remain;
What sails on our great fishing banks are unfurl'd!
What shoals fill our streams from the depths of the main!

Chorus—Then Freedom, &c.

VIII.

The fruits of our country, our flocks and our fleeces,
The treasures immense in our mountains that lie,
While discord is tearing old Europe to pieces,
Shall amply the wants of our people supply:
New *Roads* and *Canals*, on their bosoms conveying,
Refinement and wealth, through our forests shall roam;
And millions of freemen, with rapture surveying,
Shall shout out, "O LIBERTY! *this* is thy home!"

Chorus—Then Freedom, &c.

IX.

Great shades of our Fathers! unconquer'd, victorious!
To whom under Heaven, our Freedom we owe,
Bear witness, that Peace we revere still as glorious—
For Peace every gain for a while we forego;
But should the great son of ambition and plunder—
Should Ocean's proud scourges our Liberty claim—
Your spirit shall ride in the roar of our thunder,
That sweeps to the gulph of perdition their name.

Chorus—For Freedom, &c.

X.

Our strength and resources defy base aggression—
Our courage—our enterprize—both have been try'd;
Our nation unstained with the crimes of oppression,
Hath Heaven's own thunderbolts all on its side;
Then henceforth let freeman with freeman be brother,
Our Peace and our liberty, both to assert,
Nor ever resign up the one or the other
For all that ambition's proud pomp can impart.

Chorus—Then Freedom and Peace we will cherish together,
We'll guard them with valor—we'll crown them with art!
Nor ever resign up the one or the other,
For all that ambition's proud pomp can impart.

**Figure 5.2.** Alexander Wilson, "Freedom and Peace." *Washington Expositor*, 23 July 1808. Readex/NewsBank.

composition. Under the headline "National Airs," Duane's Philadelphia *Aurora* and other Republican newspapers had called for submissions for a national musical contest. The organizers, officers of the first division of the Pennsylvania militia, explained that the nation was "insulted abroad and in our own ports—menaced by the augmentation and array of foreign troops in our neighbourhood." They launched the musical contest amid this "crisis calculated to inspire the genius of our country, to awaken the virtuous spirit, and to swell the noble soul with such emotions as those that warmed and animated the sages and heroes to whom we owe independence as a nation, and liberty as men and citizens." Songs submitted were supposed to be "expressive of the spirit of the times, and calculated to raise the military ardor of the nation." The contest's rhetoric echoed the spirit evoked by demonstrations of modern military tactics before huge crowds in Philadelphia and detailed by the *Aurora* and other Republican newspapers. "Aware of the great influence of national music, on national character and heroism," the organizers offered a gold medal worth $50 to the author of "the best national *song* or *martial tune*."[51] Seven worthy song submissions were ultimately circulated in Republican newspapers like Duane's *Aurora*. Those songs, along with worthy instrumental submissions, also circulated in a sheet music collection published by William M'Culloch, the American-born son of Scottish immigrant printer John M'Culloch. William M'Culloch's novel incorporation of detachable individual instrumental parts on coarse paper indicated an intended regimental use. Duane was among the many figures from Boston to Savannah who accepted subscriptions for this collection.[52]

Duane's support for the contest and printed collection should not be surprising: he had advocated war shortly after the *Chesapeake* incident, and he championed the militia. His long-standing commitment to citizen militia prepared to fight to maintain their citizenship was likely nurtured in Ireland in the late 1770s and early 1780s when Volunteers formed in emulation of American revolutionary citizen militias. After being beaten by Federalist militia officers of McPherson's Blues outside the *Aurora* office in 1799, Duane had spurred the formation of Republican militia in Philadelphia. He became captain of the Republican Greens and even designed their uniforms. Eager to serve in war, Duane was appointed lieutenant colonel of riflemen and wrote and published a militia manual designed to end reliance on British military theory.[53]

Duane's interests were reflected in the song contest's call for "martial" and "animating" submissions. Wilson's peace-promoting lyrics, poorly aligned with these interests, were made more martial in M'Culloch's collection, where they were set to a march by Philadelphia composer Rayner Taylor. Without a heroic and inspiring leader in the White House, several songwriters turned to George Washington to conjure a martial spirit in the present. Two songwriters whose work was featured in M'Culloch's collection repeatedly stressed the importance of principled militarism and courage in wartime before calling for restraint in their final verses in alignment with the embargo. Indeed, the song contest generated conflicting commentaries on the embargo's purposes and value in relation to peace, war, and prosperity. The writer of "Let the Drum Beat to Arms" opened with a war call but concluded by stressing peace. Writing from Petersburg, Virginia, home to a sizable radical Irish community, Irish immigrant and merchant-poet John M'Creery offered the most energetic song submission of those circulated by M'Culloch and Duane. Densely filled with graphic wartime imagery and set to an A minor jig,[54] M'Creery's "The American Star" was an energetic response to the contest organizers' calls for martial and animating lyrics. In his third verse, M'Creery welcomed invasion as a pretext for war. His bellicose lyrics were fueled by Anglophobia, but in alignment with the contest's call for national songs, he refrained, as did other successful contestants, from naming Britain as the aggressor.

Despite these conflicting responses to the embargo and the wartime context, the contest produced a significant body of song. M'Culloch described his printing as "the first collection of airs and songs that are 'wholly original and national.'" As the nation moved closer to war in subsequent years, M'Creery's "The American Star" was reprinted in 1810 and appeared in forty-eight songsters and in many newspapers. Another contest submission was reprinted in 1811. And even before it was set to music, Wilson's song was read on the geographic periphery of the nation before a "numerous company" assembled in a Maine tavern.[55] Although the radical Republican Duane, after serving as the "architect of Jefferson's triumph" in 1800, was beleaguered by libel proceedings and marginalized by his party at the national and state levels, the song contest and the publication of worthy submissions attracted attention, including the notice of the president, who scrapbooked all the published contest lyrics.[56]

While Republican newspaper printers circulated worthy contest submissions, their Federalist counterparts expanded their application of satire from individual songs to an entire ritual. Federalist newspapers circulated a satirical account of a Georgia July 4 celebration (see Figure 5.3). First appearing in the Savannah *Columbian Museum*, the city's oldest and most conservative newspaper, the "Cracker Planter's" account of his solitary celebration of the nation's independence was significant not only as Federalist political commentary on the embargo but also because detailed

FROM THE SAVANNAH MUSEUM.

*The Fourth of July*, 1808.—This great and glorious dav was celebrated at my plantation in a comfortable style; being *solus*, I chose myself President, and will venture to assert that a more perfect unity of sentiment and harmony of disposition, never prevailed since the existence of our national independence. The following appropriate toasts were drank, accompanied with songs—after which I retired with decency and decorum:

1 The GLORIOUS DAY that I now celebrate—
Purchas'd by heroes at so dear a rate,
May every rascal get a broken pate,
And his base name become obliterate,
Who would attempt thro' malice to create
Political dissentions in this state
At such a crisis.
song—*Firm united let us be, &c.*

2 The sacred memory of the great WASHINGTON—
His virtues shine resplendent as the sun—
The day I now enjoy his valour won:
I prithee Death, do'st think it was well done
To take him from us!
song—*Faithful below he did his duty, but now he's gone aloft*, &c.

3 The Philosophick Friend of THOMAS PAINE—
A lack of firmness—not a lack of brain,
But want of nerves may make a man insane.
—Our crops are very much in want of rain,
But these embargo times I wont complain,
Because 'tis nonsense.
song—*Poor Tom's cold*—long metre.

4 The Constitution, as it was of old—
Pure as unadulterated gold:
Alas! alas! I could a tale unfold;
But no—'twould make my boiling blood run cold,
And crack my heart strings.
song—*God save the United States*, &c.

5 The State of Georgia, as it ought to be—
I hope to live the happy time to see,
Among all parties perfect harmony,
And honest dealings.
song—*A light heart and thin pair of breeches*, &c.

6 Our Sister States, throughout the Continent—
I do not think the money was well spent,
That for the Lousy-Anna purchase went
To Buonaparte.
song—*Moll in the Wad and I fell out.*

7 Nothing for Tribute, for Defence a million—
We'll make Napoleon dance a new cotillion
If arbitrary measures he keeps still on,
To rule our great men.
song—*No Foreign Land shall give us Laws*, &c.

8 The British Council—it appears to me,
They wish to take a trip across the sea,
And with us drink another dish of tea
In Massachusetts.
song—*Yankee Doodle.*

9 A free and open trade with all the world—
May every tyrant from his throne be hurl'd
And with hot pokers have his whiskers curl'd
That would prevent it.
song—*America, Commerce and Freedom.*

10 Our infant Navy—once it promis'd well—
Its nurse was chang'd, and wonderfull to tell,
Like Tarrapine it crawl'd into its shell,
At the New City.
song—*I'm safe from Davies Locker.*

11 The Chesapeake—don't let her be forgotten—
The Captain sure, (but not the ship) was rotten;
Sooner than strike, by Jove I'd eat my cotton—
I can't digest it!
song—*Hearts of Oak are our ships.*

12 Brave WARREN, MERCER, and MONTGOMERY—
Who died like Heroes for our Liberty,
Their mem'ry shall be ever dear to me—
Peace to their ashes.
song—*Soldiers Adieu!*

13. Traitors and Vagabonds of every kind—
May they like my old horse become stone blind,
And be compell'd a *bran new* road to find
To Carter's Mountain.
song—*O ye scamps, ye pads, ye divers.*

14 The American Fair—kind Heaven bless them all—
For their protection, at a moments call
Would I turn out and firmly stand or fall,
Although a coward.
song—*And when the wars are over, we'll come and live with you.*

15 My Planting Friends—the neighbourhood around—
Of honest hearts and principles right sound,
May cotton fetch us fifty cents a pound,
And rice five dollars.
song—*Hospitality, all reality, no formality, here you'll ever see.*

16 Myself—poor fellow! though the last not the least—
May I grow better as my years increase,
And when death comes—Oh! may I die in peace—
I have no friend to toast me at my feast,
'Tis hard, by gracious.
song—*In the down hill of life*, &c.

A CRACKER PLANTER.

Figure 5.3. Mock July 4 celebration written by a "Cracker Planter." *Charleston Courier*, 27 July 1808. Readex/NewsBank.

musical accounts and political songs were printed in newspapers south of Virginia less frequently than in other states. The "Cracker Planter's" satire was not intended to be performed but was written and circulated for readers' enjoyment as a commentary on the times. Praised for its wit, the satire was reprinted in several Federalist electioneering newspapers.[57] It was also preserved by Jefferson in his scrapbook of newspaper songs, one of few items he saved expressing Federalist views on the embargo.

Having selected as the vehicle for his satire a requisite annual ritual in communities large and small across the nation, the "Cracker Planter" used several of the ritual's staple songs and toasts as a relief for his witty commentary on the embargo. These staples included "Hail Columbia," "Yankee Doodle," and "America, Commerce, and Freedom." Written by Susanna Rowson and set to music by Alexander Reinagle, "America, Commerce, and Freedom" had been incorporated in the pantomime *The Sailor's Landlady* in 1794, and it circulated through sheet music editions and over sixty songsters during the next quarter-century, as well as being recorded in music manuscripts. ▶ The song proved especially useful on convivial and patriotic occasions: Rowson had avoided specific, topical references; repeated a broadly applicable slogan; and wisely included a recurring invitation to drink. Consequently, her song was often used to toast commerce, manufacturing, and agriculture. Later likened to the theatrical sea songs of Charles Dibdin, Rowson's lyrics captured sentiments attributed to sailors on the stage.[58] The song therefore suited well declarations like the "Cracker Planter's" ninth toast to "Free and open trade with all the world."

Within the framework established by these staple songs, the "Cracker Planter" programmed lyrics wholly inappropriate for such anniversary rituals to deliver his satirical commentary on the embargo. To punctuate the sixth toast, the planter used the jig "Moll in the Wad," also known as "Moll in the Straw," which in some common lyrical variants told of a man and prostitute quarreling over money. Accompanying a toast asserting that the Louisiana Purchase was money not well spent, the song suggested that the transaction, which Republicans had touted as expansion through peaceful acquisition, had not freed the nation from Napoleon's schemes of conquest. Rather, as the prostitute demanded more money, the planter implied, the Louisiana Purchase simply fueled Napoleon's plans for conquest and left the nation vulnerable to his aspirations. For the penultimate toast, the planter selected the Irish song, "The Land of Potatoes Oh." Written by Robert MacOwen Owenson, an Irish comic actor and songwriter, and sung to a D major Irish jig called "Morgan Rattler," this was one of many potato-related songs symbolizing Ireland. Owenson's song was put to political use on both sides of the Atlantic: it was included in an 1804 song collection designed to foster British loyalty in Ireland during the Napoleonic Wars,[59] while through the Georgia satirist's pen, its highlighting of Ireland's symbolic crop made it an ideal commentary on the South's staple crops. From 1806, excess US exports had sent prices down, and prices on commodities, especially cotton and rice, remained low through most of 1808.[60] With the Irish song, the planter highlighted southern claims of sectional sacrifice.

The "Cracker Planter" placed this sectional complaint in a larger political context. He denounced Republican "traitors" like Aaron Burr and the Yazoo land fraud in Georgia, challenged both European belligerents, and criticized Jefferson himself.[61] Defying both belligerents and rejecting submission and alliance altogether, the satirist endorsed the idea of war and cheered in recollection of the XYZ era, "Nothing for tribute; for defence a million." Indeed, as the embargo dragged on without coercive effect, more Americans came to see only two choices: submission or war. Despite the defiance of many Americans like the "Cracker Planter," the nation was unprepared in many ways for war.[62]

## "Embargo and Navy"

In addition to an ill-prepared militia, the nation had almost no navy. Since the Tripolitan War (1801–5) in the Mediterranean Sea, the navy had been portrayed as a point of national pride. Americans constructed narratives of naval strength and growth through theatrical productions, art, poetry, and music.[63] A representative example was Charles Harford and Alexander Reinagle's song "The Tars of Columbia." Honoring the war's naval heroes and martyrs, Harford maintained that "Whilst at the hostile shore/Where thundering cannons roar,/The note of each brave tar shall be/Not for tribute! But glory, we'll die or be free." Following the war, organizers of an Albany celebration honoring local veteran Lieutenant Jonathan Thorn toasted "The gallant and intrepid Heroes of the Mediterranean" with a naval reworking of "Anacreon in Heaven" that cheered, "our Navy triumphant shall ride o'ver the Main/Our Rights & our Commerce defend & maintain."[64] Such sentiments remained relevant amid the increasing commercial restrictions of the Napoleonic Wars.

But while these heroic narratives touted the nation's naval prowess, Federalists regarded the navy as woefully inadequate. The Federalist songwriter "Yankee Doodle" noted that the government had built no frigates, gunboats, or harbor fortifications. For Portsmouth Federalists' July 4 celebration in 1806, Jonathan Mitchell Sewall deplored the sorry state of the nation's defenses in a song praised by the *New York Evening Post*. Nearly sixty and in rapidly declining health, Sewall noted that "no navy guards our shore,/ And COMMERCE bleeds at ev'ry pore. . . . no bulwarks guard our land/Our capitols defenceless stand."[65] Intent on protecting commerce and the nation's seaports, the primary source of federal revenue, Federalists regularly advocated building ships of the line, additional frigates, and robust, permanent coastal fortifications.[66]

Following the *Chesapeake* incident and throughout the embargo period, Congress and Americans debated the makeup and purpose of the navy. Calculating the objectives and costs of naval investments relative to current conditions, early in his second term, Jefferson had promoted defensive measures, including gunboats, floating batteries, and coastal fortifications, but he remained unenthusiastic about ships of the line, the largest and most heavily armed warships at the heart of the British navy. In January 1807, the Antinavalist House had rejected proposals for constructing ships of the line and provided for only fortifications and gunboats. Gunboats were appreciated by Antinavalist Republicans for their peacetime storage, potential to be manned by militia, and low cost. In contrast to this primarily defensive navy focused on preventing violations of US territorial waters, the Federalists and few Republicans comprising the Navalists had wanted a navy well stocked with larger seagoing vessels like frigates and ships of the line to protect commerce, defend national honor, and expand influence in North America while Europe was consumed by war.[67] As the debate was simplified in song and the press, gunboats and frigates symbolized a defensive and offensive navy, respectively.

Songwriters carried these two positions effectively to the larger public. Federalist songwriters cast a defensive navy as insufficient and based on a faulty prioritization of economy. Navalist songwriters ridiculed the country's "Lilliputian" and mice-like gunboats and dry-dock.[68] The "Cracker Planter" lamented that "Our infant Navy" had great promise until its "nurse" changed from Federalist to Republican. The Navalists and anti-Navalists often, but not always, aligned with Federalist and Republican stances, respectively. An exception came from Maryland's eastern shore, not that far from the *Chesapeake* incident, at the close of 1807. Reminding Americans of a past commitment to naval expansion, the editor of the Easton *Republican Star* reprinted Federalist David Humphreys's 1799 "Naval Song" that had announced "Honor calls us to the main," backed by Congress's authorization of $1 million to construct battleships, sloops, and dockyards and purchase of timberlands when the militarism of the XYZ Affair intensified during the Quasi War. By early 1801 there were thirteen frigates, and six ships of the line were slated for construction.[69] The latter were insufficiently financed, however, and were never constructed. Years later, while Navalist songwriters lamented that the nation's ships were useless, Republican songwriters like Boston printer Samuel G. Snelling maintained faith in the nation's modest navy against either Britain or France. One of these printer-songwriters—Anthony Haswell of Bennington, Vermont—even maintained that the American frigates and small craft would torment British vessels like a chased crow.[70]

As American patience with the embargo wore thin, Congress labored with another round of naval legislation. In January 1809, Congress appropriated $1 million for coastal defenses. The House agreed to man the 171 available gunboats. Navalist proposals to man all existing frigates and other armed vessels resulted, after complex congressional efforts, in a bicameral compromise to outfit and man just four existing frigates for defensive purposes.[71] This defensive concept of the navy limited the nation's options for dealing with the belligerents' commercial restrictions and depredations.

Both sides of this naval debate were captured by the writer of "Embargo and Navy," a song first printed by the Trenton *True American* and scrapbooked by Jefferson. While acknowledging the Federalists' argument that the "navy's neglect" was the cause of "All the evils we feel," the songwriter also recounted the Republicans' view—"do not the large navies swallow the small?" and supported it by recalling the fate of the Danish navy, which fell to Britain " 'at one fell swoop,' a prey." Britain used both construction and capture to amass its 800 naval vessels, and Republicans felt that Britain would not tolerate any challenges to its dominance of the seas. The Republican songwriter therefore concluded in support of the embargo, "A cheaper and safer defence is, by far,/To exclude all their goods, all our products retain;/This will punish *them* worse than a seven years war,/Yet will injure *us* less than a single campaign."[72]▶ Other common components of Republicans' arguments can be seen in Alexander Wilson's "Freedom and Peace": Wilson called navies "cancers of nations" and portrayed them as tools of plunder used by emperors and kings (see Figure 5.2).

A coastally defensive navy incapable of protecting the nation's commerce on the high seas continued to draw the Federalists' criticism. Members of a "private circle in Charleston, S.C." lamented in song that America's "ships are harmless to her foes, and only hurt the nation."[73] Navalists blasted the embargo as the result of not having built a seagoing navy in peacetime as Federalists had wished. Among many Federalist songwriters targeting Jefferson's defensive navy,[74] the anonymous writer of "War with England" used the tune "Derry Down" to mock it as a fantasy. The songwriter envisioned Britain being scared off by American cannons loaded with "capers and sugar plums" and "empty glass bottles turn'd into grenades!"[75] A songwriter selecting "Yankee Doodle" to carry this argument had the New England country bumpkin character observe, "Congress thought as how they'd raise,/A navy big as France floats,/So after taking yeas and nays,/They built some shabby gunboats./Yankee doodle boats of war,/I wish I may be shot Sir,/If one broad side from man of war,/Wouldn't send them all to pot Sir."[76] One songwriter sarcastically celebrated the anniversary of Jefferson's inauguration in a reworking of "Hail Columbia." The songwriter crowed with mock national pride, "How our gallant *Navy* rides!/*Gun-boats* blacken all our tides!/And *Wasps* and *Hornets* scour the coast;/And *Wasps* and *Hornets* scour the coast;/While *Frigates* spread our fame afar,/And triumph over Neptune's car./The haughty *tyrants of the sea*,/Before our flag ignobly flee;/And *Gallia's monarch*, stain'd with gore,/Must still respect *our* happy shore." With the final line, "To Jefferson and *Liberty!*," the songwriter highlighted Republicans' failed diplomacy and inability to extract the country from the belligerents' web of commercial restrictions without a seagoing navy.[77] ▶ With such lyrics, Federalists mocked Jefferson for dreaming gunboats into ships, underestimating the need for maritime defense, and ruining the navy through diminution.

The latter argument was voiced in "A Parody" of "Robert Kidd," one of four reworkings circulated in Harry Croswell's Albany *Balance* and sung at a local Federalist celebration when the party gained control of the New York State Assembly (see Figure 5.4). ▶ Among reworkings of "Anacreon in Heaven," "Hail Columbia," and "Yankee Doodle," the songwriter penned new lyrics for a song about William Kidd (1645–1701). Kidd was a Scottish privateer who was hired by the British to attack French vessels

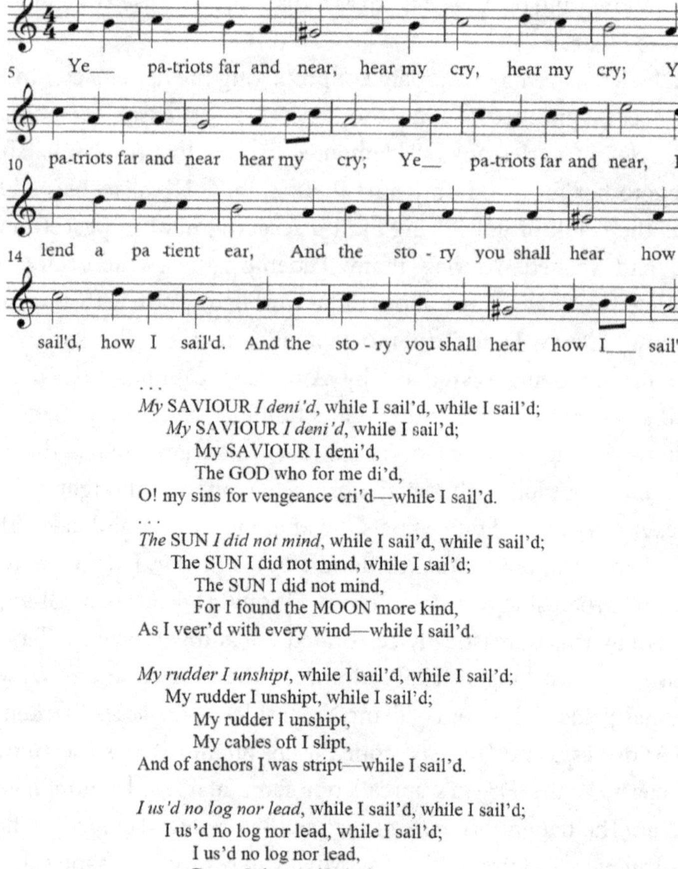


. . .

*My* SAVIOUR *I deni'd*, while I sail'd, while I sail'd;
*My* SAVIOUR *I deni'd*, while I sail'd;
My SAVIOUR I deni'd,
The GOD who for me di'd,
O! my sins for vengeance cri'd—while I sail'd.

. . .

*The* SUN *I did not mind*, while I sail'd, while I sail'd;
The SUN I did not mind, while I sail'd;
The SUN I did not mind,
For I found the MOON more kind,
As I veer'd with every wind—while I sail'd.

*My rudder I unshipt*, while I sail'd, while I sail'd;
My rudder I unshipt, while I sail'd;
My rudder I unshipt,
My cables oft I slipt,
And of anchors I was stript—while I sail'd.

*I us'd no log nor lead*, while I sail'd, while I sail'd;
I us'd no log nor lead, while I sail'd;
I us'd no log nor lead,
But as I *dream'd* in bed,
The course to steer came in my head—as I sail'd.

. . .

*I wav'd my magic wand*, while I sail'd, while I sail'd;
I wav'd my magic wand, while I sail'd;
I wav'd my magic wand,
O'er *Frigates Eggs* in sand,
And GUN BOATS hatch'd along the strand—while I sail'd.

. . .

*My maps and charts I tore*, while I sail'd, while I sail'd;
My maps and charts I tore, while I sail'd;
My maps and charts I tore,
And I've run my ship ashore,
O, the wreck I must deplore—while I sail.

. . .

*O let my mournful fate*, while I sail'd, while I sail'd;
O let my mournful fate, while I sail'd;
O let my mournful fate
Teach those who rule the state
TO STEER BY COMPASS e'er 'tis too late—while they sail

**Figure 5.4.** "Jefferson's Confession." Albany *The Balance and New-York State Journal*, 16 May 1809. Readex/NewsBank.

and then tried and hanged in England after assaulting a large treasure-laden Armenian vessel sailing for the East India Company under a falsely flown French flag. "Robert Kidd" was part of a complex multicentury network of criminal confession songs united by a distinctive repetitive lyrical structure. The songwriter extended this network with the reworking titled "Jefferson's Confession." In addition to maintaining the repetitive structure, the songwriter retained and applied to Jefferson the fictionalized Kidd's rejection of God, admission of sin, and concluding warning to audiences to learn from his erring ways. Along with well-worn accusations of cowardice, misguided purchase of Louisiana swamplands, and submission to French demands, the songwriter ridiculed Jefferson as a philosopher and dreamer who destroyed the navy. The songwriter had Jefferson admit, "I wav'd my magic wand/O'er *Frigates Eggs* in sand,/And Gun Boats hatch'd along the strand."[78] While Robert Kidd's fictional confession centered on piratical prowess, Jefferson's centered on wrecking the nation-as-ship by navigating it without log, lead, rudder, able crew, maps, charts, or compass. The haunting aeolian melody enhanced this extended confession. The central theme of Jefferson's inept leadership was only reinforced in the Federalists' celebration at the Eagle Tavern by other lyrics written for the occasion and circulated for a larger audience in the *Balance*.

While Anti-Navalists stressed the importance of coastal defense, Navalists stressed the defense of national honor. Federalist songwriters accused Republicans of giving up honor through the embargo. Beneath this discourse of honor was an intense dedication to commercial interests and mercantile profit. Overseas trade, especially the carrying trade that flourished during the Napoleonic Wars, had benefited the merchants, shipbuilders, and elites of the northern port cities. With that trade thwarted, opponents of the embargo called for greater national naval investment to protect commerce. This discourse of honor also reflected an increasing association between commercial interests and national interest, intensely supported by American interpretations of maritime law that stressed the basic principle that "free ships make free goods." But while northern merchants wanted naval protection of commerce, their representatives were not willing to use the navy against Britain.[79] As Congress supported a defensive navy and rejected the construction of additional seagoing vessels, ongoing impressment and commercial restrictions highlighted the nation's insufficient naval capabilities and a fundamental conflict between the nation's aspirations and its actual institutions.

## Submission or War

As the Napoleonic Wars dragged on, the embargo proved ineffective. Initially conceived as a defensive, temporary preparation for war, the embargo was turned into a protracted form of peaceable economic coercion and retaliation. But the embargo had not changed British policy on impressment and neutral trade. Additionally, the increasingly stringent enforcement of the embargo required an unacceptable degree of control over individual citizens' economic affairs and was not compatible with republican society. Support for the embargo waned from mid-1808 and declined dramatically at the year's end, the time when Jefferson had indicated that he anticipated the embargo would be repealed.[80]

When Congress did not promptly repeal the embargo in late 1808, northern outcries and smuggling intensified as low prices in Britain finally rose. The one-year anniversary of the embargo was deemed the "death of commerce" and treated as a day of mourning in Massachusetts and Rhode Island communities; Republicans responded with countercelebrations. Residents in Wells, Maine, marked the anniversary with a funeral dirge written for the occasion. To situate current events in a national historical narrative, Providence mobs sang Revolutionary-era liberty songs on the passage of the final embargo act in January 1809.[81] Boston's *New England Palladium* circulated such Revolutionary-era lyrics to accuse embargo proponents of being "Tories" in their support of a "tyrannical system" to "enslave their country." In contrast to this New England outrage, there were almost no protests in the South, and half of the southern members of the House of Representatives voted to extend the embargo in early 1809.[82]

In the mid-Atlantic, which had fared better due to growth in manufacturing, various perspectives were expressed through music. Some representatives similarly supported the embargo's extension. But Federalist outlets in the region circulated stinging criticism. In Philadelphia, George Helmbold's pioneering comic paper *The Tickler* distributed a scathing anti-Republican reworking of "Hail Columbia." The anonymous songwriter cast Republicans as cowards and villains, highlighted the embargo's cost, and blamed Jefferson for running the nation-as-ship aground. The final verse of the scathing attack declared, "Lo! then the chief who now commands,/No more to enslave his country stands,/But sunk into oblivion's vale,/But sunk into oblivion's vale,/Detested as he liv'd, shall die;/His fame expire with his last sigh."[83] For Robert Y. Sidney, a multimovement anthem was more appropriate for performance in a complex event designed to both commemorate the abolition of the international slave trade and urge New York African Americans to vote for Federalist candidates around the one-year anniversary of the embargo. Robert was possibly a relative of black activist Joseph Sidney. Featuring choruses and recitative and solo passages, Robert's anthem extended a decades-long tradition of using multimovement odes for celebratory political expression in America and illustrated the broader efforts of African American abolitionist, philanthropic, educational, and religious activists to legitimate their celebrations and public political voice by leveraging established ritual forms. In his anthem, Robert Sidney described America as a "hapless nation deprived of peace" as long it engaged in the international slave trade, suggesting that the nation's moral wrongs brought on its struggles with European powers. Turning from the transatlantic slave trade to domestic partisan politics, Joseph Sidney, in his oration, sought additional black votes that were key in elections determined with a margin as slim as one vote.[84]

For other mid-Atlantic performances, songwriters frequently turned to "Anacreon in Heaven." This was the basis for "The Pilots Whom Washington Plac'd at the Helm,"[85] a song performed at a Philadelphia dinner honoring Timothy Pickering and other Federalists who strenuously argued the minority position in Congress in debates over the fate of the embargo. The dinner was attended by Commodore Truxton, the naval hero of the Quasi War of the late 1790s, and featured a large portrait of Washington.[86] The anonymous songwriter lauded the Federalist minority as a "Leonidas band," likening them to the tiny Greek army that Leonidas led against Xerxes's vastly larger Persian forces at Thermopylae in 480 BC (see Figure 5.5). Such references to ancient history and culture were well suited to the tune of "Anacreon in Heaven," the original lyrics of which memorialized an ancient Greek poet. Incorporating other ancient references, the Federalist songwriter noted that Europe was not simply plagued by war but shrouded in "Cimmerian darkness," a state of perpetual darkness assigned in English literature to an ancient nomadic people who occupied Asia Minor in the seventh century BC. Yet the songwriter complemented these ancient references with thoroughly American ones. Any European tyrant would have to "win his way through our hearts," like Washington decades before. The songwriter not only traced the Federalist minority's lineage back to Washington through the song's title and refrain, but he also positioned Jefferson in opposition to Washington. Using alliteration, elevated vocabulary, and noble

*The following Song was composed for the occasion and sung at the festival.*

SONG.

THE PILOTS WHOM WASHINGTON PLAC'D AT THE HELM.

TUNE—"*Anacreon in Heaven.*"

I.

Ye patriots bold, a *Leonidas band*,
Our pilots in freedom's tempeſtuous ocean,
The chiefs whom our WASHINGTON choſe to command,
Sheet-anchors of hope, 'mid the world's dread commotion!
With hearts firm and true,
May you guide the bark through,
In ſpite of the ſtorm, and the Jacobin crew;
For the tempeſt of Faction cannot overwhelm
The pilots whom WASHINGTON plac'd at the helm.

II.

Though Europe diſtracted with war's dire alarm,
With more than Cimmerian darkneſs, is ſhrouded,
Yet, led by our WASHINGTON's comrades in arms,
The ſun of our glory can never be clouded.
The powers are defied
Of the old world allied,
By men who in danger's dark hour have been tried,
For war's rudeſt tempeſt cannot overwhelm
The pilots whom WASHINGTON plac'd at the helm.

III.

If Europe ſhould fall by the arms or the arts
Of Bonaparte's demons of dire deſolation,
The tyrant muſt firſt win his way through our hearts,
Before he ſubdues the American nation.
Philoſophiſts' dreams,
And Frenchified ſchemes,
Avaunt; for the falchion of WASHINGTON gleams.
And J———n's follies cannot overwhelm
The pilots whom WASHINGTON plac'd at the helm.

IV.

Ye "generous ſons of illuſtrious ſires,"*
With their blood who cemented fair freedom's foundations,
Your patriot boſoms inherit their fires,
And yours is the meed of a world's acclamations,
Your names you ſhall find
In our boſoms enſhrin'd,
With life's deareſt ligaments ever entwin'd:
And you ſhall unite, leſt the ſtorm overwhelm,
With the pilots, whom WASHINGTON plac'd at the helm.

* Mr. Quincy's Speech.

Figure 5.5. "The Pilots Whom Washington Plac'd at the Helm." *Trenton Federalist*, 27 March 1809. Readex/NewsBank.

V

Your efforts of wiſdom your country reveres,
Your counſels alone can enſure her ſalvation
Your preſence is welcom'd, with gratitude's tears,
THE ROCKS TO WHICH CLING THE LAST HOPES OF
THE NATION.
Let each honour'd name
Swell the trumpet of Fame,
While it peals with its longeſt and loudeſt acclaim;
And we ALL WILL UNITE, leſt the ſtorm overwhelm,
With the pilots whom *Waſhington* placed at the helm.

Figure 5.5. Continued.

imagery, the songwriter created a song well in line with the American tradition of reworking "Anacreon in Heaven" and one that was well suited for performance.

As partisans elaborated their arguments in song, the nation had only two options: war or submission. The House refused to declare war in early 1809, largely due to the votes of New York and New England representatives. Instead, the embargo was replaced with a less restrictive Non-Intercourse Act. The act closed US ports to British and French vessels and prohibited US citizens from trading with Britain or France. The compromise legislation did not address fundamental foreign policy issues, and impressment and ship seizures continued. Northern merchants still faced shipping delays, bad exchange rates, huge tariffs, high insurance rates, inability to sell goods, seizures in port, privateering, and natural disasters.[87]

As the Non-Intercourse Act was about to expire in 1810, Republicans, who had previously worked so hard to stress the importance of maintaining peace when defending the embargo, led calls for war.[88] A good example came from the one New England state that had remained supportive of Madison in the 1808 presidential election: Vermont. In "Freedom and Navigation," a reworking of "Anacreon in Heaven" written for the Windsor *Vermont Republican*, a Vermont songwriter charged that the British had "turnpik'd" the seas and promised that American forces would fight against Britain "for the rights of all nations." Going further, the songwriter supported Napoleon's efforts to conquer Spain to ensure the freedom of the seas from a British monopoly. Inflamed by special British envoy Francis "Copenhagen" Jackson, whose arrogance and indiscretion in the United States compounded his reputation for destroying Copenhagen when Denmark refused to give Britain its navy, the Anglophobic songwriter envisioned the fall of Britain to France.[89]

Federalist songwriters stressed that Britain needed Americans' support in fighting a common French enemy. Federalist and Harvard graduate John Lathrop Jr. (1772–1820) made this argument by literally calling Americans the "sons" of Britain who owed her support. In a song performed in Faneuil Hall for Federalist-organized July 4 festivities, Lathrop told his fellow Bostonians, "our ancestor Britain her enemy braves--/. . . she knows/That the love of her sons, is the death of her foes." Lathrop asked the audience if their fathers' ghosts should see them conquered by Napoleon. Drawing on his characteristically vivid imagery, Robert Treat Paine's ode for the day's subscription dinner concluded with a scene of French aggression that hit close to home, as he invoked a gallant sailor grieving "in fierce Napoleon's midnight cells."[90]

While lyrical rhetoric intensified, American legislation loosened and the country moved closer to war. Two months before Americans celebrated the anniversary of the nation's independence in 1810, the Non-Intercourse Act was replaced by Macon's Bill No. 2, which legalized US trade with both Britain and France. Barely removed from submission to British definitions of neutral trade rights and a British commercial monopoly, the act sought diplomatic leverage by allowing commercial retaliation against the power that would not lift sanctions against American neutral trading rights and promise to stop harassing US ships.[91] The bill was intended to make both belligerents accept the terms in quick succession, but only the French appeared to do so. Madison proclaimed non-intercourse against Britain.[92]

War calls grew. While the Northwest is now remembered as a strong advocate for war with Britain, Republican war calls came from and circulated through many regions.[93] Even in New England, the pro-navy, pro-war Joseph Story, soon to become a Supreme Court justice, had his fellow Salem Republicans celebrate July 4 with a reworking of "Anacreon in Heaven" that ended in anticipation of war, "Our hearts leap in union to combat oppression. . . . To DIE or be FREE, is the right of the brave!"[94] Diplomatic solutions failed and shifting British justifications of the orders in council reinforced long-standing American concerns of British designs on a complete maritime monopoly. Anticipating more vocal Republican disunity in advance of the 1812 presidential election—disunity that would harden Britain's stance—and knowing that war preparations would unite the American people and apply pressure to Britain, Madison, with the support of Congress, moved the country toward war.[95]

## Notes

1. Cripe, *Thomas Jefferson and Music*; Gordon-Reed and Onuf, *"Most Blessed of the Patriarchs*, 211–35.
2. Carl E. Prince, "James J. Wilson: Party Leader, 1801–1824," *Proceedings of the New Jersey Historical Society* 8 (1965): 24–31.
3. Mlada Bukovansky, "American Identity and Neutral Rights from Independence to the War of 1812," *International Organization* 51, no. 2 (Spring 1997): 212, 215, 221–3, 227; Brian Schoen, "Calculating the Price of Union: Republican Economic Nationalism and the Origins of Southern Sectionalism, 1790–1828," *Journal of the Early Republic* 23, no. 2 (Summer 2003): 183, 192; Burton Spivak, *Jefferson's English Crisis: Commerce, Embargo, and the Republican Revolution* (Charlottesville: University of Virginia Press, 1979), 14, 31, 39–40, 59–63, 67; James H. Broussard, *The Southern Federalists, 1800–1816* (Baton Rouge: Louisiana State University Press, 1978), 75; James Sofka, "American Neutral Rights Reappraised: Identity of Interest in the Foreign Policy of the Early Republic?" *Review of International Studies* 26, no. 4 (October 2000): 615; Donald R. Adams Jr., "American Neutrality and Prosperity, 1793–1808: A Reconsideration," *Journal of Economic History* 40, no. 4 (December 1980): 733; Ian W. Toll, *Six Frigates: The Epic History of the Founding of the U.S. Navy* (New York: W. W. Norton, 2006), 14–15; Donald R. Hickey, *Don't Give Up the Ship! Myths of the War of 1812* (Urbana: University of Illinois, 2006), 26–7; John H. Reinoehl, "Post-Embargo Trade and Merchant Prosperity: Experiences of the Crowninshield Family, 1809–1812," *Mississippi Valley Historical Review* 42, no. 2 (September 1955): 229–30.
4. Sofka, "American Neutral Rights Reappraised," 612, 615–6; Spivak, *Jefferson's English Crisis*, 65; Hickey, *Don't Give Up the Ship!*, 23.
5. Robert E. Cray Jr., "Remembering the USS *Chesapeake*: The Politics of Maritime Death and Impressment," *Journal of the Early Republic* 25, no. 3 (Fall 2005): 445, 447, 453–4.
6. Sofka, "American Neutral Rights Reappraised," 603.
7. Bukovansky, "American Identity and Neutral Rights," 224, 234; Dumas Malone, *Jefferson the President: Second Term, 1805–1809* (Boston: Little, Brown, 1974), 496; Sofka, "American Neutral Rights Reappraised," 603.
8. *Salem Gazette*, 17 July 1798; New Haven *Connecticut Herald*, 7 July 1807; Elizabethtown *New Jersey Journal*, 7 July 1807; Hanover *Dartmouth Gazette*, 8 July 1807; Philadelphia *Poulson's American Daily Advertiser*, 13 July 1807; Charleston *City Gazette*, 23 July 1807; Concord *American Patriot*, 1 November 1808.
9. Portsmouth *New Hampshire Gazette*, 4 August 1807; Troy *Farmers' Register*, 22 September 1807; Portland *Eastern Argus*, 17 December 1807; Gross, *Jefferson's Scrapbooks*, 78–9.
10. Hartford *American Mercury*, 6 August 1807; Gross, *Jefferson's Scrapbooks*, 73–5; Cooperstown *Otsego Herald*, 20 August 1807; Trenton *True American*, 7 September 1807; Northampton *Republican Spy*, 23 December 1807; Salem *Essex Register*, 5 March 1808.

11. Gross, *Jefferson's Scrapbooks*, 91–3; Trenton *True American*, 20 June 1808; Boston *Independent Chronicle*, 27 October 1808.
12. New York *Public Advertiser*, 30 June 1807; Trenton *True American*, 7 September 1807; Gross, *Jefferson's Scrapbooks*, 73–5.
13. Schoen, "Calculating the Price of Union," 187.
14. Spivak, *Jefferson's English Crisis*, 73–4, 81–98; Malone, *Jefferson the President*, 453, 456–7, 459–63, 466–8; Thomas Jefferson, *The Works of Thomas Jefferson*, ed. Paul Leicester Ford. Federal Edition, vol. 10 (New York: G.P. Putnam's Sons, 1904–5), 503–26. http://oll.libertyfund.org/titles/806; John J. McCusker and Kenneth Morgan, eds., *The Early Modern Atlantic Economy* (Cambridge: Cambridge University Press, 2000), 313.
15. Spivak, *Jefferson's English Crisis*, 69, 77, 100–5, 110, 115, 120; Sofka, "American Neutral Rights Reappraised," 616–17; Malone, *Jefferson the President: Second Term*, 481, 563, 579–80, 590; New York *Republican Watch-Tower*, 29 December 1807; "From Thomas Jefferson to William Duane, 20 July 1807," *Founders Online*, http://founders.archives.gov/documents/Jefferson/99-01-02-5996; *Salem Gazette*, 23 September 1808; Scott A. Silverstone, *Divided Union: The Politics of War in the Early American Republic* (Ithaca, NY: Cornell University Press, 2004), 79.
16. Trenton *True American*, 20 June 1808; Boston *Independent Chronicle*, 27 October 1808.
17. *Newburyport Herald*, 8 July 1808; *Trenton Federalist*, 27 March 1809.
18. Philadelphia *Spirit of the Press*, 1 August 1808; *New York Evening Post*, 29 October 1808.
19. *New York Commercial Advertiser*, 6 April 1808; *Portsmouth Oracle*, 9 July, 15 October 1808; Boston *New England Palladium*, 25 March 1806; *Charleston Courier*, 14 October 1806.
20. *Portsmouth Oracle*, 9 July 1808; Schoen, "Calculating the Price of Union," 178–9; Craig L. Symonds, *Navalists and Antinavalists: The Naval Policy Debate in the United States, 1785–1827* (Newark: University of Delaware Press, 1980), 143; Malone, *Jefferson the President: Second Term*, 486, 641; Boston *Repertory*, 2 September 1808; Philadelphia *Spirit of the Press*, 1 August 1808; Brattleboro *Reporter*, 27 August 1808; Boston *Columbian Centinel*, 29 October 1808.
21. *New York Commercial Advertiser*, 4 April 1808; New York *Spectator*, 6 April 1808; Boston *Columbian Centinel*, 16 April 1808; *Newburyport Herald*, 26 April 1808; Hartford *Connecticut Courant*, 11 May 1808; Salem *Gazette*, 3 June 1808.
22. Fisher Ames, *Works of Fisher Ames Compiled by a Number of His Friends* (Boston: T. B. Wait, 1809), 492; Fessenden, *Original Poems*, vi; *The Hull Packet*, 22 March 1808; *New York Evening Post*, 15 June 1808; Boston *Columbian Centinel*, 25 June 1808; Springfield *Hampshire Federalist*, 7 July 1808; *Charleston Courier*, 12 July 1808; Silverstone, *Divided Union*, 83, 89; Malone, *Jefferson the President: Second Term*, 474, 604; Shalhope, *Roots of Democracy*, 148.
23. Gibbs, *Performing the Temple of Liberty*, 38; Michael Fortune, *Jefferson and Liberty. A New Song* (Philadelphia: N. G. Dufief, 1801); Michael Fortune, "The Acquisition of Louisiana: A National Song" (Philadelphia: G. Willig, 1804); "To Thomas

Jefferson from Michael Fortune, 23 June 1801," *Founders Online*, http://founders.archives.gov/documents/Jefferson/01-34-02-0333; "To Thomas Jefferson from Michael Fortune, 3 August 1804," *Founders Online*, http://founders.archives.gov/documents/Jefferson/99-01-02-0170; Absalom Jones, *A Thanksgiving Sermon, Preached January 1, 1808, In St. Thomas's, or the African Episcopal, Church, Philadelphia* (Philadelphia: 1808), [23–4].

24. Washington *Monitor*, 22 October 1808; Sofka, "American Neutral Rights Reappraised," 606; Silverstone, *Divided Union*, 19; *The Papers of Thomas Jefferson*, vol. 33 (Princeton, NJ: Princeton University Press, 2006), 148–52; Bukovansky, "American Identity and Neutral Rights," 224.
25. Worcester *National Aegis*, 29 June 1808, 4 July 1810; Lexington *Reporter*, 10 October 1808.
26. *New York Public Advertiser*, 10 May 1808; Portsmouth *New Hampshire Gazette*, 16 August 1808; *New York Commercial Advertiser*, 6 April 1808.
27. "From Thomas Jefferson to Ma., Citizens of Beverly, 2 September 1808," *Founders Online*, http://founders.archives.gov/documents/Jefferson/99–01–02–8617; Harvey Strum, "Reluctant Warriors and the Federalist Resurgence in New York, 1808–1815," *Courier* 16, no.1 (1979): 14; Sofka, "American Neutral Rights Reappraised," 606, 611; David A. Wilson, *United Irishmen, United States: Immigrant Radicals in the Early Republic* (Ithaca, NY: Cornell University Press, 1998), 81.
28. *New York Herald*, 23 April 1808; *Georgetown Gazette and Commercial Advertiser*, 6 August 1808; *Portsmouth Oracle*, 20 August 1808; Boston *New England Palladium*, 26 April 1808; Schoen, "Calculating the Price of Union," 178–80, 183; Lawrence A. Peskin, "How the Republicans Learned to Love Manufacturing: The First Parties and the 'New Economy,'" *Journal of the Early Republic* 22, no. 2 (Summer 2002): 243–5, 258.
29. Steven Watts, *The Republic Reborn: War and the Making of Liberal America, 1790–1820* (Baltimore: Johns Hopkins University Press, 1989), 224–39; Ronald Schultz, *The Republic of Labor: Philadelphia Artisans and the Politics of Class, 1720–1830* (New York: Oxford University Press, 1993), 3–35; James L. Huston, *Securing the Fruits of Labor: The American Concept of Wealth Distribution, 1765–1900* (Baton Rouge: Louisiana State University Press, 2015), 3–28; Spivak, *Jefferson's English Crisis*, 9, 110, 206, 209; Peskin, "How the Republicans Learned to Love Manufacturing," 251; Shankman, " 'A New Thing on Earth,' " 336–42; Sag Harbor *Suffolk Gazette*, 2 July 1808; Newark *Centinel of Freedom*, 5 January 1808.
30. J. C. A. Stagg, "James Madison and the 'Malcontents': The Political Origins of the War of 1812," *William and Mary Quarterly* 33, no. 4 (October 1976): 561; *Pennsylvania Herald and Easton Intelligencer*, 19 October 1808; Ronald L. Hatzenbuehler and Robert L. Ivie, *Congress Declares War: Rhetoric, Leadership, and Partisanship in the Early Republic* (Kent, OH: Kent State University Press, 1983), 82–3.
31. Schoen, "Calculating the Price of Union," 175, 179–80, 183, 188–92; New Haven *Connecticut Herald*, 7 July 1807; Charleston *City Gazette*, 28 July 1808; Silverstone, *Divided Union*, 86, 89.
32. Keller, *Music of the War of 1812*, 41; *Portland Gazette*, 14 March 1808.

33. *New York Commercial Advertiser*, 30 March 1808; *New York Spectator*, 27 April 1808; Worcester *Massachusetts Spy*, 10 July 1811.
34. Silverstone, *Divided Union*, 79; Schoen, "Calculating the Price of Union," 181–2; D. Adams Jr., "American Neutrality and Prosperity," 725–6, 728, 731–2.
35. *Middlebury Mercury*, 13 July 1808.
36. Peskin, "How the Republicans Learned to Love Manufacturing," 245, 247, 256; Boston *Democrat*, 1 June 1808; Gross, *Jefferson's Scrapbooks*, 96–7. The song of "spunky Jonathan" was widely reprinted in Republican newspapers in New York, New Jersey, Massachusetts, and Vermont.
37. *The Papers of Thomas Jefferson*, vol. 33, 148–52; *New York Herald*, 23 April 1808; *Boston Gazette*, 18 July 1808; Baltimore *Federal Republican*, 17 July 1810.
38. Schoen, "Calculating the Price of Union," 190, 193, 195; Silverstone, *Divided Union*, 86; Malone, *Jefferson the President: Second Term*, 628; Thorp Lanier Wolford, "Democratic-Republican Reaction in Massachusetts to the Embargo of 1807," *New England Quarterly* 15, no. 1 (March 1942): 47; Doron Ben-Atar and Barbara B. Oberg, "The Paradoxical Legacy of the Federalists," in *Federalists Reconsidered*, edited by Doron Ben-Atar and Barbara B. Oberg (Charlottesville: University of Virginia Press, 1998), 5; Hickey, *Don't Give Up the Ship!*, 28–9.
39. Trenton *True American*, 20 June 1808; Portland *Eastern Argus*, 21 July 1808.
40. Wolford, "Democratic-Republican Reaction," 49, 56; Spivak, *Jefferson's English Crisis*, 140; Malone, *Jefferson the President: Second Term*, 565, 600, 606, 608, 643.
41. Malone, *Jefferson the President: Second Term*, 487, 489; Bennington *World*, 11 July 1808; *Middlebury Mercury*, 13 July 1808.
42. Worcester *National Aegis*, 29 June 1808; "From Thomas Jefferson to Ma., Citizens of Beverly, 2 September 1808," *Founders Online*, http://founders.archives.gov/documents/Jefferson/99-01-02-8617.
43. Salem *Essex Register*, 5 March 1808; Boston *Independent Chronicle*, 4 July 1808; Gross, *Jefferson's Scrapbooks*, 94–5; Strum, "Reluctant Warriors," 4–6, 8; "To Thomas Jefferson from William Duane, 9 August 1808," *Founders Online*, http://founders.archives.gov/documents/Jefferson/99-01-02-8472; Fischer, *Revolution of American Conservatism*, 175–7; *Salem Gazette*, 23 September 1808.
44. Spivak, *Jefferson's English Crisis*, 187; *St. Albans Adviser*, 24 March 1808; Portsmouth *New Hampshire Gazette*, 16 August 1808; Walpole *Political Observatory*, 22 August 1808.
45. Sherburne *Olive Branch*, 30 January 1808.
46. Sag Harbor *Suffolk Gazette*, 2 July 1808; Peskin, "How the Republicans Learned to Love Manufacturing," 258; Schoen, "Calculating the Price of Union," 178–80, 183.
47. Spivak, *Jefferson's English Crisis*, x, 69; Sofka, "American Neutral Rights Reappraised," 608; Lexington *Reporter*, 10 October 1808; Gross, *Jefferson's Scrapbooks*, 89–90.
48. Salem *Essex Register*, 13 July 1808; *Washington Expositor*, 3 July 1808; Boston *Democrat*, 9 July 1808; Danville *North Star*, 6 August 1808; Walpole *Political Observatory*, 8 August 1808; *Carthage Gazette*, 13 August 1808; Cooperstown *Otsego Herald*, 24 September 1808; *Lexington Reporter*, 3 October 1808; Newburyport *Statesman*, 6 October 1808; Portland *Weekly Argus*, 20 October 1808;

Providence *Columbian Phenix*, 12 November 1808; Concord *American Patriot*, 15 November 1808.

49. "To Thomas Jefferson from Alexander Wilson, 18 March 1805," *Founders Online*, National Archives, http://founders.archives.gov/documents/Jefferson/99-01-02-1405; "From Thomas Jefferson to Alexander Wilson, 7 April 1805," *Founders Online*, http://founders.archives.gov/documents/Jefferson/99-01-02-1509; Robert Plate, *Alexander Wilson: Wanderer in the Wilderness* (New York: David McKay, 1966), 53–4, 61–2, 82–3, 112.
50. Boston *New England Palladium*, 19 February 1808; *Albany Gazette*, 31 March 1808; Keller, *Music of the War of 1812*, 37, Gross, *Jefferson's Scrapbooks*, 84–6; *New York Spectator*, 27 April 1808; Boston *Columbian Centinel*, 29 October 1808; Albany *Balance and New York State Journal*, 27 June 1809.
51. New York *L'Oracle and Daily Advertiser*, 15 April 1808; *New York Public Advertiser*, 5, 6 May 1808; Portland *Eastern Argus*, 26 May 1808; Philadelphia *Poulson's American Daily Advertiser*, 11 August 1808; Morristown *Palladium of Liberty*, 11 July 1808.
52. Bennington *World*, 25 July 1808; Boston *Democrat*, 13, 30 July 1808; Salem *Essex Register*, 20, 30 July 1808; Providence *Columbian Phenix*, 3 September 1808; Norwich *Olive Branch*, 3 September 1808; Newburyport *Statesmen*, 8 September 1808; Sag Harbor *Suffolk Gazette*, 17 September 1808; Morristown *Palladium of Liberty*, 17 October 1808; Richard B. Sher, *The Enlightenment and the Book: Scottish Authors and Their Publishers in Eighteenth-Century Britain, Ireland, and America* (Chicago: University of Chicago Press, 2008), 548; Philadelphia *Poulson's American Daily Advertiser*, 11 August 1808; *National Martial Music and Songs* (Philadelphia: William M'Culloch, 1809); Clyde S. Shive Jr., "National Martial Music and Songs: A Musical First," *American Music* 9, no. 1 (Spring 1991): 92–101.
53. Little, *Transoceanic Radical, William Duane*, 10, 25–6, 89–92, 144–5, 156–7, 169–70; "To Thomas Jefferson from William Duane, 8 July 1807," *Founders Online*, http://founders.archives.gov/documents/Jefferson/99-01-02-5905; "To Thomas Jefferson from William Duane, 5 December 1807," *Founders Online*, http://founders.archives.gov/documents/Jefferson/99-01-02-6915; "To Thomas Jefferson from William Duane, 14 July 1807," *Founders Online*, http://founders.archives.gov/documents/Jefferson/99-01-02-5959; "To Thomas Jefferson from William Duane, 4 February 1809," *Founders Online*, http://founders.archives.gov/documents/Jefferson/99-01-02-9711; M. Ruth Kelly, *The Olmsted Case: Privateers, Property, and Politics in Pennsylvania, 1778–1810* (Selinsgrove: Susquehanna University Press, 2005), 56; Daniel, *Scandal and Civility*, 261–2; William Duane, *The American Military Library, or, Compendium of the Modern Tactics* (Philadelphia, William Duane, 1809); Wilson, *United Irishmen*, 83; Stagg, "James Madison and the 'Malcontents,'" 562.
54. New York *L'Oracle and Daily Advertiser*, 15 April 1808; Bennington *The World*, 25 July 1808; Minot Baker, *Minot Baker's Favourite Collection of Ancient and Modern Songs*, Boston, 1809, musical manuscript, American Antiquarian Society; L. H. Baker, *Florae Memoriae*, 1825, musical manuscript, American Antiquarian Society; Wilson, *United Irishmen*, 61, 79, 82; Keller, *Music of the War of 1812*, 51.

55. Philadelphia *Poulson's American Daily Advertiser*, 11 August 1808; Keller, *Music of the War of 1812*, 51; Worcester *Massachusetts Spy*, 14 August 1811; Hunter, *Life and Letters*, 289.
56. Daniel, *Scandal and Civility*, 281–3.
57. Hudson *Balance*, 6 September 1808; *Charleston Courier*, 27 July 1808; Haverhill *Merrimack Intelligencer*, 20 August 1808. Other newspapers circulating it included *Newburyport Herald*, 16 August 1808; *Alexandria Gazette*, 17 August 1808; Trenton *Federalist*, 22 August 1808; New Haven *Connecticut Herald*, 23 August 1808; Pittsfield *Berkshire Reporter*, 27 August 1808; Hudson *Balance*, 6 September 1808.
58. Richard J. Wolfe, *Secular Music in America, 1801–1825: A Bibliography*, vol. 2 (New York: New York Public Library, 1964), 729–30; Robert M. Keller, Raoul F. Camus, Kate Van Winkle Keller, and Susan Cifaldi, *Early American Secular Music and Its European Sources, 1589–1839* (Annapolis, MD: Colonial Music Institute, 2002); *Maryland Herald and Hager's-Town Weekly Advertiser*, 26 June 1800; New York *Morning Chronicle*, 12 March 1806; Philadelphia *Aurora*, 4 July 1807; *Brooklyn Minerva*, 14 November 1807; New York *Republican Watch-Tower*, 25 December 1807; Newark *New Jersey Telescope*, 19 May 1809; Baltimore *Federal Republican*, 28 February, 9 July 1810; Keller, *Music of the War of 1812*, 13–17; Hosmer, *Music Book*.
59. Thomas Crofton Croker, *The Popular Songs of Ireland* (London: Henry Colburn, 1839), 56–60; William Tait and Christian Isobel Johnstone, *Tait's Edinburgh Magazine*, vol. 6 (Edinburgh: W. Tait, 1839), 291; *The Patriot's Vocal Miscellany; or, A Collection of Loyal Songs* (Dublin, 1804), 99–100. Owenson's song had inspired a contrafact by "an American abroad," circulated in the *New York Weekly Museum*, 4 March 1797.
60. Spivak, *Jefferson's English Crisis*, 199–200; Schoen, "Calculating the Price of Union," 190; Douglas Irwin, *Clashing over Commerce: A History of U.S. Trade Policy* (Chicago: University of Chicago Press, 2017), 105.
61. After being exposed for organizing an invasion of Mexico and creation of an independent republic, Burr was repeatedly arraigned on charges of treason before finally being indicted. While Jefferson pushed the Supreme Court to find him guilty, Burr was found not guilty due to lack of credible evidence.
62. Spivak, *Jefferson's English Crisis*, 192; Robert L. Kerby, "The Militia System and the State Militias in the War of 1812," *Indiana Magazine of History* 73, no. 2 (June 1977): 110–20.
63. *New York Commercial Advertiser*, 27 February 1806; New York *Morning Chronicle*, 7 March 1806; Philadelphia *Aurora*, 2 July 1806; New York *Weekly Inspector*, 25 October 1806; Philadelphia *Poulson's American Daily Advertiser*, 11 April 1807; Sherburne *Olive Branch*, 31 October 1807; Lexington *Reporter*, 3 November 1810; James, *Cradle of Culture*, 81–2, 86–90; Susan L. Porter, *With an Air Debonair: Musical Theatre in America, 1785–1815* (Washington, DC: Smithsonian Institution Press, 1991), 491.
64. Alexander Reinagle and Charles Harford, "The Tars of Columbia" (Philadelphia: Blake's Musical Repository, 1804); New York *Morning Chronicle*, 12 March 1806.

65. Batchellor, ed., *Early State Papers of New Hampshire*, 846–7; *New York Spectator*, 30 April 1806; *Newburyport Herald*, 8 July 1806; *New York Evening Post*, 19 July 1806.
66. Donald R. Hickey, "Federalist Defense Policy in the Age of Jefferson, 1801–1812," *Military Affairs* 45, no. 2 (April 1981): 64–7; Symonds, *Navalists and Antinavalists*, 115–16.
67. Symonds, *Navalists and Antinavalists*, 107–8, 111–15, 118, 121, 125–7, 130, 167; Malone, *Jefferson the President: Second Term*, 463, 500.
68. *Portsmouth Oracle*, 15 October 1808; *Salem Gazette*, 8 March 1808; Boston *Repertory*, 2 September 1808; *Trenton Federalist*, 29 October 1808; Boston *Columbian Centinel*, 29 October 1808.
69. Easton *Republican Star*, 22 December 1807; Malone, *Jefferson the President: Second Term*, 456–7; Hickey, "Federalist Defense Policy," 65; *Federalist Songster*, 81–3.
70. Boston *Repertory*, 2 September 1808; Salem *Essex Register*, 12 September 1810; Bennington *Green Mountain Farmer*, 28 August 1809.
71. Symonds, *Navalists and Antinavalists*, 137–43.
72. Trenton *True American*, 29 August 1808; Washington *Monitor*, 13 September 1808; Lexington *Reporter*, 10 October 1808; *Washington Reporter*, 31 October 1808; Gross, *Thomas Jefferson's Scrapbooks*, 89–90; Symonds, *Navalists and Antinavalists*, 107–8, 122, 139.
73. Boston *Repertory*, 2 September 1808.
74. Symonds, *Navalists and Antinavalists*, 138; Albany *Balance*, 27 June 1809; Worcester *Massachusetts Spy*, 15 August 1810.
75. Worcester *Massachusetts Spy*, 6 December 1809.
76. Philadelphia *Spirit of the Press*, 1 August 1808.
77. Newark *New Jersey Telescope*, 28 February 1809.
78. Albany *Balance and New York State Journal*, 16, 19, 26 May, 27 June 1809; Springfield *Hampshire Federalist*, 25 May 1809; Bertrand Harris Brunson, *The Ballad as Song* (Berkeley: University of California Press, 1969), 18–36.
79. Boston *Columbian Centinel*, 29 October 1808; Bukovansky, "American Identity and Neutral Rights," 226; Symonds, *Navalists and Antinavalists*, 136, 143–5.
80. Malone, *Jefferson the President: Second Term*, 484, 578, 587, 590–1, 601; Spivak, *Jefferson's English Crisis*, x–xi, 67, 105, 107–8, 111, 116–17; Washington *National Intelligencer*, 28 December 1807; *Salem Gazette*, 23 September 1808; *Pennsylvania Herald and Easton Intelligencer*, 19 October 1808.
81. Malone, *Jefferson the President: Second Term*, 642; Wolford, "Democratic-Republican Reaction," 47; Boston *Repertory*, 27 December 1808; *New York Commercial Advertiser*, 28 December 1808; Providence *American*, 23 December 1808; Salem *Essex Register*, 24 December 1808; Portland *Gazette*, 26 December 1808; Spivak, *Jefferson's English Crisis*, 170, 201–2.
82. Boston *New England Palladium*, 20 January 1809; John Dickinson, *The Writings of John Dickinson* (Bedford, MA: Applewood Books, 2009), 428–9; Irwin, *Clashing over Commerce*, 103, 107.
83. Philadelphia *Tickler*, 22 February 1809; David E. E. Sloane, "The Comic Writers of Philadelphia: George Helmbold's *The Tickler*, Joseph C. Neal's *City Worthies*, and the

Beginning of Modern Periodical Humor in America," *Victorian Periodicals Review* 28, no. 3 (Fall 1995): 188–94.

84. Mitch Kachun, *Festivals of Freedom: Meaning and Memory in African American Emancipation Celebrations, 1808–1915* (Amherst: University of Massachusetts Press, 2006), 20–36; Joseph Sidney, *An Oration, Commemorative of the Abolition of the Slave Trade in the United States 1809* (New York: Seymour, 1809); Sarah L. H. Gronningsater, "'Expressly Recognized by Our Election Laws': Certificates of Freedom and the Multiple Fates of Black Citizenship in the Early Republic," *William and Mary Quarterly* 75, no. 3 (July 2018): 489, 491, 494; Gilje and Rock, "'Sweep O! Sweep O!'" 518, 520; Dorothy Porter Wesley, *Early Negro Writing, 1760–1837* (Boston: Beacon Press, 1995), 565–6.
85. Baltimore *Federal Republican*, 15 March 1809; *Trenton Federalist*, 27 March 1809. The song was also printed in newspapers in Pennsylvania, Massachusetts, New Hampshire, New York, and Rhode Island.
86. *New York Mercantile Advertiser*, 14 March 1809.
87. Spivak, *Jefferson's English Crisis*, 108, 170, 181–97; Wolford, "Democratic-Republican Reaction," 53–5; Silverstone, *Divided Union*, 81–4; Irving Bryant, *James Madison: The President, 1809–1812* (New York: Bobbs Merrill, 1956), 38–9; Malone, *Jefferson the President: Second Term*, 649; Reinoehl, "Post-Embargo Trade," 233–48.
88. Worcester *National Aegis*, 21 February 1810.
89. Bryant, *James Madison*, 125; Charles Town *Farmer's Repository*, 22 January 1810; *Boston Patriot*, 14 April 1810; Windsor *Vermont Republican*, 19 March 1810; Richmond *Virginia Patriot*, 10 July 1810; Newport *Rhode-Island Republican*, 11 July 1810.
90. *Boston Gazette*, 2 July 1810; Boston *Repertory*, 10 July 1810; Richmond *Virginia Patriot*, 10 July 1810; Boston *Columbian Centinel*, 13 July 1811; New Haven *Connecticut Herald*, 5 August 1811.
91. Schoen, "Calculating the Price of Union," 197.
92. J. C. A. Stagg, *Mr. Madison's War: Politics, Diplomacy, and Warfare in the Early American Republic, 1793–1830* (Princeton, NJ: Princeton University Press, 1983), 55–7; Stagg, "James Madison and the 'Malcontents,'" 564; Bryant, *James Madison*, 194–5; J. C. A. Stagg, *The War of 1812: Conflict for a Continent* (Cambridge: Cambridge University Press, 2012), 36. The French agreement was insincere.
93. Washington *National Intelligencer*, 8 October 1810; Providence *Rhode Island Republican*, 26 October 1810; Morristown *Palladium of Liberty*, 30 October 1810; Windsor *Vermont Republican*, 5 November 1810; Sag Harbor *Suffolk Gazette*, 17 November 1810; Richmond *Virginia Patriot*, 6 November 1810; Lexington *Reporter*, 12 October 1811; New York *Shamrock*, 12 October 1811; Salem *Essex Register*, 1 July 1812; Cooperstown *Otsego Herald*, 6 July 1811; "Rodgers & Victory. Tit for Tat Or, The Chesapeake Paid for in British Blood," *Isaiah Thomas Broadside Ballads Project*, accessed November 11, 2017, http://www.americanantiquarian.org/thomasballads/items/show/320; Hudson *Bee*, 21 June 1811; Paul Gilje, *Free Trade and Sailors' Rights in the War of 1812* (Cambridge: Cambridge University Press, 2013), 153; Quentin Scott King, *Henry Clay and the War of 1812* (Jefferson, NC: MacFarland, 2014), 80;

Burlington *Vermont Centinel*, 18 July 1811; Symonds, *Navalists and Antinavalists*, 136–46.

94. Salem *Essex Register*, 3 July 1811; Lexington *Palladium*, 5 October 1811; R. Kent Newmyer, *Supreme Court Justice Joseph Story: Statesman of the Old Republic* (Chapel Hill: University of North Carolina Press, 2004), 53, 59–63; Symonds, *Navalists and Antinavalists*, 139–40. Story wrote additional lyrics calling for wartime valor in 1813 once the War of 1812 was under way. Joseph Story, *Life and Letters of Joseph Story*, ed. William W. Story (Boston: Little, Brown, 1851), 59–60, 246; Boston *Columbian Centinel*, 7 July 1813.
95. Stagg, *Mr. Madison's War*, 70–81.

# 6
# Musical Myth-Making and the War of 1812

Most Americans' image of the War of 1812 is that shaped by Francis Scott Key—the "star-spangled banner" waving unfailingly over Fort McHenry as a symbol of American military might. Yet of the same war, Key's contemporary Samuel Griswold Goodrich admitted, "It was begun without preparation, it was carried on in weakness; it was characterized by failure, it was terminated by a treaty which left us where we began—save only that a hundred millions of dollars and thirty thousand lives had been expended in the inglorious struggle." The two Federalists' accounts highlight the power of mythologizing the War of 1812. Despite a tripling of the national debt and the cost of many lives, the war accomplished nothing in military, diplomatic, or territorial terms. A war that, like eyewitness Goodrich, subsequent historians considered a disaster, most contemporaries reported as a major American victory. With the war's major engagements far from large cities, the war took shape in American minds through ubiquitous commentary. As Eustace has stressed, "People's feelings about the war, and the moral judgments they made based on those feelings, would come not from direct experience but from the stories told and opinions expressed all around them." Myths about the war fulfilled important functions: explaining contradictory phenomena, addressing emotional needs, and articulating societal values and ideals. Such myths were created because, as Hickey has explained, they "help us make sense out of complicated or frightening events; they provide us with heroes and fulfill our need for inspiring stories; they promote local, regional and national pride; and they put a human face on history and demonstrate that we can indeed influence the course of events." Significantly, though, myth is not separate from history. Instead, as Hickey continued, myths "help us construct a history that we are comfortable with and that meets certain deep-seated needs."[1]

Myths of the War of 1812 were widely and lastingly circulated through music. These myths were regularly set to music, because music—particularly

*Hail Columbia.* Laura Lohman, Oxford University Press (2020). © Oxford University Press.
DOI: 10.1093/oso/9780190930615.001.0001

vocal music—was recognized as an important tool in shaping public opinion. Two years into the war, Washington Irving could note "the thousand pens" that Americans had "drawn forth in every part of the union" to comment on the conflict through song. These pens were wielded not only by lawyers and editors but also by teens, farmers, seamen, and soldiers.[2] The war they mythologized was conducted amid continued partisan and sectional conflict: New England states refused to send militia, Maryland mobs killed and maimed Revolutionary War veterans, and New England Federalists gathered at the Hartford Convention in what was seen as the prologue to secession.[3] Yet Americans used music to mythologize the war in ways that transcended partisan rhetoric and stressed uplifting narratives of national development. Circulated in iterative and broad ways, musical articulations of these myths obscured the war's non-accomplishment of its central goals and helped embed these myths in Americans' wartime experience and ongoing understanding of their nation.

## "Each Party Claims the Navy"

Wartime musical myth-making promptly focused on the navy. Songwriters, editors, and printers circulated appealing tales of naval prowess for varied audiences and purposes ranging from recruiting new crewmen to domestic entertainment.[4] Many song collections were dedicated in whole or part to the navy and life at sea (see Table 6.1). Compilers stimulated pride in the navy, its officers, and crews and featured selective, often exaggerated accounts of naval engagements. Theaters and circuses offered war-inspired productions. Although these entertainments seemed "foolish" and "ridiculous" to those engaged in the fighting, they too reinforced naval myths.[5] Naval songs and songsters circulated not only in port cities, where they aided recruitment, but also nationally, including far inland.[6] Naval songs were printed and sold as sheet music for domestic use and the pleasure of middling ranks.[7] Songsters and sheet music supplemented the continued circulation of naval songs in newspapers and cheaper broadsides and carried a large body of songs into domestic and convivial spheres in more durable forms. Circulated in these ways, music provided varied means of engagement with the war and furthered powerful myth-making that shaped how Americans could understand the war.

**Table 6.1.** American Song Collections Containing Naval Songs and Printed during and Shortly after the War of 1812.

| Title | City | Publisher | Year |
|---|---|---|---|
| *The American Patriotic Song-Book: A Collection of Political, Descriptive, and Humourous Songs, of National Character and The Production of American Poets Only Interspersed with a Number Set to Music* | Philadelphia | William M'Culloch | 1813 |
| *Free Trade and Sailors' Rights. American Glory. The Victories of Hull, Jones, Decatur, Bainbridge; as Detailed in Their Official Letters and the Letters of Other Officers. Together with a Collection of the Public Testimonials of Respect; and the Songs and Odes Written in Celebration of Those Events. Illustrated with Engravings of the Actions. The Designs by Woodside, the Engravings by Mason* | Philadelphia | Dennis Heartt | 1813 |
| *The Columbian Naval Songster; Being a Collection of Original Songs, Odes, &c. Composed in Honor of the Four Great Naval Victories* | New York | Edward Gillespy | 1813 |
| *The Columbian Naval Songster; Being a Collection of Original Songs, Odes &c. Composed in Honor of the Five Great Naval Victories Obtained by Hull, etc.* | New York | Edward Gillespy | 1813 |
| *A National Song-Book, being a Collection of Patriotic, Martial, and Naval Songs and Odes, Principally of American Composition* | Trenton | James J. Wilson | 1813 |
| *The Columbian Naval Melody. A Collection of Songs and Odes Composed on the Late Naval Victories and Other Occasions* | Boston | Hans Lund | 1813 |
| *The Naval Songster, or the Sailor's Pocket Companion* | Boston | Nathaniel Coverly Jr. | 1813 |
| *Odes, Naval Songs, and Other Occasional Poems (never before published) by Edwin C. Holland, Esq. Author of the Several Communications under the Signature of 'Orlando'* | Charleston | John Hoff | 1813 |

*(continued)*

Table 6.1. Continued

| Title | City | Publisher | Year |
|---|---|---|---|
| *The Columbian Harmonist: Containing the Newest and Much Admired Naval and Patriotic Songs, As Well As a Great Variety of Fashionable, Sentimental, and Other Polite Songs, Together with Most of Those Elegant Odes, Occasioned by the Recent Successes of the American Heroes, Hull, etc.* | Philadelphia | Thomas Simpson | 1814 |
| *The Naval Songster, Containing a Collection of the Best Selected American Naval Songs, Relating to the Victories Which Our Gallant Seamen Have So Gloriously Atchieved [sic] during the Present War* | Fredericktown, Maryland | Matthias Bartgis | 1814 |
| *American Patriotic and Comic Modern Songs Commemorative of Naval Victories* | Newburyport | W. & J. Gilman | 1814 |
| *National Songster, or A Collection of the Most Admired Patriotic Songs on the Brilliant Victories achieved by the Naval and Military Heroes of the United States of America, over Equal and Superior Forces of the British from the Best American Authors* | Hagerstown, MD | John Gruber and Daniel May | 1814 |
| *The Naval Songster: Being A Collection of Naval Victories, and Other Excellent Songs* | Charlestown | J. White | 1815 |
| *American Song Book: Being a New Collection of the Best Patriotic, Military, Naval, Amatory, Quizical, and Sentimental Songs* | Printed for the New York and Boston book-sellers | | 1815 |
| *Sailor's Rights; or, Yankee Notions; Being a Collection of American Patriotic, Sentimental and Comic Songs* | New York | Samuel A. Burtus | 1815 |
| *The Sky-Lark, or a New Collection of Choice, Naval, Patriotic and Sentimental Songs* | Hartford | B. & J. Russell | 1816 |
| *The Star Spangled Banner: Being a Collection of the Best Naval, Martial, and Patriotic Songs. . . Chiefly Written during, and in Relation To the Late War* | Wilmington, DE | James Wilson | 1816 |

**Table 6.1.** Continued

| Title | City | Publisher | Year |
|---|---|---|---|
| *Naval Songster. Or Columbian Naval Melody. Being a Choice Collection of the Most Approved Naval Songs* | Boston | Nathaniel Coverly Jr. | 1816 |
| *American Patriotic and Comic Modern Song-Book* | Newburyport | W. & J. Gilman | 1816 |
| *The American Patriotic Song-Book, a Collection of Political, Descriptive, and Humorous Songs, of National Character, and the Production of American Poets Only* | Philadelphia | John Bioren | 1816 |
| *The New American Songster; Being a Collection of Naval, Martial, Patriotic Songs.... Chiefly Written during the Late War; Some of Which Have Never before Appeared in Print* | Philadelphia | D. Dickinson | 1817 |
| *Magazine of Wit, and American Harmonist. Containing a Collection of the Most Admired Anecdotes, and a Variety of the Best Songs, Chiefly Composed in Honour of the Naval and Military Victories Gained during the Late War. Embellished with a Representation of Perry's Victory* | Philadelphia | M'Carty and Davis | 1818 |

The sheer volume of naval music established a pervasive discourse about the war through extensive repetition. As this large body of naval song grew, songwriters, compilers, editors, and printers highlighted an important area of bipartisan pride and circulated inspiring narratives of national development. Although many Federalists opposed the war, they supported the expansion and use of the navy. They were proud of their historical contributions to the offensive, seagoing navy that enabled wartime victories. Although most Republicans had opposed an offensive navy, the pursuit of war led some to cease that opposition and many to laud the navy's wartime successes. These successes were achieved in a Republican-supported war with Federalist-supported vessels—the frigates that Federalists had championed from the 1790s. Not surprisingly, naval songs were written by members of both parties. As one New York songwriter succinctly put it, "Each party claims the Navy."[8]

One song readily illustrates the overlap recognized between the two parties' projects, the war and an offensive navy. Writing lyrics for the Washington

Benevolent Society of Philadelphia's celebration of the first president's birthday on February 22, 1813, an anonymous songwriter turned away from past Federalist criticism of the war to the importance of loyalty and commercial benefits of the war waged with the Federalist-supported seagoing navy. Sung at a dinner attended by over 500 members of the Federalist society at the Olympic Theatre, the song opened, "Columbia's glory, claims our lays,/ A work of prosp'rous Federal days,/Let our applauding voices raise,/Huzza for our Federal Navy." Although the toasts made clear that the gathering was a partisan occasion, the song directed attention to the overlap between the parties' projects while claiming Federalist credit for naval successes.[9]

While individual naval songs were put to such partisan use and presented in partisan terms in some newspapers, compilers of naval song collections included few very partisan lyrics.[10] This larger body of naval songs appeared to transcend party. Compilers offered narratives of naval development and triumph that seemed to encompass and represent the success of both Federalist and Republican projects without partisan allusion. Unlike prose writers in the press, many songwriters ignored the parties' divergent, historical views on the navy's purpose and represented naval successes in nonpartisan terms. The songwriters and compilers who disseminated this larger body of song created a pantheon of naval heroes and compelling, inventive narratives of national naval development. Through carefully constructed cultural products and rituals, they created a mythology of the American navy that helped shape perceptions of the war and the shifting partisan landscape from which it had emerged.

Many songwriters transcended partisan rhetoric and inspired national pride by foregrounding compelling naval heroes. Songwriters highlighted individual human characters and the positive impact of human effort amid disruptive, frightening events. The first new naval hero created from the war was Captain Isaac Hull. Hull's destruction of the *Guerriere* far off the coast of Halifax came in fall 1812, just three days after his uncle, Major General William Hull, had cowardly surrendered Detroit, part of a series of humiliating army failures near Canada.[11] Hull's defeat of the *Guerriere* was touted through dozens of songs, and many perpetuated a myth of spectacular naval prowess that, as is common of myths, can be traced back to the participants themselves. Without question, the defeat was definitive: the *Guerriere's* mizzen mast was blown off and her foremast and main mast collapsed; taking on water and unnavigable, she was deliberately blown up. However, the four-hour engagement included questionable American judgments and two damaging collisions, one of which nearly resulted in the British boarding the *Constitution*. In contrast, Hull's short published report selectively explained that the *Guerriere* was destroyed through just thirty minutes of close action (difficult to believe given the large amount of ammunition used) and included no mention of collision or error. An even more skewed, widely reprinted account, based on information from an officer of *Constitution*, claimed that the *Guerriere* surrendered after just twenty-five minutes of close action and boasted, "The American frigate received no material injury in her action with the Guerrier."[12]

Songwriters quickly continued this myth-making process started by those on board the *Constitution*. Making Hull an instant hero and confidence-instilling face of the navy, songwriters touted the supposed brevity of the action and exaggerated its significance by having Captain James Richard Dacres seeking to take the *Constitution* in twenty-five or thirty minutes instead. The dropping of the *Guerriere*'s foremast and main mast—the product of a collision but implicitly attributed by Hull to the *Constitution*'s gunners—became in song proof of American naval prowess: songwriter after songwriter claimed that all three masts were blown off by just one or two American broadsides. To enhance such lyrical mythologizing, Hull's misleading account and the lists of casualties were incorporated in G. E. Blake's edition of "Hull's Victory," a song written by Philadelphia schoolmaster Joseph Hutton (1787–1828) and composed by English immigrant John Bray (1782–1822) (see Figure 6.1). Songwriters like Hutton noted the "submissive" British surrender and presented the exaggerated victory as a harbinger of future naval triumphs.[13] Significant in solidifying Hull's mythical status was the sheer volume of song generated: at least fifteen songs about Hull appeared in just two of the song collections published in 1813.[14]

After Hull, songwriters lauded a pantheon of naval heroes for their skilled action, leadership, and willingness to sacrifice their lives for their nation and the values ostensibly defended through the war, such as "free trade and sailors' rights."[15] Crews, like that of the *Constitution*, were invited to theaters for special performances designed to honor their bravery and to please "an American audience" rather than a partisan one.[16] Stephen Decatur, William Bainbridge, Oliver Hazard Perry, James Lawrence, Jacob Jones, and Thomas Macdonough were lauded in song and honored in public dinners often touted as celebrations that crossed partisan divides.[17] As one anonymous songwriter noted of Perry, "Both Feds and Demos claim him." Music was so central to these dinners that when the band at a New York naval dinner honoring

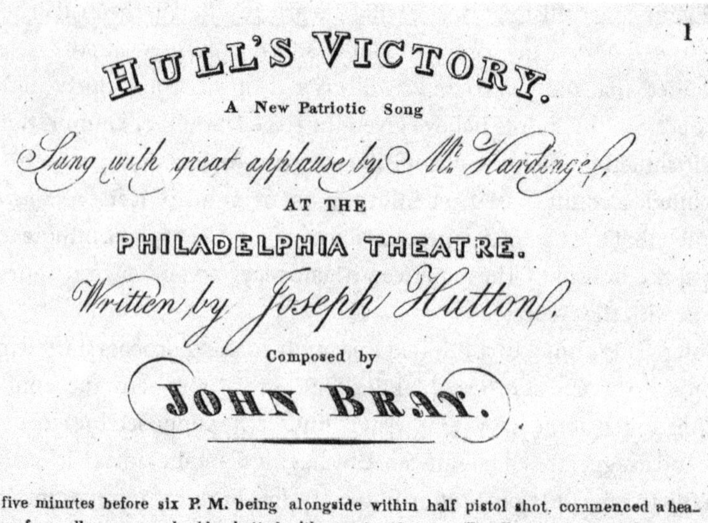


**Figure 6.1.** John Bray and Joseph Hutton, "Hull's Victory: A New Patriotic Song," as printed in Philadelphia by G. E. Blake, 1812. Clements Library, University of Michigan.

Hull, Decatur, and Jones proved poorly prepared, amateur gentlemen in attendance were praised for performing songs, glees, and catches to entertain the crowd of over 400 gentlemen of both parties. Writing to his brother about the evening, Washington Irving effused, "The whole entertainment went off with a soul and spirit which I never before witnessed. I never in my life before felt the national feeling so strongly aroused, for I never before saw in this country so true a cause for national triumph."[18] The Federalist who had mocked Jefferson in his 1809 *A History of New York* had been won over by national rhetoric that transcended party.

Naval dinners not only provided local occasions for the communal celebration of heroes and valor but also prompted widespread representations of political agreement. These events often called for new songs, which were then circulated more broadly through newspapers and song collections. Music was integral to a Boston procession and dinner honoring Isaac Hull in early September. These events were organized by leading Federalists like Harrison Gray Otis (who would later play a key role in organizing the Hartford Convention) along with merchants and at least one Republican. They were represented as opportunities for members of both parties to join and "throw off all party feelings and prejudices." Representations of bipartisan consensus expanded from pride in one engagement to pride in and support of an entire institution. As the Federalist *Salem Gazette* commented on the Faneuil Hall dinner, "It was the most pleasing part of this celebration of American valor, that both parties united in it, and thus bore their testimony in favor of a Naval Force (not Embargoes and Bonaparte's Continental System) for the Protection of Commerce." Decorations emphasized previous use of the navy in conflicts waged by both parties, while a prohibition on volunteer toasts ensured no public expression of partisan rancor.[19]

In a new ode for the dinner, "Yankee Thunders," Lucius Manlius Sargent (1786–1867) mythologized the victory in non-partisan terms as a demonstration of America's "arrival" as Britain's naval peer (see Figure 6.2). Sargent stressed repeatedly how the *Constitution* rode "In battle, side by side" with the vessel of the nearly thousand-year-old British navy commemorated in Sargent's musical inspiration and melodic source, Thomas Campbell's "Ye Mariners of England." Sargent reinforced this peer status by describing the officers and symbols of both belligerents' navies as "gallant."▶ The term captured not only bravery and skill but also morality. In British and American usage, the terms "gallant" and "gallantry" were commonly associated with zeal, ability, honor, generosity, humane conduct, courtesy, and especially bravery, skill, and determination in fighting against overwhelming force or difficult circumstances. Gallant conduct contrasted with cowardice, plunder, and barbarity. Thus, Sargent posited America as Britain's peer in both naval ability and moral conduct.[20] Citing "fortune" as the war's basis in

ODE

*Sung at the Dinner given to the Officers of the United States' frigate Constitution, after the Victory over the British frigate Guerriere.*

BY L. M SARGENT, ESQ.

TUNE—" *Ye Mariners of England.*"

BRITANNIA'S gallant streamers
Float proudly o'er the tide;
And fairly wave Columbia's stripes,
In battle, side by side.
And ne'er did bolder foemen meet,
Where ocean's surges pour,
O'er the tide, now they ride,
While the bell'wing thunders roar,
While the cannon's fire is flashing fast,
And the bell'wing thunders roar.

When Yankee meets the Britain,
Whose blood congenial flows,
By Heav'n created to be friends,
By fortune render'd foes;
Hard then must be the battle fray,
Ere well the fight is o'er.
Now they ride, side by side,
While the bell'wing thunders roar,
While the cannon's fire is flashing fast,
And the bell'wing thunders roar.

Still, still for noble England,
Bold DACRES' streamers fly;
And, for Columbia, gallant HULL'S,
As proudly and as high.
Now louder rings the battle din,
More thick the volumes pour;
Still they ride, side by side,
While the bell'wing thunders roar,
While the cannon's fire is flashing fast,
And the bell'wing thunders roar.

Why lulls Britannia's thunder,
That wak'd the wat'ry war?
Why stays that gallant Guerriere,
Whose streamer wav'd so fair?
That streamer drinks the ocean wave!
That warrior's fight is o'er!
Still they ride, side by side,
While Columbia's thunders roar,
While her cannon's fire is flashing fast,
And her Yankee thunders roar.

Hark! 'tis the Briton's lee gun!
Ne'er bolder warrior kneel'd!
And ne'er to gallant mariners
Did braver seamen yield.
Proud be the sires, whose hardy boys
Then fell, to fight no more;
With the brave, mid the wave,
When the cannon's thunder roar,
Their spirits then shall trim the blast,
And swell the thunder's roar.

Vain were the cheers of Britons,
Their hearts did vainly swell,
Where virtue, skill, and bravery,
With gallant MORRIS fell.
That heart, so well in battle tri'd,
Along the Moorish shore,
Again o'er the main,
When Columbia's thunders roar,
Shall prove its Yankee spirit true,
When Columbia's thunder roar.

Hence be our floating bulwarks
Those oaks our mountains yield;
'Tis mighty Heaven's plain decree—
Then take the wat'ry field!
To ocean's farthest barrier then
Your whit'ning sail shall pour;
Safe they'll ride o'er the tide,
While Columbia's thunder roar,
While her cannon's fire is flashing fast,
And her Yankee thunders roar.

**Figure 6.2.** Lucius Manlius Sargent, "Yankee Thunders." New York *Commercial Advertiser*, 9 September 1812. Readex/NewsBank.

his second verse, Sargent quickly glossed over the conflict's partisan origins. Part of a prominent Boston Federalist merchant family, Sargent lauded the victory in a war waged by Republicans with deserved respect for British naval prowess. Sensitive to the dinner's historically Anglophilic Federalist attendees, Sargent carefully refrained from exulting in the British defeat. In his fourth verse, Sargent's questions—"Why lulls Britannia's thunder?"—expressed surprise over weak British firepower and skirted details of the broadsides and close action, facts humiliating to the British. Sargent concluded by stressing the same theme articulated by former president John Adams on the occasion: the navy's future growth. Sargent's ode was widely reprinted in song collections where it contributed to a larger mythology of American naval prowess. Based on Sargent's lyrics, his brother Henry's highly praised naval decorations for the dinner, and his brother Daniel's contributions through the committee of arrangements, McCloskey's assertion that "Federalists manifested little or no enthusiasm over naval victories" does not stand up to scrutiny.[21]

Other songwriters and publishers transcended partisan rhetoric with cumulative accounts of naval prowess and historical narratives of naval growth. In prose, Republican printer Mathew Carey and Federalist former president John Adams joined forces to create a national naval history.[22] In music, individual songwriters narrated as many as seven naval engagements in one song, and they updated and expanded their songs to feature the latest victories or martyrdoms. Song collections like *Free Trade and Sailors' Rights* and *The Columbian Naval Songster* also presented such cumulative accounts.[23] These accounts offered extended historical narratives that stressed continuities rather than partisan differences. The writer of "The Navy" told a tale of growth and success by tracing the institution's history back to the Quasi War and the Tripolitan War, conflicts waged by Federalists and Republicans, respectively. The songwriter recalled "How Truxton fought, how Somers fell!/How gallant Preble's daring host/Triumph'd along the Moorish coast" and, in a piece of revisionist history, "Forc'd the proud infidel to treat,/And brought the Crescent to their feet!" The most noteworthy naval incident in the Tripolitan War was the deliberate burning of the USS *Philadelphia* by Lieutenant Stephen Decatur after the frigate ran aground and over 300 men were taken captive in Tripoli. Despite this reality, the songwriter wondered what American could hear such a tale of growing "naval glory" and not feel "patriot-warmth, and fire."[24] Writing from the theater, where it had long been important to avoid partisan conflict, William Dunlap traced the nation's naval history back to Columbus, "The ocean's first great conqueror."[25] Such songs and compilations showcased an expanding pantheon of naval heroes, wove convincing tales of naval successes, and offered a comforting narrative of the navy as an integral part of the nation's history and a source of future pride that transcended partisan divides.

The historiographical intent of song compilers is most clear in their reprinting of naval songs from previous wars alongside current ones. Collections like *The Columbian Naval Melody* offered a musical history of the navy, gathering songs about recent victories with older songs written about the Revolutionary War, Quasi War, and Tripolitan War. For a new generation, printers circulated Philip Freneau's songs about Revolutionary naval victories and Francis Hopkinson's "Battle of the Kegs,"[26] which mocked the British "victory" over American floating mines near Philadelphia in 1777. It mattered not to compilers that such lyrics had previously appeared in partisan publications like *The Federal Songster*, or that victories had occurred in highly partisan wars.[27] Their mission was to write, rewrite, and circulate a national naval history in more broadly appealing fashion through their new compilations. Such an approach not only could boost sales and profits but also could articulate powerful myths. Compilers' historical narratives foregrounded the naval skills underlying various victories, a continuity of heroism, and national naval development, regardless of historical shifts in naval funding and vision or the partisan orientations of most wars. Accordingly, these song collections, although offered amid a war initiated by Republicans and, in some cases, printed or compiled by Republicans like James Jefferson Wilson, were not presented as "Republican" in scope, but instead as "American," "Columbian," and "National."

The articulation of the navy as a national, rather than partisan, institution developed in tandem with interest in various forms of "national" cultural production. While Abigail Adams had previously called "Hail Columbia" a "National Song" when Federalists sought to silence Republican opposition and William M'Culloch had designated the songs in his collection as "wholly original and national," the War of 1812 prompted a sustained, aspirational discourse centered on the urgent development of national songs and literature. This went beyond one party's efforts to silence opposition in a time of crisis—rather, it reflected a desire for cultural independence from Britain and a reaction to the instability fueled by regionalism and sectional conflict.[28] Calls for the end of cultural dependence echoed fundamental desires to free American commerce and seamen from the vicissitudes of European conflict. Americans of two partisan orientations—writer Washington Irving and fellow New Yorker, Congressman Samuel Latham Mitchill—bemoaned derivative forms of culture, such as singing British songs with substitutions of "Columbia" for "Britannia." "National" cultural forms were increasingly valued as signs of national independence and identity, and paralleled the commercial independence sought through the war.[29] Goods and broadsides were advertised as being of "American production" and "American materials." Literary works were praised for their "Americanisms" and lack of reliance on foreign ideas. As for songs, Irving maintained that they should "be of our own manufacturing, however coarse. We would rather hear our victories celebrated in the merest doggerel that sprang from native invention, than beg, borrow, or steal from others." Revealing similar concerns, printers issued naval song collections with titles and subtitles that stressed American authorship (see Table 6.1).[30]

The intent behind these calls for national songs was clear in the *Port Folio*'s naval song contest. The Philadelphia magazine entreated Americans to build the base of "national poetry" by submitting naval songs that could inspire patriotism rather than faction and urge those "of all parties, and of all classes" to "unite in celebrating our own institutions, our own manners, our own statesmen, our own soldiers." Calling the lack of traditional music and "national airs" a "great and prominent defect in our social and political existence," editor Nicholas Biddle noted the absence of "an undefined something of national feeling, and of general sympathy which unites societies." Referencing sectional and partisan divisions, he deemed "the consciousness of mutual esteem, the sense of common dangers" that could be inspired by naval songs to be more powerful than "a cold and prudent calculation of the benefits of union and the dangers of dissention." [31]

The *Port Folio*'s conclusion of the contest ultimately fueled the national circulation of non-partisan statements of naval triumph and destiny. Biddle, when announcing the two winning submissions, stressed the *Port Folio*'s lack of "partiality" to any party; shifting from the strong Federalist bent at its founding, Joseph Dennie had softened the magazine's partisan discourse in pursuit of a national, bipartisan audience before his death in 1812, and Biddle, in concluding the contest, maintained this stance. One winning submission was "The Pillar of Glory," written by Charleston native and proslavery ideologue Edwin C. Holland. Holland's lyrics were twice set to music. Although Washington Irving criticized Holland's excessive, illogical imagery, the song circulated widely in newspapers, sheet music, performance, and numerous collections through the early twentieth century where it sustained the non-partisan touting of American naval prowess.[32] ▶

Such naval songs served several functions—generating profits for printers, recruiting new sailors, and myth-making. When Nicholas Biddle called for songs with which "we might forget the divisions which distract us, and remember only our native land," he called for myth-making. He did not deny that divisions existed. Rather, he called for the manipulation of memory, attention, and emotion through song. He directed contestants' attention to "the glorious achievements of our navy, which have kindled a new and holy spirit of nationality" and urged the submission of lasting songs: "These generous ebullitions of feeling should not be permitted to pass with the occasion that inspired them."[33] Even if many individual songs did not gain such lasting status, they collectively articulated a powerful myth of national naval growth and prowess that transcended partisan divides.

## The War on Land

Wartime myth-making extended to the land campaign, which from the war's start had been "generally disastrous." Central to this myth-making was the erasure of key events. A major humiliation came quickly in August 1812 with William Hull's premature surrender at Detroit, a surrender that led to a court martial and death sentence (later commuted) for neglect of duty and cowardice. The first significant American land victory came over a year later with William Henry Harrison's campaign into Canada, when the Battle of the Thames ended British control of the Detroit area. Meanwhile, the land campaign against Montreal proved futile for most of 1813 due to poor timing, ineffective leadership, and New England governors' refusal to provide militia. While the Federalist press excoriated William Hull,[34] Republican songwriters' optimistic accounts of the land campaign denied its failures, inflated its sporadic victories, and circulated hyperbolized, demonic portrayals of the British-Native American alliance.[35]

The longest-lasting and most widely circulated song mythologizing the land campaign was penned by a Federalist—Francis Scott Key's "Defense of Fort M'Henry." Key, a Georgetown lawyer, created the war's most enduring song, known today as "The Star-Spangled Banner."[36] Central to Key's song was the notion that God had determined American success in the battle and the war. Key delivered this message through a song that avoided both partisan language and topical reference to any specific person or place in the war. Shunning inflated, hyperbolic language and details of the human toll of combat, Key wrote a song that could both spread wartime mythology and stimulate reconciliation during a divisive war. That Key's lyrics effectively transcended partisan and regional differences was demonstrated by their appearance in both parties' newspapers and all sections of the country.

Key penned his lyrics at a national nadir. Despite William Henry Harrison's success in chasing Major General Henry Procter back into Canada, the northwest campaign lacked a broader impact and the invasion of Canada near Montreal remained at a stalemate. States became reluctant to send more volunteers until soldiers were paid for past service. Meanwhile, the British blockade of Atlantic seaports expanded. Poorly equipped American forces quickly fled at the Battle of Bladensburg, an embarrassment derided as "the Bladensburg races." Just hours later came the devastating burning of Washington, razing the Capitol, the president's house, and the Treasury Building. In the president's house, British officers feasted on a dinner abandoned by the Americans upon hearing news of the British advance.[37]

Key responded to these devastating events with a song that performed functions typically fulfilled by myths: instilling pride, addressing emotional needs, and constructing comforting narratives. Rather than relying on bombastic, regional, or partisan rhetoric to describe the battle, Key explained the American "triumph" at Fort McHenry as an outcome determined by God in service of a unified nation (see Figure 6.3). America was the "Heav'n-rescued land" that would be "Blest with vict'ry and peace." Deeply spiritual and expressing a sentiment central to American Protestantism, Key saw the British invasion as God's punishment for the nation's erring ways. For Key, the British retreat from Baltimore was a sign from God. Key had feared that the city would be burned and plundered, and he called the avoidance of this fate a "most merciful deliverance" that convinced him of God's mercy. He provided a narrative about the bombardment and the war that, like myths, could help people deal with frightening events, like the recent destruction of the nation's capital and uncertainty about the war's outcome.[38] Key offered a simple explanation in which others could place faith, hope, and, as he made explicit in his final verse, trust: he called Americans to "Praise the power that hath made and preserv'd us a nation!" Key's consistent invocation of the nation through "we" and "our" conveyed unity and contrasted with the typical third-person references to the nation.

Key could have offered an alternative but less comforting explanation of the battle. Attributing the fort's defense to sound planning and execution, while accurate, would have highlighted the anomalous strength of local defenses and underscored disappointment and skepticism about the war's progress. In Baltimore, controls over the military and its integration with the community were stronger than in Bladensburg and Washington. The attack on the capital had been facilitated by army leaders' rejection of additional fortifications as too costly and the secretary of war's belief that Washington was not the intended target.[39] As was widely understood, sound planning and execution, which were at the heart of Fort McHenry's defense, were the very things that should have been implemented across the country.

## DEFENCE OF FORT M'HENRY.

[From a Baltimore paper.]

[The annexed song was composed under the following circumstances:—A gentleman had left Baltimore, in a flag of truce, for the purpose of getting released from the British fleet a friend of his, who had been captured at Marlborough. He went as far as the mouth of the Patuxent, and was not permitted to return, lest the intended attack on Baltimore should be disclosed. He was therefore brought up the bay to the mouth of the Patapsco, where the flag was kept under the guns of a frigate, and he was compelled to witness the bombardment of Fort M'Henry, which the Admiral had boasted that he would carry in a few hours, and that the city must fall. He watched the flag at the Fort through the whole day with an anxiety that can be better felt than described, until the night prevented him from seeing it. In the night he watched the bomb-shells, and at early dawn his eye was again greeted by the proudly-waving flag of his country.]

TUNE—ANACREON IN HEAVEN.

O! say can you see, by the dawn's early light,
What so proudly we hail'd at the twilight's last gleaming,
Whose broad stripes and bright stars through the perilous fight;
O'er the ramparts we watch'd were so gallantly streaming?
And the Rocket's red glare, the Bombs bursting in air,
Gave proof through the night that our Flag was still there;
O! say, does that star-spangled banner yet wave,
O'er the land of the free, and the home of the brave?

On the shore, dimly seen through the mists of the deep,
Where the foe's haughty host in dread silence reposes,
What is that, which the breeze o'er the towering steep,
As it fitfully blows, half conceals, half discloses?
Now it catches the gleam of the morning's first beam,
In full glory reflected now shines on the stream,
'Tis the star-spangled banner. O! long may it wave
O'er the land of the free and the home of the brave.

And where is that band who so vauntingly swore,
That the havock of war and the battle's confusion
A home and a country should leave us no more?
Their blood has wash'd out their foul footsteps' pollution,
No refuge could save the hireling and slave,
From the terror of flight or the gloom of the grave;
And the star spangled banner in triumph doth wave,
O'er the land of the free and the home of the brave.

O! thus be it ever when freemen shall stand,
Between their lov'd home, and the war's desolation,
Blest with vict'ry and peace, may the Heav'n-rescued land,
Praise the power that hath made and preserv'd us a nation!
Then conquer we must, when our cause it is just,
And this be our motto—"In God is our Trust!"
And the star-spangled banner in triumph shall wave,
O'er the land of the free and the home of the brave.

**Figure 6.3.** Francis Scott Key, "Defense of Fort M'Henry." *Norwich Courier*, 19 October 1814. Readex/NewsBank.

Ironically, Republican administrations' lack of military preparation, due in part to an emphasis on lowering the debt, was now obscured by a Federalist who looked beyond partisan histories and blame to offer a transcendent and broadly appealing explanation.

Key created a powerful account of the war by making no specific reference to the place or people involved in the engagement that inspired him to write it. Other songwriters had often recounted the war's battles—including the battle for Baltimore—in highly detailed, ballad-like descriptions extending to thirteen and fourteen stanzas.[40] But Key portrayed the fort's defense as a major feat and heroic accomplishment without reference to any specific location, landmark, or region. He avoided conventional references to recent regional engagements, references that could have highlighted contrasting sectional perspectives on the war. Through his general language, the defense seemed a collective success of national significance. Key's reference in the third verse to the Chesapeake Bay slaves who enlisted in the British navy and participated in the Battle of Bladensburg and the burning of Washington was expressed without any such specificity of place. He also avoided reference to any specific person, a common reference in wartime songs, including his own "The Warrior's Return," which honored Stephen Decatur at the end of the Tripolitan War and included Key's earlier use of the descriptor "star-spangled."[41] Key now avoided articulating such a hero or noting any individual participants who could symbolize a state or region.

Instead, Key invoked the battle through a small but significant part of the fort: its flag. As contemporary printings often explained, he wrote the lyrics while trapped in an unusual location—amid the British fleet. To secure the release of local physician Dr. William Beanes, who had been taken prisoner by the British, Key had boarded a British vessel and was detained until the bombardment's end so he could not reveal the British attack. He had supposedly been directed to watch the flag by cocky British officers and a nervous, poorly sighted Beanes.[42] Key focused his lyrics on the flag—still standing after roughly twenty-four hours of bombardment—as a representation of success in the battle and the nation's projected success in the war as a whole. While a flag may seem an obvious focal point today, it had not yet become the standard symbol of the nation—the eagle and the goddess Columbia were national symbols used in songwriting and art for decades. However, the flag was the part of the fort that was replicated (with variations in size) across the nation. It was part of every land or sea battle and therefore had increasingly been referenced in passing in wartime songs, particularly naval songs.[43]

Key's treatment of the flag was different. His opening question about the flag not only engaged the reader, singer, or listener with "you" but also encompassed, with "we," Americans collectively. Key engaged this audience emotionally by extending the question attributed to Beanes—whether the flag had been lowered in surrender—across the first two verses, paralleling Americans' uncertainty about the outcome of the war as a whole. Through his treatment of the flag, Key conveyed the futility of British fire, which instead of destroying or prompting the surrender of the fort, simply illuminated the flag as a symbol of military and moral superiority. While the British troops' "foul footsteps' pollution" was washed out by their own blood, the American flag "gallantly" streamed its stripes and stars in the air until victory was assured. At the war's nadir, he treated the still-flying flag as a powerful symbol conveying optimism about the war's outcome. As the central image of Key's song, the flying flag was a metonym for the fort and the nation. Reflecting the broad influence of Key's lyrics, from the following year, writers and celebrants across the nation referred to the "star-spangled banner."[44]

Supporting his central image and avoidance of local references, Key fit his lyrics to a melody that had national appeal and could transcend divisive partisan rhetoric. While a fellow songwriter used "Yankee Doodle" to offer a humorously overconfident battle account that made light of the recent burning of Washington, Key turned to a tune that was normally used for serious lyrical treatments of current events, "Anacreon in Heaven." This was one of the most frequently used tunes for new American political lyrics.[45] It was regularly chosen as the basis for serious lyrics written for anniversaries of national significance, like July 4 and Washington's birthday, as well as public dinners honoring military and political figures. The tune had acquired more than a "patriotic coloring," as Richard Hill dubbed it. Instead, it had been used for partisan purposes by both Federalists and Republicans. With it, Americans had sung "Adams and Liberty" and then "Jefferson and Liberty." Referring to "Adams and Liberty," Fischer suggested that "Key took the song of a political party [the Federalist party] that in 1814 was identified with peace and sectionalism and made it a hymn to martial courage and national unity." Key could do so because "Anacreon" had already escaped such narrow partisan significance when "Adams and Liberty" was transformed by William C. Foster into a Republican election and inauguration song "Jefferson and Liberty" from 1800. Moreover, "Adams and Liberty" was used during the war by both Federalists and Republicans to express a variety of sentiments, including toasts to the Constitution, the war, and the freedom of the press and debate.[46] Given the tune's American history and Key's own personal transformations, "Anacreon in Heaven" was an ideal choice for transcending partisan divisions and conveying an uplifting message of national significance.

Although Key wrote his lyrics quickly, he produced a song of literary quality. He drafted the song while still detained by the British on September 14 and finalized it at a Baltimore inn that night after being released.[47] This timeline might be questioned except that Key had previously written a song honoring veterans of the Tripolitan War on about an hour's notice. It too received high praise, and it too reworked "Anacreon in Heaven."[48] In his second quick production, Key struck a noble but unaffected tone, appropriate to what was increasingly being called "national song." In an article that had recently caught Key's attention, Washington Irving had complained of the "taste for gorgeous finery, and violent metaphor" that he found in American song. As Irving elaborated,

> Our national songs are full of ridiculous exaggeration, and frothy rant, and commonplace bloated up into fustian. The writers seem to think that huge words, and mountainous figures, constitute the sublime. Their puny thoughts are made to sweat under loads of cumbrous imagery, and now and then they are so wrapt up in conflagrations, and blazes, and thunders and lightnings, that, like Nick Bottom's hero [in *A Midsummer Night's Dream*], they seem to have "slipt on a brimstone shirt, and are all on fire!"

In contrast, Irving praised verses marked by simplicity, directness, and a "vigorous and perspicuous tone." He cautioned that "true taste always evinces itself in pure and noble simplicity, and a fitness and chasteness of ornament." Key's account of the Battle of Baltimore exemplified Irving's recommendations. Avoiding bombastic, cumbersome, or overworked imagery like that used by Robert Treat Paine and Edwin Holland, Key presented one simple primary image—the flag. With his restrained and deft handling of tone and imagery, Key's lyrics promptly received the praise of Irving, who printed them in a literary magazine because "their merit entitles them to preservation in some more permanent form than the columns of a daily paper."[49]

Key wrote "Defense of Fort M'Henry," like Irving, as a moderate mid-Atlantic Federalist. Key may seem an unlikely author for a song memorializing a war brought on by Republicans: he was not only a Federalist, but he had opposed war on religious grounds. On the eve of war, Key agreed with Federalist leaders that war was "unnecessary, unwise, and unrighteous."

But his perspective was changed by the extremes of partisan politics and the burning of Washington. His Federalism had transformed into a disgust with American partisanship. Like fellow Federalist Washington Irving, Key enlisted in the militia, motivated by devastating British attacks in the mid-Atlantic.[50] As a result, his perspective and personal transformation enabled him to respond to a critical moment in the war with lyrics expressing a noble voice of moderation that transcended partisan rhetoric.

The potential and impact of Key's verse were foreseen in 1806. The editor of the New York *Weekly Inspector* had noted of Key's earlier song,

> "Nothing contributes more essentially to foster that high sense of national honor and thirst of glory, which are the soul of national independence, than songs like the following. Dibdin has perhaps effected little less for the British navy than the famous Navigation Act, and a National Songster in America, who would reward merit and valour with strains like these might awaken those energies which become a great and Independent nation."[51]

Eight years later, Key fulfilled this vision when he mythologized the battle for Baltimore as a work of God that could inspire all Americans' trust and faith, regardless of sectional or partisan divisions. Key crafted his lyrics to foreground non-partisan symbols and a generic sense of pride, ideas that could appeal to many Americans, regardless of political or regional identification, and that aligned with growing interest in "national song." Key offered a comforting narrative of the battle that sent a powerful message about the war's trajectory, and through his careful handling of tone and reference, restraint of imagery, and selection of tune, his account gained both broad circulation and lasting appeal.

## The End of the War

When Key offered his optimistic account, the nation was in a crisis. The federal government was bankrupt, and the heads of the army, navy, and treasury quit or were fired. Land engagements were hampered by insufficient, poorly equipped troops, and the conquest of Canada, which Jefferson had envisioned in 1812 as "a mere matter of marching," was impossible. The navy's large vessels were trapped in port by a British blockade, and "gallant" naval engagements were replaced by the unheroic raiding and destruction of British commerce. By this point, in Budiansky's assessment, the war was "unwinnable."[52]

Meanwhile, New England Federalists complained of the expense of regional defense, called for constitutional amendments, and demanded the war's end. Their complaints culminated in the Hartford Convention, where Federalist delegates from New England states met in secret proceedings from December 15, 1814, to January 5, 1815. Although later seen as a moderating vehicle—delegates were chosen to exclude extremists—the convention fueled speculation about renewed plans for secession and the prospect of civil war. These concerns were only intensified by the pursuit of local neutrality and peace agreements with Britain.[53]

Had the war not ended with the Treaty of Ghent, the outcome, political effects, and memory of the conflict would have been vastly different. A protracted war amid a worsening crisis would have exposed Republican administrations' flawed prioritization of economy over defense. Yet the peace, along with the victory at New Orleans (achieved after the treaty's negotiation but before its news reached the United States), prompted a powerful new wave of myth-making that quickly cast the war as a complete triumph. In the end, the coincidence of peace, a pride-instilling land battle, and the impression of Federalist disloyalty fueled such a surge of myth-making that, in the words of Taylor, "a war that had exposed the republic's weaknesses became, in memory, a war that had proven its strengths."[54]

Central to this reversal was myth-making about the Battle of New Orleans. Although characterized by later historians like Taylor as "exceptional" and the "most lopsided battle" of the war, the victory at New Orleans, along with news of the peace, quickly fueled mythologized assessments of the entire war. The battle included key myth-making ingredients: a hero (General Andrew Jackson), a decisive outcome, an impressive scale of casualties, and a memorable motto. A prominent part of war mythology was the land campaign's reduction to this battle that Nivola called "the one truly telling blow dealt to the enemy on land." Boastful songwriters even claimed that the battle brought about the peace, erroneous claims reinforced by the simultaneous arrival of news about the battle and the peace treaty previously signed in Europe.[55] Songwriters and composers of battle sonatas for keyboard hyperbolized the victory: the British were "totally routed" and suffered such "Terrible Carnage" that "The streams ran with blood," while the Americans left with merely a broken shin and skinned nose.[56] An often reprinted "American Patriotic Song" recounted that "Jackson with his fearless few/The *invincibles* by thousands slew," and songwriters predicted that the "immortal" Jackson would be praised along with Washington himself.[57]

Aiding such skewed memory of the battle was the motto it produced: "beauty and booty." Songwriters repeated these purported British passwords that conveyed, as federal judge George Poindexter quickly suggested, a British intent to plunder New Orleans and rape its women following a British victory.[58] The subject of debate then and now, Poindexter's reporting of the British watchword and countersign (passwords changed daily to help distinguish friend from foe) was consistent with other American efforts to ensure that the British lost the battle of morality: songwriters portrayed the British as a "savage" and "degenerate" collection of "miscreants" who committed "horrid crimes" and "barb'rous deeds."[59] The "beauty and booty" myth framed the war as a battle between Americans who fought out of national duty and British who were so devoid of such loyalty that they could only be motivated by sexual debauchery and greed. To make this point, one songwriter chastised the British, "Disgrace to thy country! Thou monster accurst!/To inflame thy foul soldiers with av'rice and lust./Was honor and courage extinct in each breast?/To rouse them must passions like these be addrest?"[60] "The Battle of New Orleans" presented the moral contrast between the two nations in stark terms. Writing in "imitation" of the verse structure and rhyme scheme of Thomas Campbell's "Hohenlinden" (commemorating an 1800 battle of the same name), the anonymous songwriter even invented a slogan for the American side to clarify the dichotomy:

> "Beauty and Booty" were the words
> That steel'd the hearts, unsheath'd the swords
> Of foreign—vassal—Vandal hordes,
>   To murder, rape, and robbery!
> "God and our Country!" was the reply
> Of Jackson's men—the matron's sigh!
> Those sounds ne'er fail to reach the sky,
>   And sanctify a victory![61]

In contrast to these claims of British moral deficit, songwriters and the composer of a keyboard sonata bolstered American moral superiority by touting American charity and medical care given to wounded British troops. As Eustace has argued, "The watchword scandal polished the U.S. image as a uniquely virtuous nation bent on preserving the most fundamental form of liberty—sexual consent—from British perfidy."[62]

Two characteristic songs played a key role in popularizing and sustaining the "beauty and booty" myth. One was "The Guinea Boy," a song that was widely reprinted after it first appeared in the Carlisle *American Volunteer*.[63] The *Volunteer*'s founder, William B. Underwood, had left Maryland to begin the new paper in Carlisle, Pennsylvania, in September 1814. Previously a printer in Fredericktown and Baltimore, Underwood had spent years in the Chesapeake Bay area where British admiral George Cockburn focused demoralizing raids in the spring and summer of 1814 and accepted hundreds of escaped slaves as enlistees.[64] The satirical song Underwood printed was written as if sung by one of those slaves who joined the British and later fought the Americans at New Orleans. Underwood presented the lyrics as "intended to be sung in character, with unbounded applause at the next opening of the Theatres Royal, Covent Garden and Drury Lane." This character, "Cuffee," abandons the first-person singular used to narrate his enslavement and enlistment once he reaches New Orleans to speak as part of the British forces. The songwriter has "Cuffee" report to both American readers and imagined British audiences, "When we come ashore, great big gun we shute-e,/For make Yankee run,/den we could get de 'booty.'" As he explained, the British had put their hopes on having fun "wid pretty garl" and getting "de plunder."

The *Volunteer*'s songwriter and editor did far more than sustain the "beauty and booty" myth. The songwriter marshalled three types or characters—black slave, western rifleman, and Irishman—to construct this imagined musical transatlantic reporting of American triumph in war. At the *Volunteer*'s direction, the reader could have sung—or imagined hearing on the British stage—the tale of American victory at New Orleans to "Love and Whiskey," a song of the Irish Volunteers that likely recalled the Battle of Carrickfergus in the Seven Years' War. This melody's original lyrics underscored the "beauty and booty" myth's attribution of immoral motivations to the British forces: "Love and whiskey can/To anything persuade us;/No other power we fear/That ever can invade us." The other tune indicated for the new lyrics was Thomas Dibdin's "Jack of Guinea," a song in West Indian dialect published in 1805 and later performed in Isaac Bickerstaff's comic opera *The Padlock*, the farce in which Thomas's father Charles Dibdin had created a sensation with his blackface performance of the slave Mungo.[65] While Thomas Dibdin's lyrics were sung in the character of a black slave who told how his masters separated other people from their money, the mid-Atlantic writer of "The Guinea Boy" used the character of a runaway slave to narrate how British motivation by lust and greed proved insufficient in battle against Americans motivated by national duty.

Central to the enlistee's narrative of American triumph in the Battle of New Orleans was the character of the western rifleman. The British fought for "beauty and booty," "But de backwood Yankee/He note much good nater/He say he 'one half horse, Half an alligator.'" These lines described a character that had emerged in the previous decade: the rough Kentucky backwoodsman. The animal references were part of an elaborate vocabulary of boasting and brawling used by boatmen and recorded by New Yorker Christian Schultz during his travels on the Mississippi River in 1808. They were applied in a cutting New York satire on Aaron Burr in the same year and incorporated by Washington Irving in his 1809 *A History of New York*.[66] By early 1815, the exotic Kentucky frontiersman on the geographical and cultural periphery of the nation had become a convenient national symbol. As Arthur Moore later elaborated this character, "being simplified to fang and belly, he is utterly competent to secure life, liberty, and the pursuit of happiness for himself if not for others. He is accordingly an ideal figure for that part of the metropolis which acknowledges the 'call of the wild.'" Indeed, as Ward has argued, the wartime invocation of the backwoodsman suggested that nature itself was responsible for American victory in the war.[67] Whether William Underwood wrote "The Guinea Boy" himself or simply printed it, he offered a multilayered representation through which an often white newspaper reader played a black slave-turned British tar who used the animalistic portrayal of a backwoodsman to report to British subjects the Americans' resounding military defeat of the British empire through the war's final land battle.

A far simpler and more popular song gave the "beauty and booty" myth greater longevity: "New Orleans." This song gained widespread popularity under the title "The Hunters of Kentucky" (see Figure 6.4) but has been surrounded by misinformation. Later mistaken as an expression of westerners' pride in their contributions to the war, "The Hunters of Kentucky" was a product of New York. And while authors have suggested that the song was written or printed in 1815 shortly after the war's end or written later in 1822 as part of Andrew Jackson's presidential campaign, it was written in late 1819, first published in 1820, and first performed in public in 1822.[68] It was written for the benefit night of a New York actor who was known for his portrayal of country boys, Scotsmen, and old veterans. Actor Hopkins Robinson (or Robertson) had already popularized Micah Hawkins'

# HUNTER'S OF KENTUCKY.

## *Or Half Horse and half Alligator.*

YE gentlemen and ladies fair
  Who grace this famous city,
Just listen, if you've time to spare,
  While I rehearse a ditty;
And for the opportunity
  Conceive yourselves quite lucky,
For 'tis not often that you see
  A hunter from Kentucky.
Oh Kentucky, the hunters of Kentucky!
Oh Kentucky, the hunters of Kentucky!

We are a hardy, free-born race,
  Each man to fear a stranger;
Whate'er the game, we join in chase,
  Despising toil and danger.
And if a daring foe annoys,
  Whate'er his strength and forces,
We'll show him that Kentucky boys
  Are alligator horses.
    Oh Kentucky, &c.

I s'pose you've read it in the prints,
  How Packenham attempted
To make old Hickory Jackson wince,
  But soon his scheme repented;
For we, with rifles ready cock'd,
  Thought such occasion lucky,
And soon around the gen'ral flock'd,
  The hunters of Kentucky.
    Oh Kentucky, &c.

You've heard, I s'pose, how New-Orleans
  Is fam'd for wealth and beauty—
There's girls of ev'ry hue, it seems,
  From snowy white to sooty.
So Packenham he made his brags,
  If he in fight was lucky,
He'd have their girls and cotton bags,
  In spite of old Kentucky.
    Oh Kentucky, &c.

But Jackson he was wide awake,
  And was not scar'd at trifles,
For well he knew what aim we take,
  With our Kentucky rifles:
So he led us down by Cypress swamp,
  The ground was low and mucky;
There stood John Bull in martial pomp,
  And here was old Kentucky.
    Oh Kentucky, &c.

A bank was rais'd to hide our breasts,
  Not that we thought of dying,
But that we always like to rest,
  Unless the game is flying.
Behind it stood our little force,
  None wished it to be greater,
For ev'ry man was half a horse,
  And half an alligator.
    Oh Kentucky, &c.

They did not let our patience tire,
  Before they show'd their faces;
We did not choose to waste our fire,
  So snugly kept our places.
But when so near we saw them wink,
  We thought it time to stop 'em,
And 'twould have done you good, I think,
  To see Kentuckians drop 'em.
    Oh Kentucky, &c.

They found, at last, 'twas vain to fight,
  Where *lead* was all their *booty*,
And so they wisely took to flight,
  And left *us* all the *beauty*.
And now, if danger e'er annoys,
  Remember what our trade is;
Just send for us Kentucky boys,
  And we'll protect ye, ladies.
    Oh Kentucky, &c

Sold Wholesale and Retail, by L. Deming, No. 1, Market Square—Boston.

**Figure 6.4.** Samuel Woodworth, "The Hunters of Kentucky" (1819), printed as a broadside in Boston by Leonard Deming. The Filson Historical Society.

(1777–1825) “Back Side Albany” or “The Siege of Plattsburg,” a comical battle account sung in the character of a black sailor, prompting Sanjek to deem Robinson “the founding father of theatrical burnt-cork minstrelsy.”[69] For his benefit night in the 1819–20 season, Robinson requested a characteristic song, one that he could perform “in the character and dress of a Kentucky Rifleman.” Although he died in November 1819 before his benefit night, Robinson's request had been fulfilled by war chronicler, writer, and newspaper editor Samuel Woodworth (1784–1842).[70]

Woodworth had already produced much war commentary, drawing on his experience as writer and printer. Born in Scituate, Massachusetts, to a Revolutionary War veteran, Woodworth moved to Boston when he was unable to fund his college education and apprenticed with Federalist printer Benjamin Russell. Woodworth also wrote and published poetry under the pseudonym “Selim.” In 1809, he moved to New York, where he joined the Knickerbocker circle of writers gathered around Washington Irving. With the war's outbreak, Woodworth began a weekly newspaper *The War* (1812–13). He commemorated Perry's victory in the Battle of Lake Erie and General William Harrison's victory at the Battle of the Thames in the epic poem *The Heroes of the Lake* (1814) and fused war reportage with fiction in his novel *The Champions of Freedom* (1816). Woodworth went on to write more odes, songs, and poems and engaged in many periodical ventures. In the nineteenth century, Woodworth was best known for his song “The Old Oaken Bucket.”[71]

Through Woodworth's New York pen, the Kentucky rifleman became the persona of “The Hunters of Kentucky” and the iconic battle hero who protected New Orleans and left the city's “beauty” intact as the British fled. Jackson had no fear in battle, Woodworth's western rifleman boasted, “For well he knew what aim we take/With our Kentucky rifles.” Woodworth portrayed the Kentucky riflemen as a small but disciplined force with the restraint to save their fire until the British were “so near we saw them wink.” This was quite a tale. In fact, Jackson's main line artillery did the most damage and British were subjected to cannon fire before they came within range of small arms. The Kentucky militia lacked proper arms and scattered after firing two rounds, prompting Jackson to criticize their lack of discipline.[72] Yet Woodworth had his Kentucky rifleman proclaim “ev'ry man was half a horse/And half an alligator.” The rifleman passed on British General Edward Pakenham's brag that “He'd have their girls,” and Woodworth's choice of tune highlighted the contrast between the lustful British soldier of the watchword myth and the faithful Kentucky rifleman who delivered his lyrics. Woodworth wrote "The Hunters of Kentucky" to the tune "Unfortunate Miss Bailey." Performed in the 1803 London comic opera *Love Laughs at Locksmiths*, "Unfortunate Miss Bailey" told of a "wicked Captain Smith" in Halifax who "Seduced a maid who hang'd herself one Morning in her garters." The British in New Orleans, like Captain Smith, had intended to have their way with the city's women and its goods, Woodworth's lyrics implied. Driving the message home, in the final verse the rifleman told the audience, "And now, if danger e'er annoys/Remember what our trade is,/Just send for us Kentucky boys,/ And we'll protect ye, ladies."

The song's first known performance was in 1822 by Noah Ludlow, dressed in a "buckskin hunting-shirt and leggins" borrowed from a "river man" like those in the pit of the New Orleans theater. Scholarly interest in this performance has deflected attention from important patterns surrounding the song's emergence. The "Hunters of Kentucky," "The Guinea Boy," and "Back Side Albany Lake Champlain" emerged from transatlantic theatrical traditions, and they were inspired, written, and first published in mid-Atlantic states. Moreover, the connection made in the Carlisle *Volunteer*'s "The Guinea Boy" between the backwoodsman, Virginia slaves, and British soldier surfaced elsewhere in the mid-Atlantic states shortly after the war, such as a comical narrative in verse attributed to J. C. Gilleland and widely reprinted from his *Pittsburgh Gazette*.[73]

Such mid-Atlantic writers and editors used music to shape a particular vision of the nation's future. Their characteristic songs about the War of 1812, as part of a larger struggle to define the nation, were commentaries on who was in the national community and who was not. Waldstreicher has argued that race and nationalism were closely entwined as the war prompted a "reinvention of American nationhood." Black sailors were among the *Chesapeake* sailors seized by the British in 1807, and in "Backside Albany," as Waldstreicher has noted, a black sailor functioned as a "spokesperson of national-popular will." The other two mid-Atlantic characteristic songs presented different visions of race in relation to the nation. Likely scripted by a white songwriter, "Cuffee" in "The Guinea Boy" gave much credit for the American victory to the white frontiersman, and Woodworth had the Kentucky backwoodsman erase the contributions of free blacks and slaves in New Orleans. Ward has estimated that Woodworth's song dismissed the contributions of 41 percent of the combatants in the battle on the American side, among them free blacks and slaves who were integral to the city's defense. Such erasure may be seen not simply as a whitening of the war but also as part of a larger white backlash against the increasing assertiveness of blacks in previous years as celebrants of the international slave trade's end and as a rapidly growing part of the electorate in Woodworth's New York.[74] It may also be seen as part of a decades-long process of envisioning the American West. As Pierce has outlined, the West was conceived as a vehicle for racial cleansing and segregation: New England and mid-Atlantic writers envisioned the American West and specifically the Louisiana Territory as a separate and distant place for blacks, while Jefferson had envisioned a white West made possible by transporting freed slaves outside the nation. This approach was pursued by the American Colonization Society, organized in December 1816 by a small group of mid-Atlantic residents, including Francis Scott Key, and which led to the founding of Liberia. Locating "Cuffee" on a London stage was consonant with this vision of an American community in which whiteness was equated with citizenship. As a result, the song illustrated such removal while simultaneously demonstrating an American superiority in military might and, as the song ended with "Cuffee" longing to return home, culture.[75]

The Kentucky hunter emerged through such lyrics as a means of representing American empire. Irving had already situated the backwoodsmen in the colonization of the American West in his 1809 *A History of New York* when he distinguished them from settlers: "the back-woodmen of Kentucky are styled half man, half horse and half alligator, by the settlers on the Mississippi, and held accordingly in great respect and abhorrence." Woodworth continued the shaping of an American empire in print. Woodworth collapsed Irving's distinction between backwoodsman and settlers, having his Kentucky rifleman be simultaneously an exotic Other and an integral part of the nation and its success in battle. While "despising toil," a common characterization of the colonized, the Kentucky hunters, in Woodworth's representation, are also a "free-born race" who could be relied on to maintain liberty and protect the integrity of the nation's "beauty and booty."[76] In contrast to the West Indies dialect of "Cuffee," carried over from Thomas Dibdin's "Jack of Guinea," Woodworth's Kentucky hunter, once secured inside the performative frame set with "ye," is allowed to represent himself and the American West in standard printed English. His performance delivers an idealized vision of an American empire, the rights to which had been defended years before through a war waged in what Eustace has called "a contest over the meaning and validity of American claims to champion liberty in an expansionist age." Such an empire had its roots in the nation's founding: in 1783 Washington called America a "rising empire" and John Adams proclaimed two years later that America was "destined to be the greatest power on earth." Central to this notion of empire was continental expansion, which Jefferson's administration ensured and Washington Irving reinforced as he revised and updated *A History of New York*.[77] When Woodworth was writing in 1819 after the war's end, America's status as a continental empire seemed secure. That "The Hunters of Kentucky" effectively engaged with this ongoing envisioning and realization of American continental expansion was born out by a Waltham, Massachusetts, correspondent of the *Columbian Centinel* who invoked the song when bemoaning the emigration of New England youth to the west a decade after the war. The Waltham resident's connection was not accidental, for the Kentucky hunter, an iconic and mythical western figure, represented a further erosion of New England's cultural and political centrality amid ongoing western expansion and mid-Atlantic commercial growth.[78]

While a cursory consideration of wartime lyrics may suggest that this was a period of nationalism based on unity, it was in fact a time of sectional divisions obscured through myth-making. The wartime surge in nationalism was a sectional nationalism—it was promoted by moderates in the Mid-Atlantic and the West and was weaker in the South, while in New England extremist voices fomented partisan rancor and a regionalist outlook that alarmed Americans in other regions.[79] These sectional differences were captured in the very different accounts of the war left by Francis Scott Key and Samuel Griswold Goodrich—while the Maryland Federalist fostered a wartime mythology that stimulated national pride, his Connecticut counterpart strove to expose such accounts as myths. The mid-Atlantic, which saw some of the most dramatic wartime destruction, produced the most strongly nationalist sentiments and the most lasting musical account of this nationalism. While not representative of national unity, such texts strove to transcend partisan and sectional differences while providing an inspiring account of the war. Writing from this mid-Atlantic perspective, Secretary of the Treasury Albert Gallatin reflected that before the war, Americans had been "above all, too much confined in [their] political feelings to local and State objects." But the conflict "renewed and reinstated the national feelings and character which the Revolution had given and which were daily lessened. The people have now more general objects of attachment with which their pride and political opinions are connected. They are more American; they feel and act more as a nation."[80] To the extent that Gallatin's observation was true, musical myth-making about the war played an important role in the cultivation of those feelings of national attachment.

Victories delivered by an iconic western hunter, divine providence, and a navy capable of uniting political parties were central to the musical accounts that helped cloak the War of 1812 in myth for generations. Musical myth-making about the war accomplished several things: it cultivated pride in naval heroes and the navy as an institution, voiced messages of hope that transcended partisan and sectional rhetoric, articulated a vision for the expanding American empire, and offered comforting narratives of the war as triumph and worthwhile endeavor. Myths about the war addressed long-standing anxiety over the status of the nation as a republic and obscured the possibility that the only viable national political party and source of future leadership had wasted lives and money on a failed war.[81] Even in New England, where anti-war rhetoric had been so strong, newspaper printers circulated songs that exaggerated the entire war as a triumph.[82] Songwriters magnified the nation's accomplishments in the war by claiming a defeat not simply of the British, but rather of "*Wellington*'s troops" who had triumphed in the Napoleonic Wars.[83] Songwriters placed mythical wartime gains in a larger narrative of national development, portraying the United States as Britain's maritime peer.[84] Through new lyrics, Americans touted what the war supposedly gained: maritime rights, freedom, and national honor.[85] The majority of such claims were false. American negotiators had repeatedly backed off from earlier demands regarding impressment; it was Napoleon's abdication that ended Britain's need to impress, not the treaty, which said nothing about the issue. As the war failed to gain territory or concessions on impressment and trade, its proponents defined victory in other terms, such as national honor and international respect.[86] Such mythologizing colored accounts for generations to come. As Theodore Roosevelt explained the war's end, "After our humiliating defeats in trying to repel the invasions of Virginia and Maryland, the signal victory of New Orleans was really almost a necessity for the preservation of the national honor. . . . [T]he fact that we were victorious, not only saved our self respect at home, but also gave us a prestige abroad which we should otherwise have totally lacked." Yet it was not so much that the war gained the nation honor but that its timely conclusion prevented national dishonor.[87] Nevertheless, Americans were elated by the news of a peace treaty regardless of the terms, and few were interested in challenging the exaggerated accounts that immediately followed. Those who did—New England Federalists—had already been discredited.[88] Amid such conditions, postwar myth-making—including song—rapidly transformed the goals of the war into apparent accomplishments.

## Notes

1. Goodrich, *Recollection of a Lifetime*, vol. 1, 506–7; Alan Taylor, "Dual Nationalisms: Legacies of the War of 1812," in *What So Proudly We Hailed: Essays on the Contemporary Meaning of the War of 1812*, ed. Pietro S. Nivola and Peter J. Kastor (Washington, DC: Brookings Institution Press, 2012), 82–3; Donald R. Hickey, "Federalist Party Unity and the War of 1812," *Journal of American Studies* 12, no. 1 (April 1978): 39; Hickey, *Don't Give Up the Ship!*, xviii; Sidney Hart and Rachael L. Penman, *1812: A Nation Emerges* (Washington, DC: Smithsonian Institution Scholarly Press, 2012), 21; Pietro S. Nivola, "The 'Party War' of 1812: Yesterday's Lessons for Today's Partisan Politics," in *What So Proudly We Hailed: Essays on the Contemporary Meaning of the War of 1812*, ed. Pietro S. Nivola and Peter J. Kastor (Washington, DC: Brookings Institution Press, 2012), 22; Michael Allen, "'Sired by a Hurricane': Mike Fink, Western Boatmen and the Myth of the Alligator Horse," *Arizona and the West* 27, no. 3 (Autumn 1985): 237–52; Alfred A. Cave, "The Shawnee Prophet, Tecumseh, and Tippecanoe: A Case Study of Historical Myth-Making," *Journal of the Early American Republic* 22, no. 4 (Winter 2002): 640, 653, 657–8, 661–3, 670–2; Carl Benn, *The War of 1812* (New York: Routledge, 2003), 82–3; Nicole Eustace, *1812: War and the Passions of Patriotism* (Philadelphia: University of Pennsylvania Press, 2012), xi, xvi; Michael Fellman, "The Earthbound Eagle: Andrew Jackson and the American Pantheon," *American Studies* 12, no. 2 (Fall 1971): 67.
2. New York *Public Advertiser*, 14 July 1812; Cooperstown *Otsego Herald*, 8 August 1812; Wilkes-Barre *Gleaner*, 25 September 1812; *The Chronicle or Harrisburgh Visitor*, 21 March 1814; [James Campbell], "A New Song" (Boston: Nathaniel Coverly, 1812); American Sailor, "New Songs" (Boston: Nathaniel Coverly, 1812).
3. Ralph Ketcham, "James Madison: The Unimperial President," *Virginia Quarterly Review* 54 (Winter 1978); Ralph Ketcham, *James Madison: A Biography* (Charlottesville: University Press of Virginia, 1990), 537; Lawrence Delbert Cress, "'Cool and Serious Reflection': Federalist Attitudes toward War in 1812," *Journal of the Early Republic* 7, no. 2 (Summer 1987): 123–45; Donald R. Hickey, *The War of 1812: A Forgotten Conflict* (Urbana: University of Illinois, 1989), 69–70, 257–80; Harvey Strum, "New York Federalists and Opposition to the War of 1812," *World Affairs* 142, no. 3 (Winter 1980): 172, 175–9; Pasley, *Tyranny of Printers*, 255; James M. Banner Jr., *To the Hartford Convention: The Federalists and the Origins of Party Politics in Massachusetts, 1789–1815* (New York: Alfred A. Knopf, 1970), 264–5, 300–50; *Washington Reporter*, 11 May 1812; *Portsmouth New Hampshire Gazette*, 11 March 1815; Anthony S. Pitch, *The Burning of Washington: The British Invasion of 1814* (Annapolis, MD: Naval Institute Press, 2000), 1–12; Broussard, *Southern Federalists*, 157; Alan Taylor, *The Civil War of 1812: American Citizens, British Subjects, Irish Rebels, and Indian Allies* (New York: Alfred A. Knopf, 2010), 288–9.

4. "A Happy New-Year to Commodore Rodgers, or, Huzza for the President and Congress" (Boston: N. Coverly Jr., 1812); Brian Roberts, *Blackface Nation: Race, Reform, and Identity in American Popular Music, 1812–1925* (Chicago: University of Chicago Press, 2017), 65.
5. Amos A. Evans, "Journal Kept on Board the United States Frigate 'Constitution,' 1812, by Amos A. Evans, Surgeon United States Navy," *Pennsylvania Magazine of History and Biography* 19, no. 3 (1895): 385; *Baltimore Patriot*, 29 December 1813; New York *Columbian*, 4 May 1813; Lucile Gafford, "The Boston Stage and the War of 1812," *New England Quarterly* 7, no. 2 (June 1934): 327–35.
6. Keller, *Music of the War of 1812*, 59; "Naval Recruiting Song," *Isaiah Thomas Broadside Ballads Project*, http://www.americanantiquarian.org/thomasballads/items/show/306; [Washington Irving], "Review of *Odes, Naval Songs, and Other Occasional Poems. By Edwin C. Holland, Esq. Charleston,*" *Analectic Magazine* 3 (1814): 248; Charles Town *Farmers' Repository*, 10 November 1814; *Carthage Gazette*, 24 April 1813; Georgetown *Telegraph*, 22 July 1813; Louisville *Western Courier*, 16 May 1814; Clinton *Ohio Register*, 29 March, 7 May, 22 October 1814; Williamsburg *Western American*, 8 October 1814; Windsor *Washingtonian*, 21 September 1812; Windsor *Vermont Republican*, 23 November 1812.
7. John Bray and Joseph Hutton, "Hull's Victory: A New Patriotic Song" (Philadelphia: G. E. Blake, [1812]); Uri K. Hill, "The Heroes of the Ocean" (Philadelphia: G. Willig, 1813); William Strickland, "Decatur's Victory: A Favorite Song" (Philadelphia: G. Willig, [1812–13]); Joseph Hutton, "Perry's Victory" (N.p., n.d.); "Lawrence the Brave" (Philadelphia: G. E. Blake, 1813); "Perry's Victory" (Philadelphia: G. Willig [ca. 1813]); Keller, *Music of the War of 1812*, 177–84.
8. Clinton *Ohio Register*, 22 February 1814. For example, Republican John D. Goodwin wrote "Perry's Tid-Re-I" and Federalist Lucius Manlius Sargent wrote a naval ode and "Yankee Thunders." *Bennington News-Letter*, 18 March 1813; Keller, *Music of the War of 1812*, 139–44.
9. *Lancaster Journal*, 4 March 1813; *New York Evening Post*, 16 March 1813; William Alexander Robinson, "The Washington Benevolent Society in New England: A Phase of Politics during the War of 1812," *Proceedings of the Massachusetts Historical Society*, 49 (March 1916): 274–86.
10. Windsor *Washingtonian*, 14 December 1812; *Bennington News-Letter*, 11 March 1813. Rare examples of partisan lyrics in songsters are *The Patriotic Songster* (Alexandria: Benjamin L. Bogan, 1816), 37–9; *The Columbian Harmonist* (Philadelphia: Thomas Simpson, 1814), 19–21; *The Naval Songster* (Fredericktown, MD: M. E. Bartgis, 1814), 19–21; William Dunlap, *Yankee Chronology; or, Huzza for the Constitution!* (New York: D. Longworth, 1812), 14–6; *The Columbian Naval Melody* (Boston: Hans Lund, 1813), 50–2.
11. Lee A. Wallace Jr., "The Petersburg Volunteers, 1812–1813," *Virginia Magazine of History and Biography* 82, no. 4 (October 1974): 458; Taylor, *Civil War*, 161–6, 169–70.
12. Hickey, *Don't Give Up the Ship*, xviii; Cave, "Shawnee Prophet," 640, 653, 657–8, 661–3, 670–2; Tyrone G. Martin, "Isaac Hull's Victory Revisited," *American Neptune* 47 (1987): 14, 18–20; Stephen Budiansky, *Perilous Fight: America's Intrepid War*

*with Britain on the High Seas, 1812–1815* (New York: Vintage Books, 2011), 142–7; New York *Columbian*, 10 September 1812; Boston *Independent Chronicle*, 31 August 1812.

13. *The American Patriotic Song-Book* (Philadelphia: W. M'Culloch, 1813), 9–15, 18; *Free Trade and Sailors' Rights* (Philadelphia: Dennis Heartt, 1813), 52–5; *The Columbian Naval Songster, Being a Collection of Original Songs, Odes &c. Composed in Honor of the Five Great Naval Victories Obtained by Hull etc.* (New York: Edward Gillespy, 1813), 61–2; *Naval Songster* (1814), 62–4; Keller, *Music of the War of 1812*, 147, 151–5.
14. *American Patriotic Song-Book* (1813), 4–21; *Free Trade and Sailors' Rights*, 51–6.
15. Paul A. Gilje, "'Free Trade and Sailors' Rights': The Rhetoric of the War of 1812," *Journal of the Early Republic* 30, no. 1 (Spring 2010): 1–23.
16. David Hildebrand, "New York in Song: The War of 1812," *New York History* 94, no. 3–4 (Summer/Fall 2013): 285, 288, 290; *New England Palladium*, 9 April 1813; New York *Columbian*, 4 May 1813. A counterexample to such heroes was John Rodgers, who profited from taking British merchantmen but found no real combat in the war, and was both criticized and defended. See Keller, *Music of the War of 1812*, 77–8, 171–5.
17. New York *Columbian*, 2 October 1813, 12 January 1814; *Port Folio*, December 1813, 583–4; Salem *Essex Register*, 25 December 1813; Elizabethtown *New Jersey Journal*, 28 December 1813; Bedford *True American*, 5 January 1814; Washington *Daily National Intelligencer*, 27 January 1814; Wilmington *American Watchman*, 9 February 1814; Bouchell, *Music Book*; Baker, *Florae Memoriae*; Keller, *Music of the War of 1812*, 165–9, 185–7, 190; Hickey, *Don't Give Up the Ship!*, 124–5.
18. Wilkes-Barre *Gleaner*, 5 November 1813; New York *Columbian*, 2 January 1813; Washington Irving, *The Life and Letters of Washington Irving*, vol. 1 (New York: G. P. Putnam, 1869), 218–19.
19. New York *Shamrock*, 5 September 1812; *Salem Gazette*, 4, 8 September 1812; Boston *Columbian Centinel*, 9 September 1812; Boston *The Yankee*, 18 September 1812; Boston *New England Palladium*, 8 September 1812.
20. Eustace, *1812*, 86; Philadelphia *Gazette of the United States*, 29 January 1799; New York *Spectator*, 13 March 1799; Philadelphia *Aurora*, 5 January 1805; Salem *Gazette*, 18 September 1812; William Goldsmith, *The Naval History of Great Britain* (London: J. Jaques and W. Wright, 1825), 63, 93, 187, 246, 545, 563, 598, 607, 632, 684, 715, 724, 772, 784, 795.
21. Keller, *Music of the War of 1812*, 139–44; *Norwich Courier*, 16 September 1812; *American Patriotic Song-Book* (1813), 9–11; *Free Trade and Sailors' Rights*, 51–2; *A National Song-Book* (Trenton: James J. Wilson, 1813), 185–7; *Columbian Naval Melody*, 12–14; *Columbian Harmonist*, 34–6; *American Patriotic and Comic Modern Songs Commemorative of Naval Victories* (Newburyport: W[hittingham] & J[ohn] Gilman, 1814), 27–9; *American Song Book* (N.p.: N.p., 1815), 23–6; *Boston Musical Miscellany* (Boston: J. T. Buckingham, 1815), 29–32; *The Star Spangled Banner: Being a Collection of the Best Naval, Martial, and Patriotic Songs . . . Chiefly Written during, and in Relation to the Late War* (Wilmington, DE: J[ames] Wilson, 1816), 97–9; John C. McCloskey, "The Campaign of Periodicals after the War of 1812 for National American Literature," *PMLA* 50, no. 1 (March 1935): 262–3. As John Adams was

unable to attend the dinner, his toast was delivered by the chair; the prohibition on volunteer toasts remained.

22. Edward C. Carter II, "Mathew Carey, Advocate of American Naval Power, 1785–1814," *American Neptune* 26 (July 1966): 177–8, 182, 184–8.
23. Dunlap, *Yankee Chronology*, 14–16; *American Song Book*, 26–8; *National Aegis*, 27 October 1813; *Free Trade and Sailors' Rights*, 57; *American Patriotic Song-Book* (1813), 89–90; *Columbian Naval Songster*, 3, 12–15, 50–2, 56–9, 68–71, 85–6, 90–2; *Columbian Naval Melody*, 40–2, 46–8, 52–4, 57–8, 71–6; *National Song-Book*, 193, 197–9, 202–4; *Star Spangled Banner*, 82–3, 96–7; *Naval Songster* (1814), 12–15, 19–21, 32–4; *Port Folio* (1815), 298–300; *Patriotic Songster*, 67–9; Philadelphia *Tickler*, 12 May 1813; *Columbian Harmonist*, 19–21; Keller, *Music of the War of 1812*, 66–8; Samuel Woodworth, *The Poems, Odes, Songs and Other Metrical Effusions of Samuel Woodworth* (New York: Abraham Asten and Matthias Lopez, 1818), 126–44.
24. *Columbian Naval Songster*, 38–9.
25. Dunlap, *Yankee Chronology*, 13–14; *Eagle and Harp* (Baltimore: J. and T. Vance and J. Cole, 1812), 35–6; *Columbian Naval Songster*, 59–61.
26. *Eagle and Harp*, 97–8; *National Song-Book*, 160–5; *American Patriotic Song-Book* (1813), 24–8, 48–50, 55–8, 62–3, 86–7, 91–4; *Columbian Naval Songster*, 55–6, 65–8; *Columbian Naval Melody*, 81–5; *Naval Songster* (1815), 6–8; *The Sky-Lark, or a New Collection of Choice, Naval, Patriotic and Sentimental Songs* (Hartford: B. & J. Russell, 1816), 51–2.
27. *Washington Reporter*, 11 October 1813; Keller, *Music of the War of 1812*, 127–30; *Eagle and Harp*, 57–60; *American Patriotic Song-Book* (1813), 24–8, 75–8; *National Song-Book*, 160–5; *Federal Songster*, 27–9.
28. "From Abigail Smith Adams to Thomas Boylston Adams, 1 May 1798," *Founders Online*, http://founders.archives.gov/documents/Adams/99-03-02-0001; *United States Chronicle*, 12 July 1798; Joseph J. Letter, "Reincarnating Samuel Woodworth: Native American Prophets, the Nation, and the War of 1812," *Early American Literature* 43, no. 3 (2008): 689, 691.
29. Irving, "Review," 244–5; *American Patriotic and Comic Modern Songs*, 3; New York *Spectator*, 18 April 1812; New York *Western Star*, 7 March 1813; Clinton *Ohio Register*, 29 March 1814; *Baltimore Patriot and Evening Advertiser*, 4 January 1815; Maysville *Eagle*, 19 January 1815; Boston *Repertory*, 11 March 1815; *Bennington Newsletter*, 27 March 1815; Portsmouth *Intelligencer*, 13 July 1815; Utica *Patrol*, 31 July 1815; Philadelphia *Weekly Aurora*, 22 August 1815; McCloskey, "Campaign of Periodicals," 262–4, 273; Hart and Penman, *1812: A Nation Emerges*, 40–1.
30. Jonathan Clark, "The First Great Western Empire: or, the United States of America" (Albany: R. Packard, 1812); Thomas Robert Price, "Samuel Woodworth and Theodore Sedgwick Fay: Two Nineteenth-Century American Literati" (EdD diss., Pennsylvania State University, 1970), 45; Irving, "Review," 244–5.
31. *Port Folio* II, no. I (July 1813), 113–6, II, no. V (November 1813), 541–3.
32. Catherine O'Donnell Kaplan, *Men of Letters in the Early Republic: Cultivating Forums of Citizenship* (Chapel Hill: University of North Carolina Press, 2008), 226, 228; Irving, "Review," 248–50; New York *Olio*, 20 November 1813; *Dedham Gazette*, 17 December

1813; Edwin C. Holland and Jacob Eckhard, "The Pillar of Glory" (Philadelphia: G. E. Blake, 1813); Edwin C. Holland and Charles Gilfert, "The Pillar of Glory" (New York: J. Appel, 1813); *National Songster*, 9–10; *Patriotic and Naval Songster* (Philadelphia: Charles H. Walsh, 1898), 194–5; Albert Bushnell Hart and Annie Bliss Chapman, eds., *How Our Grandfathers Lived* (New York: Macmillan, 1912), 283–4.

33. *Port Folio* II, no. I (July 1813), 113–16, II, no. V (November 1813), 541–3.
34. Nivola, "The 'Party War' of 1812," 22; Theodore Roosevelt, *The Naval War of 1812*, vol. 2 (New York: The Review of Reviews, 1904), 210; A. Taylor, *Civil War*, 161–6, 169–70; Hickey, *Don't Give Up the Ship!*, 124; Hickey, *War of 1812*, 143–4; Windsor *Washingtonian*, 14 December 1812.
35. Albany *Geographical and Military Museum*, 7 March 1814; Spargo, *Anthony Haswell*, 224–6; Charleston *City Gazette*, 10 November 1813.
36. George Svejda, *History of the Star Spangled Banner from 1814 to Present* (Washington, DC: US Division of History Office of Archeology and Historic Preservation, 1969), 86, 100–1, 111–23, 133, 146–9, 162–200; P. W. Filby and Edward G. Howard, *Star-Spangled Books: Books, Sheet Music, Newspapers, Manuscripts, and Persons Associated with "The Star-Spangled Banner"* (Baltimore: Maryland Historical Society, 1972), 90–105, 113–22, 133–5; Crawford, *America's Music Life*, 240–1; David Hackett Fischer, *Liberty and Freedom*, vol. 3 (New York: Oxford University Press, 2005), 172–3.
37. Hickey, *Don't Give Up the Ship!*, 128; David S. Heidler and Jeanne T. Heidler, *The War of 1812* (Westport: Greenwood Press, 2002), 472; Eustace, *1812*, 189; Anthony S. Pitch, *Burning of Washington*, 71–85, 104–24; Edward S. Delaplaine, *Francis Scott Key: Life and Times* (New York: Biography Press, 1937), 134, 137–44; John T. Silkett, *Francis Scott Key and the History of the Star Spangled Banner* (Washington, DC: Vintage America, 1978), 15–20.
38. Cress, "'Cool and Serious Reflection,'" 134; Delaplaine, *Francis Scott Key*, 65, 105, 112–16, 145–7; 168, 173; Hickey, *Don't Give Up the Ship!*, xviii.
39. A thousand men in Fort McHenry withstood roughly twenty-four hours of bombardment. Only four Americans were killed and twenty-four wounded, despite 1,800 British shells being fired. Silkett, *Francis Scott Key*, 26, 31, 34; John H. Schroeder, *Commodore John Rodgers: Paragon of the Early American Navy* (Gainesville: University Press of Florida, 2006), 136–40.
40. William McCarty, *Songs, Odes, and Other Poems, on National Subjects*, vol. 3 (Philadelphia: W. McCarty, 1842), 198–203; Keller, *Music of the War of 1812*, 85–8; *National Songster*, 28–30.
41. David Waldstreicher, "Minstrelization and Nationhood: 'Backside Albany,' Backlash, and the Wartime Origins of Blackface Minstrelsy," in *Warring for America: Cultural Contest in the Era of 1812*, ed. Nicole Eustace and Fredrika J. Teute (Chapel Hill: University of North Carolina Press, 2017), 41; Gene Allen Smith, "'Sons of Freedom': African Americans Fighting the War of 1812," *Tennessee Historical Quarterly* 71, no. 3 (Fall 2012): 212–15; Delaplaine, *Francis Scott Key*, 40–2; Windsor *Post-Boy*, 7 January 1806.
42. Delaplaine, *Francis Scott Key*, 16, 21, 44, 121, 156–7, 163–4, 167, 169–70, 173; Silkett, *Francis Scott Key*, 35; Fischer, *Liberty and Freedom*, 171.

43. Claudia L. Bushman, *America Discovers Columbus: How an Italian Explorer Became an American Hero* (Hanover, NH: University Press of New England, 1992), 50, 57; Laura Auricchio, "Two Versions of General Washington's Resignation: Politics, Commerce, and Visual Culture in 1790s Philadelphia," *Eighteenth-Century Studies* 44, no. 3 (Spring 2011): 386–7, 391; Louise Conway Belden, "Liberty and the American Eagle on Spoons by Jacob Kucher," *Winterthur Portfolio* 3 (1967): 110–1; Thomas J. Schlereth, "Columbia, Columbus, and Columbianism," *Journal of American History* 79, no. 3 (December 1992): 937–42. Representative references to the goddess Columbia, eagle, and American flag as national symbols are found in *Columbian Naval Melody*, 11–12, 17, 22, 26, 29, 37, 42, 45, 47, 55, 58, 60, 66–7, 70, 75, 77–8, 84–5; Middlebury *Columbian Patriot*, 28 September 1814.
44. *Bennington Newsletter*, 6 March 1815; Cooperstown *Otsesgo Herald*, 23 March 1815; Richmond *Virginia Patriot*, 1 April 1815; Lexington *Reporter*, 24 May 1815; Concord *New Hampshire Patriot and State Gazette*, 4 July 1815; Worcester *National Aegis*, 13 December 1815; Washington *Daily National Intelligencer*, 25 December 1815; *The New American Songster* (Philadelphia: D. Dickinson, 1817), 18–19; Woodworth, *Poems*, 96.
45. Keller, *Music of the War of 1812*, 85–8; *National Songster* (1814), 28–30; Sonneck, *Report*, 18–23; David K. Hildebrand, "Two National Anthems? Some Reflections on the Two Hundredth Anniversary of 'The Star-Spangled Banner' and Its Forgotten Partner, 'The Battle of Baltimore,'" *American Music* 32, no. 3 (Fall 2014): 253–71. Hill lists sixty-six parodies documented between 1790 and 1813 in the United States alone. Richard S. Hill, "The Melody of the Star-Spangled Banner in the United States before 1820," in *Essays Honoring Lawrence C. Wroth*, ed. Frederick R. Goff (Portland, ME: Anthoensen Press, 1951), 162, 164–75, 192.
46. Fischer, *Liberty and Freedom*, 172; Foster, *Poetry*, 115–17; Boston *Constitutional Telegraphe*, 20 August 1800; Ballston Spa *Independent American*, 23 March 1813; New York *Commercial Advertiser*, 16 July 1812; Washington *Universal Gazette*, 9 September 1813.
47. Delaplaine, *Francis Scott Key*, 16, 21, 44, 121, 156–7, 169–70, 173; Silkett, *Francis Scott Key*, 35; Fischer, *Liberty and Freedom*, 171.
48. New York *American Citizen*, 21 December 1805; *Pittsfield Sun*, 10 February 1806; New York *Weekly Inspector*, 25 October 1806.
49. Delaplaine, *Francis Scott Key*, 123, Irving, "Review," 244–5, 247–9; Irving, *Works of Washington Irving*, 320–1; *Analectic Magazine* 4 (1814), 433–4.
50. Delaplaine, *Francis Scott Key*, 39, 48–9, 63, 75, 77, 83–5, 91–2, 95–6, 98, 129–31, 143–7; Fischer, *Liberty and Freedom*, 168; A. Taylor, *Civil War of 1812*, 39; Silkett, *Francis Scott Key*, 13–14; Brian Jay Jones, *Washington Irving: An American Original* (New York: Arcade, 2008), 64–5, 121–2, 124, 330; Donna Hagensick, "Irving: A Littérateur in Politics," in *Critical Essays on Washington Irving*, ed. Ralph M. Aderman (Boston: G. K. Hall, 1990), 178–81, 184.
51. New York *Weekly Inspector*, 25 October 1806.
52. Nivola, "The 'Party War' of 1812," 18; Hickey, *War of 1812*, 221–54; A. Taylor, *Civil War*, 319–29; Murrin, "Jeffersonian Triumph," 20; Budiansky, *Perilous Fight*, 279–85, 317, 338–9, 343.

53. Banner, *To the Hartford Convention*, 326–50; A. Taylor, *Civil War*, 415–16; Hickey, *War of 1812*, 221–80; Nivola, "The 'Party War' of 1812," 21; J. S. Martell, "A Side Light on Federalist Strategy during the War of 1812," *American Historical Review* 43, no. 3 (April 1938): 553–66.
54. Nivola, "The 'Party War' of 1812," 15; Thomas M. Meagher, *Financing Armed Conflict*, vol. 1 (New York: Palgrave Macmillan, 2016), 119; Malone, *Jefferson the President: First Term*, 435; A. Taylor, *Civil War*, 439.
55. A. Taylor, *Civil War*, 420–1; Goodrich, *Recollection of a Lifetime*, 505; Nivola, "The 'Party War' of 1812," 22; Hickey, *Don't Give Up the Ship!*, 124–5, 278; *Carlisle Gazette*, 21 April 1815; *New York Evening Post*, 22 March 1815; Williamsburg *Western American*, 25 February 1815.
56. *Carlisle Gazette*, 3 March 1815; J. Bunker Clark, *The Dawning of American Keyboard Music* (Westport: Greenwood Press, 1988), 251–2; Peter Ricksecker, *The Battle of New Orleans: For the Piano Forte* (Philadelphia: G. Willig, 1816), 6; *New York Evening Post*, 22 March 1815; Williamsburg *Western American*, 25 February 1815; C. Edward Skeen, *Citizen Soldiers in the War of 1812* (Lexington: University Press of Kentucky, 1999), 172.
57. Elizabethtown *New Jersey Journal*, 4 April 1815; Lexington *Reporter*, 21 April 1815; Bedford *True American*, 4 May 1815.
58. *Carlisle Gazette*, 3 March 1815; *New York Evening Post*, 22 March 1815; Brattleboro *Reporter*, 19 April 1815; Elizabethtown *New Jersey Journal*, 4 April, 13 June 1815; Bennington *Green Mountain Farmer*, 21 August 1815; Middlebury *National Standard*, 6 December 1815; *Patriotic Songster*, 127–8.
59. Hickey, *Don't Give Up the Ship!*, 279-81; Eustace, *1812*, 211–15; *Baltimore Patriot*, 13 February 1815; Providence *Patriot and Columbian Phenix*, 18 February 1815; New Haven *Connecticut Journal*, 20 March 1815; Hartford *American Mercury*, 12 April 1815; Rutland *Vermont Herald*, 12 April 1815; Brattleboro *Reporter*, 19 April 1815; Jennifer Clark, *The American Idea of England, 1776–1840: Transatlantic Writing* (London: Routledge, 2016), 92; *Patriotic Songster*, 17–19; Keller, *Music of the War of 1812*, 235–8.
60. Lexington *Reporter*, 21 April 1815.
61. Norfolk *American Beacon*, 3 December 1816; *New American Songster*, 25–6; *The Pocket Encyclopedia of Scottish, English, and Irish Songs* (Glasgow: Andrew and James Duncan, 1816), 19; Oskar Cox Jensen, *Napoleon and British Song, 1797–1822* (New York: Palgrave Macmillan, 2015), 48–9.
62. J. Bunker Clark, *Dawning of American Keyboard Music*, 246; Philip Laroque, *Battle of the Memorable 8th of January 1815* (Philadelphia: G. Willig, 1815), 10–11; Philadelphia *Weekly Aurora*, 22 August 1815; Eustace, *1812*, 213–14.
63. The song was reprinted in Lexington *Kentucky Gazette*, 10 April 1815; New York *Columbian*, 12 April 1815; New York *National Advocate*, 13 April 1815; *Baltimore Patriot*, 19 April 1815; Elizabethtown *New Jersey Journal*, 25 April 1815; Middlebury *Columbian Patriot*, 26 April 1815; Wilmington *American Watchman*, 3 May 1815; Newport *Rhode Island Republican*, 3 May 1815; Cooperstown *Otsego Herald*, 4 May 1815; Salem *Essex Register*, 13 May 1815; *Providence Patriot and Columbian Phenix*,

13 May 1815; *Carthage Gazette*, 26 May 1815; Williamsburg *Western American*, 27 May 1815; *Patriotic Songster*, 127–8; *Star Spangled Banner*, 26–7.

64. John Thomas Scharf, *History of Western Maryland*, vol. 1 (Clearfield Co. and Willow Bend Books, 1995), 530; Waldstreicher, "Minstrelization and Nationhood," 41; G. Smith, " 'Sons of Freedom,' " 212–15.
65. Bryan Coleborne, "'They Sate in Counterview': Anglo-Irish Verse in the Eighteenth Century," in *Irish Writing: Exile and Subversion*, ed. Paul Hyland and Neil Sammells (New York: Palgrave Macmillan, 1991), 51; Monica L. Miller, *Slaves to Fashion: Black Dandyism and the Styling of Black Diasporic Identity* (Durham, NC: Duke University Press, 2009), 27–41; Roxann Wheeler, "Sounding Black-*ish*: West Indian Pidgin in London Performance and Print," *Eighteenth-Century Studies* 51, no. 1 (Fall 2017): 75–6.
66. Christian Schultz Jr., *Travels on an Inland Voyage*, vol. 2 (New York: Isaac Riley, 1810), 145–6; *New York Evening Post*, 9 July 1808; Paul Schneider, *Old Man River: The Mississippi River in North American History* (New York: Macmillan, 2013), 212; Richard Hopwood Thornton, *An American Glossary*, vol. 1 (Philadelphia: J. B. Lippincott, 1912), 410–13; Washington Irving, *A History of New York*, vol. 2 (New York: Inskeep and Bradford, 1809), 85.
67. Arthur K. Moore, *The Frontier Mind: A Cultural Analysis of the Kentucky Frontiersman* (Louisville: University of Kentucky Press, 1957), 135; John William Ward, *Andrew Jackson: Symbol for an Age* (New York: Oxford University Press, 1966), xxvi;
68. *Ladies Literary Cabinet* 1 (1820), 112; *Providence Patriot*, 10 March 1821; Baker, *Florae Memoriae*; *Grigg's Southern and Western Songster* (Philadelphia: John Grigg, 1829), 81–2; *The Northern and Eastern Songster* (Boston: Charles Gaylord, 1835), 41–3; Ward, *Andrew Jackson*, xviii–xxix; *Compiler*, 31 January 1823; Stoutamire, *Music of the Old South*, 267.
69. Russell Sanjek, *American Popular Music and Its Business: The First Four Hundred Years*, vol. 2 (New York: Oxford University Press, 1988), 166; *New York Mirror* 7 (1829), 143; Thomas Allston Brown, *History of the American Stage* (New York: Dick and Fitzgerald, 1870), 317; *Ladies Literary Cabinet* 1 (1819), 7; Meredith Henne Baker, *The Richmond Theatre Fire: Early America's First Great Disaster* (Baton Rouge: Louisiana State University Press, 2012), 37. Hawkins's song was first performed in Albany in the play *The Battle of Lake Champlain* in 1815 and was printed in *American Song-Book*, 55–6; *Patriotic Songster*, 75–7; *Star Spangled Banner*, 24–6.
70. *Ladies Literary Cabinet* 1 (1820), 112; *New York Mirror* 7 (1829), 143.
71. Letter, "Reincarnating Samuel Woodworth," 693; Price, "Samuel Woodworth," 6–7; Samuel Woodworth, *Melodies, Duets, Trios, Songs, and Ballads, Pastoral, Amatory, Sentimental, Patriotic, Religious, and Miscellaneous. Together with Metrical Epistles, Tale and Recitations* (New York: James M. Campbell, 1826), 221–3; Woodworth, *Poems*, iii–xii; 126–44
72. Hickey, *Don't Give Up the Ship!*, 279, 284–5, 347–8; James Wallace Hammack Jr., *Kentucky and the Second American Revolution: The War of 1812* (Lexington: University Press of Kentucky, 1976), 26–8; Roosevelt, *Naval War of 1812*, vol. 2, 258; Kerby, "Militia System," 102–24; Skeen, *Citizen Soldiers*, 1–2, 170–2, 175.

73. Noah Miller Ludlow, *Dramatic Life as I Found It: A Record of Personal Experience* (St. Louis: G. I. Jones, 1880), 237–8; The verse attributed to Gilleland was reprinted in *Albany Register*, 11 October 1815 and numerous other newspapers.
74. Nicole Eustace and Fredrika J. Teute, eds., *Warring for America: Cultural Contest in the Era of 1812* (Chapel Hill: University of North Carolina Press, 2017), 12–14; Waldstreicher, "Minstrelization and Nationhood," 33–4, 40, 44–6; Jared Gardner, *Master Plots: Race and the Founding of an American Literature, 1787–1845* (Baltimore, MD: Johns Hopkins University Press, 2000), 1–2, 7–8; Ward, *Andrew Jackson*, xviii–xx, xxvii–xxix; G. Smith, "'Sons of Freedom,'" 218–22.
75. Jason E. Pierce, *Making the White Man's West: Whiteness and the Creation of the American West* (Boulder: University Press of Colorado, 2016), 29, 31–4, 41–2; Murrin, "Jeffersonian Triumph," 4; St. George Tucker, *Reflections on the Cession of Louisiana* (Washington, DC: Samuel Harrison Smith, 1803), 24–6; Marc Leepson, *What So Proudly We Hailed: Francis Scott Key, A Life* (New York: Macmillan, 2014), 78–87; Peter J. Kastor, *The Nation's Crucible: The Louisiana Purchase and the Creation of America* (New Haven, CT: Yale University Press, 2008), 5.
76. Irving, *A History of New York*, 85; Michael Fellman, "Alligator Men and Cardsharpers: Deadly Southwestern Humor," *Huntington Library Quarterly* 49, no. 4 (Autumn 1986): 311–3; William J. Mahar, "'Backside Albany' and Early Blackface Minstrelsy: A Contextual Study of America's First Blackface Song," *American Music* 6, no. 1 (Spring 1988): 18.
77. Richard H. Immerman, *Empire for Liberty: A History of American Imperialism from Benjamin Franklin to Paul Wolfowitz* (Princeton, NJ: Princeton University Press, 2012), 1, 7–11, 28, 31–2, 65, 68, 72; Eustace, *1812*, 213–14; Murrin, "Jeffersonian Triumph," 8; Jerome McGann, "Washington Irving, *A History of New York*, and American History," *Early American Literature* 47, no. 2 (2012): 359–60, 365.
78. Boston *Columbian Centinel*, 24 December 1825; Craig T. Friend, "Merchants and Markethouses: Reflections on Moral Economy in Early Kentucky," *Journal of the Early Republic* 17, no. 4 (Winter 1997): 553–74.
79. A. Taylor, "Dual Nationalisms," 83; Broussard, *Southern Federalists*, 162.
80. Henry Adams, ed. *The Writings of Albert Gallatin*, vol. I (Philadelphia: J. B. Lippincott, 1879), 700.
81. A. Taylor, *Civil War*, 438; Jennifer Clark, *American Idea of England*, 94–5.
82. Keller, *Music of the War of 1812*, 57; *Vermont Republican*, 19 June 1815, *Niles Weekly Register Supplement* 9 (February 1816), 85; Boston *Repertory*, 11 March 1815; Rutland *Herald*, 22 March 1815; Baltimore *Mechanic's Gazette*, 13 July 1815; Burlington *Vermont Centinel*, 24 February 1815; Newport *Rhode Island Republican*, 1 March 1815.
83. Williamsburg *Western American*, 25 February 1815; *New York Evening Post*, 22 March 1815; Pittsfield *Sun*, 30 March 1815; Brattleboro *Reporter*, 19 April 1815; Lexington *Reporter*, 21 April 1815; *Carlisle Gazette*, 21 April 1815; New York *Shamrock*, 3 August 1815; *Niles Weekly Register Supplement* 9 (February 1816), 94; *Patriotic Songster*, 14–17, 26–8.

84. Newport *Rhode Island Republican*, 1 March 1815; Elizabethtown *New Jersey Journal*, 11 April 1815; Salem *Essex Register*, 26 August 1815; Newark *Centinel of Freedom*, 29 August 1815.
85. Raleigh *Star*, 30 June 1815; "A New Song on the Causes—Beginning, Events, End and Consequences of the Late War with Great Britain" (New York: E. Riley, [ca. 1819]); Keller, *Music of the War of 1812*, 234–8; Williamsburg *Western American*, 25 February 1815; Newport *Rhode Island Republican*, 1 March 1815; Pittsfield *Sun*, 30 March 1815; Utica *Patrol*, 23 March 1815.
86. Budiansky, *Perilous Fight*, 320, 344; Hickey, *War of 1812*, 284, 286, 288–9; Hickey, *Don't Give Up the Ship!*, 294; A. Taylor, *Civil War*, 420; Baltimore *Mechanic's Gazette*, 13 July 1815; Keller, *Music of the War of 1812*, 234–8; Williamsburg *Western American*, 25 February 1815.
87. H. Adams, ed. *Writings of Albert Gallatin*, vol. 2, 500; Roosevelt, *Naval War of 1812*, vol. 2, 253–4; Broussard, *Southern Federalists*, 170.
88. Goodrich, *Recollection of a Lifetime*, 503–4; "To John Adams from John Quincy Adams, 29 May 1816," *Founders Online*, http://founders.archives.gov/documents/Adams/99-03-02-3109.

# Conclusion

## The Legacy of Early American Political Song

Songwriters, composers, editors, and printers created and circulated an impressive quantity of political music throughout the early national period. Americans used this music to voice opposition, delegitimate opposition, electioneer, propagandize, and compete for political power. Through music, they contested the meaning of liberty, the place of citizens in governance, the structure of government, the nation's relation to European powers, and the best means to pursue peace and prosperity. For political purposes, they used music to construct powerful narratives about the nation's history, values, and institutions, often using the hyperbolic discourse of the time to combine fact and fiction into compelling and engaging accounts of national development. During every major political development, music was prominently and effectively used as a discursive tool.

An expansive consideration of this music reveals several important aspects of this musical and political culture. First, while often perceived as ephemeral and circulated through ephemera, this music was clearly retained in Americans' memories and was regularly recirculated and reworked to serve new political ends. Americans made sense of the nation's development and influenced political thought by regularly tapping into a body of song retained in memory. Members of both parties regularly brought older music back into print and reworked older songs to address new political events, justify particular political action, and persuade their fellow Americans of the validity of their views. Second, supporters of both parties deployed the same techniques of rhetoric, narrative, and symbolism. To undermine their opponents and advocate their own views, partisans regularly reclaimed the vocabulary and symbols previously wielded by their adversaries and used them for opposing purposes. In this way, calls to unite, invocations of the Revolutionary War, metaphorical expressions of the nation-as-ship, and accusations of sedition and violence appeared in songs of both parties, written to many of the same tunes. Third, these songs garnered far more

*Hail Columbia*. Laura Lohman, Oxford University Press (2020). © Oxford University Press.
DOI: 10.1093/oso/9780190930615.001.0001

attention and engagement than previously thought. While often dismissed as doggerel in modern scholarship, this music drew the attention of presidents and a first lady, prompted literary praise and criticism, and was treated as a form of political capital that could be exchanged for various forms of political patronage. Finally, this music was created by an astonishingly varied group of Americans. Among them were a governor and his daughter, a signer of the Declaration of Independence, lawyers, a future Supreme Court justice, printers, craftsmen, sailors, immigrant actresses, theater fans, psalmodists, professional musicians, and leading playwrights and poets of the day.

Some of this music proved surprisingly durable. Not only were songs from the early national period still performed, printed, and compiled in the following decades, but tune networks continued to expand as old melodies were used to carry new lyrics responding to contemporary political developments. Political music from the nation's founding era was put to both old and new uses in subsequent years. An instructive example is Joseph Hopkinson's "Hail Columbia."

The nationalist sentiments inspired by the War of 1812 were transformed, with the Federalists' decline and James Monroe's election in 1816, into a respite from partisan politics. When Monroe began a series of state tours in 1817, these sentiments were represented in the press as part of an "era of good feelings." While Federalists first pronounced this era seeking electoral gains and expiation following the embarrassing Hartford Convention, the reprinting of the phrase "era of good feelings" captured Americans' hopes that "the destructive forces of parties" had been eliminated. In these conditions, "Hail Columbia," itself first used for partisan purposes, was transformed into a national song. It was increasingly given a prominent place in July 4 festivities and performed as a "national air" for presidential inaugurations and passing vessels' musical honors.[1] As the first party system collapsed, "Hail Columbia" came to represent a nation undivided by partisan politics.

"Hail Columbia" and other early American political songs reached generations to come through song collections. The interest in American cultural productions stimulated during the War of 1812 generated new national song collections. William McCarty's *Songs, Odes, and Other Poems on National Subjects* (1842) was an unusually thorough collection.[2] Other compilers maintained a historical perspective as well, including those who reprinted "The Raising" through 1855, nearly seventy years after Francis Hopkinson wrote his verses in support of ratification.[3]

Many Americans, though, did not need to review such compilations, for songs like "Hail Columbia" remained a nearly requisite aspect of American life. Nineteenth-century men still gathered for convivial dinners enlivened with toasts, songs, and instrumental music. In this way, songs like "Hail Columbia" were a ubiquitous part of July 4 festivities and celebratory gatherings of various immigrant and benevolent societies.[4] "Hail Columbia" was but one item on a nineteenth-century "playlist" for such convivial and anniversary gatherings, along with "Adams and Liberty," "Jefferson and Liberty," "America, Commerce, and Freedom," "The Tars of Columbia," "Jackson's March," "The Star-Spangled Banner," and Edwin Holland's "Pillar of Glory." The last three were variously used to toast the national institutions of the navy and army in the decades following the war.[5]

In this playlist, "Hail Columbia" was one of three songs that rose to ubiquity and ultimately the status of unofficial national anthem before Key's lyrical response to the defense of Fort McHenry was officially made the national anthem by Congress in 1931. Along with "Yankee Doodle" and, increasingly as the nineteenth century wore on, "The Star-Spangled Banner," "Hail Columbia" was highlighted as a "national ode," "national song," and "national anthem."[6] With such status "Hail Columbia" was frequently incorporated into concerts, developed into new fantasia-like compositions, and sold as sheet music.[7] It was used in local, national, and international ceremonies, performed to mark July 4 and other anniversaries, and featured to demonstrate the power of new technologies.[8] In the Mexican War and Civil War, brass bands played "Hail Columbia" to inspire soldiers, intimidate enemies, define new nationalisms, and announce victories (see Figure C.1).[9]

Yet "Hail Columbia" was also used for sectional purposes. Despite claims of national cultural production during the War of 1812, and despite scholars' attraction to the concept of American nationalism, there was no one unifying nationalism by the war's end. Postwar debates over protectionist measures and northern attacks on slavery fueled resurgent sectionalism.[10] Northern opponents of slavery invoked "Hail Columbia" to highlight hypocritical claims of an exceptional American land of liberty and to condemn the use of intimidation tactics and violence against slaves and those protesting slavery.[11] Songwriters reworked "Hail Columbia" and "The Star-Spangled Banner" along with more recently popularized songs "Auld Lang Syne" and "America" to protest slavery and highlight southern hypocrisy.[12] Meanwhile, southern celebrants used "Hail Columbia" to toast "The Union of the

Figure C.1. "Hail! Columbia and Hail Forever! Hail the Cause," Philadelphia, G. E. Blake, 1840. Library of Congress, Music Division.

States" as a rejection of northern efforts to end slavery through newspapers, pamphlets, orations, and petitions.[13]

Alongside these new political uses, many older songs were tapped once again for election purposes. Monroe's tours of the states from 1817 furthered the collapse of the first party system.[14] From 1828, new parties emerged and ultimately took shape as the Democrats and Whigs of the second party system. New parties cultivated popular support with a new wave of election songs. Some of these election songs stemmed from a familiar song inspired by the War of 1812—Samuel Woodworth's "The Hunters of Kentucky." When Andrew Jackson sought the presidency for the second time in 1828, "The Hunters of Kentucky" was used to rally his supporters.[15] Woodworth's multivalent creation was considered both "warlike and manly" and comic, grouped with the blackface minstrel songs performed by George Washington Dixon.[16] In a similar vein, as northerners wrote new songs, including election songs, they incorporated degrading representations of black speech and action.[17]

In the decades to come, other early national period songs were repurposed as election songs in the second party system. For another hero of the War of 1812, Whig strategists mounted a successful, highly organized campaign that appealed directly to the white male voters who, with property requirements removed, had been turning out at the polls in ever-greater numbers since 1828. Popular support for William Henry Harrison was generated in part through songbooks featuring the war-invoking slogan "Tippecanoe and Tyler Too" and a humble "log-cabin" image that obscured Harrison's origins in a wealthy Virginia family. Collections and newspapers featured reworkings of "The Hunters of Kentucky," "The Star-Spangled Banner,"[18] "Yankee Doodle," "Marseilles Hymn," and "John Anderson My Jo."[19] Running with log cabin imagery, one song collection even featured a populist reworking of Francis Hopkinson's 1788 song "The Raising." The song, which Hopkinson had written to foster support for ratification of the Constitution, was now reworked as "The Log Cabin Raising" to serve a thoroughly populist campaign that inverted Hopkinson's fifty-year old vision of an orderly republic based on the masses' deference to the wisdom of the elite few.[20] Campaign songbooks and newspapers included such reworkings until the Civil War.[21]

Now reaching a larger audience and being written and circulated in advance of elections through national party organization and nominating conventions, these songs were an important extension of much older musical practices. While these populist campaigns of the mid-nineteenth century may be better known to Americans than the electoral and policy battles that preceded them, in fact they were rooted in decades of writing, circulating, performing, reading, and enjoying American political music. Long obscured and overlooked by scholars, the nation's earliest political music proved a valuable resource for debating the structure of government, contesting the nature of liberty, vying for political control, and narrating powerful myths of national development and political authority as America's leaders strove to assure the country's future as an emerging republic and expanding empire.

## Notes

1. Norfolk *American Beacon*, 24 May 1819; Newark *Centinel of Freedom*, 13 July 1819; *St. Louis Enquirer*, 19 July 1820; *Washington Gazette*, 5 March 1821.
2. McCarty, *Songs*, 7, 250–2.
3. *The Wreath: A Collection of Songs, from the Most Admired Authors* (Philadelphia: E. Little, 1822), 148–51; *Grigg's Southern and Western Songster*, 205–7; *The Universal Songster and Museum of Mirth: A Collection of Popular Songs* (Boston: Charles Gaylord, 1835), 17–19; *The Raising. A Patriotic Song for the Mechanic* (Philadelphia A. H. Senseman) https://www.loc.gov/item/amss.cw104710/; McCarty, *Songs*, 44–6; *The American Minstrel* (Philadelphia: Henry F. Anners, 1844), 168–70; Evert Augustus Duyckinck and George Long Duyckinck, *Cyclopædia of American Literature*, vol. 1 (New York: Charles Scribner, 1855), 219.
4. St. Augustine *East Florida Herald*, 11 July 1826; Charleston *Southern Patriot*, 26 April 1832, 21 March 1840; *Salem Register*, 8 July 1852.
5. Philadelphia *Franklin Gazette*, 8, 30 July 1818, 6, 14 July 1819; *New York Columbian*, 18 May 1820; Augusta *Chronicle and Georgia Advertiser*, 9 July 1823, 1 July 1827; *Richmond Enquirer*, 12 July 1825, 14 July, 4 August 1826, 16 July 1830; Baltimore *Gazette and Daily Advertiser*, 3 February 1835; Baltimore *Sun*, 22 March 1842, 18 March 1853.
6. Washington *Whig*, 9 July 1825; New Orleans *Daily Picayune*, 19 April 1838, 4 March 1840, 4 May 1843; *Baltimore Sun*, 25 June 1840; Columbus *Ohio Statesman*, 12 May 1841; William Lichtenwanger, "The Music of 'The Star-Spangled Banner': Whence and Whither?" *College Music Symposium* 18, no. 2 (Fall 1978): 68. The many uses of "The Star-Spangled Banner" in this period are traced in Svejda, *History of the Star Spangled Banner*, 113–57, 162–217.
7. *Baltimore Gazette*, 8 December 1836; Baltimore *Sun*, 25 June 1840; New Orleans *Daily Picayune*, 4 May 1843; W. A. King, *Hail Columbia: As Performed by the Author with the Greatest Success: Arranged as a Brilliant Fantasia* (New York: Firth and Hall, 1839); *Hail Columbia: The Celebrated National Air: With Variations for the Piano Forte* (Philadelphia: George Willig, 1842); Charles Grobe, *Hail Columbia Happy Land with Variations* (Philadelphia: Edward L. Walker, 1853); Max Braun, arr., *Hail Columbia*

(New York: William Hall and Son, 1857); *Savannah Daily Republican*, 8 July 1851; Keene *New Hampshire Sentinel*, 2 January 1851.

8. *Salem Register*, 10 March 1821, 5 November 1849; *New York Spectator*, 14 October 1823; Washington City *The Madisonian*, 2 October 1841; Boston *Daily Evening Transcript*, 16 February 1844; New Orleans *Daily Picayune*, 24 November 1844, 27 July 1849; *Honolulu Friend*, 1 March 1848; *Litchfield Republican*, 18 December 1851; *New York Herald*, 10 August 1856; Great Salt Lake City *Deseret News*, 15 April 1857; Philadelphia *Inquirer*, 1 January 1890; Svejda, *History of the Star Spangled Banner*, 165–6.
9. Robert W. Johannsen, *To the Halls of the Montezumas: The Mexican War in the American Imagination* (New York: Oxford University Press, 1988), 53–4, 62, 157; Christian McWhirter, *Battle Hymns: The Power and Popularity of Music in the Civil War* (Chapel Hill: University of North Carolina Press, 2012), 34, 60–1, 68, 107, 110, 130–1, 165–6, 173; *Macon Daily Telegraph*, 18 August 1866.
10. Goodman, "American Identities," 131; Michael Wala, "From Celebrating Victory to Celebrating the Nation: The War of 1812 and American National Identity," in *Celebrating Ethnicity and Nation: American Festive Culture from the Revolution to the Early Twentieth Century*, ed. Jürgen Heideking and Geneviève Fabre (New York: Berghahn Books, 2001): 74–91; Schoen, "Calculating the Price of Union," 173–206.
11. New York *The Rights of All*, 18 September 1829; Boston *Liberator*, 23 April, 24 December 1831, 7 June 1834, 7 November 1835, 23 January 1836, 22 July 1842, 9 June 1848; Philadelphia *Pennsylvania Freeman*, 27 December 1838; New York *Emancipator*, 21 November 1839; Waukesha *American Freeman*, 19 May 1847; New York *National Antislavery Standard*, 19 July 1849; *Albany Journal*, 5 April 1852.
12. New York *National Antislavery Standard*, 4 July 1841; *Boston Courier*, 24 March 1845; Vicki L. Eaklor, *American Antislavery Songs: A Collection and Analysis* (New York: Greenwood Press, 1988), 201–3, 205–6, 215–16, 489–90; Leepson, *What So Proudly We Hailed*, 78–87; Lonn Taylor, Kathleen M. Kendrick, and Jeffrey L. Brodie, *The Star-Spangled Banner: The Making of an American Icon* (New York: Harper Collins, 2008), 46–51; Marc Ferris, *Star Spangled Banner: The Unlikely Story of America's National Anthem* (Baltimore: Johns Hopkins University Press, 2014), 30.
13. *Richmond Enquirer*, 24 July 1835.
14. Shaw Livermore Jr., *The Twilight of Federalism: The Disintegration of the Federalist Party, 1815–1830* (Princeton, NJ: Princeton University Press, 1962), 2–30, 265.
15. *Saratoga Sentinel*, 21 October 1828; Concord *New Hampshire Patriot and State Gazette*, 14 January 14 July, 29 September 1828.
16. Natchez *Ariel*, 28 June 1828; Boston *Weekly Messenger*, 16 July 1829; Hagerstown *Torch-Light*, 15 August 1833.
17. Columbus *Ohio Statesman* 5 March 1841, 1, 15 October 1842; Boston *Daily Atlas*, 30 September 1842; Mahar, "'Backside Albany,'" 10–13, 15–21; Waldstreicher, "Minstrelization and Nationhood," 29–55.
18. *New Bedford Mercury*, 7 December 1838; New York *Log Cabin*, 1 August 1840; Svejda, *History of the Star Spangled Banner*, 124–9.

19. *The Log Cabin Minstrel; or, Tippecanoe Songster* (Roxbury: Patriot and Democrat Office, 1840), 13–16, 18–19, 30–1, 41–5, 50–4.
20. *Log Cabin Minstrel*, 51–2, 54–5.
21. *The Harrison Medal Minstrel* (Philadelphia: Grigg and Elliot, 1840), 64–7, 124–33, 142–3, 152–3; Boston *Daily Evening Transcript*, 18 June 1844; Taylor, Kendrick, and Brodie, *Star-Spangled Banner*, 47, 51; Svejda, *History of the Star Spangled Banner*, 124–9.

# Bibliography

## Databases of Primary Sources

*Documentary History of the Ratification of the Constitution Digital Edition*
*Founders Online*
Readex *America's Historical Newspapers*

## Historical Periodicals

*American Museum or Universal Magazine*
*Analectic Magazine*
*Collections of the New Jersey Historical Society*
*London Magazine or Gentleman's Monthly Intelligencer*
*Massachusetts Magazine*
*New York Mirror*
*Niles Weekly Register*
*Ladies Literary Cabinet*
*Port Folio*
*Walker's Hibernian Magazine; or, Compendium of Entertaining Knowledge*

## Primary and Secondary Sources

"Adams and Liberty: The Boston Patriotic Song." Boston: Thomas and Andrews, 1798.

Adams, Donald R., Jr., "American Neutrality and Prosperity, 1793–1808: A Reconsideration," *Journal of Economic History* 40, no. 4 (December 1980): 713–37.

Adams, Henry, ed. *The Writings of Albert Gallatin*. Philadelphia: J. B. Lippincott, 1879.

Adams, Willi Paul. *The First American Constitutions: Republican Ideology and the Making of the State Constitutions in the Revolutionary Era.* Translated by Rita and Robert Kimber. Chapel Hill: University of North Carolina Press, 1980.

Adgate, Andrew. *The Mechanic's Lecture: Showing the Usefulness of the Mechanic Arts.* Philadelphia: John McCulloch, 1789.

Agnew, Daniel, and Richard Howell. "A Biographical Sketch of Governor Richard Howell, of New Jersey." *Pennsylvania Magazine of History and Biography* 22, no. 2 (1898): 221–30.

Alden, John. "A Season in Federal Street: J. B. Williamson and the Boston Theatre, 1796–1797." *Proceedings of the American Antiquarian Society* (April 1955): 9–74.

Aldrich, John H., and Ruth W. Grant. "The Antifederalists, the First Congress, and the First Parties." *Journal of Politics* 55, no. 2 (May 1993): 295–326.

Allen, John L. "Thomas Jefferson and the Mountain of Salt: Presidential Image of Louisiana Territory." *Historical Geography* 31 (2003): 9–22.

Allen, Michael. "'Sired by a Hurricane': Mike Fink, Western Boatmen and the Myth of the Alligator Horse." *Arizona and the West* 27, no. 3 (Autumn 1985): 237–52.

Altman, John A. "The Articles and Constitution: Similar in Nature, Different in Design." *Pennsylvania Legacies* 3, no. 1 (May 2003): 20–1.

*The American Minstrel*. Philadelphia: Henry F. Anners, 1844.

*The American Musical Miscellany*. Introduction by H. Wiley Hitchcock. New York: Da Capo Press, 1972. Original printing: Northampton, Massachusetts: Andrew Wright, 1798.

*American Patriotic and Comic Modern Song-Book*. Newburyport: W. & J. Gilman, 1816.

*American Patriotic and Comic Modern Songs Commemorative of Naval Victories*. Newburyport: W. & J. Gilman, 1814.

*The American Patriotic Song-Book*. Philadelphia: W. M'Culloch, 1813.

*The American Patriotic Song-Book*. Philadelphia: John Bioren, 1816.

American Sailor. "New Songs." Boston: Nathaniel Coverly, 1812.

*American Song Book*. N.p., 1815.

*The American Songster; or, Federal Museum of Melody and Wit*. Baltimore, MD: Warner & Hanna, 1799.

*The American Songster*. New York: Samuel Campbell, 1788.

Ames, Fisher. *Works of Fisher Ames Compiled by a Number of His Friends*. Boston: T. B. Wait, 1809.

Anderson, Benedict. *Imagined Communities: Reflections on the Origins and Spread of Nationalism*. New York: Verso, 1991.

Anderson, Gillian B., ed. *Freedom's Voice in Poetry and Song*. Wilmington, DE: Scholarly Resources, 1977.

Anderson, William G. *The Price of Liberty: The Public Debt of the American Revolution*. Charlottesville: University Press of Virginia, 1983.

*The Anti-Levelling Songster*. London: J. Downes, 1793.

Auricchio, Laura. "Two Versions of General Washington's Resignation: Politics, Commerce, and Visual Culture in 1790s Philadelphia." *Eighteenth-Century Studies* 44, no. 3 (Spring 2011): 383–400.

Baker, L. H. *Florae Memoriae*, 1825. Musical manuscript, American Antiquarian Society.

Baker, Meredith Henne. *The Richmond Theatre Fire: Early America's First Great Disaster*. Baton Rouge: Louisiana State University Press, 2012.

Baker, Minot. *Minot Baker's Favourite Collection of Ancient and Modern Songs*. Boston, 1809. Musical manuscript, American Antiquarian Society.

Baker, Thomas E. "Guilford Courthouse: George Washington's Visit—June 2, 1791." National Park Service, US Department of the Interior, 1991.

Banner, James M., Jr. *To the Hartford Convention: The Federalists and the Origins of Party Politics in Massachusetts, 1789–1815*. New York: Alfred A. Knopf, 1970.

Barker, Hannah, and David Vincent, eds. *Language, Print and Electoral Politics, 1790–1832*. Suffolk: Boydell Press, 2001.

Barnby, H. G. *The Prisoners of Algiers: An Account of the Forgotten American-Algerian War 1785–1797*. New York: Oxford University Press, 1966.

Barnes-Ostrander, M. E. "Domestic Music Making in Early New York State: Music in the Lives of Three Amateurs." *Musical Quarterly* 68, no. 3 (July 1982): 353–72.

Barrows, John S. "The Beginning and Launching of the United States Frigate Constitution." *Proceedings of the Bostonian Society* 9 (January 1925): 22–37.

Bartlett, Ian, with Robert J. Bruce. *William Boyce: A Tercentenary Sourcebook and Compendium*. Newcastle-upon-Tyne: Cambridge Scholars, 2011.

Batchellor, Albert Stillman, ed. *Early State Papers of New Hampshire*. Vol. 22. Concord: Ira C. Evans, 1893.

Baumann, Roland M. "Philadelphia's Manufacturers and the Excise Tax of 1794: The Forging of the Jeffersonian Coalition." In *The Whiskey Rebellion: Past and Present Perspectives*, edited by Steven R. Boyd, 135–64. Westport, CT: Greenwood Press, 1985.

Belden, Louise Conway. "Liberty and the American Eagle on Spoons by Jacob Kucher." *Winterthur Portfolio* 3 (1967): 102–11.

Bell, Charles Henry. *The Bench and Bar of New Hampshire*. Boston: Houghton, Mifflin, 1894.

Bell, Whitfield. "The Federal Processions of 1788." *New York Historical Society Quarterly* 46, no. 1 (January 1962): 5–39.

Ben-Atar, Doron, and Barbara B. Oberg. "The Paradoxical Legacy of the Federalists." In *Federalists Reconsidered*, edited by Doron Ben-Atar and Barbara B. Oberg, 1–18. Charlottesville: University of Virginia Press, 1998.

Benn, Carl. *The War of 1812*. New York: Routledge, 2003.

Bentley, William. *The Diary of William Bentley, D.D., Pastor of the East Church, Salem, Massachusetts*. Vol. 2. Salem, MA: Essex Institute, 1907.

Biddle, Charles. *Autobiography of Charles Biddle, Vice-President of the Supreme Executive Council of Pennsylvania, 1745–1821*. Philadelphia: E. Claxton, 1883.

Billings, Nathaniel. *The Republican Harmony*. Lansingburgh, New York: Silvester Tiffany, 1795.

*The Boston Directory*. Boston, 1789.

*The Boston Directory*. Boston, 1796.

*Boston Directory*. Boston: Edward Cotton, 1805.

*Boston Musical Miscellany*. Boston: J. T. Buckingham, 1815.

Bouchell, Polly Elvira. *Music Book of Polly Elvira Bouchell*. 2 vols. Salem, North Carolina, 1811.

Bouton, Terry. *Taming Democracy: "The People," the Founders, and the Troubled Ending of the American Revolution*. New York: Oxford University Press, 2007.

Bradburn, Douglas. "A Clamor in the Public Mind: Opposition to the Alien and Seditions Acts." *William and Mary Quarterly* 65, no. 3 (July 2008): 565–600.

Branham, Robert James. "'God Save the _____!' American National Songs and National Identities, 1760–1798." *Quarterly Journal of Speech* 85, no. 1 (February 1999): 17–37.

Branson, Susan. *These Fiery Frenchified Dames: Women and Political Culture in Early National Philadelphia*. Philadelphia: University of Pennsylvania Press, 2010.

Braun, Max, arr. *Hail Columbia*. New York: William Hall and Son, 1857.

Bray, John, and Joseph Hutton. "Hull's Victory: A New Patriotic Song." Philadelphia: G. E. Blake, [1812].

Brewster, Charles W. *Rambles about Portsmouth*. Vol. 2. Portsmouth: New Hampshire Publishing, 1972.

Brodie, Fawn M. *Thomas Jefferson: An Intimate History*. New York: W. W. Norton, 1974.

Brooks, Lynn Matluck. "A Decade of Brilliance: Dance Theatre in Late-Eighteenth-Century Philadelphia." *Dance Chronicle* 12, no. 3 (1989): 333–65.

Broussard, James H. *The Southern Federalists, 1800–1816*. Baton Rouge: Louisiana State University Press, 1978.

Brown, Roger H. *Redeeming the Republic: Federalists, Taxation, and the Origins of the Constitution*. Baltimore, MD: Johns Hopkins University Press, 1993.

Brown, Thomas Allston. *History of the American Stage*. New York: Dick and Fitzgerald, 1870.

Brown, Walt. *John Adams and the American Press: Politics and Journalism at the Birth of the Republic*. Jefferson, NC: McFarland, 1995.

Brunson, Bertrand Harris. *The Ballad as Song*. Berkeley: University of California Press, 1969.

Bryant, Irving. *James Madison: The President, 1809–1812*. New York: Bobbs Merrill, 1956.

Budiansky, Stephen. *Perilous Fight: America's Intrepid War with Britain on the High Seas, 1812–1815*. New York: Vintage Books, 2011.

Bukovansky, Mlada. "American Identity and Neutral Rights from Independence to the War of 1812." *International Organization* 51, no. 2 (Spring 1997): 209–43.

Bushman, Claudia L. *America Discovers Columbus: How an Italian Explorer Became an American Hero*. Hanover, NH: University Press of New England, 1992.

Butler, Nicholas Michael. *Votaries of Apollo: The St. Cecilia Society and the Patronage of Concert Music in Charleston, South Carolina, 1766–1820*. Columbia: University of South Carolina Press, 2007.

Byrnside, Ronald L. *Music in Eighteenth-Century Georgia*. Athens: University of Georgia Press, 1997.

*Calliope, or English Harmony*. Vol. 2. London: John Simpson, n.d.

[Campbell, James.] "A New Song." Boston: Nathaniel Coverly, 1812.

C[apron], H[enri]. "Come Genius of Our Happy Land." Philadelphia: B. Carr, [1798].

Carr, Benjamin, and Irving Lowens. *Benjamin Carr's Federal Overture (1794)*. Philadelphia: Musical Americana, 1957.

Carter, Edward C., II. "Mathew Carey, Advocate of American Naval Power, 1785–1814." *American Neptune* 26 (July 1966): 177–88.

Cave, Alfred A. "The Shawnee Prophet, Tecumseh, and Tippecanoe: A Case Study of Historical Myth-Making." *Journal of the Early American Republic* 22, no. 4 (Winter 2002): 637–73.

Chase, Gilbert. *America's Music, from the Pilgrims to the Present*. Revised 3d ed. Urbana: University of Illinois Press, 1992.

Clapp, William W., Jr. *A Record of the Boston Stage*. New York: Greenwood, 1969.

Clark, J. Bunker. *The Dawning of American Keyboard Music*. Westport, CT: Greenwood Press, 1988.

Clark, Jennifer. *The American Idea of England, 1776–1840: Transatlantic Writing*. London: Routledge, 2016.

Clark, Jonathan. "The First Great Western Empire: or, the United States of America." Albany: R. Packard, 1812.

Cole, Donald B. *Jacksonian Democracy in New Hampshire, 1800–1851*. Cambridge, MA: Harvard University Press, 1970.

Coleborne, Bryan. "'They Sate in Counterview': Anglo-Irish Verse in the Eighteenth Century." In *Irish Writing: Exile and Subversion*, edited by Paul Hyland and Neil Sammells, 45–63. New York: Palgrave Macmillan, 1991.

Coleman, Aaron N. "A Second Bounaparty?" A Reexamination of Alexander Hamilton during the Franco-American Crisis, 1796–1801." *Journal of the Early Republic* 28, no. 2 (Summer 2008): 183–214.

Coleman, William. "'The Music of a Well Tun'd State': 'The Star Spangled Banner' and the Development of a Federalist Musical Tradition." *Journal of the Early Republic* 35, no. 4 (Winter 2015): 599–629.

Collier, Christopher. *All Politics Is Local: Family, Friends, and Provincial Interest in the Creation of the Constitution*. Hanover, NH: University Press of New England, 2003.

*The Columbian Harmonist*. Philadelphia: Thomas Simpson, 1814.

*The Columbian Naval Melody*. Boston: Hans Lund, 1813.

*The Columbian Naval Songster, Being a Collection of Original Songs, Odes &c. Composed in Honor of the Five Great Naval Victories Obtained by Hull etc.* New York: Edward Gillespy, 1813.

*The Columbian Naval Songster; Being a Collection of Original Songs, Odes, &c. Composed in Honor of the Four Great Naval Victories*. New York: Edward Gillespy, 1813. [not extant]

*The Columbian Songster*. Nathaniel Heaton Jr., 1799.

*The Columbian Songster, or Jovial Companion*. New York: Greenleaf's, 1797.

Cornell, Saul. *The Other Founders: Anti-Federalism and the Dissenting Tradition in America, 1788–1828*. Chapel Hill: University of North Carolina Press, 1999.

Cotlar, Seth. *Tom Paine's America: The Rise and Fall of Transatlantic Radicalism in the Early Republic*. Charlottesville: University of Virginia Press, 2011.

Crawford, Richard. *America's Music Life: A History*. New York: W. W. Norton, 2001.

Crawford, Richard, editor. *The Core Repertory of Early American Psalmody*. Vols. 11–12. Madison: A-R Editions, 1984.

Cray, Robert E., Jr. "Remembering the USS *Chesapeake*: The Politics of Maritime Death and Impressment." *Journal of the Early Republic* 25, no. 3 (Fall 2005): 445–74.

Cress, Lawrence Delbert. "'Cool and Serious Reflection': Federalist Attitudes toward War in 1812." *Journal of the Early Republic* 7, no. 2 (Summer 1987): 123–45.

Crew, Danny O. *American Political Music: A State-by-State Catalog of Printed and Recorded Music Related to Local, State and National Politics, 1756–2004*. Jefferson, NC: McFarland, 2006.

Cripe, Helen. *Thomas Jefferson and Music*. Charlottesville: University Press of Virginia, 1974.

Croker, Thomas Crofton. *The Popular Songs of Ireland*. London: Henry Colburn, 1839.

Crow, Jeffrey J. "The Whiskey Rebellion in North Carolina." *North Carolina Historical Review* 6, no. 1 (January 1989): 1–28.

Cummings, Harmon Dean. "Andrew Adgate: Philadelphia Psalmodist and Music Educator." PhD diss., University of Rochester, 1975.

Daniel, Marcus. *Scandal and Civility: Journalism and the Birth of American Democracy*. New York: Oxford University Press, 2009.

Dannett, Sylvia G. L. *The Yankee Doodler*. South Brunswick, NJ: A. S. Barnes, 1973.

Dauer, Manning J. *The Adams Federalists*. Baltimore, MD: Johns Hopkins University Press, 1953.

Davis, Joseph L. *Sectionalism in American Politics, 1774–1787*. Madison: University of Wisconsin Press, 1977.

de Arce, Daniel Mendoza. *Music in North America and the West Indies from the Discovery to 1850: A Historical Survey*. Lanham, MD: Scarecrow Press, 2006.

DeConde, Alexander. *The Quasi-War: The Politics and Diplomacy of the Undeclared War with France, 1797–1801*. New York: Charles Scribner's Sons, 1966.

Delaplaine, Edward S. *Francis Scott Key: Life and Times*. New York: Biography Press, 1937.

*The Democratic Songster*. Baltimore, MD: [Angell for] Keatinge, 1794.

Dickinson, John. *The Writings of John Dickinson*. Bedford, MA: Applewood Books, 2009.

Dickson, Charles Ellis. "Jeremiads in the New American Republic: The Case of National Fasts in the John Adams Administration." *New England Quarterly* 60, no. 2 (June 1987): 187–207.

Duane, William. *The American Military Library, or, Compendium of the Modern Tactics*. Philadelphia, William Duane, 1809.

Duane, William. *The American Republican Harmonist*. Philadelphia: William Duane, 1803.

Dunham, Josiah. *An Oration, for the Fourth of July, 1798*. Hanover, NH: Benjamin True, [1798].

Dunlap, William. *Yankee Chronology; or, Huzza for the Constitution!* New York: D. Longworth, 1812.

Dunn, Thomas. *A Discourse Delivered in the New Dutch Church . . . before the New York Society for the Information and Assistance of Persons Emigrating from Foreign Countries*. London: Eaton, 1795.

Durey, Michael. *"With the Hammer of Truth": James Thomson Callender and America's Early National Heroes*. Charlottesville: University Press of Virginia, 1990.

Duyckinck, Evert Augustus, and George Long Duyckinck. *Cyclopædia of American Literature*. Vol. 1. New York: Charles Scribner, 1855.

Dwight, Timothy J. *Columbia, An Ode* ([Philadelphia]: [John M'Culloch], [1794].

*The Eagle and Harp*. Baltimore, MD: J. and T. Vance and J. Cole, 1812.

Eaklor, Vicki L. *American Antislavery Songs: A Collection and Analysis*. New York: Greenwood Press, 1988.

Ebsworth, Daniel. *The Republican Harmonist*. Philadelphia: n.p., 1800. Not extant.

Ebsworth, Daniel. *The Republican Harmonist*. 2nd ed. Boston: n.p., 1801.

Eckley, Joseph. *A Sermon, Preached at the Request of the Ancient and Honourable Artillery Company, June 4, 1792*. Boston: Samuel Hall, 1792.

Elkins, Stanley M., and Eric McKitrick. *The Age of Federalism*. New York: Oxford University Press, 1993.

Estes, Todd. *The Jay Treaty Debate, Public Opinion, and the Evolution of Early American Political Culture*. Amherst: University of Massachusetts Press, 2006.

Eustace, Nicole. *1812: War and the Passions of Patriotism*. Philadelphia: University of Pennsylvania Press, 2012.

Eustace, Nicole, and Fredrika J. Teute, eds. *Warring for America: Cultural Contest in the Era of 1812*. Chapel Hill: University of North Carolina Press, 2017.

Evans, Amos A. "Journal Kept on Board the United States Frigate 'Constitution,' 1812, by Amos A. Evans, Surgeon United States Navy." *Pennsylvania Magazine of History and Biography* 19, no. 3 (1895): 374–86.

Farnsworth, H[avilah]. *An Oration on Music*. Cooperstown, NY: Elihu Phinney, 1795.

*The Federal Songster, Being a Collection of the Most Celebrated Patriotic Songs*. New London, CT: James Springer, 1800.

Fellman, Michael. "Alligator Men and Cardsharpers: Deadly Southwestern Humor." *Huntington Library Quarterly* 49, no. 4 (Autumn 1986): 307–23.

Fellman, Michael. "The Earthbound Eagle: Andrew Jackson and the American Pantheon." *American Studies* 12, no. 2 (Fall 1971): 67–76.

Ferling, John. *Adams vs. Jefferson: The Tumultuous Election of 1800*. New York: Oxford University Press, 2004.

Ferris, Marc. *Star Spangled Banner: The Unlikely Story of America's National Anthem*. Baltimore, MD: Johns Hopkins University Press, 2014.

Fessenden, Thomas Green. *Original Poems*. Philadelphia: E. Bronson, 1806.

Filby, P. W., and Edward G. Howard. *Star-Spangled Books: Books, Sheet Music, Newspapers, Manuscripts, and Persons Associated with "The Star-Spangled Banner."* Baltimore: Maryland Historical Society, 1972.

Fischer, David Hackett. *Liberty and Freedom*. Vol. 3. New York: Oxford University Press, 2005.

Fischer, David Hackett. *The Revolution of American Conservativism: The Federalist Party in the Era of Jeffersonian Democracy*. New York: Harper and Row, 1965.

Fleming, Thomas. *The Louisiana Purchase*. Hoboken, NJ: John Wiley, 2003.

Fliegelman, Jay. *Declaring Independence: Jefferson, Natural Language and the Culture of Performance*. Stanford, CA: Stanford University Press, 1993.

Foner, Philip Sheldon. *The Democratic-Republican Societies, 1790–1800: A Documentary Sourcebook of Constitutions, Declarations, Addresses, Resolutions, and Toasts*. Westport, CT: Greenwood Press, 1976.

Ford, Paul Leicester. *Washington and the Theatre*. New York: Benjamin Blom, 1967.

Forman, Ezekial. "Amusements and Politics in Philadelphia, 1794." *Pennsylvania Magazine of History and Biography* 10, no. 2 (July 1886): 182–7.

Fortune, Michael. "The Acquisition of Louisiana: A National Song." Philadelphia: G. Willig, 1804.

Fortune, Michael. "Jefferson and Liberty. A New Song." Philadelphia: N. G. Dufief, 1801.

Foster, William C. *Poetry on Different Subjects Written under the Signature of Timothy Spectacles*. Salem, NY: John M. Looker, 1805.

Freeman, Joanne B. *Affairs of Honor: National Politics in the New Republic*. New Haven, CT: Yale University Press, 2001.

*Free Trade and Sailors' Rights*. Philadelphia: Dennis Heartt, 1813.

Friend, Craig T. "Merchants and Markethouses: Reflections on Moral Economy in Early Kentucky." *Journal of the Early Republic* 17, no. 4 (Winter 1997): 553–74.

Gafford, Lucile. "The Boston Stage and the War of 1812." *New England Quarterly* 7, no. 2 (June 1934): 327–35.

Gaines, William H., Jr. "The Forgotten Army: Recruiting for a National Emergency (1799–1800). *Virginia Magazine of History and Biography* 56, no. 3 (July 1948): 267–79.

Gale, Emily, and Bonnie Gordon. "Sound in Jefferson's Virginia." October 25, 2016. *Encyclopedia Virginia*. http://www.EncyclopediaVirginia.org/Sound_in_Jefferson_s_Virginia.

Gamble, Richard M. "'The Last and Brightest Empire of Time': Timothy Dwight and America as Voegelin's 'Authoritative Present,' 1771–1787." *Humanitas* 20, no. 1–2 (2007): 13–35.

Gannon, Kevin M. "Escaping 'Mr. Jefferson's Plan of Destruction': New England Federalists and the Idea of a Northern Confederacy, 1803–1804." *Journal of the Early Republic* 21, no. 3 (Autumn 2001): 413–43.

Gardner, Jared. *Master Plots: Race and the Founding of an American Literature, 1787–1845*. Baltimore, MD: Johns Hopkins University Press, 2000.

Gibbs, Jenna M. *Performing the Temple of Liberty: Slavery, Theater, and Popular Culture in London and Philadelphia, 1760–1850*. Baltimore, MD: Johns Hopkins University Press, 2014.

Gilje, Paul A. "The Common People and the Constitution: Popular Culture in New York City in the Late Eighteenth Century." In *New York in the Age of Constitution, 1775–1800*, edited by Paul A. Gilje and William Pencak, 48–73. Rutherford, NJ: Fairleigh Dickinson University Press, 1992.

Gilje, Paul A. *Free Trade and Sailors Rights in the War of 1812*. Cambridge: Cambridge University Press, 2013.

Gilje, Paul A. "'Free Trade and Sailors' Rights': The Rhetoric of the War of 1812." *Journal of the Early Republic* 30, no. 1 (Spring 2010): 1–23.

Gilje, Paul A. "The Meaning of Freedom for Waterfront Workers." In *Devising Liberty: Preserving and Creating Freedom in the New American Republic*, edited by David Thomas Konig, 109–40. Stanford, CA: Stanford University Press, 1995.

Gilje, Paul A. *The Road to Mobocracy: Popular Disorder in New York City, 1763–1834*. Chapel Hill: University of North Carolina Press, 1987.

Gilje, Paul A., and Howard B. Rock. "'Sweep O! Sweep O!': African-American Chimney Sweeps and Citizenship in the New Nation." *William and Mary Quarterly* 1, no. 3 (July 1994): 507–38.

Gilman, Todd. *The Theatre Career of Thomas Arne*. Newark: University of Delaware Press, 2013.

Gilreath, James, ed., and Elizabeth Carter Wills, comp. *Federal Copyright Records, 1790–1800*. Washington: Library of Congress, 1987.

Goldsmith, William. *The Naval History of Great Britain*. London: J. Jaques and W. Wright, 1825.

Goodman, Glenda. "American Identities in an Atlantic Musical World: Transhistorical Case Studies." PhD diss., Harvard University, 2012.

Goodman, Glenda. "Transatlantic Contrafacta, Musical Formats, and the Creation of Political Culture in Revolutionary America." *Journal of the Society for American Music* 11, no. 4 (November 2017): 392–419.

Goodrich, Samuel Griswold. *Recollections of a Lifetime*. Ridgefield, CT: Miller, Orton and Mulligan, 1856.

Gordon-Reed, Annette. *The Hemingses of Monticello: An American Family*. New York: W. W. Norton, 2008.

Gordon-Reed, Annette, and Peter S. Onuf. *"Most Blessed of the Patriarchs": Thomas Jefferson and the Empire of the Imagination*. New York: W. W. Norton, 2016.

Gould, Roger V. "Political Networks and the Local/National Boundary in the Whiskey Rebellion." In *Challenging Authority: The Historical Study of Contentious Politics*, edited by Michael P. Hanagan, Leslie Page Moch, and Wayne Te Brake, 36–53. Minneapolis: University of Minnesota Press, 1998.

Gray, Myron. "French Revolutionary Song for Federal Philadelphia: Benjamin Carr's Music Sheets." *Common-place* 13, no. 2 (Winter 2013). http://www.common-place-archives.org/vol-13/no-02/gray/.

Gray, Myron. "Musical Politics in French Philadelphia, 1781–1801." PhD diss., University of Pennsylvania, 2014.

Gray, Myron. "A Partisan National Song: The Politics of 'Hail Columbia' Reconsidered." *Music & Politics* 11, no. 2 (Summer 2017). DOI: http://dx.doi.org/10.3998/mp.9460447.0011.201.

Griffin, Dustin. *Patriotism and Poetry in Eighteenth-Century Britain*. Cambridge: Cambridge University Press, 2002.

*Grigg's Southern and Western Songster*. Philadelphia: John Grigg, 1829.

Grobe, Charles. *Hail Columbia Happy Land with Variations*. Philadelphia: Edward L. Walker, 1853.

Gronningsater, Sarah L. H. "'Expressly Recognized by Our Election Laws': Certificates of Freedom and the Multiple Fates of Black Citizenship in the Early Republic." *William and Mary Quarterly* 75, no. 3 (July 2018): 465–506.

Gross, Jonathan, ed. *Thomas Jefferson's Scrapbooks: Poems of Nation, Family, and Romantic Love*. Hanover, NH: Steerforth Books, 2006.

Hagensick, Donna. "Irving: A Littérateur in Politics." In *Critical Essays on Washington Irving*, edited by Ralph M. Aderman, 178–91. Boston: G. K. Hall, 1990.

*Hail Columbia: The Celebrated National Air: With Variations for the Piano Forte*. Philadelphia: George Willig, 1842.

Hale, Matthew Rainbow. "'Many Who Wandered in Darkness': The Contest over American National Identity, 1795–1798." *Early American Studies: An Interdisciplinary Journal* 1, no. 1 (Spring 2003): 127–75.

Hale, Matthew Rainbow. "On Their Tiptoes: Political Time and Newspapers during the Advent of the Radicalized French Revolution, circa 1792–93." *Journal of the Early Republic* 29, no. 2 (Summer 2009): 191–218.

Hale, Matthew Rainbow. "Regenerating the World: The French Revolution, Civic Festivals, and the Forging of Modern American Democracy, 1793–1795." *Journal of American History* 103, no. 4 (March 2017): 891–920.

Hammack, James Wallace, Jr. *Kentucky and the Second American Revolution: The War of 1812*. Lexington: University Press of Kentucky, 1976.

"A Happy New-Year to Commodore Rodgers, or, Huzza for the President and Congress." Boston: N. Coverly Jr. 1812.

Hargruder, Andrew Luke. "'A Circle Form'd of Friends:' Candor, Contentiousness, and the Democratic Clubs of the Early Republic." MA Thesis, Louisiana State University, 2015.

*The Harrison Medal Minstrel*. Philadelphia: Grigg and Elliot, 1840.

Hart, Albert Bushnell, and Annie Bliss Chapman, eds. *How Our Grandfathers Lived*. New York: Macmillan, 1912.

Hart, Sidney, and Rachael L. Penman. *1812: A Nation Emerges*. Washington, DC: Smithsonian Institution Scholarly Press, 2012.

Harvey, Oscar Jewell, and Ernest Gray Smith. *A History of Wilkes-Barré, Luzerne County, Pennsylvania*. Vol. 1 Wilkes-Barre: Raeder Press, 1909.

Hastings, George Everett. *The Life and Works of Francis Hopkinson*. New York: Russell and Russell, 1968.

Hatton, Ann Julia. *The Songs of Tammany; or, The Indian Chief*. New York: Harrisson and Faulkner, 1794.

Hatzenbuehler, Ronald L., and Robert L. Ivie. *Congress Declares War: Rhetoric, Leadership, and Partisanship in the Early Republic*. Kent, OH: Kent State University Press, 1983.

Heideking, Jürgen. "Celebrating the Constitution: The Federal Processions of 1788 and the Emergence of a Republican Festive Culture in the United States." In *Celebrating Ethnicity and Nation: American Festive Culture from the Revolution to the Early Twentieth* Century, edited by Geneviève Fabre, Jürgen Heideking, and Kai Dreisbach, 25–43. New York: Berghahn Books, 2001.

Heidenrich, Donald E., Jr. "U.S. National Security and Party Politics: The Consensus on Louisiana, 1789–1803." *Arkansas Historical Quarterly* 62, no. 4 (Winter 2003): 370–85.

Heidler, David S., and Jeanne T. Heidler. *The War of 1812*. Westport, CT: Greenwood Press, 2002.

Heintze, James R. *Music of the Fourth of July: A Year-by-Year Chronicle of Performances and Works Composed for the Occasion, 1777–2008*. Jefferson, NC: McFarland, 2009.

Hickey, Donald R. *Don't Give Up the Ship! Myths of the War of 1812.* Urbana: University of Illinois, 2006.

Hickey, Donald R. "Federalist Defense Policy in the Age of Jefferson, 1801–1812." *Military Affairs* 45, no. 2 (April 1981): 63–70.

Hickey, Donald R. "Federalist Party Unity and the War of 1812." *Journal of American Studies* 12, no. 1 (April 1978): 23–39.

Hickey, Donald R. *The War of 1812: A Forgotten Conflict.* Urbana: University of Illinois, 1989.

Higginbotham, Don. *George Washington: Uniting a Nation.* Lanham, MD: Rowman and Littlefield, 2002.

Hildebrand, David. "New York in Song: The War of 1812." *New York History* 94, no. 3–4 (Summer/Fall 2013): 283–99.

Hildebrand, David K. "Two National Anthems? Some Reflections on the Two Hundredth Anniversary of 'The Star-Spangled Banner' and Its Forgotten Partner, 'The Battle of Baltimore.'" *American Music* 32, no. 3 (Fall 2014): 253–71.

Hill, Richard S. "The Melody of the Star-Spangled Banner in the United States before 1820." In *Essays Honoring Lawrence C. Wroth*, edited by Frederick R. Goff, 151–93. Portland, ME: Anthoensen Press, 1951.

Hill, Uri K. "The Heroes of the Ocean." Philadelphia: G. Willig, 1813.

Hiltner, Judith R. *The Newspaper Verse of Philip Freneau: An Edition and Bibliographical Survey.* Troy, NY: Whitson, 1986.

Hitchcock, Marcus T. *Manuscript Music Book Belonging to Marcus T. Hitchcock.* Center for Popular Music Studies, Middle Tennessee State University.

Hofstadter, Richard. *The American Political Tradition and the Men Who Made It.* New York: Alfred A. Knopf, 1948.

Hogeland, William. *Founding Finance: How Debt, Speculation, Foreclosures, Protests, and Crackdowns Made Us a Nation.* Austin: University of Texas Press, 2012.

Holland, Edwin C. *Odes, Naval Songs, and Other Occasional Poems.* Charleston: J. Hoff, 1813.

Holland, Edwin C., and Charles Gilfert. "The Pillar of Glory." New York: J. Appel, 1813.

Holland, Edwin C., and Jacob Eckhard. "The Pillar of Glory." Philadelphia: G. E. Blake, 1813.

Holmes, Isaac. *An Account of the United States of America, Derived from Actual Observation during a Residence of Four Years in That Republic.* London: Caxton Press, 1823.

Holton, Woody. "Did Democracy Cause the Recession That Led to the Constitution?" *Journal of American History* 92, no. 2 (September 2005): 442–69.

Holton, Woody. *Unruly Americans and the Origins of the Constitution.* New York: Hill and Wang, 2007.

Hopkinson, Francis. "Account of the Grand Federal Procession in Philadelphia." *American Museum* 4 (July 1788): 57–75.

Hopkinson, Francis. "Brother Soldiers All Hail!" Philadelphia: B. Carr, 1799.

Hopkinson, Joseph. *Hail Columbia, the Favorite New Federal Song.* Retrieved from the Library of Congress. https://www.loc.gov/item/ihas.100010486/.

Horgan, Kate. *The Politics of Songs in Eighteenth-Century Britain, 1723–1795.* London: Pickering and Chatto, 2014.

Hosmer, James B. *Music Book.* Connecticut Historical Society. Manuscript 38923.

Howard, John Tasker, and Eleanor S. Bowen, eds. *Music Associated with the Period of the Formation of the Constitution and the Inauguration of George Washington.* Washington, DC: United States Sesquiscentennial Commission, n.d.

Howell, Richard. *A Sonata, Sung by a Number of Young Girls . . . as General Washington Passed under the Triumphal Arch Raised on the Bridge at Trenton, April 21, 1789.* [Trenton: Isaac Collins, 1789].

Humphreys, David. *The Miscellaneous Works of David Humphreys.* New York: T. and J. Swords, 1804.

Humphreys, Frank Landon. *Life and Times of David Humphreys.* 2 vols. St. Clair Shores, MI: Scholarly Press, 1971.

Hunter, Clark, ed. *The Life and Letters of Alexander Wilson.* Vol. 154. Philadelphia: American Philosophical Society, 1983.

Hurd, Duane Hamilton. *History of Essex County, Massachusetts, with Biographical Sketches of Many of Its Pioneers and Prominent Men.* Philadelphia: J. W. Lewis, 1888.

Huston, James L. *Securing the Fruits of Labor: The American Concept of Wealth Distribution, 1765–1900.* Baton Rouge: Louisiana State University Press, 2015.

Hutton, Joseph. "Perry's Victory." N.p., n.d.

"Huzza for the Constellation." Philadelphia: B. Carr, 1799.

Immerman, Richard H. *Empire for Liberty: A History of American Imperialism from Benjamin Franklin to Paul Wolfowitz.* Princeton, NJ: Princeton University Press, 2012.

Ireland, Owen S. *Religion, Ethnicity, and Politics: Ratifying the Constitution in Pennsylvania.* University Park: Pennsylvania State University Press, 1995.

Irving, Washington. *A History of New York.* Vol. 2. New York: Inskeep and Bradford, 1809.

Irving, Washington. *The Life and Letters of Washington Irving.* Vol. 1. New York: G. P. Putnam, 1869.

[Irving, Washington.] "Review of *Odes, Naval Songs, and Other Occasional Poems. By Edwin C. Holland, Esq. Charleston.*" *Analectic Magazine* 3 (1814): 242–52.

Irving, Washington. *The Works of Washington Irving in Twelve Volumes.* Vol. 8. New York: G. P. Putnam's Sons, 1881.

Irwin, Douglas A. *Clashing over Commerce: A History of U.S. Trade Policy.* Chicago: University of Chicago Press, 2017.

James, Reese Davis. *Cradle of Culture, 1800–1810: The Philadelphia Stage.* Philadelphia: University of Pennsylvania Press, 1957.

Janiewicz, Feliks, and Charles Harford. "The Battle of Derne." Philadelphia: G. E. Blake, 1805.

Jefferson, Thomas. *The Works of Thomas Jefferson.* Federal Edition. Edited by Paul Leicester Ford. Vol. 10. New York: G. P. Putnam's Sons, 1904–5. http://oll.libertyfund.org/titles/806.

Jennings, Isaac. *Memorials of a Century: Embracing a Record of Individuals and Events, Chiefly in the Early History of Bennington, Vt., and Its First Church.* Bennington: Gould and Lincoln, 1869.

Jensen, Merrill, and Robert A. Becker, eds. *The Documentary History of the First Federal Elections, 1788–1790.* Vol. 1. Madison: University of Wisconsin Press, 1976.

Jensen, Oskar Cox. *Napoleon and British Song, 1797–1822.* New York: Palgrave Macmillan, 2015.

Jernegan, Marcus Wilson. *The Tammany Societies of Rhode Island.* Providence, RI: Preston and Rounds, 1897.

Johannsen, Robert W. *To the Halls of the Montezumas: The Mexican War in the American Imagination.* New York: Oxford University Press, 1988.

John, Richard R., and Thomas C. Leonard. "The Illusion of the Ordinary: John Lewis Krimmel's *Village Tavern* and the Democratization of Public Life in the Early Republic." *Pennsylvania History* 65, no. 1 (Winter 1998): 87–96.

Jones, Absalom. *A Thanksgiving Sermon, Preached January 1, 1808, In St. Thomas's, or the African Episcopal, Church, Philadelphia*. Philadelphia, 1808.

Jones, Brian Jay. *Washington Irving: An American Original*. New York: Arcade, 2008.

Jones, Robert F. "Economic Opportunism and the Constitution in New York State: The Example of William Duer." *New York History* 68, no. 4 (October 1987): 357–72.

"Journal of Major William Gould during an Expedition into Pennsylvania, 1849." *Proceedings of the New Jersey Historical* Society 3 (1849): 173–91.

*Jovial Songster: Containing a Variety of Patriotic and Humorous Songs*. New York: John Harrisson, 1794.

Kachun, Mitch. *Festivals of Freedom: Meaning and Memory in African American Emancipation Celebrations, 1808–1915*. Amherst: University of Massachusetts Press, 2006.

Kaminski, John P. "New York: The Reluctant Pillar." In *The Reluctant Pillar*, edited by Stephen L. Schechter, 48–117. Troy, NY: Russell Sage College, 1985.

Kaplan, Catherine O'Donnell. *Men of Letters in the Early Republic: Cultivating Forums of Citizenship*. Chapel Hill: University of North Carolina Press, 2008.

Kastor, Peter J. *The Nation's Crucible: The Louisiana Purchase and the Creation of America*. New Haven, CT: Yale University Press, 2008.

Kastor, Peter J. "'What Are the Advantages of the Acquisition?': Inventing Expansion in the Early American Republic." *American Quarterly* 60, no. 4 (December 2008): 1003–35.

Kaye, Harvey J. *Thomas Paine and the Promise of America*. New York: Hill and Wang, 2005.

Keller, Kate Van Winkle. *Music of the War of 1812 in America*. Annapolis, MD: Colonial Music Institute, 2011.

Keller, Robert M., Raoul F. Camus, Kate Van Winkle Keller, and Susan Cifaldi. *Early American Secular Music and Its European Sources, 1589–1839*. Annapolis, MD: Colonial Music Institute, 2002.

Kelly, M. Ruth. *The Olmsted Case: Privateers, Property, and Politics in Pennsylvania, 1778–1810*. Selinsgrove, PA: Susquehanna University Press, 2005.

Kennedy, John P. *Memoirs of the Life of William Wirt*. Philadelphia: 1849.

Kerber, Linda K. *Federalists in Dissent: Imagery and Ideology in Jeffersonian America*. Ithaca, NY: Cornell University Press, 1970.

Kerby, Robert L. "The Militia System and the State Militias in the War of 1812." *Indiana Magazine of History* 73, no. 2 (June 1977): 102–24.

Ketcham, Ralph. *James Madison: A Biography*. Charlottesville: University Press of Virginia, 1990.

Ketcham, Ralph. "James Madison: The Unimperial President." *Virginia Quarterly Review* 54 (Winter 1978): 116–36.

King, Quentin Scott. *Henry Clay and the War of 1812*. Jefferson, NC: MacFarland, 2014.

King, W. A. *Hail Columbia: As Performed by the Author with the Greatest Success: Arranged as a Brilliant Fantasia*. New York: Firth and Hall, 1839.

Kirtland, Jared Potter. "History." In *Song of Jefferson and Liberty*. 1874. In *American Poetry, 1609–1900: Segment II*. New Haven, CT: Research Publications, 1975.

Klarman, Michael J. *The Framers' Coup: The Making of the United States Constitution*. New York: Oxford University Press, 2016.

Knott, Sarah. *Sensibility and the American Revolution*. Chapel Hill: University of North Carolina Press, 2012.

Kohn, Richard H. *Eagle and Sword: The Federalists and the Creation of the Military Establishment in America, 1783–1802*. New York: Free Press, 1975.

Koschnik, Albrecht. *"Let a Common Interest Bind Us Together": Associations, Partisanship, and Culture in Philadelphia, 1775–1840.* Charlottesville: University of Virginia Press, 2007.

Kuntz, Andrew. "Fiddle Tune History: The Black Sloven." *Fiddler Magazine* 15, no. 1 (Spring 2008): 34–7.

Labaree, Benjamin W. *Patriots and Partisans: The Merchants of Newburyport* Cambridge, MA: Harvard University Press, 1962.

"The Ladies Patriotic Song." Boston: P. A. von Hagen, [1798].

Lambert, Frank. *The Barbary Wars: American Independence in the Atlantic World.* New York: Hill and Wang, 2005.

*The Lark: Containing a Collection of Above Four Hundred and Seventy Celebrated English and Scotch Songs.* London: John Osborn, 1740.

Larkin, Edward. "Nation and Empire in the Early U.S." *American Literary History* 22, no. 3 (Fall 2010): 501–26.

Laroque [Larroque], Philip. *Battle of the Memorable 8th of January 1815.* Philadelphia: G. Willig, 1815.

*The Launch, a Federal Song.* [Boston: n.p., 1798].

"Lawrence the Brave." Philadelphia: G. E. Blake, 1813.

Lawrence, Vera Brodsky. *Music for Patriots, Politicians, and Presidents.* New York: Macmillan, 1975.

"Lawyers and Bullfrogs." *Isaiah Thomas Broadside Ballads Project.* http://www.americanantiquarian.org/thomasballads/items/show/145.

Leepson, Marc. *What So Proudly We Hailed: Francis Scott Key, A Life.* New York: Macmillan, 2014.

Leiner, Frederick C. "The Subscription Warships of 1798." *American Neptune* 46 (Summer 1986): 141–58.

Lendler, Marc. "Equally Proper at All Times and at All Times Necessary": Civility, Bad Tendency, and the Sedition Act." *Journal of the Early Republic* 24, no. 3 (Fall 2004): 419–44.

Leonard, Thomas C. *News for All: America's Coming-of-Age with the Press.* New York: Oxford University Press, 1995.

Letter, Joseph J. "Reincarnating Samuel Woodworth: Native American Prophets, the Nation, and the War of 1812." *Early American Literature* 43, no. 3 (2008), 687–713.

Lichtenwanger, William. "The Music of 'The Star-Spangled Banner': Whence and Whither?" *College Music Symposium* 18, no. 2 (Fall 1978): 34–81.

Lienesch, Michael. *New Order of the Ages: Time, the Constitution, and the Making of Modern American Political Thought.* Princeton, NJ: Princeton University Press, 2014.

Lienesch, Michael. "The Role of Political Millennialism in Early American Nationalism." *Western Political Quarterly* 36, no. 3 (September 1983): 445–65.

Little, Nigel. *Transoceanic Radical, William Duane: National Identity and Empire, 1760–1835.* London: Pickering and Chatto, 2008.

Livermore, Edward St. Loe. *An Oration, in Commemoration of the Dissolution of the Political Union between the United States of America and France.* Portsmouth, New-Hampshire, 1799.

Livermore, Shaw, Jr. *The Twilight of Federalism: The Disintegration of the Federalist Party, 1815–1830.* Princeton, NJ: Princeton University Press, 1962.

*The Log Cabin Minstrel; or, Tippecanoe Songster.* Roxbury: Patriot and Democrat Office, 1840.

Looby, Christopher. *Voicing America: Language, Literary Form, and the Origins of the United States.* Chicago: University of Chicago Press, 1996.

Lossing, Benjamin J. *Lossing's Pictorial Field Book of the War of 1812.* New York: Harper and Brothers, 1868.

Lowens, Irving. *A Bibliography of Songsters Printed in America before 1821.* Worcester, MA: American Antiquarian Society, 1976.

Ludlow, Noah Miller. *Dramatic Life as I Found It: A Record of Personal Experience.* St. Louis: G. I. Jones, 1880.

Lutz, Donald S. "The Articles of Confederation as the Background to the Federal Republic." *Publius* 20, no. 1 (Winter 1990): 55–70.

*Magazine of Wit, and American Harmonist.* Philadelphia: M'Carty and Davis, 1818.

Mahar, William J. "'Backside Albany' and Early Blackface Minstrelsy: A Contextual Study of America's First Blackface Song." *American Music* 6, no. 1 (Spring 1988): 1–27.

Maier, Pauline. *Ratification: The People Debate the Constitution, 1787–1788.* New York: Simon and Schuster, 2010.

Main, Jackson Turner. *The Antifederalists: Critics of the Constitution, 1781–1788.* Foreword by Edward Countryman. Chapel Hill: University of North Carolina Press, 2004. First printed 1961.

Malone, Dumas. *Jefferson the President: First Term, 1801–1805.* Boston: Little, Brown, 1970.

Malone, Dumas. *Jefferson the President: Second Term, 1805–1809.* Boston: Little, Brown, 1974.

Martell, J. S. "A Side Light on Federalist Strategy during the War of 1812." *American Historical Review* 43, no. 3 (April 1938): 553–66.

Martello, Robert. *Midnight Ride, Industrial Dawn: Paul Revere and the Growth of American Enterprise.* Baltimore, MD: Johns Hopkins University Press, 2010.

Martin, Tyrone G. "Isaac Hull's Victory Revisited." *American Neptune* 47 (1987): 14–21.

Mason, Laura. *Singing the French Revolution: Popular Culture and Politics, 1787–1799.* Ithaca, NY: Cornell University Press, 1996.

McCarty, William. *Songs, Odes, and Other Poems on National Subjects.* Philadelphia: William McCarty, 1842.

McCloskey, John C. "The Campaign of Periodicals after the War of 1812 for National American Literature." *PMLA* 50, no. 1 (March 1935): 262–73.

McCullough, David. *John Adams.* New York: Simon and Schuster, 2008.

McCusker, John J., and Kenneth Morgan, eds. *The Early Modern Atlantic Economy.* Cambridge: Cambridge University Press, 2000.

McDonald, Gerald D., Stuart C. Sherman, and Mary T. Russo. *A Checklist of American Newspaper Carrier's Addresses, 1720–1820.* Worcester, MA: American Antiquarian Society, 2000.

McGann, Jerome. "Washington Irving, *A History of New York*, and American History." *Early American Literature* 47, no. 2 (2012): 349–76.

McMaster, John Bach, and Frederick D. Stone, eds. *Pennsylvania and the Federal Constitution, 1787–1788.* Philadelphia: Historical Society of Pennsylvania, 1888.

McWhirter, Christian. *Battle Hymns: The Power and Popularity of Music in the Civil War.* Chapel Hill: University of North Carolina Press, 2012.

Meagher, Thomas M. *Financing Armed Conflict.* Vol. 1. New York: Palgrave Macmillan, 2016.

Mee, Jon. *Print, Publicity, and Popular Radicalism in the 1790s: The Laurel of Liberty.* Cambridge: Cambridge University Press, 2016.

Merrill, Michael, and Sean Wilentz, eds. *The Key of Liberty: The Life and Democratic Writings of William Manning, "A Laborer," 1747–1814*. Cambridge, MA: Harvard University Press, 1993.

Mestyan, Adam. *Arab Patriotism: The Ideology and Culture of Power in Late Ottoman Egypt*. Princeton, NJ: Princeton University Press, 2017.

Miller, Monica L. *Slaves to Fashion: Black Dandyism and the Styling of Black Diasporic Identity*. Durham, NC: Duke University Press, 2009.

Milns, William, and James Hewitt. "The Federal Constitution & Liberty Forever." New York: J. Hewitt's Musical Repository, [1798].

Mitchell, Stewart, ed. "New Letters of Abigail Adams." *Proceedings of the American Antiquarian Society* (October 1945): 299–444.

Montgomery, James. *The Poetical Works of James Montgomery*. Philadelphia: Linsday and Blakiston, 1853.

Moore, Arthur K. *The Frontier Mind: A Cultural Analysis of the Kentucky Frontiersman*. Louisville: University of Kentucky Press, 1957.

Moore, Frank. *Songs and Ballads of the American Revolution*. 1855. Reprint, New York: Arno Press, 1969.

Morris, Richard B. *The Forging of the Union, 1781–1789*. New York: Harper and Row, 1987.

*Mr. Francis's Ballroom Assistant*. Philadelphia: G. Willig, n.d.

M'Skimin, Samuel. *Annals of Ulster; or, Ireland Fifty Years Ago*. Belfast: John Henderson, 1849.

Murphy, William J., Jr. "John Adams: The Politics of the Additional Army, 1798–1800." *New England Quarterly* 52, no. 2 (June 1979): 234–49.

Murrin, John M. "The Jeffersonian Triumph and American Exceptionalism," *Journal of the Early Republic* 20, no. 1 (Spring 2000): 1–25.

"Music Physically Considered." *Columbian Magazine* (February 1789): 90–93.

Nason, Elias. *A Memoir of Mrs. Susanna Rowson, with Elegant and Illustrative Extracts from Her Writings in Prose and Poetry*. Albany, NY: Joel Munsell, 1870.

Nathans, Heather S. *Early American Theatre from the Revolution to Thomas Jefferson: Into the Hands of the People*. Cambridge: Cambridge University Press, 2003.

*National Martial Music and Songs*. Philadelphia: William M'Culloch, 1809.

*A National Song-Book*. Trenton: James J. Wilson, 1813.

*National Songster*. Hagerstown, MD: John Gruber and Daniel May, 1814.

"Naval Recruiting Song." *Isaiah Thomas Broadside Ballads Project*. http://www.americanantiquarian.org/thomasballads/items/show/306.

*The Naval Songster*. Charlestown: J. White, 1815.

*The Naval Songster*. Fredericktown, MD: M. E. Bartgis, 1814.

*Naval Songster. Or Columbian Naval Melody*. Boston: Nathaniel Coverly Jr., 1816.

*The Naval Songster, or the Sailor's Pocket Companion*. Boston: N. Coverly Jr. 1813.

Nelson, William, and Charles A. Shriner. *History of Paterson and Its Environs*. Vol. 1. Paterson: Lewis Historical Publishing Company, 1920.

*The New American Songster*. Philadelphia: D. Dickinson, 1817.

*The New Ladies Memorandum-Book for the Year 1794*. London: James Evans, 1793.

Newman, Simon P. *Parades and the Politics of the Street: Festive Culture in the Early American Republic*. Philadelphia: University of Pennsylvania Press, 1997.

Newman, Simon P. "Principles or Men? George Washington and the Political Culture of National Leadership, 1776–1801." *Journal of the Early Republic* 12, no. 4 (Winter 1992): 477–507.

Newman, Simon P., and Marion Vaillant. "La Révolution française vue de loin: la celebration de Valmy à Boston, en janvier 1793," *Revue d'histoire moderne et contemporaine* 58, no. 1 (January–March 2011): 80–99.

Newmyer, R. Kent. *Supreme Court Justice Joseph Story: Statesman of the Old Republic.* Chapel Hill: University of North Carolina Press, 2004.

"A New Song on the Causes—Beginning, Events, End and Consequences of the Late War with Great Britain." New York: E. Riley, [ca. 1819].

*Nightingale of Liberty: or Delights of Harmony. A Choice Collection of Patriotic, Masonic, & Entertaining Songs.* New York: Harrison, 1797.

Nivola, Pietro S. "The 'Party War' of 1812: Yesterday's Lessons for Today's Partisan Politics." In *What So Proudly We Hailed: Essays on the Contemporary Meaning of the War of 1812*, edited by Pietro S. Nivola and Peter J. Kastor, 8–35. Washington, DC: Brookings Institution Press, 2012.

*The Northern and Eastern Songster.* Boston: Charles Gaylord, 1835.

Nourse, Nick. "Australia's First (British) Musical Import: The 'Rogue's March.'" *CHOMBEC News* 1 (Summer 2012): 1–3. http://www.bristol/ac.uk/music/.

*Ode for Election Day, 1792.* N.p.: n.p., 1792.

"Ode for His Majesty's Birth-day, 1746," *Scots Magazine* (November 1746): 521.

*Ode for the 23rd of October, 1792.* [Boston]: n.p., [1792].

Odell, George C. D. *Annals of the New York Stage.* Vol. 1. New York: Columbia University Press, 1927.

Ogasapian, John. *Music of the Colonial and Revolutionary Era.* Westport, CT: Greenwood Press, 2004.

Olmsted, Timothy. *Music Book, 1792–1822.* Connecticut Historical Society. Manuscript 95261.

Onuf, Peter S. *The Origins of the Federal Republic: Jurisdictional Controversies in the United States, 1775–1787.* Philadelphia: University of Pennsylvania Press, 1983.

Onuf, Peter S. "The Revolution of 1803." *Wilson Quarterly* 27, no. 1 (Winter 2003): 22–9.

Opal, J. M. "The Politics of 'Industry': Federalism in Concord and Exeter, New Hampshire, 1790–1805." *Journal of the Early Republic* 20, no. 4 (Winter 2000): 637–71.

Paine, Robert Treat. "Rule New England." Boston: Mallet and Graupner, 1802.

Paine, Robert Treat. *The Works in Verse and Prose of the Late Robert Treat Paine, Jun. Esq.* Boston: J. Belcher, 1812.

Paine, Thomas. *Rights of Man.* Philadelphia: D. Webster, 1797.

Paine, Thomas. *The Writings of Thomas Paine.* Edited by Moncure Daniel Conway. New York: AMS Press, 1967.

*Papers of the New Haven Colony Historical Society.* Vol. 2. New Haven, 1877.

*The Papers of Thomas Jefferson*, vol. 33. Princeton, NJ: Princeton University Press, 2006.

Pasley, Jeffrey L. "The Cheese and the Words: Popular Political Culture and Participatory Democracy in the Early American Republic." In *Beyond the Founders: New Approaches to the Political History of the Early American Republic*, edited by Jeffrey L. Pasley, Andrew Whitmore Robertson, and David Waldstreicher, 31–56. Chapel Hill: University of North Carolina Press, 2004.

Pasley, Jeffrey L. *"The Tyranny of Printers": Newspaper Politics in the Early American Republic.* Charlottesville: University Press of Virginia, 2001.

*Patriotic and Naval Songster.* Philadelphia: Charles H. Walsh, 1898.

*The Patriotic Songster.* Alexandria, VA: Benjamin L. Bogan, 1816.

*The Patriot's Vocal Miscellany; or, A Collection of Loyal Songs.* Dublin: n.p., 1804.

Pencak, William A. *Contested Commonwealths: Essays in American History.* Bethelem: Lehigh University, 2011.

Perkins, Edwin J. *American Public Finance and Financial Services, 1700–1815.* Columbus: Ohio State University Press, 1994.

"Perry's Victory." Philadelphia G. Willig [ca. 1813].

Peskin, Lawrence A. *Captives and Countrymen: Barbary Slavery and the American Public, 1785–1816.* Baltimore, MD: Johns Hopkins University Press, 2009.

Peskin, Lawrence A. "How the Republicans Learned to Love Manufacturing: The First Parties and the 'New Economy.'" *Journal of the Early Republic* 22, no. 2 (Summer 2002): 235–62.

Peskin, Lawrence A. *Manufacturing Revolution: The Intellectual Origins of Early American Industry.* Baltimore, MD: Johns Hopkins University Press, 2010.

Peterson, Merrill D. *The Jefferson Image in the American Mind.* Charlottesville: University of Virginia Press, 1960.

*The Philadelphiad; or, New Pictures of the City.* Vol. 1. Philadelphia: Kline and Reynolds, 1784.

Pierce, Jason E. *Making the White Man's West: Whiteness and the Creation of the American West.* Boulder: University Press of Colorado, 2016.

Pindar, Peter, Esq. [John Wolcot]. *Odes to Mr. Paine, Author of "The Rights of Man," on the Intended Celebration of the Downfall of the French Empire, by a Set of British Democrats, on the Fourteenth of July.* London: J. Evans, 1791.

Pinks, William John, and Edward J. Wood. *The History of Clerkenwell.* 2nd ed. London: Charles Herbert, 1881.

Pitch, Anthony S. *The Burning of Washington: The British Invasion of 1814.* Annapolis, MD: Naval Institute Press, 2000.

Plate, Robert. *Alexander Wilson: Wanderer in the Wilderness.* New York: David McKay, 1966.

Platt, Orville. "Negro Governors." *New Haven Historical Society Quarterly* 6 (1900): 315–35.

*The Pocket Encyclopedia of Scottish, English, and Irish Songs.* Glasgow: Andrew and James Duncan, 1816.

*Pocock's Everlasting Songster.* Gravesend: R. Pocock, 1800.

*The Poetical Works of David Garrick, Esq.* Vol. 2. London: George Kearsley, 1785.

*Politics for the People; or, Salmagundi for Swine.* London: D. I. Eaton, 1794.

*Political Sermons of the American Founding Era: 1730–1805.* 2 vols. Foreword by Ellis Sandoz. 2nd ed. Indianapolis: Liberty Fund, 1998.

Pollock, Thomas Clark. *The Philadelphia Theatre in the Eighteenth Century.* New York: Greenwood Press, 1968.

Porter, Susan L. *With an Air Debonair: Musical Theatre in America, 1785–1815.* Washington, DC: Smithsonian Institution Press, 1991.

Pownall [Wrighten], Mary Ann and James Hewitt. *Six Songs; For the Harpsichord or Piano Forte.* New York: J. Hewitt, 1794.

Price, Thomas Robert. "Samuel Woodworth and Theodore Sedgwick Fay: Two Nineteenth-Century American Literati." EdD diss., Pennsylvania State University, 1970.

Prince, Carl E. "James J. Wilson: Party Leader, 1801–1824." *Proceedings of the New Jersey Historical Society* 8 (1965): 24–39.

Prince, Carl E. *New Jersey's Jeffersonian Republicans: The Genesis of an Early Party Machine.* Chapel Hill: University of North Carolina Press, 1967.

Purcell, Richard J. "An Irish Crusader for American Democracy: Matthew Lyon, 1750–1822." *Studies: An Irish Quarterly Review* 25, no. 97 (March 1936): 47–64.

Purcell, Sarah J. *Sealed with Blood: War, Sacrifice, and Memory in Revolutionary America*. Philadelphia: University of Pennsylvania Press, 2002.

*The Raising. A Patriotic Song for the Mechanic*. Philadelphia: A. H. Senseman. https://www.loc.gov/item/amss.cw104710/.

Randall, Randolph. "Authors of the Port Folio Revealed by the Hall Files." *American Literature* 11, no. 4 (January 1940): 379–416.

Ratcliffe, Donald J., ed. "The Autobiography of Benjamin Tappan." *Ohio History* 85 (Spring 1976): 109–57.

Rath, Richard Cullen. *How Early America Sounded*. Ithaca, NY: Cornell University Press, 2003.

Ray, Thomas M. "'Not One Cent for Tribute': The Public Addresses and American Popular Reaction to the XYZ Affair, 1798–1799." *Journal of the Early Republic* 3, no. 4 (Winter 1983): 389–412.

*Records of the Grand Lodge of Free and Accepted Masons of the State of Vermont*. Free Press Association, 1879.

Reinagle, Alexander. *Federal March as Performed in the Grand Procession in Philadelphia the 4th of July 1788*. Philadelphia, 1788.

Reinagle, Alexander, and Charles Harford. "The Tars of Columbia." Philadelphia: Blake's Musical Repository, 1804.

Reinagle, Alexander, and Susanna Rowson. *The Volunteers: A Music Entertainment as Performed at the New Theatre*. N.p.: n.p., 1795. https://www.loc.gov/item/2015562334/.

Reinoehl, John H. "Post-Embargo Trade and Merchant Prosperity: Experiences of the Crowninshield Family, 1809–1812." *Mississippi Valley Historical Review* 42, no. 2 (September 1955): 229–49.

Rice, Paul F. *British Music and the French Revolution*. Newcastle: Cambridge Scholars Publishing, 2010.

Richards, Leonard. *Shays's Rebellion: The American Revolution's Final Battle*. Philadelphia: University of Pennsylvania Press, 2002.

Ricksecker, Peter. *The Battle of New Orleans: For the Piano Forte*. Philadelphia: G. Willig, 1816.

Rigal, Laura. "'Raising the Roof': Authors, Spectators and Artisans in the Grand Federal Procession of 1788." *Theatre Journal* 48, no. 3 (1996): 253–77.

Riggs, Luther G., ed. *The Anarchiad*. Introduction by William K. Bottorff. Gainesville, FL: Scholar's Facsimiles, 1967.

Riordan, Liam. "'O Dear, What Can the Matter Be?': The Urban Early Republic and the Politics of Popular Songs in Benjamin Carr's Federal Overture." *Journal of the Early Republic* 31, no. 2 (Summer 2011): 179–227.

Ritcheson, Charles R. "Thomas Pinckney's London Mission, 1792–1796, and the Impressment Issue." *International History Review* 2, no. 4 (October 1980): 523–41.

Ritchey, David. *A Guide to the Baltimore Stage in the Eighteenth Century*. Westport, CT: Greenwood Press, 1982

Robbins, Chandler. *An Address, Delivered at Plymouth, on the 24th Day of January, 1793, to the Inhabitants of That Town*. [Boston], [1793].

Roberts, Brian. *Blackface Nation: Race, Reform, and Identity in American Popular Music, 1812–1925*. Chicago: University of Chicago Press, 2017.

Roberts, Oliver Ayer. *History of the Military Company of Massachusetts, Now Called the Ancient and Honorable Military Company of Massachusetts*. Vol. 2. Boston: Alfred Mudge and Son, 1897.

Robertson, Andrew W. "Voting Rites and Voting Acts: Electioneering Ritual, 1790–1820." In *Beyond the Founders: New Approaches to the Political History of the Early American Republic*, edited by Jeffrey L. Pasley, Andrew W. Robertson, and David Waldstreicher, 57–78. Chapel Hill: University of North Carolina Press, 2009.

Robinson, James. *Philadelphia Directory, City and County Register for 1803*. Philadelphia: William W. Woodward, 1802.

Robinson, William A. *Jeffersonian Democracy in New England*. New York: Greenwood Press, 1968.

Robinson, William Alexander. "The Washington Benevolent Society in New England: A Phase of Politics during the War of 1812." *Proceedings of the Massachusetts Historical Society* 49 (March 1916): 274–86.

"Rodgers & Victory. Tit for Tat or, the Chesapeake Paid for in British Blood," *Isaiah Thomas Broadside Ballads Project*. http://www.americanantiquarian.org/thomasballads/items/show/320.

Roosevelt, Theodore. *The Naval War of 1812*. 2 vols. New York: Review of Reviews, 1904.

Rosenfeld, Richard N. *American Aurora: A Democratic-Republican Returns*. New York: St. Martin's Press, 2014.

Ross, John, ed. *The Book of Scottish Poems: Ancient and Modern*. Edinburgh: Edinburgh Publishing Company, 1878.

Roth, George L. "Verse Satire on 'Faction' 1790–1815." *William and Mary Quarterly* 17, no. 4 (October 1960): 473–85.

Rothman, Joshua D. "James Callender and Social Knowledge of Interracial Sex in Antebellum Virginia." In *Sally Hemings and Thomas Jefferson: History, Memory, and Civic Culture*, edited by Jan Ellen Lewis and Peter S. Onuf, 87–113. Charlottesville: University of Virginia Press, 1999.

Rowson, Susanna. "Truxton's Victory." N.p., 1799.

Rush, Benjamin. "Observations on the Federal Procession, on the Fourth of July, 1788, in the City of Philadelphia." *American Museum* 4 (July 1788): 75–8.

*Sailor's Rights; or, Yankee Notions; Being a Collection of American Patriotic, Sentimental and Comic Songs*. New York: S. A. Burtus, 1815.

Sanjek, Russell. *American Popular Music and Its Business: The First Four Hundred Years*. New York: Oxford University Press, 1988.

Savage, Edward Hartwell. *Police Records and Recollections, or, Boston by Daylight and Gaslight*. Boston: John P. Dale, 1873.

Scharf, John Thomas. *History of Western Maryland*. Vol. 1. Clearfield. and Willow Bend Books, 1995.

Schechter, Stephen L. "A Biographical Gazetteer of New York Federalists and Antifederalists." In *The Reluctant Pillar*, edited by Stephen L. Schechter, 157–206. Troy, NY: Russell Sage College Press, 1985.

Scherr, Arthur. "Inventing the Patriot President: Bache's 'Aurora' and John Adams." *The Pennsylvania Magazine of History and Biography* 119, no. 4 (October 1995): 369–99.

Schlereth, Thomas J. "Columbia, Columbus, and Columbianism." *Journal of American History* 79, no. 3 (December 1992): 937–68.

Schlesinger, Arthur M. "A Note on Songs as Patriot Propaganda 1765–1776." *William and Mary Quarterly* 11, no. 1 (January 1954): 78–88.

Schloss, Dietmar. "The Nation as Spectacle: The Grand Federal Procession in Philadelphia, 1788." In *Celebrating Ethnicity and Nation: American Festive Culture from the Revolution to the Early Twentieth Century*, edited by Geneviève Fabre, Jürgen Heideking, and Kai Dreisbach, 44–62. New York: Berghahn Books, 2001.

Schneider, Paul. *Old Man River: The Mississippi River in North American History*. New York: Macmillan, 2013.

Schoen, Brian. "Calculating the Price of Union: Republican Economic Nationalism and the Origins of Southern Sectionalism, 1790–828." *Journal of the Early Republic* 23, no. 2 (Summer 2003): 173–206.

Schoenbachler, Matthew. "Republicanism in the Age of Democratic Revolution: The Democratic-Republican Societies of the 1790s." *Journal of the Early Republic* 18, no. 2 (Summer 1998): 237–61.

Schrader, Arthur F. "Songs to Cultivate the Sensations of Freedom." In *Music in Colonial Massachusetts, 1630–1820: A Conference Held by the Colonial Society of Massachusetts*, 105–56. Boston: The Society, distributed by the University Press of Virginia, 1980.

Schroeder, John H. *Commodore John Rodgers: Paragon of the Early American Navy*. Gainesville: University Press of Florida, 2006.

Schultz, Christian. *Travels on an Inland Voyage*. New York: Isaac Riley, 1810.

Schultz, Ronald. *The Republic of Labor: Philadelphia Artisans and the Politics of Class, 1720–1830*. New York: Oxford University Press, 1993.

Schwartz, Barry. *George Washington: The Making of an American Symbol*. New York: Free Press, 1987.

Scrivener, Michael. *Poetry and Reform: Periodical Verse from the English Democratic Press, 1792–1824*. Detroit: Wayne State University Press, 1992.

Seilhamer, George O. *History of the American Theatre: New Foundations*. New York: Haskell House, 1969.

Sesay, Chernoh M., Jr. "Mapping Intersectionality, Imagining Music, and Excavating America's African Archives." *Journal of the Early Republic* 38, no. 2 (Summer 2018): 325–33.

Sewall, Jonathan Mitchell. *Miscellaneous Poems, with Several Specimens from the Author's Manuscript Version of the Poems of Ossian*. Portsmouth, NH: William Treadwell, 1801.

Shalhope, Robert E. *Bennington and the Green Mountain Boys: The Emergence of Liberal Democracy in Vermont, 1760–1850*. Baltimore, MD: Johns Hopkins University Press, 1996.

Shalhope, Robert E. *The Roots of Democracy: American Thought and Culture, 1760–1800*. Lanham, MD: Rowman and Littlefield, 2004.

Shankman, Andrew. "'A New Thing on Earth': Alexander Hamilton, Pro-Manufacturing Republicans, and the Democratization of American Political Economy." *Journal of the Early Republic* 23, no. 3 (Autumn 2003): 323–52.

Sher, Richard B. *The Enlightenment and the Book: Scottish Authors and Their Publishers in Eighteenth-Century Britain, Ireland, and America*. Chicago: University of Chicago Press, 2008.

Shive, Clyde S., Jr. "National Martial Music and Songs: A Musical First." *American Music* 9, no. 1 (Spring 1991): 92–101.

Sidney, Joseph. *An Oration, Commemorative of the Abolition of the Slave Trade in the United States*. New York: Seymour, 1809.

Silkett, John T. *Francis Scott Key and the History of the Star Spangled Banner*. Washington, DC: Vintage America, 1978.

Silverstone, Scott A. *Divided Union: The Politics of War in the Early American Republic*. Ithaca, NY: Cornell University Press, 2004.

Skeen, C. Edward. *Citizen Soldiers in the War of 1812*. Lexington: University Press of Kentucky, 1999.

*The Sky-Lark, or a New Collection of Choice, Naval, Patriotic and Sentimental Songs*. Hartford: B. & J. Russell, 1816.

Slaughter, Thomas P. *The Whiskey Rebellion: Frontier Epilogue to the American Revolution*. New York: Oxford University, 1986.

Sloane, David E. E. "The Comic Writers of Philadelphia: George Helmbold's *The Tickler*, Joseph C. Neal's *City Worthies*, and the Beginning of Modern Periodical Humor in America." *Victorian Periodicals Review* 28, no. 3 (Fall 1995): 186–98.

Smelser, Marshall. "George Washington and the Alien and Sedition Acts." *American Historical Review* 59, no. 2 (January 1954): 322–34.

Smith, Gene A. *"For the Purposes of Defense": The Politics of the Jeffersonian Gunboat Program*. Newark: University of Delaware Press, 1995.

Smith, Gene Allen. "'Sons of Freedom': African Americans Fighting the War of 1812." *Tennessee Historical Quarterly* 71, no. 3 (Fall 2012): 206–27.

Smith, James Morton. "Background for Repression: America's Half-War with France and the Internal Security Legislation of 1798." *Huntington Library Quarterly* 18, no. 1 (November 1954): 37–58.

Smith, James Morton. "The Enforcement of the Alien Friends Act of 1798." *Mississippi Valley Historical Review* 41, no. 1 (June 1954): 85–104.

Smith, John Stafford, and Robert Treat Paine Jr. *Adams and Liberty*. A. Wright, for D. Wright and Company, Northampton, MA, 1798. Pdf. Retrieved from the Library of Congress. https://www.loc.gov/item/ihas.100010461/.

Smith, Mark M. *Listening to Nineteenth-Century America*. Chapel Hill: University of North Carolina Press, 2001.

*Society for the Information and Advice of Immigrants. Boston, December 30, 1793*. Boston: 1794.

Sofka, James. "American Neutral Rights Reappraised: Identity of Interest in the Foreign Policy of the Early Republic?" *Review of International Studies* 26, no. 4 (October 2000): 599–622.

Sonneck, Oscar. *Early Concert-Life in America (1731–1800)*. Leipzig: Breitkopf & Härtel, 1907.

Sonneck, Oscar. *Francis Hopkinson and James Lyon*. New York: Da Capo Press, 1967. First printing 1905.

Sonneck, Oscar. *Miscellaneous Studies in the History of Music*. New York: Macmillan, 1921.

Sonneck, Oscar. *Report on "The Star-Spangled Banner" "Hail Columbia" "America" "Yankee Doodle."* New York: Dover Publications, 1972. First published 1909.

Southern, Eileen. *The Music of Black Americans: A History*. New York: W. W. Norton, 1997.

Spargo, John. *Anthony Haswell, Printer-Patriot-Balladeer: A Biographical Study with a Selection of His Ballads and an Annotated Bibliographical List of His Imprints*. Rutland, VT: Tuttle, 1925.

Spicer, Richard C. "Popular Song for Public Celebration in Federal Portsmouth, New Hampshire." *Popular Music and Society* 25 (2001): 1–99.

Spivak, Burton. *Jefferson's English Crisis: Commerce, Embargo, and the Republican Revolution*. Charlottesville: University of Virginia Press, 1979.

Sprague, Henry Harrison. *An Old Boston Institution: A Brief History of the Massachusetts Charitable Fire Society*. Boston: Little, Brown, 1893.

Stagg, J. C. A. "James Madison and the 'Malcontents': The Political Origins of the War of 1812." *William and Mary Quarterly* 33, no. 4 (October 1976): 557–85.

Stagg, J. C. A. *Mr. Madison's War: Politics, Diplomacy, and Warfare in the Early American Republic, 1793–1830*. Princeton, NJ: Princeton University Press, 1983.

Stagg, J. C. A. *The War of 1812: Conflict for a Continent*. Cambridge: Cambridge University Press, 2012.

*The Star Spangled Banner: Being a Collection of the Best Naval, Martial, and Patriotic Songs . . . Chiefly Written during, and in Relation to the Late War*. Wilmington, DE: J[ames] Wilson, 1816.

Steffen, Charles G. *The Mechanics of Baltimore: Workers and Politics in the Age of Revolution 1763–1812*. Urbana: University of Illinois Press, 1984.

Steffen, Charles G. "Newspapers for Free: The Economies of Newspaper Circulation in the Early Republic." *Journal of the Early Republic* 23, no. 3 (Autumn 2003): 381–419.

Stevenson, Burton Egbert. *Poems of American History*. Boston: Houghton Mifflin, 1908.

Stewart, Donald H. *The Opposition Press of the Federalist Period*. Albany: State University of New York Press, 1969.

Stone, Timothy. *A Sermon, Preached before His Excellency Samuel Huntington*. Hartford: Hudson & Goodwin, 1792.

Story, Joseph. *Life and Letters of Joseph Story*. Edited by William W. Story. Boston: Little and Brown, 1851.

Stoutamire, Albert. *Music of the Old South: Colony to Confederacy*. Rutherford: Fairleigh Dickinson University Press, 1972.

Strickland, William. "Decatur's Victory: A Favorite Song." Philadelphia: G. Willig, [1812–1813].

Strum, Harvey. "New York Federalists and Opposition to the War of 1812." *World Affairs* 142, no. 3 (Winter 1980): 169–87.

Strum, Harvey. "Reluctant Warriors and the Federalist Resurgence in New York, 1808–1815." *Courier* 16, no.1 (1979): 3–21.

Svejda, George J. *The History of the Star Spangled Banner from 1814 to Present*. Washington, DC: US Division of History, Office of Archeology and Historic Preservation, 1969.

Symonds, Craig L. *Navalists and Antinavalists: The Naval Policy Debate in the United States, 1785–1827*. Newark: University of Delaware Press, 1980.

Szatmary, David O. *Shays' Rebellion: The Making of an Agrarian Insurrection*. Amherst: University of Massachusetts Press, 1980.

Tait, William, and Christian Isobel Johnstone. *Tait's Edinburgh Magazine*. Edinburgh: W. Tait, 1839.

Tammany Society, or Columbian Order. "Committee of Amusement Minutes." New York Public Library Digital Collections. http://digitalcollections.nypl.org/items/0b59d950-ab40-0133-3b9c-00505686d14e.

Taylor, Alan. "'The Art of Hook & Snivey': Political Culture in Upstate New York during the 1790s." *Journal of American History* 79, no. 4 (1993): 1371–96.

Taylor, Alan. *The Civil War of 1812: American Citizens, British Subjects, Irish Rebels, and Indian Allies*. New York: Alfred A. Knopf, 2010.

Taylor, Alan. "Dual Nationalisms: Legacies of the War of 1812." In *What So Proudly We Hailed: Essays on the Contemporary Meaning of the War of 1812*, edited by Pietro S. Nivola and Peter J. Kastor, 67–96. Washington, DC: Brookings Institution Press, 2012.

Taylor, Edward, ed. *Hymns and Miscellaneous Poems of John Taylor of Norwich*. N.p.: n.p., 1863.

Taylor, Lonn, Kathleen M. Kendrick, and Jeffrey L. Brodie. *The Star-Spangled Banner: The Making of an American Icon*. New York: Harper Collins, 2008.

Theriault, Sean M. "Party Politics during the Louisiana Purchase." *Social Science History* 30, no. 2 (Summer 2006): 293–324.

Thompson, Katrina Dyonne. *Ring Shout, Wheel About: The Racial Politics of Music and Dance in North American Slavery*. Urbana, IL: University of Chicago Press, 2014.

Thompson, Peter. *Rum Punch and Revolution: Taverngoing and Public Life in Eighteenth-Century Philadelphia*. Philadelphia: University of Pennsylvania Press, 1999.

Thomson, R. *A Tribute to Liberty; or, a New Collection of Patriotic Songs*. London: Thomson, 1793.

Thomson, R. *A Tribute to the Swinish Multitude, Being a Choice Collection of Patriotic Songs*. New York: Samuel Loudon, 1795.

Thornton, Richard Hopwood. *An American Glossary*. Vol. 1. Philadelphia: J. B. Lippincott, 1912.

Toll, Ian W. *Six Frigates: The Epic History of the Founding of the U.S. Navy*. New York: W. W. Norton, 2006.

*Tom Paine's Jests*. Philadelphia: Richard Folwell for Mathew Carey, 1794.

Travers, Len. *Celebrating the Fourth: Independence Day and the Rites of Nationalism in the Early Republic*. Amherst: University of Massachusetts Press, 1997.

Tucker, St. George. *Reflections on the Cession of Louisiana*. Washington, DC: Samuel Harrison Smith, 1803.

Turner, Lynn Warren. *The Ninth State: New Hampshire's Formative Years*. Chapel Hill: University of North Carolina Press, 1983.

Underhill, Lora Altine Woodbury. *Descendants of Edward Small of New England, and the Allied Families with Tracings of English Ancestry*. Vol. 1. Cambridge, MA: Riverside Press, 1910.

*The Universal Songster and Museum of Mirth: A Collection of Popular Songs*. Boston: Charles Gaylord, 1835.

Van Dover, J. K. "The Design of Anarchy: *The Anarchiad*, 1786–1787." *Early American Literature* 24, no. 3 (1989): 237–47.

Van Schaack, Henry Cruger. *Memoirs of the Life of Henry Van Schaack*. Chicago: A. C. McClurg, 1892.

*The Vocal Magazine, Containing a Selection of the Most Esteemed English, Scots, and Irish* Songs. Vol. 1. Edinburgh: C. Stewart, 1797.

Von Hagen, Peter Albrecht. "Adams and Washington: A New Patriotic Song." Boston: P. A. von Hagen, 1798.

Wakelyn, Jon L. *Birth of the Bill of Rights: Encyclopedia of the Antifederalists*. Vol. 1. Westport, CT: Greenwood, 2004.

Wala, Michael. "From Celebrating Victory to Celebrating the Nation: The War of 1812 and American National Identity." In *Celebrating Ethnicity and Nation: American Festive Culture* from the Revolution to the Early Twentieth Century, edited by Jürgen Heideking and Geneviève Fabre, 74–91. New York: Berghahn Books, 2001.

Waldstreicher, David. *In the Midst of Perpetual Fetes: The Making of American Nationalism, 1776–1820*. Chapel Hill: University of North Carolina Press, 1997.

Waldstreicher, David. "Minstrelization and Nationhood: 'Backside Albany,' Backlash, and the Wartime Origins of Blackface Minstrelsy." In *Warring for America: Cultural Contest in the Era of 1812*, edited by Nicole Eustace and Fredrika J. Teute, 29–55. University of North Carolina Press, 2017.

Wallace, Lee A., Jr. "The Petersburg Volunteers, 1812–1813." *Virginia Magazine of History and Biography* 82, no. 4 (October 1974): 458–85.

Ward, John William. *Andrew Jackson: Symbol for an Age*. New York: Oxford University Press, 1966.

Warren, Mercy Otis. *Poems, Dramatic and Miscellaneous*. Boston: I. Thomas and E. T. Andrews, 1790.

*Washington's Reception by the Ladies of Trenton Together with the Chorus Sung as He Passed under the Triumphal Arch*. New York: Society of Iconophiles, 1903.

Watson, John Fanning. *Historic Tales of Olden Time, Concerning the Early Settlement and Progress of Philadelphia and Pennsylvania*. Philadelphia: E. Littell and T. Holden, 1833.

Watts, Steven. *The Republic Reborn: War and the Making of Liberal America, 1790–1820*. Baltimore, MD: Johns Hopkins University Press, 1989.

Welles, Elijah. *Music Book*. Connecticut Historical Society Manuscript 90474.

Wesley, Dorothy Porter. *Early Negro Writing, 1760–1837*. Boston: Beacon Press, 1995.

West, Benjamin. *Bickerstaff's Boston Almanack*. Boston: E. Russell, 1787.

Wewers, Daniel Corbett. "The Specter of Disunion in the Early American Republic, 1783–1815." PhD diss., Harvard University, 2008.

Wheeler, Roxann. "Sounding Black-*ish*: West Indian Pidgin in London Performance and Print." *Eighteenth-Century Studies* 51, no. 1 (Fall 2017): 63–88.

Whipple, A. B. C. *To the Shores of Tripoli: The Birth of the U.S. Navy and Marines*. Annapoli, MD: Naval Institute Press, 1991.

Willis, Eola. *The Charleston Stage in the XVIII Century*. New York: Benjamin Blom, 1968.

Wills, Garry. *Cincinnatus: George Washington and the Enlightenment*. Garden City, NY: Doubleday, 1984.

Wilson, Alexander. *The Poems and Literary Prose of Alexander Wilson, the American Ornithologist*. Vol. 1. Paisley, Scotland: A. Gardner, 1876.

Wilson, David A. *United Irishmen, United States: Immigrant Radicals in the Early Republic*. Ithaca, NY: Cornell University Press, 1998.

Wolfe, Richard J. *Secular Music in America, 1801–1825: A Bibliography*. New York: New York Public Library, 1964.

Wolford, Thorp Lanier. "Democratic-Republican Reaction in Massachusetts to the Embargo of 1807." *New England Quarterly* 15, no. 1 (March 1942): 35–61.

Wood, Gordon S. "Conspiracy and the Paranoid Style: Causality and Deceit in the Eighteenth Century." *William and Mary Quarterly* 39, no. 3 (July 1982): 401–41.

Wood, Gordon S. *Empire of Liberty: A History of the Early Republic, 1789–1815*. New York: Oxford University Press, 2009.

Wood, Kirsten E. "'Join with Heart and Soul and Voice': Music, Harmony, and Politics in the Early American Republic." *American Historical Review* 119 (October 2014): 1083–16.

Woodworth, Samuel. *Melodies, Duets, Trios, Songs, and Ballads, Pastoral, Amatory, Sentimental, Patriotic, Religious, and Miscellaneous. Together with Metrical Epistles, Tale and Recitations*. New York: James M. Campbell, 1826.

Woodworth, Samuel. *The Poems, Odes, Songs and Other Metrical Effusions of Samuel Woodworth*. New York: Abraham Asten and Matthias Lopez, 1818.

Worrall, David. "Blake and the 1790s Plebeian Radical Culture." In *Blake in the Nineties*, edited by Steve Clark and David Worrall, 194–211. New York: St. Martin's Press, 1999.

Worrall, David. "Robert Hawes and the Millenium Press: A Political Microculture of Late-Eighteenth-Century Spitalfields." In *Romanticism and Millenarianism*, edited by Tim Fulford, 167–182. New York: Palgrave, 2002.

*The Wreath: A Collection of Songs, from the Most Admired Authors.* Philadelphia: E. Little, 1822.

Young, Alfred F. *The Democratic-Republicans of New York: The Origins, 1763–1797.* Chapel Hill: University of North Carolina Press, 2012.

Young, Christopher J. "Connecting the President and the People: Washington's Neutrality, Genet's Challenge, and Hamilton's Fight for Public Support." *Journal of the Early Republic* 31, no. 3 (Fall 2011): 435–66.

Zall, Paul M., ed. *Comical Spirit of Seventy-Six: The Humor of Francis Hopkinson.* San Marino, CA: Huntington Library, 1976.

# Index

*For the benefit of digital users, indexed terms that span two pages (e.g., 52–53) may, on occasion, appear on only one of those pages.*

Figures are indicated by *f* following the page number.